CINCINNATI'S
COLORED CITIZENS

CINCINNATI'S
COLORED CITIZENS

WENDELL P. DABNEY

Commonwealth Book Company
ST. MARTIN, OHIO

Copyright © 1926 by Wendell P. Dabney. Copyright © 2019 by Commonwealth Book Company, Inc. All rights reserved. Printed in the United States of America.

ISBN: 978-1-948986-04-5

COVER BACKGROUND PHOTOGRAPH: Cincinnati's West End, before it was razed and redeveloped in the 1950's, making way for the construction of Interstate-75 and industrial development. Many considered the West End, in particular its Kenyon Barr neighborhood, the center of Cincinnati's African American community.

FRONT COVER PHOTOGRAPH: Mrs. Laura Troy Knight and Ms. Laura Knight (p. 287).

TITLE PAGE PHOTOGRAPH: James Hathaway Robinson & Family (pp. 290-291).

SECTIONAL INDEX

I.

A summary of Cincinnati history from pre-historic times to 1877 7

II.

Excerpt from "Negroes of Cincinnati prior to Civil War," by Woodson, in Vol. 1, Journal of Negro History 31

III.

Ante Bellum Days—Incidents, tragedies............... 48

IV.

A few of the men who made history.................... 58

V.

Colored school history to 1902, by Shotwell. Teachers in colored schools, 1925........................... 100

VI.

Sketches, pictures, churches, streets, etc. Pioneers, pathfinders and items................................ 112

VII.

Institutions, biographical sketches, pictures............ 210

VIII.

Sociological and statistical business, postal employees, lodges 362

IX.

Prominent property owners............................ 420

PREFACE

OR many years there had dwelt with me the idea of publishing a booklet setting forth the history and achievements of the colored people of Cincinnati. Such information, I felt, would go far to eradicate much of the prejudice against us, that owes its origin to the ignorance or superficial knowledge of our white citizens. To my great surprise, I found that apart from tradition, a few scattered church notes and the recollections of several survivors of the past, there was little Negro history, other than scattered remnants of records, left by white men whose lives and ideals were interwoven with the tragedy of the days when the dark cloud of slavery cast its sombre shadow over "this land of liberty." In three months the work was begun and done. There is some repetition, much dwelling upon certain phases and places, other signs of the rapid execution rendered necessary by the fact that almost daily the depredations of death destroyed some human landmark laden with the lore of our ancient days.

The deeper the digging in the past the richer the ore. "The booklet" grew into a book, and still there remains untold much of rarest historical and literary wealth.

The beginning of this volume is devoted to a general description and history of Cincinnati, for the reason that such knowledge is necessary for a thorough understanding of the circumstances surrounding, and condition of, its Colored Citizens.

A most embarrassing feature in connection with this work has been the thought that imputation of egotism will be registered against me by some persons who note the frequency with which my name occurs in this work, but unfortunately, no one else arose, despite the extreme urgency, to write the history, and as records are useless unless accurate, the name could not well be omitted, since its owner has been "a Stormy Petrel" in politics and active in every branch of human endeavor in this community during the last third of a century. About myself,

I could, in truth, have said more; in justice to the narrative, I could not have said less.

Have strayed far from the cold, formal, stereotyped historical volume in efforts to show the soul as well as the body of a people, who are so little known, so little understood and, for so many years, so much oppressed because of such misunderstanding.

For the information compiled I am deeply indebted to many sources and people, among them Howe's Historical Collections of Ohio, Greve's Centennial History of Cincinnati, Levi Coffin's Reminiscences, Joseph Early, John Dixon, Wm. Copeland, Wm. Brown, A. Lee Beaty, Geo. W. Hays, Sr., Prof. John R. Blackburn, and Dr. Charles A. Schooley. To Rev. R. A. Moody, for collection of biographical matter, and Anderson's Print Shop, for a few cuts of old citizens. Acknowledgment and thanks are also due Arthur A. Schomburg of New York (president of The Negro Academy, famous Bibliophile, Connoisseur and Collector of Negro Literature and Art) for valuable data of ante bellum days; to Alain Le Roy Locke, Ph. D., Washington, D. C. (a product of Harvard, Oxford, Berlin Universities, winner of Rhodes Scholarship, author of "The New Negro") for many suggestions concerning compilation; to Henry P. Slaughter, Washington, D. C. (editor of the Odd Fellows' Journal) for inspection of his extensive library of Negro history. Others from whom statistics or articles have been obtained are given due credit in connection with the matter furnished.

To Cincinnati's colored citizens, this book is respectfully dedicated by

WENDELL P. DABNEY.

COPYRIGHT, PAUL A. BRIOL

Cincinnati, "the City of Rivers and Hills"

Cincinnati's Colored Citizens

Section I

A Summary of Cincinnati History From Prehistoric Times to 1877

"The country in the vicinity of Cincinnati owes its unsurpassed beauty to the operations of nature during the glacial era. It was the ice movements that gave it those fine terraces along the valleys and graceful contours of formation on the summits of the hills that were so attractive to the pioneers. Here it was that the great ice movement from the north ended. As has been remarked, "those were the days of the beautiful lake rather than the beautiful river."

No single cause has done more to diversify the surface of the country, to add to the attractiveness of the scenery and to furnish the key by which the condition of the Ice Age can be reproduced to the mind's eye than glacial dams. To them we owe the present existence of nearly all the waterfalls in North America, as well as nearly all the lakes.

A glacial dam across the Ohio river is supposed to have existed at the site of Cincinnati during the Ice Age.

The bottom of the Ohio river at Cincinnati is 447 feet above the sea level.

Madisonville, eight miles northeast of Cincinnati (in a cross valley about five miles in length, connecting Millcreek with the Little Miami back of Avondale, Walnut Hills and the Observatory), is an extremely interesting region, as connected with the glacial period. It is occupied by a deposit of gravel, sand and loam, belonging to the glacial terrace epoch. In the article, "Glacial Man in Ohio," by Prof. Wright, in Vol. I, page 93, is given a map of this region. The article also speaks of the discoveries of Dr. C. L. Metz of two palaeolithic implements, which prove that man lived in Ohio before the close of the glacial period, say from 8,000 to 10,000 years ago, before which there were no Niagara Falls and no Lake Erie.

Mounds and Earthworks

The territory comprising Hamilton County appears to have been one of the great centres of the aboriginal inhabitants. This is evidenced by the great number of earthwords, mounds and extensive burial places found throughout the country.

The mounds and the earthworks are found most numerous in the valleys of the Little and Great Miami, and in the region between the Little Miami and Ohio rivers. Of the mounds, 437 have been observed in the county. Many mounds were found in Cincinnati, some very large ones between Broadway and Sycamore, between Third and Sixth Streets, and one on lower Vine. An immense one was located at Fifth and Mound."

Hamilton County

Hamilton was the second county established in the Northwestern Territory. It was formed January 2, 1790, by proclamation of Governor St. Clair, and named from Alexander Hamilton, bosom friend of George Washington, and the greatest Secretary of the Treasury the United States ever had. *He, the real founder of its financial system, was a colored man.*

Its original boundaries were thus defined: "Beginning on the Ohio river, at the confluence of the Little Miami, and down the said Ohio to the mouth of the Big Miami; and up said Miami to the standing stone forks or branches of said river, and thence with a line to be drawn due east to the Little Miami, and down said Little Miami river to the place of beginning." The surface is generally rolling; soil on the uplands clay, and in the valleys deep alluvion, with a substratum of sand. Area about 400 square miles.

Before the war much attention was given to the cultivation of vineyards upon the hillsides of the Ohio for the manufacture of wine, and it promised to be a great business, when the change in climate resulted disastrously.

The Indians occupying the Great Middle West were the Iroquois, Algonquins, and later the Five Nations, consisting of Mohawks, Oneidas, Onondagas, Cayugas and Senecas. They fought so much among themselves that they were weakened into easy victims for the whites.

The First Settlements

The country between the Great and Little Miami had been the scene of so many fierce conflicts between the Kentuckians and Indians in their raids to and fro that it was termed the "Miami Slaughter House." In June 1780, the period of the Revolutionary War, Captain Byrd, in command of 600 British and Indians, with artillery from Detroit, came down the Big Miami and ascended the Licking opposite Cincinnati, on his noted expedition into Kentucky, when he destroyed several stations and did great mischief. And in the August following, General Rogers Clark, with his Kentuckians, took up his line of march from the site of Cincinnati for the Shawnee towns on Little Miami and Mad rivers, which he destroyed. On this campaign he erected two blockhouses on the north side of the Ohio. These were the first structures known to have been built on the site of the city.

The beautiful country between the Miamis had been so infested by the Indians that it was avoided by the whites and its settlement might have been procrastinated for years but for the discovery and enterprise of Major Benjamin Stites, a trader from New Jersey. In the summer of 1786, Stites happened to be at Washington, just back of Limestone, now Maysville, where he headed a party of Kentuckians in pursuit of some Indians who had stolen some horses. They followed for some days; the Indians escaped, but Stites gained by it a view of the rich valleys of the Great and Little Miami as far up as the site of Xenia. Charmed by the beauty of the country, he hurried back to New Jersey and revealed his discovery to Judge John Cleves Symmes, of Trenton, at that time a member of Congress and a man of great influence. The result was a formation of a company of twenty-four gentlemen of the state. Symmes, in August of next year, 1787, petitioned Congress for a grant of the land, but before the bargain was closed he made arrangements with Stites to sell him 10,000 acres of the best land.

Under the contract with Symmes, Stites, with a party of eighteen or twenty, landed on the 18th of November, 1788, and laid out the village of Columbia, below the mouth of the Little Miami; it is now within the limits of the city, five miles east of Fountain Square.

Settlement of Cincinnati

The facts connected with the settlement of Cincinnati are these: In the winter of 1787-1788, Matthias Denman, of Springfield, New Jersey, purchased of John Cleves Symmes, a tract of land comprising 740 acres, now but a small part of the city, his object being to form a station, lay out a town on the Ohio side opposite the mouth of the Licking river, and establish a ferry, which last was especially important. The old Indian war-path from the British garrison at Detroit here crossed the Ohio, and here was the usual avenue by which savages from the north had invaded Kentucky. Denman paid five shillings per acre in Continental scrip, or about fifteen pence per acre in specie, or less than $125 in specie for the entire plot.

Denman, the next summer, associated with him two gentlemen of Lexington, Ky., each having one-third interest, Col. Robert Patterson and John Filson. The first was a gallant soldier of the Indian wars, and John Filson, a schoolmaster and surveyor, and author of various works upon the West, of which he had been an explorer, one of them "The Discovery, Settlement and Present State of Kentucky," published in 1784; also a map of the same. Filson was to survey the site and lay it out into lots, thirty in-lots of half an acre and thirty out-lots of four acres, to be given thirty settlers on their paying $1.50 for deed and survey. He called the proposed town Losantiville, a name formed by him from the Latin "os," mouth; the Greek "anti," opposite, and the French "ville," city, from its position opposite the mouth of the Licking river. And this name it retained until the advent of Governor St. Clair, January 2, 1790, who, being a member of the old Revolutionary Army Society of Cincinnatus, expressed a desire the name should be changed to Cincinnati, when his wish was complied with.

Early Beginnings of Cincinnati

Soon as the settlers of Cincinnati landed (December, 1788), they commenced erecting three or four cabins, the first of which was built on Front, east of and near Main Street. The lower table of land was then covered with sycamore and maple trees, and the upper with beech and oak. Through this dense forest the streets were laid out, their corners being marked upon the trees. This survey extended from Eastern Row, now Broadway, to Western Row, now Seventh Street.

Fort Washington was built in the fall of 1789 by Major Doughty. The site selected was a little east of what is now Broadway where Third Street crosses it. The fort was a solid, substantial fortress of hewn timber about 180 feet square with block-houses at the four angles and two stories high. Fifteen acres were reserved there by the government. It was the most important and extensive military work then in the Territories, and figured largely in the Indian wars of the period. General Harmar arrived and took command late in December, its garrison then comprising seventy men.

In January, 1790, Gen. Arthur St. Clair, then governor of the Northwest Territory, arrived at Cincinnati to organize the the county of Hamilton. In the succeeding fall Gen. Harmar marched from Fort Washington on his expedition against the Indians of the Northwest. In the following year (1791) the unfortunate army of St. Clair marched from the same place. On his return St. Clair gave Major Zeigler the command of Fort Washington and repaired to Philadelphia. Soon after the latter was succeeded by Col. Wilkinson. This year Cincinnati had little increase in its population. About one-half of the inhabitants were attached to the army of St. Clair, and many killed in the defeat.

In 1792 about fifty persons were added by immigration to the population of Cincinnati, and a house of worship erected. In the spring following the troops which had been recruited for Wayne's army landed at Cincinnati and encamped on the bank of the river, between the village of Cincinnati and Mill Creek. In the fall, after the army had left, the small-pox broke out in the garrison at Fort Washington. Nearly one-third of the soldiers and citizens fell victims. In July, 1794, the army on the 20th of August defeated the enemy at the battle of "The Fallen Timbers," in what is now Lucas County, a few miles above Toledo.

Judge Burnet Thus Describes Cincinnati at About This Period

"In Cincinnati, Fort Washington was the most remarkable object. That rude but highly interesting structure stood between Third and Fourth Streets, east of Eastern Row, now Broadway, which was then a two-pole alley, and was the eastern boundary of the town, as originally laid out.

The artificers' yard was an appendage to the fort, and stood on the bank of the river immediately in front. It contained about two acres of ground, enclosed by small contiguous buildings, occupied as work-shops and quarters for laborers. Within the enclosure there was a large two-story frame house, familiarly called the "yellow-house," built for the accommodation of the quartermaster-general, which was the most commodious and best finished edifice in Cincinnati."

On the north side of Fourth Street, immediately behind the fort, Col. Sargent, secretary of the territory, had a convenient frame house and a spacious garden, cultivated with care and taste. This space ran from Broadway over and beyond McAllister and was known as Sargent's Square. Now the site of the Western and Southern Life Insurance Co. and McAllister Street. The house and grounds were the finest in town. On the east side of the fort, Dr. Allison, the surgeon-general of the army, had a plain frame dwelling in the center of a large lot, cultivated as a garden and fruitery, which was called Peach Grove. Probably included what became the Longworth residence, later "Dave" Sinton's, now the Chas. P. Taft estate.

"The Presbyterian Church, an interesting edifice, stood on Main Street in front of the spacious brick building now occupied by the First Presbyterian congregation. It was a substantial frame building about forty feet by thirty, enclosed with clapboards, but neither lathed, plastered nor ceiled. The floor was of boat plank, resting on wooden blocks. In that humble edifice the pioneers and their families assembled stately for public worship; and, during the continuance of the war, they always attended with loaded rifles by their sides. That building was afterwards neatly finished, and some years subsequently (1814) was sold and removed to Vine Street, where it now (1847) remains the property of Judge Burke.

On the north side of Fourth Street, opposite where St. Paul's Church now stands, there stood a frame school-house, enclosed, but unfinished, in which the children of the village were instructed. On the north side of the Public Square there was a strong log building erected and occupied as a jail. A room in the tavern of George Avery, near the frog-pond, at the corner of Main and Fifth Streets, had been rented for the accommodation of the courts; and as the penitentiary system had not been adopted, and Cincinnati was a seat of justice, it was ornamented with a pillory, stocks and whipping-post, and occasionally with a gallows.

The first jail was on Water Street west of Main. The whipping post was 100 feet west of Main, and 50 feet north of Fifth. Levi McLean the jailer did the whipping; when he got drunk he would amuse himself by whipping prisoners with a cowhide.

The fort was then commanded by William H. Harrison, a captain in the army, but afterwards President of the United States. In 1797, General Wilkinson, the commander-in-chief of the army, made it his headquarters for a few months, but did not apparently interfere with the command of Captain Harrison, which continued till his resignation in 1798.

During the period now spoken of, the settlements of the territory, including Cincinnati, contained but a few individuals, and still fewer families, who had been accustomed to mingle in the circles of polished society. That fact put it in the power of the military to give character to the manners and customs of the people. Idleness, drinking and gambling prevailed in the army to a greater extent than it has done at any subsequent period.

In 1800 there was a big pond on Broadway near Columbia, four acres in extent. Fine spot for duck shooting. In 1795, ninety-four cabins, ten frame houses, and five hundred people. In 1800, seven hundred and fifty people; in 1805, nine hundred and sixty people; in 1810, twenty-five hundred and forty people.

Cumminsville was probably named from David Cummins, said to have been one of the first children born in this city. Ludlow Station was made in Cumminsville in 1790 and the block-house was located on what is now Knowlton's Corner.

A very large proportion of the officers under General Wayne, and subsequently under General Wilkinson, were hard drinkers. As a natural consequence the citizens indulged in the same practices and formed the same habits. As a proof of this it may be stated that when Mr. Burnet came to the bar there were nine resident lawyers engaged in the practice, of whom he is and has been for many years the only survivor. They all became confirmed sots, and descended to premature graves, excepting his brother, who was a young man of high promise, but whose life was terminated by rapid consumption in 1801."

On the 9th of November, 1792, William Maxwell established at Cincinnati The Centinel of the Northwestern Territory, with the motto, "open to all parties—influenced by none." It was on a half-sheet, royal quarto size, and was the first newspaper printed north of the Ohio River. In 1796, Edward Freeman became the owner of the paper, which he changed to Freeman's Journal, which he continued until the beginning of 1800, when he removed to Chillicothe. On the 28th of May, 1799, Joseph Carpenter issued the first number of a weekly paper entitled the Western Spy and Hamilton Gazette. On the 11th of January, 1794, two keel-boats sailed from Cincinnati to Pittsburgh, each making a trip once in four weeks. Each boat was so covered as to be protected against rifle and musket-balls, and had port-holes to fire out of, and was provided with six pieces carrying pound balls, a number of muskets and ammunition, as a protection against the Indians on the banks of the Ohio. In 1801, the first sea-vessel equipped for sea—of 100 tons, built at Marietta—passed down the Ohio, carrying produce, and the banks of the river at Cincinnati were crowded with spectators to witness this novel event. December 19, 1801, the Territorial Legislature passed a bill removing the seat of government from Chillicothe to Cincinnati.

January 2, 1802, the Territorial Legislature incorporated the town of Cincinnati, and the following officers were appointed: David Ziegler, President; Jacob Burnet, Recorder; Wm. Ramsay, David E. Wade, Chas. Avery, John Riley, Wm. Stanley, Samuel Dick, and Wm. Ruffner, Trustees; Jo. Prince, Assessor; Abram Cary, Collector; and James Smith, Town Marshal.

Cutler's book in 1812 states that Cincinnati contains about 400 dwellings, an elegant court-house, jail, three market-houses, a land-office for the sale of Congress lands, two printing-offices, issuing weekly gazettes, thirty mercantile stores, and the various branches of mechanism are carried on with spirit. Industry of every kind being duly encouraged by the citizens, it is likely to become a considerable manufacturing place. It has a bank, issuing notes under the authority of the State, called the Miami Exporting Company. A considerable trade is carried on between Cincinnati and New Orleans in keel-boats, which return laden with foreign goods. The passage of a boat, of forty tons, down to New Orleans, is computed at about twenty-five, and its return at about sixty-five days.

In 1819, a charter was obtained from the State Legislature, by which Cincinnati was incorporated as a city. This, since repeatedly amended and altered, forms the basis of its present municipal authority.

In 1819 two fire engines were in use. In 1820, Mayor's office at Front and Main Streets, during Miami Bank.

In 1826 the police department was increased to two captains and eighteen men. (New charter in 1834.)

On celebration of Independence Day, July 4, 1824, General Sam Findlay delivered the oration at the meeting in the chapel of the Cincinnati College; 1,104 white and 208 black children of the Sabbath schools took part in the procession.

February, 1832, first of great floods recorded. The land for a mile west of what is now John Street was submerged. Ferry boats landed at Main and Pearl Streets. The largest steamboats could have passed down Second or Front Street for over a mile.

The Little Miami Railroad, after years of effort, was built. In 1843, thirty miles of track were in operation and in 1846 the road was completed to Springfield.

Years later the Cincinnati Southern was built. The first and possibly only railroad owned by an American municipality. It is now one of our greatest assets.

Description of Cincinnati in 1847

Cincinnati is 116 miles southwest of Columbus; 120 miles southeast of Indianapolis, Indiana; 90 miles north-northwest of Lexington, Kentucky; 270 miles north-northeast of Nashville, Tennessee; 455 miles below Pittsburgh, Pennsylvania, by course of the river; 132 miles above Louisville, Kentucky; 494 miles above the mouth of the Ohio river and 1,447 miles above New Orleans by the Mississippi and Ohio rivers; 518 miles by post-route west of Baltimore; 617 miles west by south of Philadelphia; 950 miles from New York by Lake Erie, Erie Canal and Hudson river, and 492 miles from Washington City. It is situated on the north bank of the Ohio river, opposite the mouth of the Licking river, which enters the Ohio between Newport and Covington, Kentucky.

This city is near the eastern extremity of a valley about twelve miles in circumference, surrounded by beautiful hills, which rise to the height of 300 feet by gentle and varying slopes, and mostly covered with native forest trees. The summit of these hills presents a beautiful and picturesque view of the city and valley. The city is built on two-table lands, the one elevated from forty to sixty feet above the other. Low-water mark in the river, which is 108 feet below the upper part of the city, is 432 feet above tide-water at Albany, and 133 feet below the level of Lake Erie. The population in 1800 was 750; in 1847, over 90,000.

Cincinnati seems to have been originally laid out on the model of Philadelphia with great regularity. North of Main Street, between the north side of Front Street and the bank of the river, is the landing, an open area of 10 acres, with about 1,000 feet front. This area is of great importance to the business of the city, and generally presents a scene of much activity. The corporate limits include about four square miles. The central part is compactly and finely built, with spacious warehouses, large stores, and handsome dwellings; but in its outer parts it is but partially built up and the houses irregularly scattered. Many of them are of stone or brick, but an equal or greater number are of wood and are generally from two to four stories high. The city contains over 11,000 edifices, public and private; and of those recently erected, the number of brick exceeds those of wood, and the style of architecture is constantly improving. Many of the streets are well paved, extensively shaded with trees, and the houses ornamented with shrubbery. The climate is more variable than on the Atlantic coast in the same latitude. Snow rarely falls sufficiently deep or lies long enough to furnish sleighing. Few places are more healthy, the average annual mortality being one in forty. The inhabitants are from every state in the Union and from various countries in Europe. Besides natives of Ohio, Pennsylvania and New Jersey have furnished the greatest number; but many are from New York, Virginia, Maryland and New England. Nearly one-fifth of the adult population are Germans, but England, Ireland, Scotland, France and Wales have furnished considerable number.

The Ohio river at Cincinnati is 1,800 feet, or about one-third of a mile wide, and its mean annual range from low to high water is about 50 feet; the extreme range may be about 10 feet more. The greatest depressions are generally in August, September and October, and the greatest rise in December, March, May and June. The upward navigation is generally suspended by floating ice for eight or ten weeks in the winter. Its current at its mean height is about three miles an hour; when higher and rising, it is more; and when very low, it does not exceed two miles. The quantity of rain and snow which falls annually at Cincinnati is near 3 feet 9 inches. The wettest month is May and the driest, January. The average number of clear and fair days in a year is 146; of variable, 114; of cloudy, 105. There have been, since 1840, from thirty to thirty-eight steamboats built annually, with an average aggregate tonnage of 6,500 tons.

Among the public buildings of Cincinnati is the court-house, on Main Street; it is a spacious building. The edifice of the Franklin and Lafayette Bank, of Cincinnati, on Third Street, has a splendid portico of Grecian Doric columns, 4 feet 6 inches in diameter, extending through the entire front, was built after the model of the Parthenon, and is truly classical and beautiful. The First and Second Presbyterian churches are beautiful edifices, and the Unitarian church is singularly neat. There are several churches, built within the last three years, which possess great beauty, either internally or externally. But the most impressive building is the Catholic Cathedral, which, at far less cost, surpasses in beauty and picturesque effect the metropolitan edifice at Baltimore. There are many fine blocks of stores on Front, Walnut, Pearl, Main and Fourth Streets, and the eye is arrested by many beautiful private habitations. The most showy quarters are Main Street, Broadway, Pearl and Fourth Street, west of its intersection with Main.

There are 76 churches in Cincinnati, viz.: 7 Presbyterian (4 old and 3 new school); 2 Congregational; 12 Episcopal Methodist; 2 Methodist Protestant; 2 Wesleyan Methodist; 1 Methodist Episcopal, South; 1 Bethel; 1 Associate Reformed; 1 Reformed Presbyterian; 6 Baptist; 5 Disciples; 1 Universalist; 1 Restorationist; 1 Christian; 8 German Lutheran and Reformed; English Lutheran and Reformed, 1 each; 1 United Brethren; 1 Welsh Calvinistic; 1 Welsh Congregational; 1 Unitarian; 2 Friends; 1 New Jerusalem; 8 Catholic, 6 of which are for Germans; 2 Jewish synagogues; 5 Episcopal, and 1 Second Advent.

There are five market houses and three theaters, of which one is German.

Cincinnati contains many literary and charitable institutions. The Cincinnati College was founded in 1819. The building is in the center of the city, and is the most beautiful edifice of the kind in the state. It is of the Grecian Doric order, with pilaster fronts and facade of Dayton marble, and cost about $35,000. It has seven professors or other instructors, about 160 pupils, one-quarter of whom are in the collegiate department. Woodward College, named from its founder, who gave a valuable block of ground in the north part of the city, has a president and five professors or other instructors, and including its preparatory department, near two hundred students.

The Catholics have a college called St. Xavier's, which has about one hundred students and near 5,000 volumes in its libraries. Lane Seminary, a theological institution, is at Walnut Hills, two miles from the center of the city. It went into operation in 1833, has near one hundred students and over 10,000 volumes in its libraries. There is no charge for tuition. Rooms are provided and furnished at $5.00 per annum, and the students boarded at 90 and 62½ cents per week. The Medical College was chartered and placed under trustees in 1825. The Cincinnati Law School is connected with Cincinnati College, has three professors and about thirty students. The Mechanics' Institute, chartered in 1828, has a valuable philosophical and chemical apparatus, a library and a reading room. The common free schools of the city are of a high order, with fine buildings, teachers, and apparatus. In the high schools there are not less than 1,500 pupils; in the common and private,

5,000; and, including the students in the collegiate institutions, there are 7,000 persons in the various departments of education. In 1831 a college of teachers was established, having for its object the elevation of the profession and the advancement of the interest of schools in the Mississippi Valley, which holds an annual meeting in Cincinnati in October. The Young Men's Mercantile Library Association has a fine library and reading room. The library contains over 3,800 volumes, and the institution promises to be an honor and a blessing to the commercial community. The Apprentices' Library, founded in 1821, contains 2,200 volumes.

The charitable institutions of the city are highly respectable. The Cincinnati Orphan Asylum is in a building which cost $18,000. Attached is a library and well organized school, with a provision even for infants, and it is surrounded by ample grounds. It has trained over 300 children for usefulness. The Catholics have one male and female orphan asylum. The commercial hospital and lunatic asylum of Ohio was incorporated in 1821. The edifice, in the northwest part of the city, will accommodate 250 persons; 1,100 have been admitted within a year. A part of the building is used for a poorhouse, and there are separate apartments for the insane.

The city is supplied by water raised from the Ohio river by a steam engine of forty horsepower, and forced into two reservoirs on a hill 700 feet distant, from whence it is carried in pipes to the intersection of Broadway and Third Streets, and thence distributed through the principal streets in pipes. These works are now owned by the city.

Cincinnati is an extensive manufacturing place. Its natural destitution of water power is extensively compensated at present by steam engines and by the surplus water of the Miami canal, which affords 3,000 cubic feet per minute. But the Cincinnati and White Water canal, which extends twenty-five miles and connects with the White Water canal of Indiana, half a mile south of Harrison, on the state line, will furnish a great increase of water power, equal to ninety runs of millstones. The manufactures of the city, already large, may be expected to greatly increase. By a late enumeration it appears that the manufactures of Cincinnati, of all kinds, employ 10,647 persons, a capital of $14,541,842, and produce articles of over seventeen millions of dollars value.

The trade of Cincinnati embraces the country from the Ohio to the lakes, north and south; and from the Scioto to the Wabash, east and west. The Ohio river line, in Kentucky, for fifty miles down, and as far up as the Virginia line, make their purchases here. Its manufactures are sent into the upper and lower Mississippi country.

There are six incorporated banks, with aggregate capital of $5,800,000, besides two unincorporated banks. Cincinnati is the greatest pork market in the world. Not far from three millions of dollars worth of pork are annually exported.

Cincinnati enjoys great facilities for communication with the surrounding country. The total length of canals, railroads and turnpikes which center here, completed and constructing, is 1,125 miles. Those who have made it a matter of investigation predict that Cincinnati will eventually be a city of a very great population. A writer, J. W. Scott, editor of the Toledo Blade, in Cist's "Cincinnati in 1841," in a long article on this subject, commences with the startling announcement: "Not having before my eyes the fear of men, 'who—in the language of Governor Morris—with too much pride to study and too much wit to think, undervalue what they do not understand, and condemn what they do not comprehend,' I venture the prediction that within one hundred years from this time Cincinnati will be the greatest city in America; and by the year of our Lord 2000 the greatest city in the world." We have not space here to recapitulate the arguments on which this prediction is based. The prediction itself we place on record for future reference— Old Edition." We regret to say that at this late date, 1925, the possibility or probability of the realization of Editor Scott's predictions are exceedingly remote.

Reminiscences of Cincinnati in the War Time

"Cincinnati, up to the outbreak of the rebellion, largely sympathized with the slave-holders so far as to deprecate any restrictions upon what was termed "their rights under the laws." Many of the leading families by blood and kindred were connected with the South; indeed, largely came from there. Through trade with the South its citizens had been greatly sustained. The establishment of an anti-slavery newspaper had resulted in its destruction by a mob, in which were some of the most prominent citizens, and the driving of its editor, Mr. Birney, to a distant city. The quarters of the negro population at times were subject to attacks from the scum of the city, aided by the rabble from the Kentucky side of the Ohio. Free speech, if it took the form of public protests against the continuance of slavery, was dangerous. Wendell Phillips was driven from the stage at Pike's Opera House, and waited for in the streets to be hung up by a howling slavery mob, the mayor refusing to allow the police to suppress it. At the same era, Mr. Yancey, of Alabama, was allowed therein to utter the most bitter disloyal tirade, with threats against the North, without a whisper of dissent from an audience of three thousand.

With the firing upon Sumter, April 12, 1861, a spirit of vengeance for the insult to the flag seemed at once to take possession of the entire population. All thoughts of trade and money-getting were swept completely from the minds of the people as in any northern city.

What made the position of Cincinnati at this trying era especially interesting was that no large northern city was so exposed, so inviting to attacks from its location and great wealth. If Kentucky should secede the city would have to be defended from her own hills instead of from those on the south side of the river. By wise management Kentucky was saved, but multitudes of her young men from her rich slave-holding centers enlisted under the banner of secession.

"During the first week after the fall of Sumter, active work was done in recruiting and drilling companies and in perfecting regimental organizations. Four regiments were started in the city and recruiting was so active that it became a question who was not to go. The Germans turned out with a magnificent soldierly body of men, over 1,000 strong, the regiment known as the famous Ninth Ohio." This regiment was commanded by Colonel Robert L. McCook. He was a large-hearted man with a frank, open, laughing manner, a lawyer and a partner with the eminent German lawyer, J. B. Stallo.

The Irish element in Cincinnati was not far behind the Germans in their alacrity to spring to the cause of the Union and "the well-known regiment, the Tenth Ohio, that did splendid work under Colonel William H. Lytle, the 'Soldier Poet,' was ready for camp." The Fifth Ohio, with Colonel J. H. Patrick, with many of the most promising young men of the city as members, formed during the week, and the ranks of the Guthrie Grays—the Sixth Ohio—were well filled, over one thousand strong, with the most prominent young men in all branches of society and business in the city, under W. K. Bosley.

A meeting of gentlemen and ladies was held at Smith and Nixon's hall to learn from O. M. Mitchell what he knew about war. He was an object of pride with the Cincinnatians. Through his exertions they had the honor of having established the first observatory, built by the contributions of a people, on the globe. On this occasion he spake with fiery energy.

Judge Bellamy Storer was another of Cincinnati's fiery, enthusiastic orators. At a meeting in Greenwood hall, Judge Storer gave one of his fervid appeals, calling upon the young men to volunteer. As he closed, he drew his tall, imposing form to its utmost height and spreading out his arms, exclaimed, "I'm an old man, rising of sixty years." Then with a look as though about ready to spring into a fight, added, "And I now volunteer."

A few days later our eyes were greeted with the sight of a company of old substantial citizens called the "Storer Rifles," clad in handsome uniforms, marching through the streets to the sound of drum and fife—old, mostly wealthy, gray-headed men, some of them very obese, with aldermanic protuberances; they were splendidly equipped, each at his own expense, and were named the "Storer Rifles." Among them was the judge himself, bearing his shooting-piece and evidently as proud of his trainer clothes as any school boy. This company was organized to act as Home Guards for the protection of the city and to stimulate "the boys" to enlist for the war.

After a little it seemed as though the entire force of ablebodied men were drilling, and, where not for the army, to act as Home Guards. Within a week from the fall of Sumter at least ten thousand men were drilling in the city.

The famed Literary Club, converting their rooms into a drilling hall, formed into a military company. They were largely young lawyers, their business for the time crushed and they had no resource for occupation but to turn from law to war, from courts to camps.

Cincinnati was especially prominent for the large number of eminent characters she supplied for the cabinet and the field. Hon. Salmon P. Chase, the great war secretary, and two of Ohio's war governors, Dennison and Brough, and many of the distinguished Union generals, as Major-Generals Rosecrans, McClennan, Mitchell and Godfrey Weitzell; Brevet Major-Generals R. B. Hayes, August Willich, Henry B. Banning, Manning F. Force, August V. Kautz and Kenner Garrard; Brigadier-Generals Robert L. McCook, William H. Lytle, A. Saunders Piatt, E. P. Scammon, Nathaniel McLean, M. S. Wade and John P. Slough; and Brevet Brigadier-Generals Andrew Hickenlooper, Benjamin C. Ludlow, Israel Garrard, William H. Baldwin, Henry V. N. Boynton, Charles E. Brown, Henry L. Bennet, Henry M. Cist, Stephen J. McGroarty, Granville Moody, August Moore, Reuben D. Mussey, George W. Neff, Edward F. Noyes, Augustus C. Parry, Durbin Ward and Thomas L. Young; also Joshua L. Bates of the Ohio militia. A host of other Cincinnatians served in various civil and military capacities.

The most marked events in the war history of the city were what has been termed the "Siege of Cincinnati" in 1862 and the raid of John Morgan in the following year.

The Siege of Cincinnati

"After the unfortunate battle of Richmond, on the 29th of August, Kirby Smith, with his 15,000 rebel veterans, advancing into the heart of Kentucky, took possession of Lexington, Frankfort and Maysville. Bragg, with his large army, was then crossing the Kentucky line, while Morgan, with his guerrilla cavalry, was already joined to Smith.

General Lewis Wallace was at once placed in command at Cincinnati by order of Major-General Wright. Soon as he arrived in the city on Thursday, the 4th of September, he put Cincinnati and the two cities on the Kentucky side of the Ohio, Newport and Covington, under martial law, and, within an hour of his arrival, he issued a proclamation suspending all business, stopping the ferry boats from plying the river, and summoning all citizens to enroll themselves for defense. Of course, there were a few timid creatures who feared to obey the summons. Sudden illness overtook some. Others were hunted up by armed men with fixed bayonets, ferreted from back kitchens, garrets and cellars, closets and even under beds where they were hiding. One peacefully excited individual was found in his wife's clothes, scrubbing at the wash-tub.

An almost endless stream of sturdy men rushed to the rescue from the rural districts of Ohio and Indiana. These were known as the Squirrel Hunters. They came in files, numbering thousands upon thousands, in all kinds of costumes, and armed with all kinds of firearms, but chiefly the deadly rifle, which they knew so well how to use.

The shrewd leaders of the rebel army learned of our preparations. Taking advantage of the darkness of night and the violence of a thunder storm, they made a hasty and ruinous retreat. Wallace was anxious to follow and was confident of success, but was overruled by those higher in authority.

The colored men were roughly handled by the Irish police. From hotels and barber shops, in the midst of their labors, these helpless people were pounced upon and often bareheaded and in shirtsleeves, just as seized, driven in squads, at the point of the bayonet, and gathered in vacant yards and guarded. What rendered this act more than ordinarily atrocious was that they, through their head men, had, at the first alarm, been the earliest to volunteer their services to our mayor for the defense of our common homes. It was a sad sight to see human beings treated like reptiles.

At this stage of affairs the idea that our colored citizens possessed war-like qualities was a subject for scoffing; the scoffers forgetting that the race, in ancestral Africa, including even the women, had been in war since the days of Ham; strangely oblivious also to the fact that our foreign-born city police could only by furious onslaughts, made with Hibernian love of the thing, quell the frequent pugnacious outbreaks of the crispy-haired denizens of our own Bucktown. From this view, or more probably a delicate sentiment of tenderness, instead of being armed and sent forth to the dangers of battle, they were consolidated into a peaceful brigade of workers in the trenches back of Newport, under the philanthropic guidance of the Hon. William M. Dickson.

The daily morning march of the corps down Broadway to labor was a species of the mottled picturesque. At their head was the stalwart, manly form of the landlord of the Dumas house, Colonel Harlan. Starting back on the honest, substantial, coal-black foundation, all shades of color were exhibited, degenerating out through successive gradations to an ashy white, the index of Anglo-Saxon fatherhood of the chivalrous American type. Arrayed for dirt-work in their oldest clothes, apparently the fags of every conceivable kind of cast-off, kicked-about, and faded-out garments; crownless and lop-eared hats, diverse boots; with shouldered pick, shovel, and hoe; this merry, chattering, piebald, grotesque body, shuffled along amid grins and jeers."

From a Cincinnati Newspaper

"In a deserted rebel camp, Laurel Hill, Western Virginia, was found "a love letter" in which was expressed the bottom thought of at least one poor secessionist: "I sa agen, dear Melindy, weer fitin for our libertis to do gest as we pleas, and we will fit for them so long as Goddlemity gives us breth."

"*Contraband Soldiers.*—Ordinarily, men in uniform are so transformed that it was rarely that we could tell, on seeing a regiment marching through the streets, whether it was Irish, German, or American. In regard to one class of Union soldiers there could be no mistake—the Negro. On Fifth Street, close to Main, on the large space in front of the present Government building, was reared a huge shed-like structure, one story high, for barracks. Late in the war it was occupied briefly by a regiment or more of plantation blacks, clad in the Union uniform. They were a very different looking people from our Northern blacks, many of whom possess bright, interesting faces. These were stolid-appearing, their faces with but little more expression than those of animals. When I saw them they had finished their suppers and were engaged in whiling away their time singing plantation melodies in the gathering shadows of the evening. The voices of this immense multitude went up in a grand orchestra of sound. The tunes were plaintive, weird-like, and the whole exhibition one that could not but affect the thoughtful mind. It was singularly appealing to one's best instincts to look upon these poor simple children of nature."

Cincinnati in 1877

"*Temperance Crusade in 1877.*—When the temperance crusade opened, the Germans were dumbfounded. Beer is with them as water is with us, and is used from infancy to old age. They received the crusading bands with stolid silence, looking at the ladies from out of their round blue eyes with an expression that showed that their sensations must have been queer, indescribable. Not a saloon in the city was closed. The ladies might as well have prayed and sang before the Rock of Gibraltar.

One day the crusade among the Germans came to a sudden end. An entire band of ladies, wives and mothers of the very best citizens, were arrested by the city police, respectfully arrested and escorted to the police station and charged with violating the city laws in obstructing the sidewalks. As is usual with criminals, they were compelled to register their names, residence and age. As they were not put in "the lock-up," their pockets were saved the usual emptying.

During these exciting times the temperance meetings were crowded, and men and women alike addressed the multitudes, the exercises being varied with prayer and song. At some of these meetings the narratives were so touching that hundreds were melted in tears.

And the speaker who so aroused our emotions by the plaintive melody of her voice and the heart-melting scenes of her narrative, was a woman, and she with crispy hair black as the ace of spades! The earthly tabernacle is as nothing, but it is the divine spirit, wherever it enters, that gives dignity to its possessor, lifts and unites with the Infinite."

In 1877—The Cause of Cincinnati's Pre-Eminence

It may be asked, why has Cincinnati obtained its pre-eminence in art, literature and public spirit over other western cities, for instance, Chicago? We answer, Cincinnati is older than this century. More than forty years ago, when Chicago was a mere fort and Indian trading post, Cincinnati was a city of 25,000 people with a cultured society noted even then for its fostership of literature and art. In those days Cincinnati had such men as Chief Justice McLean, Salmon P. Chase, Jacob Burnett, Dr. Daniel Drake, James C. Hall, Nicholas Longworth, Nathaniel Wright, Nat G. Pendleton, Charles Hammond, Henry Starr, Bellamy Storer, Larz Anderson, Bishop McIlvain, Lyman Beecher, D. K. Este, John P. Foote, Nathan Guilford, General William Lytle, General William H. Harrison, Colonel Jared Mansfield, etc. The last named had been Surveyor-General of the Northwest Territory and Professor of Mathematics at West Point.

In 1888, the German population formed a most important element, enough to make a large city—more than a hundred thousand. It is liberty loving and distinguished for thrift and intelligence. The Germans are devoted patrons of education and the arts, and especially music. German is taught in the public schools. The Irish element is also large and powerful.

Cincinnati, by the accident of her geographical position, became the focus of Abolitionism, and also of the opposite sentiment. In this city Birney was mobbed; Phillips was egged; colored men persecuted. In this city "Uncle Tom's Cabin" was planned, and here the Republican party was born. When the war came on Cincinnati did not waver. All sects and all parties, foreign and native, followed the Union flag. As soon as the war was over the citizens resumed their discussions. The Queen City is the arena of wrestling thoughts.

In the period of its early life it was largely visited by foreign travelers (for it was regarded as the brightest, most interesting place in the West), such as Volney, Ashe, Basil Hall, the Duke of Saxe-Weimar, Captain Marryat, Harriett Martineau, Chas. Dickens and Mrs. Trollope. The latter, with her four children, resided here two years, from 1828 to 1830, and lost thousands in what she named "The Bazaar," which came to be known as "Trollope's Folly." It stood on Third Street, just east of Broadway. Among its attractions was a splendid ball-room, long the pride of the city.

The Civil War wrought miracles in the development of Cincinnati. Its manufacturing enterprises have developed prodigiously, property value multiplied and large individual fortunes accumulated. A population of fully half a million dwells within a radius of ten miles, and the city proper has a third of a million. A wide and rich field of traffic and investment has of late years opened in the South by means of the Cincinnati Southern Railroad, and also by that through the Virginias by the Chesapeake and Ohio.

The Cincinnati Southern Railway was built at a total cost of $20,000,000, and runs to Chattanooga, a distance of 336 miles, into the heart of the South. It was leased in 1880 until the close of the century to the Erlanger Syndicate.

Cincinnati is a composite city, an aggregation of towns once separate, which, however, retain their old names, as Walnut Hills, Pendleton, and etc., and just outside lie some charming villages which practically enjoy the benefits of the city, yet control their own affairs by a mayor and aldermen, as Clifton and Avondale. Then, on the Kentucky side of the Ohio are Covington and Newport, with the Licking dividing them, and Bellevue, Dayton and Ludlow. Several bridges connect Cincinnati with Kentucky, among them the beautiful suspension bridge to Covington, completed in 1866 by the engineer Roebling, at a cost of $1,800,000. It is 103 feet above low water, and is the largest single span of its class in the world. The towers over which the gigantic cables pass are 1,057 feet apart, are 230 feet in height, and thus are higher, and each contains more stone than the Bunker Hill monument. The others are pier bridges, and built to accommodate railroads, viz.: the Cincinnati Southern Railroad, the Louisville Short Line Railroad, and the Chesapeake and Ohio. This last cost nearly $5,000,000 and was opened January 1, 1889.

Access to the hill-tops is by steeply graded roads, cable car and horse car roads, and by four inclined planes up which cars are drawn by powerful engines. The principal lines converge at Fountain Square.

The pavements are excellent, consisting of granite, asphalt and Ohio river boulders. The sewerage and underdrainage is perfect, and few cities are so healthy. Within the city limits is Eden Park, which is on the hills above the city plain, a pleasure ground of 240 acres, on which is the reservoir which supplies the city with water. Burnet Woods, a tract of beautiful forest of 170 acres, is also on the hills not far from the Zoological

Gardens, which last front on the Carthage pike. They are the largest and finest in America, and the buildings are as costly and substantial as those of the Zoological Gardens in Europe. The grounds, sixty acres in extent, are beautifully improved. There are about 1,000 specimens of animals and birds from all parts of the world. Frequently there are balls, picnics and special attractions, and on Thursday evening there is a fete. The gardens were opened in 1875, and since then over $300,000 has been expended.

Each of the four inclined planes leads to a famous resort. On the east is the Highland House, on the north, Lookout and Bellevue, and on the west, Price Hill. Thousands flock to these, especially summer evenings and on Sundays.

Spring Grove Cemetery is six miles from the river, in the valley of Mill Creek, on Spring Grove Avenue. It comprises 600 acres, and has had therein about 35,000 interments. Its numerous springs and groves suggest the name. It is probably the most picturesque, as it is the largest cemetery in the world. It is on the plan of a park, to relieve the ground of the heavy, incumbered air of a church-yard, and to present the appearance of a natural park. It is exquisitely laid out, with far-stretching lawns, miniature lakes and shrubbery, and ornamented with stately monuments, chapels, vaults and statues. There are about 7,000 lot holders. The more prominent objects are the Mortuary Chapel, the Dexter Mausoleum and the Soldiers' Monument. Many eminent historical characters are interred here. The spot is so enchanting that it seems as an earthly paradise rather than a home of the dead.

The Tyler-Davidson Fountain is the grandest fountain on the continent. It stands on the Esplanade in the center of Fountain Square, which is a raised stone structure twenty-eight inches in height. This square is near the center of the city and from which distances are calculated and the car lines mostly start. The fountain is a work in bronze consisting of fifteen large figures, of which the most prominent represents a woman from whose outstretched prone hands water is falling in fine spray. She is the Spirit of Rain. The head of this figure rises forty-five feet above the street level. The fountain was designed and cast in Munich, at a cost of $200,000. The work was presented to Cincinnati in 1871 by one of her public-spirited citizens, Henry Probasco, a patron of arts and literature, whose magnificent residence is one of the palaces of the suburbs.

The Government building is on the same street near it and is a magnificent and convenient structure. Herein are the custom house, court rooms and post-office. It is built of gray stone and cost $5,000,000, the most expensive building in the city. Close by it also is the Emery Arcade, one of the largest in the world, extending between two streets, a passage way of 400 feet protected by a glass roof.

Section II

Excerpts From "Negroes of Cincinnati Prior to Civil War," by Woodson, in Vol. I, Journal of Negro History

The following article is an abridgement of an account written by DR. C. G. WOODSON for the *Journal of Negro History*, January, 1916:

"The study of the history of the Negroes of Cincinnati is unusually important for the reason that from no other annals do we get such striking evidence that the colored people generally thrive when encouraged by their white neighbors. This story is otherwise significant when we consider the fact that about a fourth of the persons of color settling in the State of Ohio during the first half of the last century made their homes in this city. Situated on a north bend of the Ohio where commerce breaks bulk, Cincinnati rapidly developed, attracting both foreigners and Americans, among whom were not a few Negroes. Exactly how many persons of color were in this city during the first decade of the nineteenth century is not yet known. It has been said that there were no Negroes in Hamilton County in 1800. It is evident, too, that the real exodus of free Negroes and fugitives from the South to the Northwest Territory did not begin prior to 1815, although their attention had been earlier directed to this section as a more desirable place for colonization than the shores of Africa. As the reaction following the era of good feeling toward the Negroes during the Revolutionary period had not reached its climax, free persons of color had been content to remain in the South. The unexpected immigration of these Negroes into this section and the last bold effort made to drive them out marked epochs in their history in this city. The history of these people prior to the Civil War, therefore, falls into three periods, one of toleration from 1800 to 1826, one of persecution from 1826 to 1841, and one of amelioration from 1841 to 1861.

In the beginning the Negroes were not a live issue in Cincinnati. The question of their settlement in that community was debated but resulted in great diversity of opinion rather than a fixedness of judgment among the citizens. The question came up in the Constitutional Convention of 1802 and provoked some discussion, but reaching no decision, the convention simply left the Negroes out of the pale of the newly organized body politic, discriminating against them together with Indians and foreigners, by incorporating the word white into the fundamental law. The legislature to which the disposition of this question was left, however, took it up in 1804 to calm the fears of those who had more seriously considered the so-called menace of Negro immigration. This body enacted a law, providing that no Negro or mulatto should be allowed to remain permanently in that state, unless he could furnish a certificate of freedom issued by some court in the United States. Negroes then living there had to be registered before the following June, giving the names of their children. No man could employ a Negro who could not show such a certificate. Hiring a delinquent black or harboring or hindering the capture of a runaway was punishable by a fine of $50 and the owner of a fugitive thus illegally employed could recover fifty cents a day for the services of his slave.

As the fear of Negro immigration increased the law of 1804 was found to be inadequate. In 1807, therefore, the legislature enacted another measure providing that no Negro should be permitted to settle in Ohio unless he could within twenty days give bonds to the amount of $500, guaranteeing his good behavior and support. The fine for concealing a fugitive was raised from $50 to $100, one-half of which should go to the informer. Negro evidence against the white man was prohibited. This law together with that of 1830 making the Negro ineligible for service in the state militia, that of 1831 depriving persons of color of the privilege of serving upon juries, and that of 1838 prohibiting the education of colored children at the expense of the state, constituted what were known as the "Black Laws."

Up to 1826, however, the Negroes of Cincinnati had not become a cause of much trouble. Very little mention of them is made in the records of this period. They were not wanted in this city but were tolerated as a negligible factor. D. B. Warden, a traveler through the West in 1819, observed that the blacks of Cincinnati were "good-humoured, garrulous, and profligate, generally disinclined to laborious occupations, and prone to the performance of light and menial drudgery." Here the traveler was taking effect for cause. "Some few," said he, "exercise the humbler trades, and some appear to have formed a correct conception of the objects and value of property, and are both industrious and economical. A large proportion of them are reputed, and perhaps correctly, to be habituated to petit larceny." But this had not become a grave offense, for he said that not more than one individual had been corporally punished by the courts since the settlement of the town.

When, however, the South reached the conclusion that free Negroes were an evil, and Quakers and philanthropists began to direct these unfortunates to the Northwest Territory for colonization, a great commotion arose in southern Ohio and especially in Cincinnati. How rapid this movement was, may be best observed by noticing the statistics of this period. There were 337 Negroes in Ohio in 1800; 1,890 in 1810; 4,723 in 1820; 9,586 in 1830; 17,342 in 1840; and 25,279 in 1850. Now Cincinnati had 410 Negroes in 1819; 690 in 1826; 2,255 in 1840; 3,237 in 1850.

It was during the period between 1826 and 1840 that Cincinnati had to grapple with the problem of the immigrating Negroes and the poor whites from the uplands of Virginia and Kentucky. With some ill-informed persons the question was whether that section should be settled by white men or Negroes. The situation became more alarming when the Southern philanthropic minority sometimes afforded a man like a master of Pittsylvania County, Virginia, who settled 70 freedmen in Lawrence County, Ohio, in one day. It became unusually acute in Cincinnati because of the close social and commercial relations between that city and the slave state. Early in the nineteenth century Cincinnati became a manufacturing center to which the South learned to look for supplies of machinery, implements, furniture, and food. The business men prospering thereby were not advocates of slavery, but rather than lose trade by acquiring the reputation of harboring fugitive slaves or frightening away whites by encouraging the immigration of Negroes, they began to assume the attitude of driving the latter from those parts.

[2]

From this time until the forties the Negroes were a real issue in Cincinnati. During the late twenties they not only had to suffer from the legal disabilities provided in the "Black Laws," but had to withstand the humiliation of a rigid social ostracism. They were regarded as intruders and denounced as an idle, profligate and criminal class with whom a self-respecting white man could not afford to associate. Their children were not permitted to attend the public schools and few persons braved the inconveniences of living under the stigma of teaching a "nigger school." Negroes were not welcome in the white churches and when they secured admission thereto they had to go to the "black pew." Colored ministers were treated with very little consideration by the white clergy, as they feared that they might lose caste and be compelled to give up their churches. The colored people made little or no effort to go to white theaters or hotels and did not attempt to ride in public conveyances on equal footing with members of the other race. Not even white and colored children dared to play together to the extent that such was permitted in the South.

This situation became more serious when it extended to pursuits of labor. White laborers there, as in other Northern cities during this period, easily reached the position of thinking that it was a disgrace to work with Negroes. This prejudice was so much more inconvenient to the Negroes of Cincinnati than elsewhere because of the fact that most of the menial labor in that city was done by Germans and Irishmen. Now, since the Negroes could not follow ordinary menial occupations there was nothing left them but the lowest form of "drudgery," for which employers often preferred colored women. It was, therefore, necessary in some cases for the mother to earn the living for the family because the father could get nothing to do. A colored man could not serve as an ordinary drayman or porter without subjecting his employer to a heavy penalty.

The trades unions were then proscribing the employment of colored mechanics. Many who had worked at skilled labor were by this prejudice forced to do drudgery or find employment in other cities. The president of a "mechanical association" was publicly tried in 1830 by that organization for the crime of assisting a colored youth to learn a trade. A young man of high character who had at the cabinet-making trade in Kentucky saved enough to purchase his freedom, came to Cincinnati about this time, seeking employment. He finally found a position in a shop conducted by an Englishman. On entering the establishment, however, the workmen threw down their tools, declaring that the Negro had to leave or they would. The unfortunate "intruder" was accordingly dismissed. He then entered the employ of a slave holder, who at the close of the Negro's two years of service at common labor discovered that the black was a mechanic. The employer then procured work for him as a rough carpenter. By dint of perseverance and industry this Negro within a few years became a master workman, employing at times six to eight men, but he never received a single job of work from a native-born citizen from a free state.

The hardships of the Negroes of this city, however, had just begun. The growth of a prejudiced public opinion led not only to legal proscription and social ostracism but also to open persecution. With the cries of the Southerners for the return of fugitives and the request of white immigrants for the exclusion of Negroes from that section, came the demand to solve the problem by enforcing the "Black Laws." Among certain indulgent officials these enactments had been allowed to fall into desuetude. These very demands, however, brought forward friends as well as enemies of the colored people. Their first clash was testing the constitutionality of the law of 1807. When the question came up before the Supreme Court, however, this measure was upheld. Encouraged by such support, the foes of the Negroes forced an execution of the law. The courts at first hesitated but finally took the position that the will of the people should be obeyed. The Negroes asked for ninety days to comply with the law and were given sixty. When the allotted time had expired, however, many of them had not given bonds as required. The only thing to do then was to force them to leave the city. The officials again hesitated but a mob quickly formed to relieve them of the work. This was the riot of 1829. Bands of ruffians held sway in the city for three days, as the police were unable or unwilling to restore order. Negroes were insulted on the streets, attacked in their homes, and even killed. About a thousand or twelve hundred of them found it advisable to leave for Canada West, where they established a settlement known as Wilberforce.

This upheaval, though unusually alarming, was not altogether a bad omen. It was due not only to the demands which the South was making upon the North and the fear of the loss of Southern trade, but also to the rise of Abolition Societies, the growth of which such a riotous condition as this had materially fostered. In a word, it was the sequel of the struggle between the proslavery and the antislavery elements of the city. This was the time when the friends of the Negroes were doing most for them. Instead of frightening them away a group of respectable white men in that community were beginning to think that they should be trained to live there as useful citizens. Several schools and churches for them were established. The Negroes themselves provided for their own first school about 1820; but one Mr. Wing had sufficient courage to admit persons of color to his evening classes after their first efforts had failed. By 1834 many of the colored people were receiving systematic instruction. To some enemies of these dependents it seemed that the tide was about to turn in favor of the despised cause. Negroes began to raise sums adequate to their elementary education and the students of Lane Seminary supplemented these efforts by establishing a colored mission school which offered more advanced courses and lectures on scientific subjects twice a week. These students, however, soon found themselves far in advance of public opinion. They were censured by the faculty and to find a more congenial center for their operations they had to go to Oberlin in the Western Reserve, where a larger number of persons had become interested in the cause of the despised and rejected of men.

During the years from 1833 to 1836 the situation in Cincinnati grew worse because of the still larger influx of Negroes driven from the South by intolerable conditions incident to the reaction against the race. To solve this problem various schemes were brought forth. Augustus Wattles tells us that he appeared in Cincinnati about this time and induced numbers of the Negroes to go to Mercer County, Ohio, where they took up 30,000 acres of land. Others went to Indiana and purchased large tracts on the public domain. Such a method, however, seemed rather slow to the militant proslavery leaders who had learned not only to treat the Negroes as an evil but to denounce in the same manner the increasing number of abolitionists by whom it was said the Negroes were encouraged to immigrate into the state. The spirit of the proslavery sympathizers was well exhibited in the upheaval which soon followed.

This was the riot of July 30, 1836. It was an effort to destroy the abolition organ, *The Philanthropist*, edited by James G. Birney, a Southerner who had brought his slaves from Huntsville, Alabama, to Kentucky and freed them.

Undaunted by this persistent opposition the Negroes of Cincinnati achieved so much during the years between 1835 and 1840 that they deserved to be ranked among the most progressive people of the world. Their friends endeavored to enable them through schools, churches and industries to embrace every opportunity to rise. These 2,255 Negroes accumulated, largely during this period, $209,000 worth of property, exclusive of personal effects and three churches valued at $19,000. Some of this wealth consisted of land purchased in Ohio and Indiana. Furthermore, in 1839 certain colored men of the city organized "The Iron Chest Company," a real estate firm, which built three brick buildings and rented them to white men. One man who a few years prior to 1840 had thought it useless to accumulate wealth from which he might be driven away, had changed his mind and purchased $6,000 worth of real estate. Another Negro who had paid $5,000 for himself and family had bought a home worth $800 or $1,000. A freedman, who was a slave until he was twenty-four years old, then had two lots worth $10,000, paid a tax of $40 and had 320 acres of land in Mercer County. Another, who was worth only $3,000 in 1836, had seven houses in Cincinnati, 400 acres of land in Indiana, and another tract in the same county. He was worth $12,000 or $15,000. A woman who was a slave until she was thirty was then worth $2,000. She had also come into potential possession of two houses on which a white lawyer had given her a mortgage to secure the payment of $2,000 borrowed from this thrifty woman. Another Negro who was on the auction block in 1832 had spent $2,600 purchasing himself and family and had bought two brick houses worth $6,000 and 560 acres of land in Mercer County, said to be worth $2,500.

This unusual progress had been promoted by two forces, the development of the steamboat as a factor in transportation and the rise of the Negro mechanic. Negroes employed on vessels as servants to the traveling public amassed large sums received in the form of tips. Furthermore, the fortunate few constituting the stewards of these vessels could, by placing contracts for supplies and using business methods, realize handsome incomes. Many Negroes thus enriched purchased real estate and went into business in Cincinnati. The other force, the rise of the Negro mechanic, was made possible by overcoming much of the prejudice which had at first been encountered. A great change in this respect had taken place in Cincinnati by 1840. Many who had been forced to work as menial laborers then had the opportunity to show their usefulness to their families and to the community. Colored mechanics were then getting as much skilled labor as they could do. It was not uncommon for white artisans to solicit employment of colored men because they had the reputation of being better paymasters than master workmen of the more favored race. White mechanics not only worked with colored men but often associated with them, patronized the same barber shop, and went to the same places of amusement.

In this prosperous condition the Negroes could help themselves. Prior to this period they had been unable to make any sacrifices for charity and education. Only $150 of the $1,000 raised for Negro education in 1835 was contributed by persons of color. In 1839, however, the colored people raised $889.30 for this purpose, and thanks to their economic progress, this task was not so difficult as that of raising the $150 in 1835. They were then spending considerable amounts for evening and writing schools, attended by seventy-five persons, chiefly adults. In 1840 Reverend Mr. Denham and Mr. Goodwin had in their schools sixty-five pupils each paying $3 per quarter, and Miss Merrill a school of forty-seven pupils paying the same tuition. In all, the colored people were paying these teachers about $1,300 a year. The only help the Negroes were then receiving was that from the Ladies Anti-Slavery Society, which employed one Miss Seymour at a salary of $300 a year to instruct fifty-four pupils. Moreover, the colored people were giving liberally to objects of charity. Some Negroes burned out in 1839 were promptly relieved by members of their own race. A white family in distress was befriended by a colored woman. The Negroes contributed also to the support of missionaries in Jamaica and during the years from 1836 to 1840 assisted twenty-five emancipated slaves from Cincinnati to Mercer County, Ohio.

During this period they had made progress in other than material things. Their improvement in religion and morals was remarkable. They then had four flourishing Sabbath Schools with 310 regular attendants, one Baptist and two Methodist churches with a membership of 800, a "Total Abstinence Temperance Society" for adults numbering 450, and a "Sabbath School or Youth's Society" of 180 members. A few of these violated their pledges, but when we consider the fact that one-fourth of the entire colored population belonged to temperance organizations while less than one-tenth of the whites were thus connected, we must admit that this was no mean achievement. Among the Negroes public sentiment was then such that no colored man could openly sell intoxicating drinks. This growing temperance was exhibited, too, in the decreasing fondness for dress and finery. There was less tendency to strive merely to get a fine suit of clothes and exhibit one's self on the streets. Places of vice were not so much frequented and barber shops which on Sundays formerly became a rendezvous for the idle and the garrulous were with few exceptions closed by 1840. This influence of the religious organizations reached also beyond the limits of Cincinnati. A theological student from the state of New York said after spending some time in New Orleans, that the influence of the elevation of the colored people of Cincinnati was felt all the way down the river. Travelers often spoke of the difference in the appearance of barbers and waiters on the boats.

It was in fact a brighter day for the colored people. In 1840 an observer said that they had improved faster than any other people in the city. The *Cincinnati Gazette*, after characterizing certain Negroes as being imprudent and vicious, said of others: "Many of these are peaceable and industrious, raising respectable families and acquiring property." Mr. James H. Perkins, a respectable citizen of the city, asserted that the day school which the colored children attended had shown by examination that it was as good as any other in the city. He said further "there is no question, I presume, that the colored population of Cincinnati, oppressed as it has been by our state laws as well as by prejudice, has risen more rapidly than almost any other people in any part of the world." Within three or four years their property had more than doubled; their schools had become firmly established, and their churches and Sunday Schools had grown as rapidly as any other religious institutions in the city. Trusting to good conduct and character, they had risen to a prosperous position in the eyes of those whose prejudices would "allow them to look through the skin to the soul."

The colored people had had too many enemies in Cincinnati, however, to expect that they had overcome all opposition. The prejudice of certain labor groups against the Negroes increased in proportion to the prosperity of the latter. That they had been able to do so well as they had was due to the lack of strength on the part of the labor organizations then forming to counteract the sentiment of fair play for the Negroes. Their labor competed directly with that of the whites and began again to excite "jealousy and heart burning." The Germans, who were generally toiling up from poverty, seemed to exhibit less prejudice; but the unfortunate Irish bore it grievously that even a few Negroes should outstrip some of their race in the economic struggle.

In 1841 there followed several clashes which aggravated the situation. In the month of June one Burnett, referred to as "a mischievous and swaggering Englishman running a cake shop," had harbored a runaway slave. When a man named McCalla, his reputed master, came with an officer to reclaim the fugitive, Burnett and his family resisted them. The Burnetts were committed to answer for this infraction of the law and finally were adequately punished. The proslavery mob which had gathered undertook to destroy their home but the officials prevented them. Besides, early in August, according to a report, a German citizen defending his blackberry patch near the city, was attacked by two Negroes and stabbed so severely that he died. Then about three weeks thereafter, according to another rumor, a very respectable lady was insultingly accosted by two colored men and in fleeing from them two others rudely thrust themselves before her on the sidewalk. But in this case, as in most others growing out of rumors, no one could ever say who the lady or her so-called assailants were. At the same time, too, the situation was further aggravated by an almost sudden influx of irresponsible Negroes from various parts, increasing the number of those engaged in noisy frolics which had become a nuisance to certain white neighbors.

Accordingly, on Tuesday, the twenty-ninth of August, 1841, there broke out on the corner of Sixth and Broadway a quarrel in which two or three persons were wounded. On the following night the fracas was renewed. A group of ruffians attacked the Dumas Hotel, a colored establishment, on McAllister Street, demanding the surrender of a Negro who, they believed, was concealed there. As the Negroes of the neighborhood came to the assistance of their friends in the hotel the mob had to withdraw. On Thursday night there took place another clash between a group of young men and boys and a few Negroes who seriously wounded one or two of the former. On Friday evening the mob, incited to riotous acts by an influx of white ruffians, seemingly from the steamboats and the Kentucky side of the river, openly assembled in Fifth Street Market without being molested by the police, armed themselves and marched to Broadway and Sixth Street, shouting and swearing. They attacked a colored confectionery store nearby, demolishing its doors and windows. James W. Piatt, an influential citizen, and the mayor then addressed the disorderly persons, vainly exhorting them to peace and obedience to the law. Moved by passionate entreaties to execute their poorly prepared plan, the assailants advanced and attacked the Negroes with stones. The blacks, however, had not been idle. They had secured sufficient guns and ammunition to fire into the mob such a volley that it had to fall back. The aggressors rallied again, however, only to be in like manner repulsed. Men were wounded on both sides and carried off and reported dead. The Negroes advanced courageously, and according to a reporter, fired down the street into the mass of ruffians, causing a hasty retreat. This mêlée continued until about one o'clock when a part of the mob secured an iron six pounder, hauled it to the place of combat against the exhortations of the powerless mayor, and fired on the Negroes. With this unusual advantage the blacks were forced to retreat, many of them going to the hills. About two o'clock the mayor succeeded in bringing out a portion of the "military" which succeeded in holding the mob at bay.

On the next day the colored people in the district under fire were surrounded by sentinels and put under martial law. Indignation meetings of law-abiding citizens were held on Saturday to pass resolutions, denouncing abolitionists and mobs and making an appeal to the people and the civil authorities to uphold the law. The Negroes also held a meeting and respectfully assured the mayor and citizens that they would use every effort to conduct themselves orderly and expressed their readiness to give bonds according to the law of 1807 or leave the city quietly within a specified time. But these steps availed little when the police winked at this violence. The rioters boldly occupied the streets without arrest and continued their work until Sunday. The mayor, sheriff and marshal went to the battle ground about three o'clock but the mob still had control. The officers could not even remove those Negroes who complied with the law of leaving. The authorities finally hit upon the scheme of decreasing the excitement by inducing about 300 colored men to go to jail for security after they had been assured that their wives and children would be protected. The Negroes consented and accordingly were committed, but the cowardly element again attacked these helpless dependents like savages. At the same time other rioters attacked the office of *The Philanthropist* and broke up the press. The mob continued its work until it dispersed from mere exhaustion. The Governor finally came to the city and issued a proclamation setting forth the gravity of the situation. The citizens and civil authorities rallied to his support and strong patrols prevented further disorder.

It is impossible to say exactly how many were killed and wounded on either side. It is probable that several were killed and twenty or thirty variously wounded, though but few dangerously. Forty of the mob were arrested and imprisoned. Exactly what was done with all of them is not yet known. It seems that few if any of them, however, were severely punished. The Negroes who had been committed for safe-keeping were thereafter disposed of in various ways. Some were discharged on certificates of nativity, others gave bonds for their support and good behavior, a few were dismissed as non-residents, a number of them were discharged by a justice of the Court of Common Pleas and the rest were held indefinitely.

This upheaval had two important results. The enemies of the Negroes were convinced that there were sufficient law-abiding citizens to secure to the refugees protection from mob violence;

and because of these riots their sympathizers became more attached to the objects of their philanthropy. Abolitionists, Free Soilers and Whigs fearlessly attacked the laws which kept the Negroes under legal and economic disabilities. Petitions praying that these measures be repealed were sent to the legislature. The proslavery element of the state, however, was equally militant. The legislators, therefore, had to consider such questions as extradition and immigration, state aid and colonization, the employment of colored men in the militia service, the extension of the elective franchise, and the admission of colored children to the public schools. Most of these "Black Laws" remained until after the war, but in 1848 they were so modified as to give the Negroes legal standing in courts and to provide for their children such education as a school tax on the property of colored persons would allow and further changed in 1849 so as to make the provision for education more effective. The question of repealing the other oppressive laws came up in the Convention of 1850. It appeared that the cause of the Negroes had made much progress in that a larger number had begun to speak for them. But practically all of the members of the Convention who stood for the Negroes were from the Western Reserve. After much heated discussion in this Convention the colored people were, by a large majority of votes, still left under the disabilities of being disqualified to sit on juries, unable to obtain a legal residence so as to enter a charitable institution supported by the state, and denied admission to public schools established for white children.

The greatest problem of the Negroes, however, was one of education. There were more persons interested in furnishing them facilities of education than in repealing the prohibitive measures, feeling that the other matters would adjust themselves after giving them adequate training. But it required some time and effort yet before much could be effected in Cincinnati because of the sympathizers with the South. The mere passing of the law of 1849 did not prove to be altogether a victory. Complying with the provisions of this act the Negroes elected trustees, organized a system, and employed teachers, relying on the money allotted them by the law on the basis of a per capita division of the school fund received by the Board of Education. So great was the prejudice of people of the city that the school officials refused to turn over the required funds on the grounds that the colored trustees were not electors and therefore could not be office-holders, qualified to receive and disburse funds. Under the leadership of John I. Gaines, therefore, the trustees called an indignation meeting and raised sufficient money to employ Flamen Ball, an attorney, to secure a writ of mandamus. The case was contested by the city officials, even in the Supreme Court, which decided against the officious whites.

This decision did not solve the whole problem in Cincinnati. The amount raised was small and even had it been adequate to employ teachers they were handicapped by another decision that no portion of it could be used for building school houses. After a short period of accomplishing practically nothing the law was amended in 1853 so as to transfer the control of such schools to the managers of the white system. This was taken as a reflection on the blacks of the city and tended to make them refuse to co-operate with the white board. On account of the failure of this body to act effectively prior to 1856 the people of color were again given power to elect their own trustees.

During this contest certain Negroes of Cincinnati were endeavoring to make good their claim to equal rights in the public schools. Acting upon this contention a colored man sent his son to a public school which, on account of his presence, became a center of unusual excitement. Isabelle Newhall, the teacher to whom he went, immediately complained to the board of education requesting that he be expelled because of his color. After "due deliberation" the board of education decided by a vote of 15 to 10 that the colored pupil would have to withdraw. Thereupon two members of that body, residing in the district of the timorous teacher, resigned.

Many Negroes belonging to the mulatto class, however, were more successful in getting into the white schools. In 1849 certain parents complained that children of color were being admitted to the public schools, and in fact there were in one of them two daughters of a white father and a mulatto mother. On complaining about this to the principal of the school in question, the indignant patrons were asked to point out the undesirable pupils. They could not; for, says Sir Charles Lyell, "the two girls were not only among the best pupils, but better looking and less dark than many of the other pupils."

Thereafter, however, much progress in the education of the colored people among themselves was noted. By 1844 they had six schools of their own and before the war two well-supported public schools. Among their teachers were such useful persons as Mrs. M. J. Corbin, Miss Lucy Blackburn, Miss Anne Ryall, Miss Virgina C. Tilley, Miss Martha E. Anderson, William H. Parham, William R. Casey, John G. Mitchell and Peter H. Clark. The pupils were showing their appreciation by regular attendance, excellent deportment, and progress in the acquisition of knowledge. Speaking of these Negroes in 1855, John P. Foote said that they shared with the white citizens that respect for education and the diffusion of knowledge, which has been one of their "characteristics," and that they had, therefore, been more generally intelligent than free persons of color not only in other parts of this country but in all other parts of the world. It was in appreciation of the worth of this class to the community that in 1844 Nicholas Longworth helped them to establish an orphan asylum and in 1858 built for them a comfortable school building, leasing it with a privilege of purchasing it within four years. They met these requirements within the stipulated time and in 1859 secured through other agencies the construction of another building in the western portion of the city.

The most successful of these schools, however, was the Gilmore High School, a private institution founded by an English clergyman. This institution offered instruction in the fundamentals and in some vocational studies. It was supported liberally by the benevolent element of the white people and patronized and appreciated by the Negroes as the first and only institution offering them the opportunity for thorough training. It became popular throughout the country, attracting Negroes from as far South as New Orleans. Rich Southern planters found it convenient to have their mulatto children educated in this high school.

The work of these schools was substantially supplemented by that of the colored churches. They directed their attention not only to moral and religious welfare of the colored people but also to their mental development. Through their well-attended Sunday Schools these institutions furnished many Negroes of all classes the facilities of elementary education. Such opportunities were offered at the Baker Street Baptist Church, the Third Street Baptist Church, the Colored Christian Church, the New Street Methodist Church, and the African Methodist Church. Among the preachers then promoting this cause were John Warren, Rufus Conrad, Henry Simpson, and Wallace Shelton. Many of the old citizens of Cincinnati often refer with pride to the valuable services rendered by these leaders.

In things economic the Negroes were exceptionally prosperous after the forties. Cincinnati had then become a noted pork-packing and manufacturing center. The increasing canal and river traffic and finally the rise of the railroad system tended to make it thrive more than ever. Many colored men grew up with the city. A Negro had, in the East End on Calvert Street, a large cooperage establishment which made barrels for the packers. Knight and Bell were successful contractors noted for their skill and integrity and employed by the best white people of the city. Robert Harlan made considerable money buying and selling race horses. Thompson Cooley[1] had a successful pickling establishment. On Broadway, A. V. Thompson, a colored tailor, conducted a thriving business. J. Pressley and Thomas Ball[2] were the well-known photographers of the city established in a handsomely furnished modern gallery which was patronized by some of the wealthiest people. Samuel T. Wilcox, who owed his success to his position as a steward on an Ohio river line, thereafter went into the grocery business and built up such a large trade among the aristocratic families that he accumulated $59,000 worth of property by 1859.

A more useful Negro had for years been toiling upward in this city. This man was Henry Boyd, a Kentucky freedman, who had helped to overcome the prejudice against colored mechanics in that city by exhibiting the highest efficiency. He patented a corded bed which became very popular, especially in the Southwest. With this article he built up a creditable manufacturing business, employing from 18 to 25 white and colored men. He was, therefore, known as one of the desirable men of the city. Two things, however, seemingly interfered with his

---

[1] An error—should be Schooley and Thompson.
[2] Should be Ball and Thomas; their names were Pressley Ball and Alexander Thomas.

business. In the first place, certain white men who became jealous of his success, burned him out and the insurance companies refused to carry him any longer. Moreover, having to do chiefly with white men he was charged by his people with favoring the miscegenation of races. Whether or not this was well founded is not yet known, but his children and grandchildren did marry whites and were lost in the so-called superior race."

Section III

Ante-Bellum Days—Incidents—Tragedies

NEGROES VICTIMS OF EVERY ATROCITY

The year of 1810 was remarkable for the tide of immigration that set in from the adjoining state of Kentucky. Thousands of the colored inhabitants, black and brown, abandoned their homes, swam the river and landed on the banks of the Ohio. They came unarmed, without sword or spear, musket or ammunition, or other munitions of war than those bestowed upon them by nature. Immediately upon landing they dispersed among the woods, prepared themselves log cabins or built more temporary structures and set up housekeeping. Nothing could be more peaceable than their intentions. No class of citizens could have been more active, industrious, frugal or cleanly in their habits. But though as a class they were conceded to be productive, in political economy they were ranked an non-producers and accordingly were doomed to suffer persecution. Then every white man was a ranger. Middlemen had not found their way out west; so war was declared immediately against the intruders and every man, woman and child arrayed themselves against these unarmed and inoffensive immigrants. War to the knife, bitter, relentless, exterminating war was waged and speedily raged. From the township the war sentiment extended to the county; from the county to the state, until the legislature actually passed a law for the extinction of the races, black and brown, indiscriminately. Every atrocity was practiced and encouraged, and scalping commanded a high premium.—(Nelson's Suburban Homes, page 621.)

MOB OF 1836

In 1836, Central Avenue was known as Western Row. One day a colored boy had a row with a white boy. Words were followed by blows. "Unfortunately the colored boy won the fight." The whites took the part of the white boy while Negroes rushed to the support of the colored, and soon a riot was in progress which resulted in the death and damage of many people. The actual result is not known but it is reasonable to conclude that victory followed the advantage that rested with the whites. The Negroes took refuge in the swamps and forest, now the region comprising the West End.

THE MOB OF 1841

(From the *Daily Gazette*, September 6, 1841, Cincinnati, Ohio.)

"This city has been in a most alarming condition for several days, and from about eight o'clock on Friday evening until about three o'clock yesterday morning, almost entirely at the mercy of a lawless mob, ranging in number from two to fifteen hundred.

On Tuesday evening last, a quarrel took place near the corner of Sixth Street and Broadway, between a party of Irishmen and some Negroes, in which blows were exchanged and other weapons, if not firearms, used. Some two or three of each party were wounded.

On Wednesday night the quarrel was renewed in some way, and some time after midnight a party of excited men, armed with clubs, etc., attacked a house occupied as a negro boarding house, on McAllister Street, demanding the surrender of a Negro who they said had fled into the house and was there secreted, and uttering the most violent threats against the house and the Negroes in general. Several of the adjoining houses were occupied by Negro families, including women and children. The violence increased and was resisted by those in or about the houses. An engagement took place, several were wounded on each side, and some say guns and pistols were discharged from the house. The interference of some gentlemen in the neighborhood succeeded in restoring quiet, after about three-quarters of an hour, when a watchman appeared. But it is singular that this violent street disturbance elicited no report to the police, no arrest—indeed, that the Mayor remained ignorant of the affair until late in the day, when he casually heard of it.

On Thursday night another encounter took place in the neighborhood of the Lower Market, between some young men and boys, and some Negroes, in which one or two boys were badly wounded, as it was supposed, with knives.

On Friday, during the day, there was considerable excitement, threats of violence and lawless outbreaking were indicated in various ways, and came to the ears of the police and of the Negroes. Attacks were expected upon the Negro residences in McAllister, Sixth and New Streets. The Negroes armed themselves, and the knowledge of this increased the excitement. But we do not know that it produced any known measure of precaution on the part of the police to preserve the peace of the city.

Before eight o'clock in the evening, a mob, the principal organization of which, we understand, was arranged in Kentucky, openly assembled in Fifth Street Market, unmolested by the police or citizens. The number of this mob, as they deliberately marched from their rendezvous toward Broadway and Sixth Street, is variously estimated, but the number increased as they progressed. They were armed with clubs, stones, etc. Reaching the scene of operations, with shouts and blasphemous imprecations, they attacked a negro confectionery on Broadway, and demolished the doors and windows. This attracted an immense crowd. Savage yells were uttered to encourage the mob onward to the general attack upon the Negroes. About this time the Mayor came up and addressed the people, exhorting them to peace and obedience to law. The savage yell was instantly raised, "Down with him." "Run him off," was shouted, intermixed with horrid imprecations, and exhortations to the mob to move onward.

They advanced to the attack with stones, etc., and were repeatedly fired upon by the Negroes. The mob scattered, but immediately rallied again, and again were in like manner, repulsed. Men were wounded on both sides and carried off, and many reported dead. The Negroes rallied several times, advanced upon the crowd, and most unjustifiably fired down the street into it, causing a great rush in various directions. These things were repeated until past one o'clock, when a party procured an iron six-pounder from near the river, loaded it with boiler punchings, etc., and hauled it to the ground, against the exhortations of the Mayor and others. It was posted on Broadway, and pointed down Sixth Street. The yells continued, but there was a partial cessation of firing. Many of the Negroes had fled to the hills. The attack upon houses was recommenced with firing of guns on both sides, which continued during most of the night, and exaggerated rumors of the killed and wounded filled the streets. The cannon was discharged several times. About two o'clock a portion of the military, upon the call of the Mayor, proceeded to the scene of disorder and succeeded in keeping the mob at bay. In the morning, and throughout the day, several blocks, including the battle-ground, were surrounded by sentinels, and kept under martial law—keeping within the Negroes there, and adding to them such as were brought during the day, seized without particular charge, by parties who scoured the city, assuming the authority of the law.

A meeting of citizens was held at the court house, on Saturday morning, at which the Mayor presided. This meeting was addressed by the Mayor, Judge Reed, Mr. Piatt, Sheriff Avery and Mr. Hart. They resolved to observe the law, to discountenance mobs, invoked the aid of the authorities to stay the violence, and pledged themselves to exertion in aid of the civil authority to arrest and place within reach of the law the Negroes who wounded the two white boys on Columbia Street; that the Township Trustees enforce the law of 1807, requiring security of Negroes, pledging themselves to enforce it to the very letter, until the city is relieved of the effect of "modern abolitionism," assuring our "Southern brethren" to carry out that act in good faith and to deliver "up, under the law of Congress, forthwith" every negro who escapes from his master and comes within our borders. They requested the Mayor, sheriff, and the civil authorities to proceed at once to the dwellings of the blacks and disarm them of all offensive weapons—and recommended search for offenders against the laws, immediate legal proceedings against them, and an efficient patrol to protect the persons and property of the blacks, during the existence of the present excitement, and until they give the bonds required by the act of 1807, or leave the city. They requested the parents and guardians of boys to keep them at home, or away from the scene of excitement. They resolved, "That we view with abhorrence the proceedings of the abolitionists in our city, and that we repudiate their doctrines, and believe it to be the duty of every good citizen, by all lawful means, to discountenance every man who lends them his assistance." These resolutions adopted unanimously and signed by the Mayor. They were afterward printed in handbills and posted in all parts of the city.

The City Council also held a special session and passed resolutions invoking the united exertions of orderly citizens to the aid of the authorities to put down the violent commotion existing in the city, to preserve order and vindicate the law against the violence of an excited and lawless mob—requesting all officers, watchmen and firemen to unite for the arrest of the rioters and violators of law, and the marshal to increase his deputies to any number required—not exceeding five hundred—to preserve life and protect property; requiring the Mayor and marshal to call in the aid of the county militia to preserve order, and the captain of the watch to increase his force. These proceedings were posted in handbills. Intense excitement continued during the day, the mob and the leaders boldly occupying the streets without arrest, or any effort to arrest them, so far as we have heard.

The Negroes held a meeting in a church, and respectfully assured the Mayor and the citizens that they would use every effort to conduct themselves as orderly, industrious and peaceable people—to suppress any imprudent conduct among their population, and to ferret out all violation of order and law. They deprecated the practice of carrying about their persons any dangerous weapons, pledged themselves not to carry or keep any about their persons or houses, and expressed their readiness to surrender all such. They expressed their readiness to conform to the law of 1807, and give bond, or to leave within a specified time, and tendered their thanks to the Mayor, watch officers and gentlemen of the city for the efforts made to save their property, their lives, their wives and their children.

At three o'clock in the afternoon the Mayor, sheriff, marshal, and a portion of the police proceeded to the battle-ground and there, under the protection of the military, though in the presence of the mob, and so far controlled by them as to prevent the taking away of any negroes, upon their complying with the law, several Negroes gave bond, and obtained the permission of the authorities to go away with sureties—some of our most respectable citizens—but were headed even within the military sentinels, and compelled to return within the ground. It was resolved to embody the male Negroes and march them to jail for security, under the protection of the military and civil authorities.

From two hundred and fifty to three hundred Negroes, including sound and maimed, were with some difficulty marched off to jail, surrounded by the military and officers; and a dense mass of men, women and boys, confounding all distinction between the orderly and disorderly, accompanied with deafening yells.

They were safely lodged, and still remained in prison, separated from their families. The crowd was in that way dispersed. Some then supposed that we should have a quiet night, but others, more observing, discovered that the lawless mob had determined on further violence, to be enacted immediately after nightfall. Citizens disposed to aid the authorities were invited to assemble, enroll themselves, and organize for action. The military were ordered out, firemen were out, clothed with authority as a police band. About eighty citizens enrolled themselves as assistants of the marshal, and acted during the night under his direction, in connection with Judge Torrence, who was selected by themselves. A portion of this force was mounted, and a troop of horse and several companies of volunteer infantry continued on duty till near midnight. Some were then discharged to sleep upon their arms; others remained on duty till morning, guarding the jail, etc. As was anticipated, the mob, efficiently organized, early commenced operations, dividing their force and making attacks at different points, thus distracting the attention of the police. The first successful onset was made upon the printing establishment of the "Philanthropist." They succeeded in entering the establishment, breaking up the press, and running with it, amid savage yells, down through Main Street to the river, into which it was thrown.

The military appeared in the alley near the office, interrupting the mob for a short time. They escaped through by-ways, and, when the military retired, returned to their work of destruction in the office, which they completed. Several houses were broken open in different parts of the city, occupied by Negroes, and the windows, doors and furniture totally destroyed. From this work they were driven by the police, and finally dispersed from mere exhaustion, whether to remain quiet or to recruit their strength for renewed assault, we may know before this paper is circulated.

Mortifying as is the declaration, truth requires us to acknowledge that our city has been in a complete anarchy, controlled mostly by a lawless and violent mob for twenty-four hours, trampling all law and authority under foot. We feel this degradation deeply—but so it is. It is impossible to learn the precise number killed and wounded, either of whites or among the Negroes; probably several were killed on both sides, and some twenty or thirty variously wounded, though but few dangerously.

The authorities succeeded in arresting and securing about forty of the mob, who are now in prison. Others were arrested but were rescued or made their escape otherwise.

Monday morning, three a. m.—No disturbances have occurred in our city during the night. The different military companies were stationed at various points through the city. Captain Taylor's troop of horse, together with a large number of citizens, formed themselves into companies of about thirty each, and kept up a patrol until about two o'clock, when the citizens generally retired, leaving the military on duty.

Governor Corwin issued a proclamation on the 5th of September (the day on which the mob demonstrated), calling upon and commanding all people who might be in the city to yield prompt obedience to the civil authorities engaged in the preservation of the peace, and enjoining upon all persons to abstain from all unlawful assemblages, or any act of violence against the persons or property of the citizens.

There was no further disturbance! and thus ended the disgraceful outbreak."

"Some particulars not given in this account may be mentioned here. While these demonstrations were in progress it was reported that a number of Negroes had fled to Walnut Hills and were concealed in Lane Seminary. The mob expressed their intention to ferret them out, and breathed many threats against those who protected them. The students of

Lane Seminary heard of this, and began preparations for defense. They formed a military company, under command of E. M. Gregory, and collected all the available weapons in the neighborhood. Governor Corwin, hearing of their organization, sent them a supply of firearms from the state arsenal. The mob mustered a company two hundred strong, and started to make an attack on the "d——d abolition hole," as they called the seminary, but hearing of the warlike preparation of the students, they concluded that prudence was the better part of valor, and relinquished their purpose."

THE JAIL RIOT OF 1848

"The most disastrous jail riot in the history of the city occurred in the summer of 1848. The details are given in the Reminiscences of Judge Carter. Two returned volunteers (Germans) from the Mexican war, who were boarding in a German family consisting of a man and wife and daughter of eleven years of age, were arrested by the parents on the charge of having committed a horrible outrage upon their child. At the examination at the old court house, the bed clothes and undergarments of the little girl were shown covered with blood which, with her testimony and that of the parents, so frenzied the spectators that it was with difficulty that the sheriff, Thomas J. Weaver, could lodge them in the jail and call in the service of the Cincinnati Grays and Citizens' Guards to protect it from the mob.

"That night the mob made an attach upon the jail. The sheriff first tried expostulation, but this was useless. Then he ordered the military to fire with blank cartridges, which only the more enraged them. Finally he repeated the order to fire, with ball, and when eleven persons fell dead, some of them innocent bystanders, the mob dispersed.

"But," writes the judge, "the sequel. I was the prosecuting attorney at the time, and know of what I speak. At the next term of court a bill of indictment against these poor volunteer soldiers was unanimously ignored on the plain and simple ground of their entire innocence. They had served their adopted country and were hard-working, industrious, honest men. They had been the victims of these Germans who, because they could not induce them to give up their land warrants entitling them each, for honorable service, to 160 acres of land, had conspired with their little daughter to get up and maintain this awful charge. After their discharge there was a hunt after their guilty prosecutors to lynch them, when it was found that father, mother and daughter had disappeared and were never heard of after."

NEARLY ONE HUNDRED YEARS AGO, NEGRO HAD BEST WHITE PRACTICE

"One of the boldest charlatans, who for awhile monopolized the best practice in town, held forth at the northeast corner of Eighth and Plum Streets, where every day the carriages of the wealthiest people drove up, while the leading physicians deplored the absence of their best patients. Drake informs us that this quack was a Negro who had followed an itinerant oculist from New Orleans and was stranded in Cincinnati. This Negro was nearly blind from gonorrheal ophthalmia. He, in some manner or another, attracted an enormous practice by the silliest kind of swindle. He would tell the patient to dip one finger into a tumbler of water, whereupon he would study and analyze the water and tell the patient what ailed him. One young lady was told by the Negro that a male had also dipped his finger into the water. She denied this, whereupon the Negro stated that she was pregnant with a male child. The girl broke down and confessed that she was pregnant. In due time she was delivered of a male child. A man was told by the Negro that a dead person's finger had been put into the water. The patient was worried and annoyed and decided to see his family physician about the matter. On his way to the doctor's office he dropped dead in the street. These and similar occurrences established the Negro's reputation. Drake tells us that one of the leading physicians proceeded to drive this Negro out of the city and in the melee which followed, the physician, whose name Drake does not give, was severely cut by the Negro. Fearing the result, the latter left the city."

The Old McAllister St.—historic ground—Dabney Buildings, 268 feet on McAllister Street, 39½ feet on Fifth Street; now site of vast Catholic Edifice—The Sacred Heart Home.

Section IV
A Few of the Men Who Made History

LEVI COFFIN

"The reputed president of the Underground Railroad, Levi Coffin, philanthropist, was born October 28, 1798, near New Garden, North Carolina, and of Quaker parentage. His ancestors were from Nantucket, and he was a farmer and teacher. His sympathies were enlisted in favor of the slaves, and when but a lad of fifteen, he began to aid in their escape. In 1826 he settled in Wayne County, Indiana, kept a country store, cured pork and manufactured linseed oil. His wife was Catharine Coffin.

Meanwhile his interest in the slaves continued, and he was active in the Underground Railroad, by which thousands of escaping slaves were aided by him on their way to Canada, including Eliza Harris, the heroine of "Uncle Tom's Cabin." In 1847 he moved to Cincinnati and opened and continued for years a store where only were sold goods produced by free labor, at the same time continuing his efforts for the escape of slaves. In the war period he aided in the establishment of the Freedmen's Bureau, visited England and held meetings in the various cities and collected funds for the Freedmen's commission. On the adoption of the Fifteenth Amendment he formerly resigned his office of president of the Underground Railroad, which he had held for more than thirty years. He died in 1877."

A grandson of Coffin worked as an engineer in the City Hall of this city and Paymaster Dabney would, in paying him, often say, Wouldn't your grandfather be surprised to see the son of a slave doing this?

Experiences of Levi Coffin, a Quaker, and President of the Underground Railroad

"When we moved to Cincinnati in the spring of 1847, my wife and I thought that perhaps our work in Underground Railroad matters was done, as we had been in active service more than twenty years.

"When in the city in business, I had mingled with the abolitionists and been present at their meetings, but some of them had died and others had moved away, and when I came to the city to live I found that the fugitives generally took refuge among the colored people and that they were often captured and taken back to slavery.

"Most of the colored people were not shrewd managers in such matters, and many white people who were at heart friendly to the fugitives, were too timid to take hold of the work themselves. They were ready to contribute to the expense of getting the fugitives away to places of safety, but were not willing to risk the penalty of the law or the stigma on their reputation.

"I was personally acquainted with all the active and reliable workers on the Underground Railroad in the city, both colored and white. There were a few wise and careful managers among the colored people, but it was not safe to trust all of them with the affairs of our work. Most of them were too careless, and a few were unworthy—they could be bribed by the slave-hunters to betray the hiding places of the fugitives. We soon found it to be the best policy to confine our affairs to a few persons, and to let the whereabouts of the slaves be known to as few people as possible.

"There seemed to be a continual increase of runaways, and such was the vigilance of the pursuers that I was obliged to devote a large share of time from my business to making arrangements for their concealment and safe conveyance of the fugitives. They sometimes came to our door frightened and panting and in a destitute condition, having fled in such haste and fear that they had no time to bring any clothing except what they had on, and that was often very scant. The expense of providing suitable clothing for them when it was necessary for them to go on immediately, or of feeding them when they were obliged to be concealed for days or weeks, was very heavy.

"We generally hired teams from a certain German livery stable. We had several trusty colored men, who owned no property and who could lose nothing in a prosecution, who understood Underground Railroad matters, and we generally got them to act as drivers, but in some instances white men volunteered to drive, generally the young and able-bodied.

"Learning that the runaway slaves often arrived almost destitute of clothing, a number of the benevolent ladies of the city, Mrs. Sarah H. Ernst, Miss Sarah O. Ernst, Mrs. Henry Miller, Mrs. Dr. Aydelott, Mrs. Julia Harwood, Mrs. Amanda E. Foster, Mrs. Elizabeth Coleman, Mrs. Mary Mann, Mrs. Mary M. Guild, Miss K. Emery, and others, organized an Anti-Slavery Sewing Society, to provide suitable clothing for the fugitives. After we came to the city they met at our house every week for a number of years and wrought much practical good by their labors.

"Our house was large and well adapted for secreting fugitives. Very often slaves would lie concealed in upper chambers for weeks without the boarders or frequent visitors at the house knowing anything about it.

"The fugitives generally arrived in the night and were secreted among the friendly colored people or hidden in the upper room of our house. They came alone or in companies, and in a few instances had a white guide to direct them.

"One company of twenty-eight that crossed the Ohio river at Lawrenceburg, Indiana, twenty miles below Cincinnati, had for conductor a white man whom they had employed to assist them. The character of this man was full of contradictions. He was a Virginian by birth and spent much of his time in the South, yet he hated slavery. He was devoid of moral principle, but was a true friend to the poor slave.

"The company of twenty-eight slaves all lived in the same neighborhood in Kentucky. This white man, John Fairfield, had been in the neighborhood for some weeks buying poultry, etc., for market.

"He was engaged by the slaves to help them cross the Ohio river and conduct them to Cincinnati. They paid him some money; the amount was small considering the risk the conductor assumed, but it was all they had. Several of the men had their wives with them, and one woman, a little child with her, a few months old. John Fairfield conducted the party to the Ohio river opposite the mouth of the Big Miami, where he knew there were several skiffs tied to the bank near a wood yard.

"The entire party waded out through mud and water and reached the shore safely, though all were wet and several lost their shoes. Their plight was a most pitiable one. They were cold, hungry and exhausted. When they reached the outskirts of the city, below Millcreek, John Fairfield hid them as well as he could, in ravines that had been washed in the sides of the steep hills, and told them not to move until he returned. He then went directly to John Hatfield, a worthy colored man, a deacon in the Zion Baptist Church, and told his story. He had applied to Hatfield before and knew him to be a great friend to the fugitives, one who had often sheltered them under his roof and aided them in every way he could.

"I suggested that someone should go immediately to a certain German livery stable in the city and hire two coaches and that several colored men should go out in buggies and take the women and children from their hiding places, then, that the coaches and buggies should form a procession as if going to a funeral. In the western part of Cumminsville was the Methodist Episcopal burying ground, where a certain lot of ground had been set apart for the use of the colored people. They should pass this and continue on the Colerain Pike until they reached a right-hand road leading to College Hill. At the latter place they would find a few colored families living in the outskirts of the village and could take refuge among them. Jonathan Cable, a Presbyterian minister, who lived near Farmer's College, on the west side of the village, was a prominent abolitionist, and I knew that he would give prompt assistance to the fugitives.

"While the carriages and buggies were being procured, John Hatfield's wife and daughter and other colored women of the neighborhood busied themselves in preparing provisions to be sent to the fugitives.

"All the arrangements were carried out, and the party reached College Hill in safety and were kindly received and cared for. But, sad to relate, it was a funeral procession not only in appearance but in reality, for when they arrived at College Hill and the mother unwrapped her sick child, she found to her surprise and grief that its stillness, which she supposed to be that of sleep, was that of death. All necessary preparations were made by the kind people of the village, and the child was decently and quietly interred the next day in the burying ground on the Hill.

"Cable kept the fugitives as secluded as possible until a way was provided for safely forwarding them on their way to Canada.

"West Elkton, twenty-five or thirty miles from College Hill, was the first Underground Railroad depot.

"In connection with the cases tried under the Fugitive Slave Law in this city, that noble anti-slavery lawyer—John Jolliffe—was especially prominent. He has gone to his reward, but the record he left is imperishable.

Kirby Smith's Threatened Raid

"The war excitement was greatly increased when the news came that the rebel General, Kirby Smith, had approached near Cincinnati with a large army. The mayor of the city issued a proclamation requiring every man, without distinction of age, color, or country, to report at the voting places in the various wards, to be organized into military companies for the protection of the city. Cannon were placed on Mount Adams and the high hills above and below the city, in position to rake the river if the rebel army attempted to cross. We soon had an army of over one hundred thousand men in Cincinnati, many of them raw, untrained soldiers, without any preparation for camping or supplies of provisions. These were called "Squirrel Hunters." Tables were spread in the market houses and parks, and (in some wards) on the public sidewalks, and bountifully furnished with provisions by the ladies, many of whom attended as waiters. Public halls and other places were used as headquarters and lodging places for the soldiers. In our ward a table was spread on the sidewalk of Franklin Street, from Broadway to Sycamore, in front of our house and Woodward College, where five hundred could be fed at one time. It was supplied with provisions for several days by the ladies of the Ninth Ward. Our basement kitchen was made the depository for the victuals between meals and our large cooking stove was used to furnish hot coffee and tea. At the table were fed the Oberlin students and other abolitionists from the northern part of Ohio, many of whom we knew. After meals, they frequently formed in line in front of our house and sang "John Brown," and other anti-slavery songs, the whole company joining in the chorus.

"The German element was strong in our city. Many of the men were veteran soldiers who had seen service in their own country and well understood military tactics.

"The Negro element, on the contrary, was utterly ignorant of all kinds of drill. Many of the colored men did not understand why they should be called upon, having never before been recognized as citizens, and neglected to report; some of them were alarmed and hid themselves. The police hunted them out and forced them into the ranks.

"Judge Dickson, who was the colored people's friend and in whom they had entire confidence, organized a separate company of colored men. They rallied willingly to him. A pontoon bridge was made across the Ohio river, between Cincinnati and Covington, and a large army marched over into Kentucky. A few miles back of Covington they went into camp and made great preparations for defense, throwing up breastworks and extending their lines so as to prevent the approach of the enemy to the city. Colonel Dickson's colored regiment was marched over to aid in making the fortifications, and was said to be the most orderly and faithful regiment that crossed. After they were released and marched back to the city, the men contributed money to buy a fine sword, which they presented to Colonel Dickson as a testimonial of their regard for him, accompanied by an able speech from one of their company selected for the occasion."

Kidnapped

An industrious, highly respected Negro, known as Tom Mitchell, had lived in Dayton, Ohio, several years. He had a wife and little boy. In 1832 a white man came from Kentucky, saw him, had him arrested as an escaped slave. He was tried under the Fugitive Slave Law. The judge claimed the evidence insufficient and released him. A few weeks later his master had him kidnapped; his cries for help brought rescue, but charges were again made and this time he was turned over to his master. The people, much aroused, put up a large sum of money, and the negro, whose real name was Ben, gave his entire savings, fifty dollars. The master refused to sell and when he came in the room to take him back to Kentucky, the slave had to be held to keep him from jumping out of a window. He was carried to Cincinnati and this letter from the Dayton Journal of that year tells what happened:

"POOR TOM IS FREE"

Cincinnati, January 24, 1832.

Dear Sir: In compliance with a request of Mr: J. Deinkard, of Kentucky, I take my pen to inform you of the death of his black man, Ben, whom he took in your place a few days ago. The circumstances are as follows: On the evening of the 22nd inst., arrived in this city on their way to Kentucky, and put up at the Main Street Hotel, where a room on the uppermost story (fourth) of the building was provided for Ben and his guard. All being safe, as they thought, about one o'clock, when they were in a sound sleep, poor Ben, stimulated with even the faint prospect of escape, or perhaps pre-determined on liberty or death, threw himself from the window, which is upwards of fifty feet from the pavement. He was, as you may well suppose, severely injured, and the poor fellow died this morning about four o'clock. Mr. D. left this morning with the dead body of his slave, to which he told me he would give decent burial in his own graveyard. Please tell Ben's wife of these circumstances.

Your unknown correspondent,

Respectfully,

R. P. Simmons.

Margaret Garner—Slavery's Greatest Tragedy

"The latter part of January, 1856, from shore to shore, the Ohio river was frozen. Many slaves crossed to Cincinnati. Among the fugitives were Margaret Garner, her husband and four children. They wandered to the house of a colored man named Kite, who lived in the West End, down below Mill Creek. The next morning the house was surrounded by officers and slave hunters. The slaves fought desperately. Margaret declared she would kill herself and children before she would return to slavery. Finally the door was battered down. Margaret's husband was wounded before being overpowered. She seeing that all was lost, grabbed a butcher knife and cut her daughter's throat and tried to kill the other children. The fugitives were jailed. The trial under the Fugitive Slave Law took place two weeks later. Attorney John Jolliffe, famous abolitionist, defended the prisoners. Margaret Garner was a very intelligent looking, brown-skinned woman about five feet high. Two old scars were on the left side of her face where, she said, 'white man struck me.' She was about twenty-three years old. During the trial she held in her arms a nine months' old baby girl, and around her feet played her two little boys, four and six years old. Lucy Stone, the well-known and very eloquent public speaker, was said, by Col. Chambers, to have visited Margaret in prison and gave her a knife to kill herself and children. She said, 'When I saw that poor fugitive, took her toil-hardened hand in mine, and read in her face deep suffering and an ardent longing for freedom, I could not help bid her be of good cheer. I told her that a thousand hearts were aching for her and that they were glad one child of her's was safe with the angels. Her only reply was a look of deep despair, of anguish such as no words can speak. The faded faces of the Negro children tell too plainly to what degradation female slaves must submit. Rather than give her little daughter to that life, she killed it. If in her deep maternal love, she felt the impulse to send her child back to God to save it from coming woe, who shall say she had no right to do so? That desire had its root in the deepest and holiest feelings of our nature, implanted alike in black and white by our Common Father. With my own teeth I would tear open my veins and let the earth drink my blood, rather than to wear the chains of slavery.' The slaves were, by the court, turned over to their owners. They took them to Covington, held them a few days, and before money could be raised to buy Margaret, she was shipped South. She jumped overboard, was dragged out of the river, but the baby was drowned."

For a full account of the case, see Reminiscences of Levi Coffin.

The Vice-President's Slave
(From Levi Coffin's Book)

"Jackson, the subject of this story, was the property of Vice-President King, of Alabama, who was elected to office with Franklin Pierce. While the master was at Washington, the slave ran away from him and came to Cincinnati. He was a barber by trade, and after remaining here unmolested for some time, he opened a shop in which he served several years, having a number of patrons and being liked by all who knew him. By some means his master learned of his whereabouts and sent an agent to secure him. The man arrived in Cincinnati, and without procuring a writ, as the law required, resolved to take forcible possession of Jackson. He gathered a posse of men with pistols and bowie-knives, had the ferry boat in waiting at the wharf at the foot of Walnut Street, in readiness to take them across to Kentucky as soon as they came on board, and about noon, one day, pounced upon Jackson at the corner of Fifth and Walnut Streets as he was going to his dinner, and dragged him down Walnut Street to the wharf. Jackson struggled with all his might and called for help, but most of the men of the stores had gone to their dinner at that hour and the policemen, who were generally on the side of the slaveholders, remained out of sight.

"He was bound and carried back to Alabama, where he remained in slavery two or three years, and where he married a free woman, a Creole of Mobile, who possessed some property. She was portly in form and had handsome features, with straight hair and olive complexion. When dressed up, she presented the appearance of an elegant southern lady. A plan was soon formed to gain Jackson's liberty. His wife was to act the part of a lady traveling to Baltimore on business, and Jackson, who was small in stature, was to be disguised as a woman and accompany her as her servant. When all the preparations were made they sent their trunks on board the regular vessel for New Orleans and took passage for that city in their newly assumed characters.

"When the boat reached the wharf at Cincinnati, the lady took a carriage, and, with her servant, drove to the Dumas House, a public hotel kept by a colored man. Jackson was well acquainted in the city and knew where to find friends. A few hours afterward I received a message requesting me to call at the Dumas House, as a lady there wished to see me on business. I went, accompanied by John Hatfield, a colored man, who was a prominent worker in the cause of freedom, and who had received a similar message. The landlord conducted us upstairs to the ladies' parlor, and introduced us to the lady from Alabama. She was a fine-looking, well-dressed Creole. She went on to say that she had a servant with her whose liberty she wished to secure, and she had been referred to us for advice. She was not very well acquainted with laws of Ohio, and felt at a loss how to proceed.

"The servant came and made a graceful curtsey to us and stood looking at us; it was Jackson, dressed in woman's clothes. It was decided that it would be unsafe for Jackson to remain in Cincinnati; he was too well known here. He concluded that he would go to Cleveland, where he was not known. It was decided that his wife should remain in Cincinnati until he had made preparations for housekeeping and established himself in business. Soon his wife joined him, and when we last heard from them they were living comfortably and happily at Cleveland. Jackson had a good business in his barbershop."

ELIZA HARRIS' ESCAPE
(Levi Coffin's Reminiscences)

Eliza Harris, of "Uncle Tom's Cabin," the slave woman who crossed the Ohio river on the drifting ice, with her child in her arms, was sheltered for several days and aided to escape by Levi Coffin, he then residing at Newport, Indiana.

Harriet Beecher Stowe's graphic description of this woman's experience is almost identical with the real facts in the case.

The originals of Simeon and Rachel Halliday, the Quaker couple alluded to in her remarkable work, were Levi and Catharine Coffin.

Eliza Harris's master lived a few miles back from the Ohio river below Ripley, Ohio. Her treatment from master and mistress was kind, but they having met with financial reverses, it was decided to sell Eliza, and she, learning of this and the probable separation of herself and child, determined to escape. That night, with her child in her arms, she started on foot for the Ohio river. She reached the river near daybreak, and instead of finding it frozen over, it was filled with large blocks of floating ice. Thinking it impossible to cross, she ventured to seek shelter in a house nearby, where she was kindly received.

She hoped to find some way of crossing the next night, but during the day the ice became more broken and dangerous, making the river seemingly impassable. Evening came on, when her pursuers were seen approaching the house. Made desperate through fear, she seized her infant in her arms, darted out the back door and ran toward the river, followed by her pursuers.

Fearing death less than separation from her babe, she clasped it to her bosom and sprang on the first cake of ice, and from that to another, and then to another, and so, on. Sometimes the ice would sink beneath her;

then she would slide her child on to the next cake, and pull herself on with her hands. Wet to the waist, her hands benumbed with cold, she approached the Ohio shore nearly exhausted. A man who had been standing on the bank watching her in amazement, assisted her to the shore. After recovering her strength, she was directed to a house on a hill in the outskirts of Ripley. Here she was cared for and after being provided with food and dry clothing, was forwarded from station to station on the Underground Railroad until she reached the home of Levi Coffin. Here she remained several days until she and her child, with other fugitives, were forwarded via the Greenville branch of the Underground Railroad to Sandusky, and from thence to Chatham, Canada, West, where she finally settled, and where years after Mr. Coffin met her.

THE BEECHER FAMILY

The Beechers lived in Cincinnati (Walnut Hills) from 1832 to 1852, twenty years, and were closely connected with the anti-slavery and educational history of this region. Dr. Lyman Beecher, the head of this remarkable family, was born in New Haven, Conn., in 1775, the son of a blacksmith and the direct descendant of the Widow Beecher, who followed the profession of midwife to the first settlers there about 1638. Lyman was educated at Yale, but could not "speak his piece" on graduating day from the inability of his father to supply him with a suit of new clothes in which to appear. To fight evil in whatever form he saw it, and help on the good, was the love of his life. Old men who remember him in his prime pronounce him the most eloquent, powerful preacher they ever heard, surpassing in his greatest flights of oratory, his highly gifted son, Henry Ward Beecher.

The Lane Theological Seminary having been established at Walnut Hills, a large sum of money was pledged to its support on the condition of Dr. Beecher accepting the presidency, which he did in 1832.

Soon after, in consequence of a tract issued by the abolition convention, at Philadelphia, the evils of slavery were discussed by the students. "Many of them were from the South; and an effort was made to stop the discussions and the meetings. Slaveholders went over from Kentucky and incited mob violence in Cincinnati, and at one time it seemed as though the rabble might destroy the seminary, and the houses of the professors. In the absence of Dr. Beecher, the board of trustees were frightened into obeying the demands of the mob by forbidding all discussions of slavery; whereupon the students withdrew en masse. A few returned, while the seceders laid the foundations of Oberlin College.

In 1846 we made his acquaintance and, walking with him on Fourth Street one day, he described the situation at the time of the mobbing of "The Philanthropist," a newspaper of that period. The seminary was some three miles distant and over a road, most of the way uphill, ankle-deep in clayey, sticky mud, through which the mob, to get there, must of necessity flounder, even without being filled, as they would undoubtedly have been, with Old Bourbon. The mud was really what probably saved the theologian. "I told the boys," said he, "that they had the right of self-defense;

that they could arm themselves and if the mob came they could shoot, but I told them not to kill 'em, aim low, hit 'em in the legs."

On one occasion a young minister was lamenting the dreadful increasing wickedness of mankind. "I don't know anything about that, young man," replied he in his whispering tones. "I've not had anything to do with running the world the last twenty-five years. God Almighty now has it in charge."

This good man was wont, after preaching a powerful sermon, to relax his mind from his highly wrought state of nervous excitement, sometimes by going down into his cellar and shoveling sand from one spot to another; sometimes by taking his "fiddle," playing "Auld Lyng Syne" and dancing a double shuffle in his parlor.

Lyman Beecher was married thrice and had thirteen children; his seven grown sons all became Congregational clergymen, and his four daughters gained literary and philanthropic distinction. Henry Ward, his most distinguished son, was educated at Lane Seminary, and it was on Walnut Hills that his daughter, Harriet Beecher Stowe, met the originals of the persons that figure in her novel of "Uncle Tom's Cabin," and got filled up for the famous work which was published on her return East.

It used to be a common expression forty years ago that the United States possessed two great things, viz., the American flag and the Beechers."

"SQUIRREL HUNTERS"

(Levi Coffin)

"Many of the colored men did not understand why they should be called upon, having never before been recognized as citizens, and neglected to report. Some hid themselves. The police hunted them out and forced them into the ranks. Judge Dickson, who was the colored people's friend and in whom they had entire confidence, organized a separate company of colored men. They rallied willingly to him. They went over and assisted in making the fortifications and was said to be the most orderly and faithful regiment that crossed. After they were released they contributed money and bought for Colonel Dickson a fine sword."

THE EVANS BROTHERS

About the year 1838 or 1840, from over the Virginia mountains in a covered wagon came two brothers, Louis and Stephen Evans. They landed in Madison, Indiana, where Louis became a successful shoe merchant, which caused much jealousy among the whites, who often chased him to the woods where he was forced to hide among the cliffs as long as a week at a time without food. Stephen came on to Cincinnati where he became a successful carpenter and was well known in the business world.

"BILLY GOAT" HILL

In the race riot which occurred September, 1841, the Negroes, when attacked in the boarding house on McAllister Street (the Old Dumas House), fought back and the battle lines extended to Sixth and Broadway, where the Negroes fought desperately from streets, Allen Chapel and the houses in Bucktown. The whites secured a cannon and opened fire. According to the newspapers of that period, the Negroes fled to the hill. The Negroes claim that, instead, they made a flank movement through Bucktown, came up Seventh Street and captured the cannon. Then that part of the city was under military control. As a proof they cite the fact that Negroes did not dare retreat to the hills, for what is now Sixth and Eighth Street Hill was then known as "Billy Goat Hill." It was said that the Irish and goats were so thick in that section that on summer afternoons and evenings you could hardly walk on the pavements without disturbing an Irishman or "Billy" Goat. In either case a fight resulted. "Andy" Brown, who is still working as a barber on East Seventh Street and who lived in the Dabney Building for thirty years, states that only two colored families were permitted to live on Billy Goat Hill in the early days. One of them, the Palmers (mulattoes) were his relatives, and because of his whiteness he could visit them without having a battle with their Hibernian neighbors.

CALAMITIES

On April 26, 1838, the new steamer, The Moselle, blew up soon after leaving the wharf. Two hundred people lost.

Asiatic Cholera came first in 1832; three hundred and fifty-one people died here. In 1849, out of a population of 116,000, the total deaths were 8,500.

RIOT OF 1884

The court-house riot of 1884 was the most disastrous uprising of citizens in the history of Cincinnati. The court-house was burned, much property destroyed, many lives lost. It was caused by the extreme laxity of law enforcement and the unbridled corruption of officials which culminated in the butchery and robbery of a reputable citizen.

The murder was planned by Wm. Berner, a young German, who was assisted in the perpetration of the atrocious deed by "Joe" Palmer, a young mulatto, well-known in this city. Berner's lawyers were too shrewd to permit them to be tried together. In consequence, the white boy was sent to the penitentiary, the colored boy to the gallows.

A NAPOLEON OF FINANCE

From Richmond, Va., to this city, in 1846, came Robert Gordon, a heavy-set, light brown-skinned, full bearded man. In his home town he labored for a coal dealer. So thorough was his work, so loyal his services, that in appreciation the owner permitted him to have the slack, which he sold to such advantage that soon he made his greatest financial deal, that is, he bought himself. Old residents are thoroughly conversant with his private affairs. His clerk and others claim that he had about $500 when he arrived. A big sum in those days. Acquiring a large yard in the bottoms, into the coal business he went. In his career he had at least two partners, one of whom, the old turnkey Jas. Clark, was quite wealthy when he died. Another was West, who succeeded him in business. Gordon was famous for close, shrewd dealing. His money grew slowly but surely. A summer came that marked the crisis in his career. A merchant from Pittsburg brought down the river a large supply of coal. A dispute arose with the dealers in regard to the price. He refused to yield and in anger went to Gordon. As usual, the latter hesitated and haggled. The Pittsburg man insisted that he take the coal. Old Gordon used his favorite expression, "I kyahnt (can't) and I shyahnt (shan't)." But the merchant left the immense amount of coal anyhow and departed. The summer was hot. The autumn also. Gordon was in despair. The white dealers were jubilant. They had only a small supply of coal and weather prophets predicted a very mild winter. Gordon was stuck with this big cargo dumped upon him, despite his "Kyahnt" and "Shyahnt." This city is noted for lightning-like changes of temperature. A day, summer-like in its balminess, was followed by a night whose coldness increased with the fast flying hours. When morning came, winter reigned. Coal was in demand. The white dealers were overrun with orders. Gordon, the Negro dealer, was left severely alone. A few days and the coal supply in the local market almost reached the vanishing point. The white dealers then came to Gordon. In their need for coal, his "color" was forgotten. As he was not in need, he did not forget theirs. They could get no coal from Gordon. That was the time that tried men's souls. Gordon showed that he had the same stock-broking brain that enthroned Jay Gould and other Wall Street manipulators. Colder and colder it grew. Over the river was a deep sheet of ice that united for many weeks Ohio and Kentucky, and over which there came by day the traffic of trade and by night hundreds of escaping Negroes. All coal was gone from Cincinnati but Gordon's. His prices went to the fabulous sum of one dollar a bushel. People were burning their furniture, rails from their fences, planks from their homes. When the thaw came, Gordon's coal was gone, but in its place thousands of dollars. This went into land and so as the years flew by, it grew and grew, until when he crossed "the great river," history recorded him as Ohio's richest colored citizen. His widow was a fine old lady and her daughter Virginia, a model of modesty, married Geo. H. Jackson, a school teacher of Cincinnati, who afterwards became a lawyer, member of the legislature, and real estate dealer. Some years after the death of Mrs. Gordon, the realty was sold and invested in Chicago properties. In that city still reside the two children, Helen, who married Dr. Thorne; Gordon, now Dr. Gordon Jackson, who married, in New York, a few years ago, Mae Walker, heiress of Madame Walker. Their mother died in the last decade and their father, Geo. H. Jackson, was brought here for interment in the spring of this year.

A GREAT INVENTOR

"The most useful inventor with a career extending into the twentieth century, however, was Granville T. Woods, who doubtless surpassed most men in his field in the number and variety of his devices. He began in Cincinnati, Ohio, 1884, where he obtained his first patent on a steam boiler furnace. Then came an amusement machine apparatus in 1880, an incubator in 1900, and electrical air brakes in 1902, 1903 and 1905. He then directed his attention to telegraphy, producing several patents for transmitting messages between moving trains, and also a number of transmitters. He thereafter invented fifteen appliances having to do with electrical railways and a number of others for electrical control and distribution. To further his interest he organized the Woods Electrical Company, which took over by assignment all of his early patents. As in the course of time, however, he found a large market for his devices with the more prosperous corporations in the United States, the records of the patent office show the assignment of a large number of his inventions to the General Electric Company of New York, the Westinghouse Air Brake Company of Pennsylvania, the American Bell Telephone Company of Boston, and the American Engineering Company of New York. During this period of his larger usefulness he had the co-operation of his brother, Lyates Woods, who, himself, invented a number of such appliances of considerable commercial value."—(Woodson.)

THE LONGWORTHS

Nicholas Longworth, born in Newark, New Jersey, in 1782, for a time a clerk in his brother's store in South Carolina, came to Cincinnati in 1803 and died in 1863, leaving an estate of many millions from early investments in Cincinnati land.

He studied law and practiced for a while, and in 1828 began the cultivation of the Catawba grape, and from it manufactured wine of high marketable value. He had 200 acres of vineyards, a large wine house, and was favorably known by his experiments on the strawberry.

Mr. Longworth lived in a huge stone cottage mansion, in the center of a three or four-acre lot, at the east end of Fourth Street, originally built by Martin Baum, now the residence of David Sinton. Forty years ago the spot was known as Longworth's Garden, and was one of the chief attractions of the city from its display of flowers and fruits, notably grapes.

"He was very shrewd, quick-witted, with great common sense and acquisitiveness. He had a quiet good humor and a readiness at repartee which made him very popular." He was a friend to artists and kindly to the poor and very eccentric.

Every Monday for a term of years he had at his house a free gift distribution to the poor. At the appointed hour strings of old ladies, German and Irish, would be seen flocking there with baskets to receive at their option a loaf of bread or a peck of corn meal or a dime.

He had continuous appeals for charity, and he was wont to say in certain cases, "Ha! a poor widow, is she? Got a struggling family of little ones? I won't give her a cent. She is the Lord's poor; plenty to help such. I will help the devil's poor, the miserable drunken dog that nobody else will do anything for but despise and kick."

His son Joseph and grandson Nicholas were noted as patrons of art, as is his granddaughter, Mrs. Maria Longworth Storer. The entire family is unusually popular from its beneficence and public spirit, especially in the fostering the things of beauty that give to life its efflorescence and fragrance."

The Longworths were always noted for their kindness to colored and 'tis a matter of record that from the earliest years helped them with the orphan asylum, schools, etc. We have known our Congressman, "Nic" Longworth, for over a quarter of a century. He judges no man by the color of his skin, and as his wife, formerly Miss Alice Roosevelt, is also devoid of racial prejudice, we feel safe in assuming that Miss Longworth has inherited this noble quality, this trait so characteristic of the genuine aristocracy.

TAFT

Judge Alphonso Taft was born in Townsend, Vermont, November 5, 1810. In 1838, admitted to the bar and after 1840 practiced in Cincinnati, where he won high reputation. In 1856 he was a delegate to the National Republican Convention. In 1875 he was a candidate for the Republican nomination for the governorship, but a dissenting opinion that he had delivered on the question of the Bible in the public schools was the cause of much opposition to him.

He became Secretary of War, March 8, 1876, on the resignation of Gen. William W. Belknap, and on the 22nd of May following, was transferred to the attorney generalship, serving until the close of Gen. Grant's administration. He was sound on the color question and was closely identified with the great abolitionists of his day.

Chas. P. Taft, owner of the Times-Star, who married Miss Sinton, and ex-president Wm. Taft, are his sons.

AN EXCERPT FROM
"THE NEGRO IN CINCINNATI"
By Frank W. Quillan

[In our issue of July 20, 1905, we printed a very significant article by Mr. Quillan, entitled "Race Prejudice in a Northern Town." It was a description of the town of Syracuse, Ohio, where no Negro is permitted to live. The following article is the result of a study of the status of the Negro in the life of Cincinnati, Ohio, prepared under the direction of the Department of History of the University of Michigan in which Mr. Quillan has been working for the degree of Ph.D. It will not be forgotten that Cincinnati is a Northern city and boasts of being the birthplace and present home of the President of the United States.—Editor, The Independent Weekly Magazine, New York City, February 24, 1910.]

Samuel J. Tilden, Democratic candidate for the presidency in 1876, called Ohio a "d——d nigger state." The writer of this article, knowing that Ohio has the most interesting Negro history of all the Northern states, spent the past summer touring Ohio and investigating the relations existing between the white and colored races today, to see whether the above statement is still true. I visited Cleveland, Akron, Columbus, Springfield, Dayton, Urbana, Xenia, Cincinnati, Hamilton, and many smaller cities, and talked with all classes of both colored and white people. My object was to learn the facts about what the two races think of one another, or more specifically, to find out how much race prejudice really exists. I believe that I started on the investigation unbiased, so far as it is possible for a man to be, and I desire to remain so, letting facts stand as they are. The Negro question is a delicate one to treat, for the reason that there are two distinct classes of readers on the subject, one reading all on the subject that is favorable to the colored man and relegating to the waste basket all that is unfavorable, and the other doing just the opposite.

The object of the writer of this article is to bring the two classes together on a common plane, to submit facts as to conditions, and let each reader draw his own conclusions.

While conditions vary in different cities, the following facts about the situation in Cincinnati are, in a broad way, typical of all the cities of Ohio, the nearest to an exception probably being Cleveland.

In the first place, no colored man is allowed to enroll in the Ohio Medical College, which is a branch of the University of Cincinnati, a public institution, nor can he enter the Eclectic Medical School. In fact, there is no school in the city where he is privileged to equip himself for the medical profession. If he leaves the city and secures his training elsewhere and then comes back again, he finds the door of opportunity closed. The colored doctor, no matter what his training has been or what his ability and standing may be, is not allowed to operate in the large City Hospital, a public institution maintained by taxation to which the colored people contribute their share. He is debarred from the Seton Hospital, on West Sixth Street, and, in fact, from all hospitals save two small charity concerns. Colored people, received with reluctance into separate wards in the City Hospital, are refused the privilege of having a physician of their own race attend them.

Recently there came up the question of having colored men in the Health Department, and the Board of Public Service, which, of course, is made up of white men, handed down the decision that it would be unwise, as the colored sanitary officer would be compelled to call at the houses of white men during the latter's absence, and their wives would be made subject to insult in having to accept orders of a colored man.

There is not a Negro to be found in the city fire department, which employs hundreds of men, all, of course, paid out of public taxation. The reason given for their absence is that white firemen will not work with them, as they would be compelled to eat and sleep alongside of them under the present manner of conducting the department.

The officers controlling the Municipal Bath House now forbid all colored people to bathe there. The privilege was granted for a short time recently under Democratic administration, but the house became practically a colored institution so quickly that the reform party had to withdraw the privilege.

All the popular parks, such as Chester, The Lagoon and Coney Island, exclude the Negroes. Some of them have one "nigger day" each year, when the colored people are allowed to pass the sacred portals which are forbidden them the rest of the year. Some Negroes are employed as waiters and porters at Coney Island, a leading park, six miles up the Ohio river. These are compelled to ride on the *deck* of the steamboat, going and coming.

Hotels, restaurants, eating and drinking places, almost universally are closed to all people in whom the least tincture of colored blood can be detected. The Bartenders' Union has passed a resolution forbidding its members to wait on a colored person, and they live up to it. On Fifth Street, between Central Avenue and Broadway, a distance of a dozen blocks, a colored man can not enter a single saloon and buy a drink, or even a ham sandwich. W. P. Dabney, a colored man of education and of recognized ability in music and other arts, the assistant paymaster of the City of Cincinnati, handling tens of thousands of dollars annually, and paying it out to the Mayor, Chief of Police, and all other city employes, personally told the writer of the following experience: He and another prominent musician had, at much financial risk and trouble, secured a famous pupil of Rubinstein, an Italian, to give a concert in Cincinnati. After the concert was over the performer asked the committee to go to a saloon and have a drink with him. They all agreed and entered, the party consisting of the Italian musician, another foreigner, and the colored man, Mr. Dabney. The conversation at the moment happened to be about America, and the Italian was congratulating his companions upon their privilege of living in this land of the free. They sat down at a table and called for something to drink. The bartender could see but two at the table, and those the foreigners. The one real American, simply because his skin was dark (no, not that, or the Italian would have been unnoticed also), though he was the trusted employe of a great city, was beneath the notice of a bartender.

At the Sinton Hotel, where Mr. Taft made his campaign headquarters, the colored man is not welcome even to standing room in the lobby. No matter how prominent he is, if he desires to see a white man on one of the upper floors he must take the freight elevator, or the lower compartment of the elevator, the "Jim Crow" compartment, we may call it.

The Pullman Car Company refuses to sell berths to colored people going South. Under stress, they will offer to put them in the drawing room, which costs more than they can afford to pay, and which if occupied would segregate them from the whites. Trains pulling out of Cincinnati for the South have their "Jim Crow" coaches, into which the colored people are asked to go. If they do not go willingly they are compelled to do so on reaching the Kentucky side of the Ohio river.

The Y. M. C. A. refuses them either active or associate membership. Recently some young colored men established a Y. M. C. A. on Walnut Hills, a prominent suburb of the city. The white Y. M. C. A. rose in holy wrath at this defilement of their name, and caused the colored organization to change its name to the Y. B(oys) C. A.

The Ohio Mechanics' Institute, probably the largest school of its kind in Ohio, has recently decided to deny them admission.

In the Children's Home, on Ninth Street, another large public institution, colored children are permitted to stay but twenty-four hours, after which they are sent to the Colored Orphans' Asylum. The Automobile Club of America has decided to give orphans of cities in which there are branches of the association a free trip to the country annually. The Cincinnati branch two years ago forgot (?) the colored children. Last year, after a very heated public discussion of the matter, it was decided that there were not enough colored chauffeurs to draw them out, so they could not take them.

Theaters universally exclude the Negro, or at the best give him a gallery seat, and that possibly at an advanced price. The large city workhouse, reformatories, city and county prisons, and hospitals, separate white and black as much as they possibly can.

The Negro can neither rent nor buy a house in a decent section of the city without paying an exorbitant price. If he does succeed in buying a desirable piece of property, his white neighbors will endeavor by all possible means to get him out of it. Sometimes they even threaten his life, but more often they buy him out, generally paying him considerably more than the property cost him. This is expensive for the white man, but he maintains his price. Many Negroes are taking advantage of this pride to better their financial condition, and many more would be doing the same if they had the capital. The following extract from a conversation with a colored preacher in one of the suburbs of Cincinnati will illustrate their attitude and their methods: "If I had a little money saved I would make the white folks pay for their prejudice. I would have some 'poor white trash' buy a lot in a fashionable neighborhood for me, and then I would declare my ownership and my intention to build. Immediately I would get many offers to buy, and when I could sell at a good profit I would let it go, and then I would buy another piece, and so continue. I could make a fine living in that way, far better than I can in the ministry, but I haven't the money to start with."

In St. James place, a fashionable residence district of Cincinnati, there lives a colored man of much prominence, being connected with the Southern Freedman's Aid Society and the Methodist Book Concern. The white neighbors have offered him big inducements to sell, but he, not being of the type represented above by the colored preacher, has refused all overtures and insists upon his rights.

But all of these prejudices, galling as they might be and would be to any white man, are small ones in comparison to one other. That other is the one that strikes at the law of self-preservation, strikes indeed at one of the basic principles of our life, namely, that every man should be permitted to earn his bread by the sweat of his brow, working in that pursuit best adapted to his ability. The colored man in earning his living is hampered on every side by race prejudice. The labor unions as a whole do not want him and will not have him, and their members will not work by the side of him. The result of this is that he is practically debarred from all mechanical pursuits requiring skill. He can join the hod carriers' union only, and this is due to the fact that not enough white men can be found to do the work. The bricklayers' union, the painters', the carpenters', the lathers', the plumbers', the barbers', the bartenders', the printers' unions, and many others deny him admission. The white man can not employ them in any skilled work if he has so large a job that he has to employ white men along with them. The white men will not work with them, there are not enough colored people prepared to do the work to do it alone, and the result is that no matter how much the white employer himself is free from prejudice, his hands are tied, he must of necessity, generally speaking, refuse to employ the colored man in any skilled capacity. Many colored men who had come from the South told the writer that there was no such condition as this existing in the South; that if a colored man became capable of laying brick or doing carpenter work or any other skilled work, he was as freely employed in it by the whites as the white laborers themselves were.

Besides their being debarred from skilled labor, they are not employed as stenographers, bookkeepers or office men in any capacity except that of janitor. Not one is employed as teacher in the public schools, none are employed as clerks in stores or factories.

The post office work is open to them because of its being under civil service rules, and we find them generally measuring up to the possibilities in this line. In the Cincinnati post office there are twelve employed as clerks and twenty-eight as carriers, making a total of forty out of a grand total of seven hundred employes, or about 5 per cent, which is the per cent of colored people in the city to the total population. In the police department there are twelve colored patrolmen out of a total of six hundred and ten, which is one-half their quota according to population. They get these places as policemen from the white people solely as a price for the colored vote.

The learned professions—the law, the ministry and medicine—are open to them, but the few who are brave enough to attempt these find that they can hardly make an honest living. The white people, of course, will not employ them, and, strange to say, their colored brothers are almost as much against them, but for different reasons, one of which is jealousy (a very strong race trait, as dozens of them themselves told the writer during the summer), and the other is lack of confidence. They will not respect the advice of one another, but will take the white man's every time, having learned during their days of slavery to look upon the word of the white man as law.

What are the causes of this strong prejudice in the City of Cincinnati? In general they are the same as are found in other cities of the state. The one big cause is that—"well, *just* BECAUSE."

The other causes are:

(1) There is a large number of ignorant colored people coming in from the South, seeking the land of the free, where they can have "their rights," many of whom mistake liberty for license.

(2) When a Negro commits a crime the newspapers always emphasize his race connection by such headlines as "A Big Black Burly Brute of a Negro" does such and such, and the whole race gets a share of the blame; while if the crime is committed by a white man, race is not mentioned, and the individual gets the blame.

(3) The mixing of the lower classes of the two races causes jealousy and ill feeling in these very classes, and much revulsion of feeling and fear in the higher classes.

(4) Cincinnati has always catered to the Southern trade and still does; therefore she adopts much of the South's attitude toward the Negroes.

(5) An unusually large number of Cincinnati's population very probably has been in the South for a time and then returned to the North. It

is almost the universal observation that such people, after their return, forever despise the Negro.

(6) The white people constantly complain of not being able to depend upon the Negro; they say he is shiftless, careless, and too prone to appropriate little things belonging to other people.

(7) The Negro more and more is entering politics as a Negro, and demanding rewards for the Negroes, in the way of positions and public offices. Naturally they are meeting with strong opposition and much secret resentment. The following words from the New York *Tribune* of June, 1877, apply so remarkably well to conditions in Cincinnati and other cities throughout the State of Ohio that I quote it in full:

"If a delegation of red-haired gentlemen should invade the White House with a petition to be recognized they would at once arouse the hostility of bald-headed patriots as well as of those whose hair was black or gray, and there would be established a color line in hair, which would complicate the difficulties of civil service reform. It is equally clear that if a deputation of citizens who wear false teeth should demand some offices for their class, the citizens who gum it would combine with those who masticate their food with natural grinders, not only to the discomfiture of the fictitious ivory party, but to the peril of our institutions. Citizens of African descent should reflect before they commit like indiscretions. The political salvation of the Negro depends upon his keeping out of politics *as* a Negro. If he keeps everlastingly besieging the Executive Mansion in squads in order to have his color recognized he will succeed in establishing a very distinct color line. It will be a blessed day when Negroes and white men both come to understand that appointment to office is not one of the inalienable rights of an American citizen, and when they can impress upon the gentlemen who are reforming the civil service that appointments are to be made solely for the purpose of transacting the business of the Government and solely upon the ground of fitness, and that race, color, previous condition of servitude, or present condition of politics are to be considered no more in the selection of place-men than they are in making out the tax list."

(8) The fact that so many Negroes appear in the police court and prisons certainly hurts their cause greatly. According to the report of the chief of police of Cincinnati for the year 1905, there were 12,138 white people arrested and 3,107 colored. According to the census of 1900 there were 325,000 people in the city and 14,482 were colored. By a little study of these figures we see that in proportion to their respective populations there were five colored people arrested to one white, and we can also see that if the white people were as criminal as the colored, the police would have made the enormous number of 68,345 arrests that one year. In 1906 there were 11,284 arrests of white people and 2,658 of colored. There were remaining in the House of Refuge, the city prison for young people, on December 31, 1907, 238 white children and 95 colored. From the annual report of the Cincinnati workhouse for 1907 we learn that there were 2,414 white prisoners and 949 colored. About the same proportion has obtained for the last several years. From a study of these figures one must conclude that in recent years and in this one city, at least, the criminality of the Negro has been fully five times as great as that of the white man.

Many "extenuating circumstances" might be offered to explain this difference, but the figures tell the more convincing story to the average man.

Many other causes possibly enter into the making of this condition of affairs in this one city. I have mentioned only such as came under my observation and such as throw extra light upon the facts presented. Here and there possibly I have appeared to favor one side and then another. I have tried very hard to present the facts and all the facts that I learned. May they help to better the relations between the two races."

EARLY

"Joe" Early will be eighty years of age June 12, 1926. Probably the oldest colored male resident born in this city. His father, Rev. Dangerfield Early, came from Virginia in the youth of the last century, and built, about 1859, the first colored church on Walnut Hills. The Earlys were the sixth colored family to move into that suburb. The father, a famous preacher, was a friend of Henry Ward Beecher, and in his wonderful tabernacle in Brooklyn, in the year 1879, Rev. Early opened and closed the great convention with prayer. "Joe" Early is our oldest politician. He was elected a constable in 1869, probably the first colored man elected to office in Ohio. Before the days of enfranchisement, light colored Negroes were allowed to vote. He was founder of the Nellie Grant Republican Club and personally uniformed 110 of its members. In a very exciting campaign, Ben Butterworth, afterwards senator, was candidate for election to convention. Early, a "Butterworth Booster," rendered great service, and on the day of election, was arrested several times for carrying a gun. That night "the big bosses," Luke Staley, Amor Smith, Henry Kessler, took Ben Butterworth and "Joe" Early with them to the St. Nicholas to celebrate. He was two days recovering from the champagne imbibed. Those were the good old days. Early was then the colored boss and many a job was gotten through his agency. His grandmother, Cornelia Jones, cooked for "Old Nick" Longworth, and the Longworths bore all expenses of her wedding supper. Joe Early was a celebrated chef and is an expert in the realms of pastry making. During the many years in which he was employed by Col. Morton in Glendale, he cooked the grand dinners tendered Grant, Hayes and Garfield. Got drunk on two cigars given him by Grant, but experienced no ill effects from shaking hands twice with President Lincoln. Early was the third colored man employed as mail carrier of the post office and served in that capacity for thirty-nine years. Though great for his time

and race when Geo. B. Cox was only a wagon driver, yet he is still hale and hearty, prominent in Masonic circles, and working daily in charge of the commissary department of The American Laundry Machinery Company.

A PIONEER PHYSICIAN

Dr. C. F. Buckner passed away in 1907, four score years of age. For many years he had been noted for marvelous cures and the most distinguished white physicians in the early days recognized and respected his ability. He was one of the very first in his time to study and use therapeutically the powerful forces of electricity. A good musician, splendid singer, he was noted for his interest in the choir and his organ playing at Allen Temple, and is said to have been the first Negro to play the big pipe organ in Music Hall. He was active until the brief illness came that carried him hence. The only surviving member of his family is his talented daughter, Mrs. Ellanette Hamilton, ex-school teacher, general secretary of the U. N. I. A. branch here and once a vocalist who sang with distinction in a concert company that made a grand tour of Europe.

SALMON P. CHASE

On January 13, 1808, in the town of Cornish, New Hampshire, there was born Salmon P. Chase. Salmon was a studious lad. He entered Dartmouth College, graduated in 1826, paid for his college expenses by school teaching. He then went to Washington, where he taught a classical school and studied law with William Wirt. Having been admitted to the bar in 1830, he settled in Cincinnati to practice his profession. His age was twenty-two years.

From his Puritan training he had early learned to view all questions in their moral aspects, and so, from the very beginning of his career, he was the friend of the slave, being, when in Washington, active in procuring signatures to a petition to Congress for the abolition of slavery in the District of Columbia.

In politics he did not then identify himself with either of the parties. When, in 1836, a mob destroyed "The Philanthropist," the anti-slavery newspaper, he was engaged by Mr. Birney, the editor, to bring the offenders to justice. About this time miscreants in and about Cincinnati not only made it a business to hunt and capture runaway slaves for the sake of reward, but to kidnap free blacks, carry them across the Ohio and sell them into slavery. In 1837, in what was known as the Matilda case, where a master brought a slave girl to the city and afterwards endeavored to take her back into slavery, Mr. Chase appeared in her behalf, as he frequently did in similar cases, without expectation of pecuniary reward. After the case had been closed a gentleman of note, who was present, said, "There goes a promising young lawyer who has ruined himself," he feeling how unpopular in those days was the defense of the enslaved and defenseless. None but a man of the highest moral courage and humanity would have been willing to endure the obloquy. Governor Hoadley said of him, "What helped him—yes, what made him, was this. He walked with God. The predominant element of his life, that which gave tone and color to his thoughts and determined the direction and color of all he did, was his striving after righteousness . . . Behind the dusky face of every black man he saw his Saviour, the divine man also scourged, also in prison, at last crucified. This is what made him what he was. To this habit of referring to divine guidance every act of his life we owe the closing words of the Proclamation of Emancipation, which Mr. Lincoln added from Mr. Chase's pen as follows: 'And upon this act, sincerely believed to be an act of justice, warranted by the constitution, upon military necessity, I invoke the favorable judgment of all mankind, and the gracious favor of Almighty God.'"

Mr. Chase defended so many blacks who were claimed as fugitives from slavery that the Kentuckians called him the "Attorney General for Negroes," and the colored people of Cincinnati presented him a silver pitcher "for his various public services in behalf of the oppressed."

Mr. Chase, almost singly, wrote the platform for the liberty party, which in 1843 nominated James G. Birney for the presidency.

In 1855 Mr. Chase was elected governor of Ohio by the newly formed Republican party.

When Mr. Lincoln was called to the presidency, March 4, 1861, he made Mr. Chase secretary of the treasury. His consummate management of the finances of the nation was such that a conspicuous leader of the rebellion said, "They had been conquered by our treasury department and not by our generalship."

As a public speaker Mr. Chase was not eloquent. His speech was at times labored and hard, but he was impressive from his earnestness and the weight of his thoughts. The listener felt that he was no common man.

In appearance he was the most imposing public man in the country—over six feet high, a blonde, with blue eyes and fresh complexion, portly, with handsome features and a massive head. His manners were dignified, but he had but little suavity, had none of the arts of the demagogue, and his great reputation was solely due to his great services and capacity, for he had but little personal popularity; the multitude never shouted for him. His great ambition arose from the patriotic conviction that he could render great public service.

Mr. Chase died in New York, May 7, 1873, of paralysis. He was buried in Washington, and on Thursday, October 14, 1886, his remains were removed to Spring Grove, Cincinnati. On this occasion ex-Gov. Hoadley, his once partner, gave a masterly oration upon his life and services, in Music Hall, and addresses were made by Congressman Butterworth, Governor Foraker and Justice Matthews; James E. Murdoch read a poetical tribute from the pen of W. D. Gallagher. Conspicuous in the crowd who had assembled to pay their last tribute to the distinguished dead were some old colored men who had been slaves, and who felt a debt of gratitude to a man who had done so much for their liberty.

Julius Hawkins
Captain of the "Attucks Blues"
Crack Colored Company of Civil War Period

Mrs. Serena Webb
Sister to Sandy Shumate,
Owner of "The Old Dumas House"

JOSEPH BENSON FORAKER

Joseph Benson Foraker was born July 5, 1846, in Highland County, Ohio. When two years old his parents moved to Reece Mills. At fifteen years of age he went to Hillsboro, lived with his uncle, James Reece, and secured a position as clerk in the County Auditor's office. In 1862, sixteen years of age, he enlisted as a private in Company A, 89th O. V. I. He served until the close of the war, when he became a student. Was graduated from Cornell University, and admitted to the practice of law in 1869. Elected Judge of the Superior Court of Cincinnati in 1879; Governor of Ohio, 1885; re-elected, 1887; elected United States Senator, 1899; re-elected, 1902.

The election of 1884 was scarcely out of the way when the Republicans of Ohio commenced discussing the campaign of 1885, and especially the nomination for governor.

"I had to defend myself against some rather vicious attacks from enemies within the party who sought to stir up opposition to my renomination, especially among the colored voters.

"A war of this kind, to alienate the colored vote, had been made upon me during the campaign of 1883 by Democrats. It was revived and made over again, this time by Republicans.

"Governor Hoadley had been a strong anti-slavery man, who was noted for his friendship for the colored race.

"The attack was made in 1883 to defeat my election. It was made in 1885 to defeat my renomination.

"It did not prove to be a very serious matter when fathered by Democrats, who made the attack in the interest of the Democratic party; but it assumed serious proportions when fathered by the Republicans.

"There were two grounds for the attack, both relied upon in 1883, and both brought forth again in 1885. They were, in the first place, a silly story to the effect that I left the Ohio Wesleyan University at Delaware and went to the Cornell University at Ithaca, New York, to finish there my education, because a colored man had been received at Delaware as a student.

"It was so easily and effectually answered when first brought forward that I supposed it had been disposed of for all time.

"The other ground was the fact that I had, in 1882, after resigning from the bench and resuming the practice of law, successfully defended William J. White, my old classmate, Superintendent of the Public Schools of Springfield, Ohio, against an action for damages that had been brought against him in the United States Circuit Court for the Southern District of Ohio, for an alleged violation by him of the Civil Rights Law, in denying to Eva Gazzaway, a colored girl, some privileges she claimed she was entitled to enjoy with respect to the public schools of Springfield.

"This, too, was effectually answered, not only by myself, but by counsel representing the plaintiff, among whom were two Negro lawyers, all of whom made public statements to the effect that I did in connection with the case only what my duties as an attorney required, and all of whom testified that I did not speak any word in the conduct or argument of the case that was in the slightest degree offensive to the colored race.

"I had the right to assume that neither of these matters would ever again be brought forward to prejudice my claims upon the colored voters of my party. It was annoying, therefore, and embarrassing to see these objections revived and urged by Republicans who had joined in their rejection and refutation in 1883.

"At that time there were a number of newspapers published in Ohio edited by Negroes. Every one of them seemed to be arrayed against me. They gave much space in their columns to reprinting these stories, with all kinds of extravagant and exaggerated and false features and amendments added.

"The Negro vote was so large that it was not only an important but an essential factor in our consideration. It would not be possible for the Republican party to carry the state if that vote should be arrayed against us.

"The situation was rapidly becoming embarrassing. I was somewhat perplexed to know how to deal with it without making myself an avowed candidate. My embarrassment in that respect was happily and most unexpectedly relieved.

"I received a letter making inquiry about the matter from Mr. S. E. Huffman, a colored man of Springfield, Ohio. I answered him at length, showing there were no facts to justify any of the criticisms that had been made." (We reprint a few extracts from Foraker's answer to the Huffman letter.)

"In 1862, when only sixteen years of age, I enlisted as a private in Co. A of the 89th Ohio Regiment. I served with this regiment for three years until the close of the war. At that time I did not know that I would ever be a candidate for any office, and certainly did not dream of such thing as ever having my attitude toward the colored people called in question. My expressions at that time ought, therefore, to be conclusive as to my sentiments in that regard.

"When a man is made a candidate for such an office as that of Governor of Ohio, everything that he ever said or did is likely to be made public. Such seemed to be my fortune when a candidate in 1883. Among other things published at that time were some of the letters I wrote home from the army. I had nothing to do with their publication.

"But it would seem now that it was well that they were published, since it enables me to point you to them as an incontestable record to disprove the charges to which you refer. For in them you will find that I then wrote that 'the war ought not to stop until slavery is abolished, and every colored man is made a citizen, and is given precisely the same civil and political rights that the white man has.'

"The war ended, and all who knew me then will testify that I was uncompromisingly in favor of the enfranchisement of the colored people as a basis of reconstruction in the South, and as a matter of justice in the North.

"And when it was proposed to amend the constitution of Ohio in 1867 by striking out the word "white," I took an active part in the campaign, although still in school at Delaware, speaking in favor of the measure and voting for it at the polls—the first vote I ever cast.

"This brings me in chronological order to the charge that I left the Ohio Wesleyan University because a colored man was admitted there as a student.

"The story that I left the Ohio Wesleyan University because he or any other colored man came there is a baseless falsehood.

"The truth was, so far as I can recollect, that there was but very little dissatisfaction manifested on the part of any one because he became a student there. In fact, I only remember one student who left on that account, and I need scarcely add that he was a Democrat then and is a Democrat still.

"The Rev. Mr. Mortimer left school at the end of his first term of his own free will and accord. I did not leave there until one year later, when I left and went to Cornell University at Ithaca, New York, where I graduated.

"The object of the civil rights bill is to prevent masked marauders from burning Negro schoolhouses, shooting Negro school teachers and keeping this innocent and inoffensive people in a state of terror, which retards their development and corrupts and demoralizes society and politics in a hundred ways. And it is right, and the Republican party is for it because it is right.

"When in Columbus the other day I stood in our Capitol building and looked with admiring gaze upon that magnificent painting which adorns its walls, of 'Perry's Victory on the Lake.' There, in the midst of the death storm of that terrible conflict, as gallant looking as any one of the grave faces surrounding the commodore, is a full-blooded representative of the African race. And so it has always been since our government was founded, on land and sea, in adversity and prosperity, through peace and through war, this race has been ever present with us, and never once has its faith faltered, its devotion lagged, or its courage failed.

"They have justly earned their citizenship and they have earned it in such a way as that for us not to protect them in it would be the basest ingratitude and wrong for which the nation would deserve to sink to rise no more.

"The Rev. Mr. Gazzaway was represented in the case by two colored men, both of whom have testified, and will again, that throughout the case I neither did nor said anything whatever that was, or could be, in the slightest degree, disrespectful or offensive to the colored people. And not only that, but the statement has been correctly made that one of Mr. Gazzaway's attorneys, who was a colored man, had not, previously to the trial, been admitted to the bar of the United States Court, and that he was admitted upon my motion and recommendation in order that he might assist in the trial of that cause.

"I believe I have now fully answered all that your letter calls for. To do so has made it necessary that I should write you at considerable length. Nevertheless, I can not stop without reminding you that it is far more important to the colored people that the Republican party should succeed than it is to the party itself.

"It has been only a few years since Democrats held colored men in slavery; now all are free; only a few years since the Democratic party of Ohio disgraced our statute books with the infamous visible admixture laws; now the statute books are clean; only as long ago as 1867 the Democratic party of Ohio declared in its platform that this was a white man's government and that Negroes should have no part in it.

"But to learn the feeling of the Democratic party toward the colored people you do not need to look further than the election of last October in the City of Cincinnati.

"The so-called Springer Investigating Committee has been taking testimony that establishes, to the satisfaction of every unprejudiced mind, that the Democratic party, as an organization, acting by its agents, deliberately planned and attempted to perpetrate the outrage of fraudulently carrying that election by arresting, beating and wounding and intimidating colored men and preventing them by wholesale from casting their ballots. In pursuance of this plan they deliberately arrested one hundred and fifty-two citizens of Cincinnati at midnight before the election and imprisoned them in the dungeon of the Hammond Street station-house, and kept them there without a bite of bread or a drop of water, or any charge against them, until after six o'clock in the evening of the day of the election.

"A more brutal outrage was never perpetrated north of the Ohio river, and yet no Democrat has condemned it. On the contrary, from the governor down to the lowest ward politician in their ranks there has been a chuckle of delight because of the success of the infamous scheme. And you will not have to live very long to see among the very first political acts of Mr. Cleveland, the granting of a pardon to the man who is now serving out a sentence of imprisonment for having perpetrated this crime."

(We may add that Lieutenant "Mike" Mullen, who made the wholesale arrests of Negroes, was acting under instructions of his superiors. He was pardoned, became a Republican, was elected to Council and until his death was idolized because of his charities by the great masses of Negroes who voted in his ward.)

"The convention was at Springfield, Ohio, June 10 and 11, 1885. Foraker went in the special train chartered by the Blaine Club. He was placed in nomination by the Honorable Miller Outcalt, at that time the president of the Young Men's Blaine Club of Cincinnati. He made a speech that abounded in felicitous expressions that pleased the convention and excited much enthusiasm.

"Walter S. Thomas, a young and eloquent representative of the colored voters, followed him in a seconding speech that was well received and did much good because of the refutations he made of the claim of serious defection among the colored voters and the pledges he gave of the support of those for whom he spoke.

"The usual committee to wait upon the nominee and ask him to appear before the convention was appointed. Again McKinley was a member of this committee, as he was in 1883. The other members were Col. Robert Harlan and Hon. Allen Miller.

"Foraker was nominated. Col. Harlan was the colored leader from Cincinnati. In the campaign the first place was given to the right of suffrage and the status of the Negro. I first spoke at length on this general subject at Wilberforce University a few days after I had been nominated.

"I recall this address and the Commencement Day occasion as among the most interesting of all such experiences. The presiding officer was the venerable Bishop Campbell. He had been a slave who was liberated by the Civil War."

Foraker ended a most eloquent speech with this: "A race that can produce such men as Frederick Douglass, Dr. Derrick, Bishop Campbell, Bishop Payne, Bishop Turner, and such men as our worthy friend, Brother Arnett, who is to be the next representative in the legislature from this county (loud applause), and a gloriously good one he will be—he will be loyal, I warrant you, to all of the highest and best interests of the state and of the colored and also of the white people. A race, I say, that can produce men of such intellect, men of such character, is deserving of the highest encouragement and must be successful and triumphant in all it undertakes." (Applause.)

Years passed. Foraker, as a senator, climbed glorious heights. He was mentioned for the presidency, but his star was setting, Roosevelt's rising. The controversy over the wholesale imprisonment and discharge of the colored companies for participation in the shooting up of Brownsville, Texas, came in the limelight. Foraker became the champion of the Negro troops. His doom was sealed. Retirement to private life gave him some years of calm philosophic happiness as well as the opportunity to write the volumes, "Notes of a Busy Life," from which we have so freely quoted in this sketch.

GEORGE HOADLEY

George Hoadley was born July 31, 1825. The young man was pale, slender, with keen, dark eyes, nimble in his movements, quick as a flash with an idea, and enthusiastic. This was George Hoadley; upon his history, blood and training have since asserted their power. He is of the old Jonathan Edwards stock; his great grandmother, Mary Edwards, who married Major Timothy Dwight, was a daughter of the great divine. His father, George Hoadley, was a graduate of Yale; was for years mayor of New Haven; moved in 1830 with his family to Cleveland, where he was elected five times mayor, 1832-1837, during which time he decided 20,000 suits; mayor, again, 1846-1847. He was a horticulturist, arborist, botanist and learned in New England family history, a gentleman of unusual elegance and accomplishments. His mother was a sister of the late President Woolsey, of Yale.

George Hoadley graduated at Western Reserve College and Harvard Law School, and in 1849 became a partner in the law firm of Chase & Ball, Cincinnati. In 1851, at the age of twenty-five, he was elected judge of the Superior Court of Cincinnati, and was city solicitor in 1855. "In 1858 he succeeded Judge Gholson on the bench of the new Superior Court. His friend and partner, Governor Salmon P. Chase, offered him a seat upon the Supreme Court bench, which he declined, as he did also, in 1862, a similar offer made by Governor Tod. In 1866 he resigned his place in the Superior Court and resumed legal practice. He was an active member of the Constitutional Convention of 1873-74, and in October, 1883, was elected Governor of Ohio, defeating Joseph B. Foraker, by whom he was in turn defeated in 1885. During the Civil War he became a Republican, but in 1876 his opposition to a protective tariff led him again to affiliate with the Democratic party. He was one of the counsel that successfully opposed the project of a compulsory reading of the Bible in the public schools, and was leading counsel for the assignee and creditors in the case of Archbishop Purcell. He was a professor in the Cincinnati Law School in 1864-1887, and for many years a trustee in the University. In March, 1887, he removed to New York and became the head of a law firm."

Hoadley was so strongly sympathetic with colored people that he was once arrested for refusing to assist the sheriff in capturing an escaped slave. As governor, he placed numbers of colored men on state boards and always recognized the rights of the race. When Davis, our last Republican governor, ruled, Negroes got little chance under his administration except in segregated sections.

BLACK LAWS REPEALED
BENJAMIN W. ARNETT, D.D.

"At this period the slavery question assumed such importance as to soon revolutionize the politics of the state. In the session of 1848-49, the legislature was nearly equally divided between the Whigs and Democrats, with two Free Soilers, namely, Messrs. N. S. Townshend, of Lorain County, and John F. Morse, of Lake County, holding the balance of power. The repeal of the Black Laws, which had long marred the statute books of Ohio, and their choice for a United States Senator, were the primary objects with the Free Soilers. Besides the election of a Senator, two judges were to be elected to the Supreme Bench. Mr. Morse made overtures to the Whigs, but there were some few from the southern counties who were opposed to the repeal of the laws and to Joshua R. Giddings, his choice for Senator, and hence he failed. Mr. Townshend was successful with the Democrats. They united with the Free Soilers, the Black Laws were repealed (in which vote most of the Whigs joined), Salmon P. Chase, the personal choice of Mr. Townshend, was elected to the Senate, and two Democratic judges to the Supreme Bench.

This legislation provided schools for colored children. They were, however, in a certain sense, Black Laws, inasmuch as a distinction was thereby shown between the races. This distinction was not entirely obliterated until the session of 1886-87, when they were repealed through the eloquent efforts of Benjamin W. Arnett, D.D., member-elect from Greene County. He was the first colored man in the United States to represent a constituency where the majority were white and the first to be foreman of a jury where all the other members were white.

The Black Laws of Ohio covered three points. (1) The settlement of black or mulatto persons in Ohio was prohibited unless they could show a certificate of their freedom and obtain two freeholders to give security for their good behavior and maintenance in the event of their becoming a public charge. Unless this certificate of freedom was duly recorded and produced it was a penal offense to give employment to a black or mulatto. (2) They were excluded from the common schools. (3) No black or mulatto could be sworn or allowed to testify in any court in any case where a white person was concerned.

Arnet was for a long time pastor of Allen Temple in Cincinnati, and later in life became Bishop and had a beautiful residence near the Wilberforce University grounds."

R. S. DUNCANSON

R. S. Duncanson, colored artist of this city, was a genius in every sense of the word. Many of the old residents of Mt. Healthy knew him well. Though self-taught, his pictures early attracted attention. The art records of England mention and describe some of the paintings he exhibited when making a tour of Europe. The great white masters of the brush knew and admitted him in their circle, for "Art has no color line." His main associations here were men of international reputation, among them Farny, Lindsay, S. Jerome, Uhl, and Henry Mosler, who afterwards located in New York. Among his paintings in this city are a full size portrait of Wm. Cary at the Ohio Military Institute, College Hill, and a life size picture at Ohio Mechanics' Institute of Nicholas Longworth I. There are several other pictures, magnificent landscapes, in existence. Their location is known to F. C. Wright, of Mt. Healthy, to whom the world is indebted for rescuing from oblivion a knowledge of the greatness of Duncanson. His trial of Shakespeare was painted after Harvey when he was only twenty-two years of age. He should, like Tanner, have stayed in Europe where, freed from the burden of color, the wings of genius would have borne him to fame's most glorious heights. The following article concerning him is from the Enquirer of December 21, 1924:

"ROBERT S. DUNCANSON, A CINCINNATIAN WHO BECAME WORLD FAMOUS AS AN ARTIST

"Early Cincinnati Artists—An Interesting Letter from Moncure D. Conway—A Tribute to American Art—'The Land of the Lotus Eaters'— Duncanson's Life in Europe—His Portraits

"In 1857, William P. Noble, long a well-known artist, made a drawing from the original sketch of Cincinnati, 122 years ago.

"Cincinnati was in that decade a large art center, the most prominent west of the Alleghenies. Already the city was known for the fame of Hiram Powers, a sculptor, and a score of painters headed by James H. Beard, Thomas Buchanan Read and Robert S. Duncanson, the phenomenal colored man, whose father was a Scotchman, of Canada, and whose mother was a mulatto.

"Seventy-five years ago, according to Charles Cist's 'Cincinnati in 1851,' Cincinnati had numerous artists who had already become, or were about to become, distinguished for work. One of these was the colored man, Robert S. Duncanson, who was then already prominent for such historical pieces as his 'Shylock and Jessica,' 'Ruins of Carthage,' 'Trial of Shakespeare,' 'Battle Ground of the River Raisin' and 'Western Hunters' Encampment.'

"Among the Cincinnatians whose parlors were graced by Duncanson's works in 1843 and until 1850 were James Foster, mathematical instrument maker, 384 West Third; W. H. Brisbane, M.D., northwest corner Sixth and College; Samuel S. Smith, capitalist, 200 West Fourth; Thomas Faris, daguerrean artist, Melodeon Building; Drs. Robert S. and Orrin E. Newton, 87 West Seventh; James H. Oliver, real estate dealer, 146 West Seventh; Calvin W. Starbuck, proprietor of the Cincinnati Daily Times; Charles Stetson, capitalist and president of O. L. and T. Company, and Nicholas Longworth, capitalist and attorney, Pike Street, near Fourth.

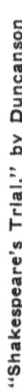

"Shakespeare's Trial," by Duncanson

"Within the scope of Mr. Cist's records up to 1851 there were over 50 painters and sculptors, beginning with Edwin B. Smith, in 1815. In gathering the facts connected with these artists of early times he called at the professional studios in Cincinnati and found that the artists had ample employment and some had even more commissions than they could accept.

"This was in the time of the Arts Union Hall, which was in the top floor of the four-story building still standing at the northwest corner of Sycamore and Fourth. This hall, now used for a leather business, was then 71 by 33 feet on its floor space and 24 feet to the skylights. Its space for exhibitions was about the same as that of the New York Arts Union. There had been at one time 300 pictures of various sizes exhibited there.

"In 1865, November 24, there appeared in the Cincinnati Daily Gazette the following item from Moncuro D. Conway, of Cincinnati, who wrote from London, England, telling of the advance of Robert S. Duncanson:

"'In walking through the gallery of miniatures, at the South Kensington Museum the other day I met Duncanson, whom some of your readers will remember as one who, a few years ago, was trying to make himself an artist in Cincinnati, and who had already produced a worthy piece of imaginative art in a picture of Tennyson's "Lotus Eaters."

"'Duncanson subsequently left Ohio and repaired to Canada, where his color did not prevent his association with other artists and his entrance into good society. He gained much of culture and encouragement in Canada, retouched his "Lotus Eaters," produced one or two still better paintings and set out for England. In Glasgow and other Scotch cities he exhibited these paintings with success.

"'He has been invited to come to London by various aristocratic personages. Among others, by the Duchess of Sutherland and the Duchess of Essex, who will be his patrons. He also received a letter from the poet laureate, Tennyson, inviting him to visit him at his home, in the Isle of Wight, where he will go and take with him the "Lotus Eaters." Think of a Negro sitting at the table with Mr. and Mrs. Alfred Tennyson, Lord and Lady of the Manor, and Mirror of Aristocracy—and so forth.

(Signed) "Aubrey" Moncure D. Conway.'

"Thus from that Cincinnati litterateur and preacher, Mr. Conway. A few years later we find him, accompanying another Cincinnati journalist, Murat Halstead, of the Commercial, tracking the dead of the great Franco-Prussian War in 1870, as over the field of Gravelotte.

"In 1866 there appeared in 'The Art Journal,' of London, England, the following tribute to American art. It was headed, 'The Land of the Lotus Eaters. Painted by R. S. Duncanson.'

"'America has long maintained supremacy in landscape art, perhaps indeed its landscape artists surpass those of England. Certainly we have no painter who can equal the works of Church; and we are not exaggerating if we affirm that the production under notice may compete with any of the modern British school. Duncanson has established high fame in the United States and in Canada. He is a native of the States and received his art education there, but it has been "finished" by a course of study in Italy, by earnest thoughts at the feet of the great masters and by a continual contemplation of nature under Southern skies.

"'The picture to which we more immediately refer (although hereafter we may describe such as make us familiar with Canadian scenery) is a composition, but one in which the national beauties of Greece are brought together with consummate skill. A bit may have been taken here and a bit there, yet there is perhaps harmony in the whole; insomuch that the scene may have been presented in its entirety, for we need the statement of the artist that it is not one of altogether truth. The painted poem has been suggested by the written poem of the poet laureate:

> "Here are cool mosses deep,
> And through the moss the ivy creep,
> And in the stream the long-leaved flowers weep,
> And from the crags' ledge the poppy hangs in sleep."

" 'The scene represents Ulysses and his warriors visiting the Lotus Islands on their way to Troy. The artist in this supplies us with an incident that gives point and value to the lovely valley surrounded by snow-topped mountains in which the simple natives—the lotus-eaters, dwell. A group is thus introduced on the borders of a river, amid richly dowered trees, the fruit-producing kind. Some have gathered around the stately Greek, while others swim in the stream, bearing their harvest. "Slender streams" come down from the mountains, and bare and barren summits contrasting with the verdure of a hundred hues at their feet, while over all is a glowing sunset that makes of the whole a very paradise of earth.

" 'Perhaps the most meritorious parts of the picture are those that represent the mountains, their tops partly hidden by the clouds, rich in the glories of a southern sunset, while the snow that covers their summits reflects the varied hues that are brightest and fairest when day is about to depart from earth. The picture is full of fancy. It is a grand conception, and a composition of infinite skill, yet every portion of it has been studied with the severest care, from "the charming sunset lingering adown in the red-west sky" to the "slender streams, some like a downward smoke" that bear the contributions of the mountains to the valley. The picture is one of large size, and has obviously been a work of time, but time well bestowed.

" 'The sight of it can not fail to be the source of intense enjoyment. As a manuscript of nature, such as nature may be in the land where even now, all but man is divine, where the loveliest of earth's products are lavished in luxurious profusion, and where the commonest things are the most beautiful. This painting may rank among the most delicious that art has given us, but it is also wrought with the skill of a master in all even the minutest of its details.

" 'We therefore may add this picture to the many works of rare value supplied to us by the landscape artists of America. They have in their richly-gifted "world" natural objects of such incalculable variety, that every student may be made a painter who looks on nature with an eye ever so little educated in art. Go where they will over their boundless forests and "everlasting prairies" they find themes for the pencil. It is not therefore surprising that we find the artists of America contending successfully in a special department of art with those of Europe; nor that recent "importations" from that country into this have raised our expectation very high as to their future.'

"The author is indebted to F. C. Wright, of Mt. Healthy, for the information concerning Duncanson. This gentleman comes of a stock that took much interest in the condition of the colored people before their emancipation, back to the days of the Underground Railroad, when white people of prominence were very enthusiastic in the freeing of the slaves and running them through to Canada.

"Mr. Wright's uncle, G. L. La Boiteaux, of a distinguished old family, had the care at one time of one of Duncanson's little sons. Mr. Wright can now vaguely recall the great artist's personal appearance. Duncanson was born in 1821, and died a raving maniac in his cell at the Detroit asylum. In 1917, Mr. Wright had correspondence with a grandson of the artist, Albert L. Duncanson, of Seattle.

"Mr. Wright, in keeping track of R. S. Duncanson's career, has had correspondence with several persons who knew him well. Henry Mosler, a great artist, who was well acquainted with Duncanson and who died in 1919, was very much interested in Mr. Wright's researches. Mr. Wright has owned and sold some of Duncanson's paintings and he has given the author information concerning some of them. The most profitable ones were produced and sold during the artist's years in Scotland, England and France. They produced for him many thousands of dollars, year after year.

"Duncanson was of a very extravagant mood while in Europe, as his vogue commanded him easy patronage and high prices. He must have been very temperamental, for his last days were clouded, in Ohio and Michigan, leading finally to his violent insanity, in which, with his great strength, he would tear apart his confining bars.

"One of Duncanson's early portraits was that of the first of the Carys, of College Hill, William Cary. There are two life-size portraits of Duncanson's—one of Miles Greenwood and one of Nicholas Longworth, which are among the historical treasures of the Ohio Mechanics' Institute. In Mr. Wright's personal collection is one which was exhibited at the first great London exhibit of 1851, which attracted Queen Victoria's commendation. It is a river and forest scene and is known as 'The Western Hunters' Encampment.'

"The well known 'Old Oaken Bucket' picture and his 'Ben Bolt' were produced in the early days of his strange artistic temperament. Fellow artists and others who saw him work at that time recalled his occasional lapses, when he would become hysterical, at times dropping his brush and laughing and weeping before he would resume his work.

"Mr. Wright has called the writer's attention to a large painting of 1868, of a forest and lake with a group of females startled out of their bathing by a dog's sudden appearance out of the woods. It now graces a wall of the Fisher tailoring shop on Walnut Street. It was first owned by Samuel Thomas, a well-known tailor in the fifties and sixties, a man known for his great skill and his high prices during the Civil War. There is also a photograph of Duncanson's 'Trial of Shakespeare' in the possession of W. P. Dabney, of McAllister Street, of the Dabney Publishing Company."

The Crawford Old Men's Home

Rev. Wallace Shelton
"Father of Zion Baptist Church"

ALEXANDER THOMAS

Mr. Alexander Thomas was a bright, ambitious boy who for years followed the lucrative calling of "steamboating." A great deal of his time was spent in New Orleans. He became a photographer of Cincinnati and finally associated with Ball and the firm name was Ball and Thomas. They had the first and finest Daguerreotype gallery in Cincinnati and became famous photographers. Locating at 28 West Fourth Street, they took the pictures of the leading statesmen, stage and other celebrities of the day. Mr. Thomas remained in business over forty years. He and Mrs. Thomas celebrated, at their residence on Hopkins Street, the golden wedding, which was finer by far than that of Harvey Young's, which took place twenty years before. Mr. Thomas moved to Chicago with his family about twenty years ago. Both he and his wife are now dead.

DR. JARED CAREY

Dr. Jared Carey opened probably the first chiropodist establishment in this city. Over fifty years had he been in that profession when death called him. He had a suite of offices in the Arcade. A splendid character in every way. His death was greatly regretted. The widow, Mrs. Eldona Carey, continued the business until her marriage to Mr. Thomas O'Banion. She passed away a few years ago and the business founded by Dr. Carey has been greatly improved and augmented by its present owner, Dr. O'Banion.

THE GRATITUDE OF CRAWFORD

In the Civil War there was a white soldier from this city named John Crawford. He experienced many, many hardships in the South, but the Negroes were so kind to him that he swore never to forget their efforts in his behalf. Years afterward he acquired a fine farm in College Hill and when he died he left that estate to be used for old colored men. The contest of the white relations proved unsuccessful, and so today we have "Crawford's Old Men's Home." It is now a beautiful place, completely renovated, a real home for its inmates, and under exclusive control of colored trustees who are appointed by the court. We are reminded of the late Col. Markbreit, though his gratitude found little expression other than in words. In a conversation during the time he was mayor of Cincinnati, he told us that he would always have a large, warm place in his heart for colored people. That when he was captured and confined in one of those loathesome, vermin-infested, foul-smelling dungeons of the South, known as prisons, he was nearly starved to death. That but for the kindness of the common Negro laborers he would have died. Often in the day or night they would come by his cell window and hand him scraps of bread and meat they had saved from lunch or stolen. Many a time they had hidden it under their shirt next to their skin, but he was glad to get, and more glad to eat, the meat scraps and bread, though they were moistened with the sweat that flowed so freely from the hides of those black workmen.

EMERY

In letters of gold the name Emery should be emblazoned upon the hearts of all Cincinnatians. The founder of that name came, and his life was an exemplification of the golden rule, that divine inspiration which has animated the soul of every truly great man since the birth of reason, the dawn of civilization. Thomas Emery had two sons, Thos. J. and J J. Emery. They were of that English stock whose blood ever fired at oppression, whose heart ever warmed to charity. Their recognition of the brotherhood of man caused them to refuse donations to any cause that recognized the color line, and so their princely gifts to institutions carried with them the admission of colored people. The Emerys gave $35,000 for the building of our Orphan Asylum and Mrs. Emery recently gave $25,000 for an addition to the building. Mr. John Emery, of New York, son of J. J. Emery, is now connected with the firm in this city and he shows every indication of being a great business man, a real gentleman, a chip off the old block. Mr. Joseph Emery, cousin of Thos. Emery, was not only an abolitionist, but a missionary of the Christ type. He wrote a book descriptive of his thirty-five years' work among the lowly. He became the Superintendent of the Baker Street Sunday School in 1850 and remained until 1890. When he donated coal or provisions to the poor, one-half always went to the colored paupers. The following incident from his book is of vital interest, as it shows the class of man he was as well as racial conditions in the religious world at that period:

"The origin of this prejudice against colored people is doubtless traceable to slavery. Ever since the arrival of the first cargo of slaves from Africa, nearly three hundred years ago, when these poor, helpless people were sold to the highest bidder, has this prejudice existed. To dislike a man because of the color of his skin is alike foolish, unreasonable and unscriptural. Has not God made of one blood all the nations of the earth? Are not all mankind brothers? Our constitution declares 'All men are free and equal.'

"The colored people were loyal, both North and South, on the battlefield; they were equally brave with their white brothers when called into action.

"As to why this prejudice against colored people should exist in a great city like Cincinnati it is difficult to explain. Some say we are close to the border; others, that many of the earlier settlers were from the South; others, that Cincinnati's chief market for her wares and manufactures was in the South. But this we know, that anti-slavery men like Levi Coffin, Dr. Boynton, Edward Harwood, the Ernsts, Colemans, Prices and others, were charged with hurting the southern trade and keeping up a useless agitation. This prejudice against our colored people had a sad and startling exhibition in our city at the first meeting of the Ohio Sabbath School Convention, which was held in Smith and Nixon's Hall, May 11 and 12, 1859.

"A committee had been previously appointed to arrange for four large mass meetings for all the Sabbath Schools of the city, including the five colored schools. The committee was unanimous on this question.

"The committee appointed the schools to four different churches and halls for the occasion. They designated the five colored Sunday Schools to Wesley Chapel, that being the nearest place to them. I happened to be the superintendent of the Union Baptist Sabbath School, then meeting on Baker Street. Children and teachers were all notified to be on hand May 12 and march to Wesley Chapel. The day before the meeting there was much talk about the trustees refusing these children admission. We little thought any Christian men could do such a foolish and unjust thing. So we marched along the streets, about two hundred in all, in perfect order, to the Chapel. A goodly number of people walked along with us. On ascending the steps we found two of the doors closed, and men stood in the front door and denied us admission. I inquired by whose authority. They replied, 'The trustees.' 'Which?' 'All,' was the reply. So we marched to the opposite side of the street and sang the hymn:

> 'Oh, do not be discouraged,
> For Jesus is your friend;
> He will give you grace to conquer,
> And keep you to the end.'

"After a few words of explanation as to why we were refused—simply because the children were colored—we marched back, in perfect order, to Baker Street Church, and there and then officers and teachers passed some decided resolutions on the injustice done by the said trustees. These were published next day in all the newspapers. All sorts of vials of wrath were poured on my head by friend and foe.

"The newspaper war which followed waxed very hot, and it lasted nearly three weeks. All the papers which took part in the controversy wrote bitterly against one solitary superintendent, who merely wished to carry out the program marked out by the committee, except the Gazette, which spoke nobly for the committee, for the colored people and the superintendent."

"THE GOLDEN RULE"

In recent years so few have been the white citizens showing an interest in colored people that when one is found we exclaim "rara avis," and congratulations for ourselves vie with commendation for him. In such class we place Mr. Henry Jonap, retired capitalist, who has made for his life's effort the promotion of truth-telling, and Mr. Chas. J. Livingood, a most important factor in the distribution of the Emery charities. Among others we find Mr. Arthur Nash, Esq., well-known philanthropist and advocate of "The Golden Rule," has done Christ-like service for his fellow man and his benefactions have even penetrated the vast wall of color prejudice to extend a helping hand to his darker brethren. His benevolence is greater than the mere charitable functioning of finance. The wisdom of his advice, the grand lesson of co-operation he teaches, will prove of far greater value to our colored citizens than gold, for self-reliance is the greatest asset of man or nation.

BISHOP HARTZELL

In late years Bishop J. C. Hartzell has stood out conspicuously in his advocacy of justice for all men. He was born in Illinois in 1842. Became a minister in 1868. After being corresponding secretary of The Freedmen's Aid Society for many years he became a Bishop in 1896. He spent many years in Africa and was retired in 1916. He has had most intimate relations with the Negro race and is one of the few white men who really knows colored people. Many years ago when he and his wife were South, they had the opportunity of attaining recognition and assistance for Tanner, then a poor, struggling young man. The Bishop still has some of the pictures he painted at that time and in his residence in the suburbs of Cincinnati this man of God delights to tell of the many fine people of the Negro race he has met in all parts of the world.

REV. HERBERT S. BIGELOW

In the white race of today there is no more outstanding defender of right than Herbert S. Bigelow, a product of Oberlin College, and for years a resident of this city. Long has he been pastor of the People's Church, a liberal and aggressive congregation that has its Sunday sessions in the afternoon at one of our leading theatres. Years ago, when the church was established in its own building, the grim specter of color arose. Among its members, a family seemingly white was found to be colored. Immediately certain of the brethren demanded its expulsion. Nobly did Bigelow stand by those colored people. He boldly announced that under no circumstances would he favor their dismissal, that his church was for all men, and those who objected to the presence of colored members could leave. His firmness won the day. A Democrat in politics, Rev. Bigelow was a prominent figure in the legislature in 1913. The intermarriage bill came up. We are eternally indebted to that gentleman for the quiet but most effective assistance he rendered in killing that pernicious measure. Had we more Americans of the type of Rev. Herbert S. Bigelow, we would have few racial troubles to mar the harmony that should permeate a country that God has showered with so many blessings.

TRIBUTE TO MARCHAND

In 1904, Dr. Otto Juetner, of this city, became author of a most valuable volume entitled, "Daniel Drake and His Followers." This Daniel Drake was the greatest doctor of his day and his fame as a writer and historian ranks equally as high. Among those to whom acknowledgments are made by Dr. Juetner for valuable assistance rendered is Mr. P. Alfred Marchand, of the Cincinnati Hospital Library. Marchand was a colored man and such tribute to him stands without precedent in this city, if not in this country. As we have before mentioned, although Marchand served this city at the hospital for a period lacking only a few months of a half century, his salary was only fifty dollars a month. He eked out an existence by doing medical and research work for the leading doctors of the white race who greatly appreciated his services.

Section V

Colored School History to 1902, by Shotwell— Teachers in Colored Schools, 1925

(From *History of Schools of Cincinnati*, by JOHN B. SHOTWELL, 1902.)

In the minutes of the Board of Trustees and Visitors of April 5, 1830, O. M. Spencer reported the following:

"The people of colour in the First Ward pray that a school may be opened in it for the benefit of their children."

This would seem to indicate that colored children were not taken special cognizance of by the authorities in 1829, when the public school system was established. It is, however, recorded that in the private schools of those years there was no distinction on account of color. Indeed, colored children of light hue were received into private schools as late as 1835, when Mr. Funk kept such a school at the southeast corner of Sixth and Vine.

According to John I. Gaines, the first school organized for colored people was in 1825, by Henry Collins, a colored man, who began in an old pork house (some say carpenter shop) on the south side of Seventh Street, between Broadway and Deer Creek. The school did not last a year. The colored population of Cincinnati at that time was about 250.

In a one-story frame building known as "King's Church," on the brink of Sixth Street Hill, looking down into Deer Creek, a colored man from Virginia, named Owen T. B. Nickens, opened the first successful colored school in 1834. The charge for tuition was one dollar per month, when he could get it, and though many paid in unredeemed promises, none were turned away for lack of payment.

In 1836 Mr. Nickens' school removed to New Street, near Broadway, where he was succeeded a few years later by John McMicken, a natural son of Charles McMicken, the founder of the University of Cincinnati. The latter was urged to do something for the education of colored youth. He responded by paying for a tract of land containing 10,000 acres, lying north of Liberia, between that republic and Sierra Leone, called it "Ohio in Africa," and told them to go there and settle.

(Baker Jones was summoned to Cincinnati and efforts were made to induce him to lead such a colony. He was willing to go, but being refused what he demanded in the way of preparation, he went back to Mercer County, his home. Peter H. Clark was then selected to go as an explorer to this "Ohio in Africa." But when he reached New Orleans he refused to embark in the dirty lumber schooner that had been chartered to carry him and one hundred and nineteen other persons. The others started.

Before getting out of the Gulf of Mexico the unfortunate emigrants were attacked by smallpox. The captain finally put into Charleston, S. C., for medical help. Here all the well ones were put into jail for coming into the state in contravention of law. After lingering there three months they were freed and set out again on their journey. In less than six months ninety per cent. of them were dead.

Having done so much, Mr. McMicken inserted a clause in his will prohibiting colored youth from sharing in the benefits of any educational facilities he might provide for the youth of the Queen City.)

In 1834, the faculty of Lane Seminary, alarmed by the threats of Kentucky mobbists, forbade their students to discuss the slavery question. A large number of students rebelled. Some went to Oberlin, which, with doors open for the discussion of all questions and for the education of all races and sexes, was at that time founded, and for the special benefit of these seceders. Some of the students came down to the city and established schools for the education of colored youth.

Three of these teachers, August Wattles and the Misses Mathews and Bishop, found employment in the East End. The ladies were in after years succeeded by Misses Lowe, Rakestraw and Merrill. One teacher, Mr. Fairchild, found pupils in the West End of the city.

It was no easy thing to secure a place in which these schools could assemble, for the mob spirit was so rampant and so powerful that there was danger of the destruction of any building so occupied, hence considerable difficulty was experienced by those determined to have schools. John O. Wattles, a white man, describes a scene of which he was an eye-witness. It was enacted at the Baptist Church, on Western Row, the site of the Central Union Depot. "The howling of the rowdies around the church, chiming with the rattling of the window shutters and the whistling of the winter winds through the vacant panes and the cracks of the door, the rattle of the stones and brickbats against the house, while the little ones within would gather up close to the teacher, and huddle closer together, trembling with fear and knowing not what to do, whether to stay and await the fire of the assailants, or rush out and brave the curses of the drunken rabble."

There was a determination not to allow the blacks to be taught, and all sorts of indignities were heaped upon teachers, who found their goods set upon sidewalks, and themselves forced to go from place to place for food and lodging.

A room for the girls of the East End was found in the Deer Creek Methodist Church, which was afterwards known as New Street Chapel. The approach to it, at that time, was by way of an alley opening into Sixth Street. Baker Jones allowed the use of two of his houses on Sixth Street, just east of Broadway (on "The Green"). In one of these Mr. Wattles taught an advanced class of boys, and in the other Miss Bishop taught the primary classes of the same sex. Mr. Jones is worthy of honorable mention in this connection. He was a man of considerable wealth for that day; also a man of intelligence and advanced ideas.

Prof. Fairchild, who taught in the colored schools here, became eminent in educational and theological work. He was for a time a professor at Oberlin College, and afterwards president of Berea College, Kentucky.

An association, the history of which has never been written, aided much in the establishment and maintenance of schools. Under its influence schools were established in Columbus, Chillicothe, Circleville, Zanesville, Dayton, and other places. The famous Liberty School House was one of their structures. Mrs. Sarah Bella Garrard, afterwards Mrs. Sarah Bella McLean, was president, and Rev. Walter Yancey agent to collect funds.

Still mob violence frequently kept the scholars from attending school, and prejudice was so intense the white teachers were refused accommodation in boarding houses, and were obliged to rent a house and board themselves. Colored men heartily co-operated in their work, and encouraged both teachers and scholars in their efforts. In 1841, Messrs. Goodwin and Denham opened a school in Baker Street Church. This was the largest of all the colored schools, having an enrollment of two or three hundred pupils. These schools continued with varying success for several years, some of them flourishing and others barely hanging on the ragged edge of existence.

The Cincinnati High School,

as Gilmore's school was called, was established in 1844 by Rev. Hiram S. Gilmore, a philanthropic gentleman of considerable wealth, who purchased a lot at the east end of Harrison Street, and erected thereon a building of five commodious rooms and a chapel. In the yard he placed a complete set of physical apparatus for gymnastic exercises.

While the building and outfit were the property of Mr. Gilmore, he was assisted in the maintenance of the school by the tuition paid by some pupils, the contributions of white friends, and by the society hitherto alluded to.

No expense was spared to make this school a success. Good teachers were employed, and besides the common branches of an English course, Latin, Greek, music, and drawing were taught.

Mr. Gilmore acted as principal, doing no teaching, and for a considerable time his brother-in-law, Joseph Moore, taught the advanced classes. Pupils were prepared for college, and quite a fair proportion of them went from this school to Oberlin and such colleges as drew no color line on matriculation.

While the enrollment reached several hundred, the receipts never equaled the expenses. Under the dirction of Dr. A. L. Childs and Prof. W. F. Colburn, respectively, the departments of elocution and music reached a high state of efficiency. Regularly during vacation the classes, under direction of the principal, journeyed through Ohio, New York and Canada, giving concerts and exhibitions, the profits of which were devoted to furnishing clothing and books and otherwise assisting indigent students.

The inspiration given to colored youth for the betterment of their individual condition and the elevation of their race, by

Peter H. Clark
Cincinnati's Most Famous Colored Citizen

Gilmore's school, was of almost incalculable benefit to the people. From its ranks came P. B. S. Pinchback, ex-governor and U. S. senator-elect (refused admission) of Louisiana; John M. Langston, ex-dean of Howard University Law School (Washington, D. C.), also congressman from Virginia and minister to Hayti; Thomas C. Ball, the artist; Peter H. Clark, ex-principal Gaines High School; Monroe Trotter, ex-United States recorder of deeds under President Cleveland; John I. Gaines, the Nestor of public school advocates; Dr. C. F. Buckner, M.D., of this city; Rev. Philip Tolliver, presiding elder of the A. M. E. Church; Joseph H. Perkins, the great orator of the Ohio Valley; and a host of others.

Public Schools.

In 1849 there was a tie in the Ohio Legislature between the Whigs and the Democrats, a handful of Free Soilers holding the balance of power. These Free Soilers made this proposition to the two parties: (a) Repeal the black laws; (b) establish free schools for colored children; (c) elect Salmon P. Chase to the United States Senate, and we will vote with you in the organization of the legislature and the distribution of state offices.

The Democrats accepted the offer, and the promised legislation was enacted. But the school and city authorities of Cincinnati held that the clause of the act which authorized colored men to elect their school directors was unconstitutional, and therefore they refused to pay over the money necessary to maintain the schools.

Six trustees were elected, teachers appointed, and houses rented, but no money was forthcoming. Led by John I. Gaines, Wm. Benkley, Richard Phillips, Dennis Hills, Jno. Woodson, Wallace Shelton, L. C. Flewellan, and others, the colored people came together in public and resolved to raise money, employ counsel, and sue the city. The city was divided into Eastern and Western Districts, with Walnut Street as the dividing line (later changed to Vine Street); teachers were employed and salaries fixed.

After serving three months, bills were presented to the council for the teachers' pay and expenses, and, as expected, payment was refused. Flamen Ball, law partner of Salmon P. Chase, was first in charge of the case, and he at once began action by asking the court for a writ of mandamus. The proceedings were begun in 1851, but a decision was not had till early in 1852. The decision affirmed the constitutionality of the act, and required the setting aside of a pro rata share of the funds, and the placing of those funds at the command of a board elected by the colored people. The delayed salaries were ordered paid, and the schools set in working order. Peter H. Clark, one of the teachers employed for that trial term, turned over his salary of one hundred and five dollars to the fund for defraying the expense incurred in the suit against the city. At first Mr. Clark was the only teacher in the Western District, but later he was assisted by Mr. Tolbert, a white man.

For the Eastern District, Owen T. B. Nickens and Miss Mary J. Hallam were employed. Miss Hallam taught the girls in a church which stood on North Street, between Sixth and New Streets. The schools were therefore fully established in 1852, under their own board of six trustees (later made nine when the Walnut Hills District was added), and with their own superintendent, Stephen L. Massey, a white man. Peter H. Clark succeeded Superintendent Massey after a brief interval; W. H. Parham succeeded Mr. Clark in 1866.

In the legislative session of 1852-3 the control of the schools was taken away from the colored people and vested in the white Board of Education. Soon that body tired of the change, and consented to the re-transfer. Then they remained under the colored board until 1874, when the management was again placed in the Board of Education.

The Eastern District school house on Seventh Street, east of Broadway, was erected in 1858. By a contract made with Nicholas Longworth in February, 1858, he covenanted to build a house on condition that he be paid 6% on the value of the house and lot, which was $12,979.49.

Five school houses composed the entire property of the colored board. Colored men could vote only for members of their board, this limited exercise of the franchise being all they had up to 1870, when Article 15 U. S. Const. was adopted. Whites did not vote for the colored board.

John Isom Gaines, after whom Gaines' High School was named, was born in Cincinnati. He was for years clerk of the colored board. He died on Thanksgiving Day, November 27,

1859. The remains were first buried in the Colored American Graveyard, Avondale, and in 1884 were removed to the Colored American Graveyard at Oakley, near Madisonville, O. In 1859 the colored people of Cincinnati and vicinity erected a monument over the grave. Mr. Gaines was a remarkable man in many respects. He was engaged in supplying provisions for steamboats, and his store on the river front, just east of Broadway, was known from Pittsburg to New Orleans. Most boats had colored stewards in those ante bellum days, and these made their purchases of Mr. Gaines, who dealt in fruits, vegetables, canned goods, etc. His home was at 415 New Street, where a daughter, Arabella E. Gaines, still resides. Mr. Gaines was a Whig and Republican sympathizer, and made speeches for the parties, although he had no right to vote. His son, Maurice Gaines, is now (1902) in London, England, manager of a theatrical troup of which he was himself some years ago the leading song and dance artist.

The inscription on Mr. Gaines' monument is as follows:

"Erected by the colored citizens of Cincinnati, in commemmoration of the invaluable services of John I. Gaines in the cause of education, and his untiring efforts to elevate his race. (*Opposite side*) John Isom Gaines. Born in Cincinnati, Nov. 6, 1821. Died Nov. 27, 1859. Aged 38 years and 21 days."

For a number of years Peter H. Clark (now in Sumner High School, St. Louis, Mo.) labored, after school hours, instructing advanced classes of young people and preparing teachers to maintain the supply demanded by the colored schools within a large radius of Cincinnati. In fact, it is safe to say that from 1859 to 1895 not a teacher in the colored schools but had been trained by him. No one realized, as he did, the pressing need of a high school for colored youth, and in 1865 he began to advocate its establishment. Always timid and apprehensive of its cost, a majority of the Board opposed the idea, but in July, 1866, the measure received a majority of one vote, and in September the school was opened under the title of Gaines' High School, with the following faculty: Peter H. Clark, principal; L. D. Easton; Alice V. Carter; R. Dempker, drawing; J. C. Christine, German; W. Schiele, music. Four years later, June, 1870, the first class of six was graduated. The following studies comprised the curriculum of the school: Algebra, geometry, trigonometry, astronomy, higher arithmetic, bookkeeping, physics, physiology, botany, chemistry, geology, history, literature, rhetoric, mensuration, Latin, German, drawing and music. The sessions were held in the Court (near John) Street building, known at first as the Western District School, and later as the Gaines' and Western School.

For more than twenty years the colored people had an abiding faith in the school and its progress. The number of young persons it was instrumental in establishing in good positions in life was its greatest recommendation to favor in their eyes, and the demand for Gaines' High School students as teachers became so urgent that it was for a time difficult to hold them until graduation, so eager were parents to have them accept places.

In 1874 the colored board was abolished never to be reestablished. Two years later the superintendency of colored schools, held by W. H. Parham, was abolished, and in 1887, when the Arnett law went into force, separate colored schools as a class were abolished, for the law now permitted colored children to attend schools for whites; the inspiring influence of Gaines' High School, Peter H. Clark, was removed. All the colored schools were, under rule 109, placed upon a plane of suffrance that is both humiliating and galling, alike to teachers and pupils. The result need hardly be told. Gaines' High School enrollment fell, in three years, from one hundred and thirty to a beggarly five pupils, and of course was abolished. With the exception of Douglass School and a one-roomed colony, all the others have been closed, and it is thought the time is near when there will be no separate schools for the colored children.*

In 1866 Wm. H. Parham was elected superintendent of colored schools, which position he filled until 1876 when the office was abolished as related above, all colored schools passing by law under the care of superintendent, John B. Peaslee. Mr. Parham was then made principal of all the colored district schools, and in 1887 he succeeded Peter H. Clark as principal of Gaines' High School, and continued there until 1890, when he resigned and entered upon the practice of law. Mr. Parham began teaching in this city in 1860. In 1863 he became principal of the Eastern District, succeeding John G. Mitchell, who resigned to become president of Wilberforce University, Xenia, Ohio. Mr. Parham was the first colored graduate of the Cincinnati Law School (1874). He was also the first colored man to become a notary in Ohio, and he was the first colored man to be nominated for the Ohio Legislature, etc. Noted men members of the colored board were: Peter F. Fossett, who had been a slave of Thomas Jefferson; Wallace Sheldon, "father of the colored Baptists of Ohio"; Col. Robert Harlan, race horse man, politician, and special agent of the Treasury under Gen. Grant; Hartwell Parham, tobacco man, father of W. H. Parham; Marshall Jones, who presented a sword and flag to Col. Wm. M. Dickson of the "Black Brigade;" Joseph C. Corbin, state school commissioner of Arkansas during reconstruction days; Robert Gordon, the coal man, the wealthiest colored man ever in Cincinnati, and father-in-law of George H. Jackson, the attorney."

1925

Principal and Teachers of Newport School

Miss Nora Ward, Principal
Mrs. Ida Lizzie Cox
Miss Luvenia Ellis
Miss Eva McComico

Principal and Teachers in Wyoming School

Mr. Edw. Minnis, Principal
Miss Julia Derrickson
Miss Annestine Guthrie
Miss Henrietta Jackson
Mrs. Ella Yates

Principal and Teachers in Lockland School

Mr. Essie Roan, Principal
Miss Carrie Beard
Miss Zenobia Jones
Miss Nellie Clarke
Miss Murphy
Miss Laura Howell
Miss Jennie Marie Griggsby

Principal and Teachers in College Hill School

Mr. W. H. Robinson, Principal
Miss Addie Bell Foster
Miss Magnolia Hummons
Miss Mary E. Whittaker
Miss Sarah Louise McGee
Mrs. Anna Hammond-Robinson

Teachers in McCall Industrial School

W. J. Decatur, Superintendent
John R. Blackburn
Rose B. Williams
Lucile P. Watts
Cora M. Haller
Ruby K. Malone
J. L. Simpson
I. P. Hobson
W. N. Lowe
John Poole

Teachers—Douglass School

Francis M. Russell, Principal
Ralph Belsinger
Beatrice Conrade
Annie E. Sanford
Margaret Bowen
Clara W. Taylor
Mary W. Rasor
Anna D. Johnson
Ida Rhodes
Sallie P. Frazier
Mrs. Cleopatra Hall Perry
Amelia C. Taylor
Sarah H. White
Willa L. Harrison
Ruth B. Johnson
Hettie G. Taylor

S. Roberts
Mayme D. Brown
Sadie B. Hinson
H. C. Walker
Myrtle Richardson
Blanche Belsinger
Sadie Samuels
Zenobia Russell
Mabel M. Blackburn
Carrie M. Smith
Jas. W. Thorpe
Marie A. Thomas
Oscar B. Brown
Rosa L. Brown
Shirley Harris
Clifford H. Gross

Teachers of Harriet Beecher Stowe School

Jennie Porter, Principal
Wm. M. Caliman
Alice Alexander
Hattie V. Feger
Kathleen S. Cannady
Margaret Clenna
Lillian Drayton
Francis Lesley
Alice Leland
Mary K. Holloway
Jessie Harris
Nancy Hawkins
Florence C. Kirtley
Ina H. Robinson
Edith Howard
Mabel Smith
Ethel Kerr
Lydia Lewis
Beatrice Morton
Ruth Alston
Maud Ragan
Katherine L. Crosby
Louise Minnes
Hazel Jones
Susie Fullman
Olive Ryder
Anna Brummitt

Henrietta Ingram
Madeline Worthington
Mattie D. Jackson
Marion Ritchie
Ethel Calimese
Lela Jackson
Zenobia C. Martin
Mayme Shaw Ford
Grace S. Slade
Lorene Miller
Mary L. Austin
Roberta Walker
Mary Roan Ross
Sanfred R. Showes
James H. Johnson
James H. Crosby
George Hayes
Mary Lee Tate
Helen Greer
Harry Martin
Jennie Austin
Oscar M. Brown
Virginia Jones
Mary E. Ross
Alice G. Showes
Marcella Farlice
Beatrice Hill

Bertram Ferguson
Bessie Smith
Anna B. Roberts
Amelia Johnson
Grace Hammond
Silas Rhodes
Katherine Wrenn
Emma Carter
Lucy Mitchell
Rose Strang
Ella Hicks
Constance Stone
Lydia Crawford
Margaret Speaks
Breta Walker
Jeanet Whittaker
Ethel Burnet
Rosetta Nolan
Castella Taylor
Caroline Welsch
Allie Collman
Oliver Crump
Richard Fox
Marcus Ramble
Arnette Radell
Louise Mason
Helen Brauchcomb

JACKSON COLONY (part of Stowe School).—*School edifice, Fifth Street, west of Mound Street.*—Built 1881-1882; cost $64,178. Lot 105 x 240 feet; cost $39,618. Building has 12 rooms, kindergarten and industrial arts rooms, penny lunch. Seats 600 pupils. Reached by East End or Sixth Street Cars. Telephone, West 305.

Teachers

Laura T. Knight, Assistant Principal in charge
Annie M. Houston
Evermont Robinson
Mary Bell Wright
Albert S. Brown
George Phillips
Gladys Warrington
Virginia Doll
Essie Lowe
Goldie D. Sweeney
Neola Robinson
Marguerite Isby

Viola G. Lockley
Althea Chapman
Angie Smith
Zelma Taylor
Reseda Berry
Ella Campbell
Hardin Spotts
Lucille Ferguson
Virginia Jones
Marie Thomas
M. Scoval Richardson
Faustina Bush

Lincoln-Grant School
Covington, Kentucky

One central plant. The Lincoln-Grant Public School located on Seventh near Scott. Two annexes with part grammar grades, Sixth Street annex and Scott Street annex. Professor R. L. Yancy, Principal. Faculty of twenty-one teachers.

Mary E. Allen
Alberta E. Booker
Vinia Claybourne
Minnie M. Corbin
Leconia Crosby
Nathan Fleming
Blanche Glenn
Elizabeth Gooch
Mrs. E. W. Henderson
Mrs. J. S. Jackson

Clara McGhee
Mrs. Lulu McLean
H. R. Merry
C. A. Rice
Eunice Simpson
Lulu Smith
Mrs. A. M. Snowden
Catherine Williams
Mrs. E. H. Wright
Jessie Johnson

The Kindergarten

The first real colored kindergarten in this city was located in the Dabney Building many years ago. It was the creation of Miss Annie Laws, who then, as now, was one of the most cultured and prominent white women of this city and state. She is a member of an old and aristocratic family, holds high rank in several national organizations, has been president of the Cincinnati Womans' Club, and was ever active in the realms of education and philanthropy. She is deeply interested in the mental development of children, and nobly bore all expenses for rent, teaching and janitorial service for the colored kindergarten. In late years Miss Laws has ably served this community as a member of the school board.

Section VI
Sketches, Pictures, Churches, Streets, Etc. Pioneers, Pathfinders and Items

---

A Political Sketch

Sentiment against Negroes was intensified when they became enfranchised. Their enemies loudly proclaimed that they would not be allowed to vote in this city. In those days the colored people who had suffered hardships, had fought their way to the front, were determined to have every right possible for manhood to obtain. Prepared to vote or die, they went to the polls. No weapons were visible, but many a gun, and those silent auxiliaries, knife, dirk, razor, reposed in pockets, easy of access. Their courage daunted the enemy. They voted. As years rolled on, the colored population was augmented both by births and immigration. Decimation by riots had become obsolete. Soon factions were formed in the Republican party and then the Negro came into his own. There were not many colored Democrats. Jesse Fosset, Sam Lewis, and others came into existence, when the Democrats got in control, for that party has always protected its adherents. Those were desperate days and murder was a recreation rather than an innovation. Little prejudice then prevailed in saloons, restaurants or places of amusement, for the city had a number of fighting Negroes who enjoyed the protection of various political cliques. Bad men were always useful at the polls. When backed by the whites, the Negro would fight for his rights, fight because of slights, fight with or without excuse, for he loves battle and if fortified by support of those in power, no man has more courage in gratification of sanguinary inclinations. Those were the golden days of Cincinnati civic and social equality. Colored men were on many committees, were well mixed in all political deals, were called on for counsel and consultation, but either through

Republican Union Trip to "Dahomey Park," Dayton, Ohio

educational inefficiency or because they were owned by the Republican party, very few positions were given them. Such conditions engendered dissatisfaction. Wise Negroes knew the cause. In that division was Peter H. Clark, Cincinnati's greatest colored product from the standpoints of intellectuality, courage and racial loyalty. In his veins coursed no bootlicking blood. At a small gathering of the leading colored men, the gravity of the situation was thoroughly discussed. All readily agreed that the division of the Negro vote between the Republican and Democratic parties would be of immense benefit, since each party would strive for its possession. The disease having been correctly diagnosed the next question arose as to who was willing to go into the Democratic party. The colored leaders hesitated. Moral courage of the strongest kind was needed, for the great mass of Negroes regarded white Democrats as the Devil's chosen children, and a Negro Democrat was a creature of such depravity that hell was far too good for him. Finally, Peter H. Clark jumped up and said, "Well, if no one else will bell the cat, I'll do it." Applauded and congratulated by those present, he entered the Democratic party, eloquently told the colored people what advantage would accrue from a division of the vote. There are none so blind as those who will not see. The colored voters stuck to the "Grand Old Party" and the colored conference leaders combined and drove Clark out of town. To St. Louis he went, "unwept, unhonored and unsung." "He was the noblest Roman of them all," the grandest school teacher Cincinnati ever produced, a statesman who, Rienzi-like, was martyred by those for whom he fought. He made a great name in the schools of St. Louis. This summer, when near the century mark, he died. Unsuccessful effort was made by some of our citizens to have his remains brought here for interment. Dead, he was no longer dangerous, therefore more desirable. Years rolled on. The "Moerlein faction" controlled the town. A young white man, George B. Cox, was rising. Ward work, the saloon and all influences of the lower world seemed embodied in his destiny. Greater than he by far, at that time, was "Bill" Copeland, a colored man who had a big saloon and a tremendous following at the polls. "Bill" and "George" became great friends. Cox, being white, continued to rise. "Cope," being colored, could climb only to certain heights. He reached those heights. On one occasion, a man desperately angry, pulled a revolver, jammed it up against the stomach of Cox, which was not so prominent then as in later years. His threat to kill died "a borning" as he felt the cold touch of Bill Copeland's blue steel 44 calibre revolver stuck against his ear, and heard Bill's stern command, "drop that gun." Never again was Cox so near death, until he died several years ago. Copeland held every position possible at that period for a colored man to hold in this "color bound" community.

George B. Cox finally became "Boss." A triumvirate was formed, for soon there became associated with him August ("Garry") Hermann, a brainy young German, very popular over the Rhine, and Rud K. Hynicka, of Pennsylvania Dutch stock. The latter was brilliant, intellectually, a master of political finesse and upon him the mantle of Cox finally fell. The Blaine Club was founded. From little acorns mighty oaks arise. One night in a saloon on Walnut Street, "Bill" Copeland and three white friends were talking. They decided to form a club. Each went out and returned with a list of members, and so, from that beginning, came the Blaine Club. When Blaine spoke here during the campaign, he was escorted out on the platform; George B. Cox held one of his arms and "Bill" Copeland, a member of the reception committee, held the other. Quite a number of colored men belonged to the Blaine Club in those days, but not one in these. Some of them were not discreet at the social entertainments given when ladies were present, and so made themselves disagreeable, if not obnoxious. White men fail to fraternize freely with colored men when white women are near. The climax came with a poker game. Gambling was prohibited in the club. One Sunday afternoon, several of the whites and one colored man, who is still living, still working daily for the city, started a poker game. It began "for fun;" it ended for money. Stakes ranged upward. The Negro was winning right along. A big "jack pot." As the "gentleman of color" laid down the winning hand and reached for the money, a man nearby yelled: "The nigger's been robbing you all!" Pandemonium reigned. The dark gentleman jumped up, grabbed the money, transferred it to his pockets, backed against the wall, and prepared for emergencies. The whites could not afford to fight because of their reputations, and so two hundred dollars departed when our "colored citizen" folded his tent and quietly walked away. From that moment Negro membership in the Blaine Club was doomed. No new ones were taken, the dues of the old ones were not collected, and so automatically their existence in one of the greatest and richest political clubs in the United States went the way of all flesh. Colored men were rapidly becoming a factor in local political life. Rev. George Williams went to the legislature after a very bitter fight. He had been pastor of the Union Baptist church. He was followed by Colonel Harlan, one of the greatest colored men of ante-bellum days, and William (Bill) Copeland, the old ally of the "Big Fellow," as George B. Cox was now called. Henry Hagerman was appointed a policeman by the Democrats. George Taylor was made Deputy Sheriff and Herbert Clark, son of Peter H. Clark, followed him. Parham was elected to the legislature but would not serve.

Fusion movements and opposition to the "Cox Gang" gave birth to bitterest partisanship.

In March, 1894, W. P. Dabney arrived. At the end of the first year he became a citizen, the second year a politician, the third year assistant license clerk in the auditor's office. In those days these men were in the vanguard of the Cox colored cohorts. Ford Stith, called by his enemies the Tuscaloosa Bull because he came from Tuscaloosa, Alabama, was a member of the campaign committee and ostensibly the King of Walnut Hills, but behind him stood Professor Andrew (Andy) DeHart, a Warwick, who had strong mentality and was well versed in every phase of political chicanery. On Walnut Hills also were Attorney Wm. H. Parham, deep thinker, a man of strategy, Peter Whitlow, Seymour Townsend, Jos. L. Jones, Henry Higgins and quite a number of lesser lights. "Dave" Irwin was Lord of Cumminsville. Down town there were "Bill" Copeland, Professor Chas. Bell and last, but not least, George W. Hayes, who was then, as now, a tower of strength with "the Lord's anointed." In church circles he reigned supreme, and was so influential with the whites that Professor DeHart, who was already a teacher and politician, found himself "called" and became a preacher. Hayes was still ahead, being court crier, politician, ex-Sunday school teacher, and a Sunday school superintendent, even at that time, of nearly twenty-five years' standing. Other strong political leaders were Attorney George H. Jackson, Bob Harlan, Sam Hill, Charlie Henson, Luke Edinburg, and the Democrats, Sam Lewis and Jesse Fossett.

The year of 1896 saw the second Fusion movement, a coalition between the Democrats and Independent Republicans. In the first one the Republican machine triumphed. All of the colored leaders named above lined up as usual with the Republican "Gang." The Ruffin Club was the great colored Republican organization. A year prior to this time, on a Sunday afternoon, seated at a table in the "Old Dumas House" bar, were "Bill" Fossett, A. Lee Beaty, "Bill" Irwin and W. Phil. Dabney. Then prohibition was not here, but loads of good beer. The plan was formed to capture the Douglass Club, a west end political organization. The next night the deed was done. It was moved to the "Old Dumas House." When the Fusion campaign opened, Beatty was over in the Republican fold, Bill Fosset was in California, Dabney had become the president, written a ritual for the club, making it The Douglass League, a secret organization. It soon sailed under the Fusion flag. The League advocated a strong doctrine, showed how the Negroes had been going backwards politically because of slavery to the Republican party; counselled independence and demanded equal rights. A terrible storm raged in consequence. The old-timers fought against such damnable principles with a fury, unbelievable in these days. As a result, other colored politicians were born. Charlie Horner, Richard (Dick) Moore, "Senator Page"; Jerry Guthrie, Ed Gaither, and from the hill came Leslie Tull, a fiery, eloquent star of the first magnitude and a graduate of Berea. The above named were all bold pirates seeking to scuttle the ship of Republicanism. The Republican forces also had recruits, Dr. Frank Johnson, Gene Matthews, Eugene Leavelle, young Geo. Hays, John Fox. Wm. L. Anderson, the well-known printer and newspaper man, who had been busy in the former campaign, took no active part in this one. Lack of space forbids a recapitulation of this great struggle. There were many big meetings, the largest among the Fusionists being on Walnut Hills, gotten up by Leslie Tull, who was the principal speaker. The Douglass League attended and its president presided. McAllister Street lived up to the traditions of early days. It became the storm center.

The Ruffin Club was a hot-bed of Republicanism. "Jim" Rawlins argued day and night. Shedd Saunders and Judge Knott only listened. The Fusionists won. A new record was made politically. Auditor H. P. Boyden appointed three colored men in his office, among them R. D. G. Troy, who made a wonderful reputation as bookkeeper. "Ed" Eshelby, who was forging to the front as boss of the Fusionists, was brilliant, brainy, a Napoleon in ambition. He wanted results and stopped neither to count cost nor color when he had an object in view. This characteristic was clearly shown when he offered to make Dabney captain of a ward. Unfortunately friction arose, factions developed. Theodore Horstman, a great lawyer and a loyal citizen, opposed Eshelby, and as two strong leaders became antagonistic, ruin resulted.

The Negroes were loud in demand for more place, more power. Tom Hill and Bill Erwin were placed in the waterworks, Dabney promoted to the treasury. Colored men continued to kick until the idea of a Negro party was evolved. Its convention was held here in Lime Hall. The big fish kept out of the pond but the little ones were largely in evidence. Samuel J. Lewis was nominated for governor. The voters had confidence in neither prospects nor promoters. They declined to give it serious consideration. As a consequence, Sam. J. Lewis only received about fifty-five votes in Hamilton County, and a total of 555 in the state. But he earned the title of Governor, and is still often called "Guv." The Fusion party split to pieces. Julius Fleischmann ran for mayor. Norman J. Keenan, president of the gas company, a man thoroughly conversant with all of the technicalities of vote production, was his personal campaign manager. Fleischman won. The Republicans were now in power. His second victory greatly enhanced that power. Dr. Frank Johnson succeeded Dabney as assistant paymaster. Sam Lewis became a Republican and assessment clerk in the auditor's office. The courthouse contingent, Bill Copeland, Sam Hill, Charlie Bell, remained unchanged.

The Negroes, during the campaigns, combined a number of small clubs into a gigantic combination known as the Hamilton

County League of Colored Clubs. What a pity it did not become independent. What a misfortune that it soon died. The Democrats finally won a victory under Dempsey, remained in power two years, 1905-1907, after which, with the exception of two years under Hunt, the Republicans have been in power continuously since 1900. In the legislature Williams, Harlan and Copeland were followed by Geo. H. Jackson, Sam B. Hill, Geo. W. Hays, who was elected three times and defeated twice, and A. Lee Beaty, two terms.

The condition of the colored people has not improved politically with the lapse of years. Servile submissiveness is as detrimental to a race as to an individual. The Republican party freed their bodies from the shackles of slavery, but the colored people here have never been able to free their souls from the shackles of party. They alone are responsible for their present unenviable condition. Beaty was the last colored man to get in the legislature from this county. Henry M. Higgins was the last one nominated. He received an overwhelming vote in the party primaries; an overwhelming defeat on election day. A martyr to party treachery! The Republican party policy engendered by the Negro's lack of reason and independence is to use him and abuse him. The total amount of salary drawn by all of the Negro clerks, deputies and messengers, in both city hall and county courthouse, does not exceed $15,000 a year! That amount is just what the city's chief engineer was formerly paid. The salary of the head of the Board of Public Service is more than one half that amount, and the same is true of the salary of the Safety Director! Not a single Negro on any important county campaign committee! Not a single Negro holding a first class city or county position! Dabney was returned to the treasury in 1907 and for years acted as head paymaster of the city, paid out millions yearly, but for himself could only draw the salary of assistant. When he really became head paymaster, because of color, he still received only the salary of assistant paymaster. He resigned for that reason two years ago. Our race lost thereby its highest political position, since Mr. Harry Friason, who followed him, is only an assistant paymaster. Hon. Wm. Copeland was for a long time a member of the State Executive Committee. That is a thing of the past for colored citizens. The men who were put on the campaign com-

West Eighth Street

mittee years ago were really doing messenger duty for their white fellow members.

Beaty and Hays hold government positions, the former Assistant U. S. District Attorney, the latter U. S. Court Crier for fifty-five years. There are over 40,000 colored people here who have had for years votes enough to elect councilmen, or bring defeat or victory to either party in a fairly close election. They had the lever of power but knew not how to use it. Women are now voters, and white women are rapidly forging to the front. They have far outstripped the "colored brother," who in the past had so many glorious opportunities. His chances are exceedingly limited. The future seems filled with gloom. A far stretch now from a Negro helping to form the Blaine Club over forty years ago. A farther stretch from the Negro fighting and bleeding at the polls over fifty years ago. The Negro of 1925 thanks God for the few crumbs that fall from the political feast he has helped in preparing, from the feast his color prevents him from sharing.

Political Clubs

"The Nellie Grant Club"

The first colored political club in this city, strange to say, was named after a woman, Nellie Grant, daughter of President U. S. Grant. The founder was "Joe" Early, one of our first colored politicians who, though eighty years old next June, still works daily. He spent a great deal of money on it. After Early entered the postal service, he got out of politics and the Nellie Grant Republican Club passed into the hands of Ford Stith, by whom it was changed into The Ford Stith Club. In a sadly depleted condition it still exists and is galvanized into some semblance of life, by Henry Higgins, when the necessity for a political demonstration on Walnut Hills arrives.

"The Ruffin Club"

The Ruffin Club, in the West End, lived many years. To it belonged the leading colored men in the city. It had great influence politically, was the rendezvous for all "high livers" in its day.

It was named in honor of Judge Ruffin, the colored judge of Boston, Massachusetts.

Strictly orthodox Republican, its adherence to the tenets of that party were as unalterable as the laws of the Medes and Persians. Socially, however, it was famous throughout the country for the excellence of its buffet service, high class whist games a la mode Hoyle, and its sub rosa seances of limitless draw poker.

The old **R. B. Elliot Club** was great in its day.

The **Maceo Club**, a big organization on Walnut Hills, Independent politically, had a large following.

The **Eighteenth Ward clubs** were composed of voters gathered from various precincts to enthuse citizens, for campaign purposes, by parading. They were generally of mushroom growth, springing into existence at the command of ward captains or precinct men who furnished the refreshments and uniforms. In 1899 a "slush fund" of $1,200 was given the colored leaders to maintain Genessee Hall as a meeting place. The club ran for a month in order to fight the independent spirit generated by the Douglass League. The Republican Union was the last of the big colored clubs. For twelve or fifteen years its headquarters in the Dabney Building were a bee-hive of industry. It did not parade but in every campaign its great meeting was a feature and many mayors, public officials, political orators and preachers held audiences spell-bound by their eloquence. Its monthly smokers kept the members together socially, and the Royal Union, an auxilliary secret organization formed for business purposes, strengthened the bond of fraternity. Picnics were given annually at "The Farm" and Frey's Park. On one such occasion, held on Sunday, Rev. Geo. Wyatt addressed an enormous crowd. The greatest affair, though, was a pilgrimage to Dahomey Park, the amusement resort in Dayton, Ohio, owned by M. C. Moore of that city, one of Ohio's wealthiest colored men.

The **Douglass League** in the East End, on McAllister Street, in its day, set a great pace. The men on parade always wore full dress suits and silk hats. In a famous campaign it turned out one hundred members and their pathway to Music Hall was a triumph of cheers only exceeded by the ovation in that magnificent auditorium. The Douglass marched behind and next to the Duckworth Club, Democracy's greatest organization, just as the Ruffin Club has marched next to the Blaine Club, the Republicans' greatest organization. We know of no other colored clubs enjoying such distinction in late years.

It was named in honor of Frederick Douglass and made some history twenty-five years ago. We briefly reprint a few letters and press notices, though we regret not being able to find press reports concerning our letter to the mayor of this city requesting that he send two colored policemen, among the fifty policemen, going south in response to an invitation from a leading city of that section. The official drilling the police, on hearing our request read, threw down his baton declaring that he would not go if any Negro police went.

Douglass League Letter to McKinley

Dabney Building, 420-22-24 McAllister Street
Cincinnati, Ohio, November 10, 1898.

President McKinley:

Your Excellency—At a called meeting of The Douglass League last night, November 9, 1898, a committee was named to write you relative to the brutal outrages now being perpetrated upon the Negroes by the whites of Wilmington, N. C. A state of anarchy evidently exists, as the governor seems completely powerless and unable, through fear, either to maintain his dignity as executive of the state, or take measures for the protection of his citizens. For several days prior to the election, hundreds of whites—leading citizens of Wilmington—have been parading with their "Red Shirts," making incendiary speeches, firing revolvers, and exhibiting their gatling gun; have been parading with brass bands, announcing to the world their contemplated butchery of American citizens, did those citizens not stay away from the polls. White Democrats and Republicans alike were implicated, and no effort was made by state or United States Government to throttle this vile public conspiracy in its incipiency. Were the colored people of that section possessed of the same facilities as the whites for the acquirement of arms, ammunition, the control of telegraph and railroads, or did they possess even one-half of the advantages, we would not lift our voices for aid, or in protest were they all slain—knowing that they would die manfully fighting, instead of being butchered like cattle. Although we are neither Cuban nor Armenian, we feel that as loyal, law-abiding American citizens we are entitled to some consideration, sympathy, and protection, even though dwelling under our own vine and fig tree in the "land of the free and home of the brave;" even though within touch of an American President and Senate and House of Representatives; even though encircled by the Star Spangled Banner and Constitution of the United States!

President McKinley, we respectfully request you to take some immediate action to relieve these citizens of the United States. Should the doctrine of "States' Rights" militate against the exercise of relief measures on your part, then, since we will not be allowed to raise regiments, or send arms and ammunition to our suffering people, kindly call off your Naval Reserves (see Cincinnati Commercial Tribune, 11st inst.), who have lent their moral support, if nothing more, to this despicable intimidation and brutal massacre—and in their stead station in the vicinity a Negro regiment.

Yours respectfully,

THE DOUGLASS LEAGUE,

W. P. Dabney, President.
A. S. Norris,
Wm. Smith,
Chas. Banks,
Samuel Richards,
Committee.

EXECUTIVE MANSION
Washington

November 15, 1898.

My Dear Sir:

Writing in behalf of the President I beg leave to acknowledge the receipt of your letter of the 10th instant with enclosure, the contents of which have been noted.

Very truly yours,
J. A. PORTER,
Secretary to the President.

"The Douglass League held a special smoker last Monday night. The occasion was most auspicious, it being the first club inspection of the rooms since their renovation. All of the work was done by Douglass League men, under the personal supervision of Architect J. E. Jackson. The bath and upper dining rooms will be completed in the near future. The quarters of this organization are as elegant and comfortably equipped as those of any other colored club in the Union. When all the improvements contemplated by the clubs are completed, the members will give a reception, to which the public will be invited."

—*Times-Star*, 1896.

WHITE MEN

NOT WANTED AS OFFICERS OF COLORED REGIMENT

Douglass League Will Petition Governor Bushnell

"The Douglass League will petition Governor Bushnell to commission only colored officers for the new regiment of colored men formed in Cincinnati.

They have addressed him an open letter, in which it is said that there are plenty of capable men in the race to command the regiment.

A petition is being circulated throughout the state, and several thousand men are expected to sign it.

President W. P. Dabney heads the list of signers. Said he: 'Colored men will go to the front first as targets. We are willing to go, but want justice.'"

—*The Post*, April, 1898.

THE DOUGLASS LEAGUE

ENTERTAINMENT IN CELEBRATION OF ITS THIRD ANNIVERSARY

An Evening Devoted to Enjoyment and Feasting— A Leading Colored Organization

The Douglass League, which boasts, and with good reason, too, of being the leading colored organization in the country, celebrated its third anniversary last night at its clubrooms, in

McAllister Street, with one of the most enjoyable entertainments in its history. Without being undignified, everything was well spiced with fun, the purpose of the affair being to bid "dull care" adieu for a season and let jest and jollity reign.

The program opened with a march, entitled "The Douglass," by the Douglass League Mandolin Orchestra, which, throughout the evening, rendered some pleasing music. After prayer by the Rev. Mr. Baltimore, W. L. Ervin sang and George H. Jackson delivered an address. C. A. Lee outlined the "Progress of the Race," and Prof. Quarles and a quartet, with Charles Trotter at the piano, gave several vocal selections.

President W. P. Dabney then gave an interesting resume of the history of the league that was as graceful in delivery as it was instructive. He said the organization had been foremost in every undertaking for the advancement of the colored man. It enjoys the distinction of never having received a cent from a white man, but relied upon its members for its support. While it is composed of loyal Republicans, it is not a partisan body nor the creature of politicians. In the view of its glorious past he predicted for it a future rich with promise.

A toothsome buffet lunch was then served, and, after cigars had been lit, Frank Hurdle responded to "The Negro Soldier," and the guests were notified that this would be the only serious toast permitted during the evening. Other numbers were: Song, Wm. Beasley; recitation, Alex. Thomas; speech, Gustave Minter; song, Messrs. Banks and Norris; address, Lawson Baker; song, Wm. Jackson; ballet, danced by Prof. Johnston and Josie Jones; song, B. Rankin and "Auld Lang Syne" by a full chorus.

The committee in charge was William Smith, Samuel Richards, Edward Berry, C. H. Woodford, Charles Banks, Wm. Ervin and Dr. E. D. Colley.

—*The Commercial Tribune,* April 8, 1899.

An Open Letter to Governor Asa S. Bushnell of Ohio

Cincinnati, Ohio, April 28, 1898.
Honorable Asa S. Bushnell, Governor of Ohio.

Your Excellency: Relative to the colored regiment now in process of formation in this city, we respectfully petition that the officers commissioned be colored men. We have in this county quite a number of capable young men anxious and ready to battle for the United States. Why not give them opportunities commensurate with their qualifications? Race prejudice stalks boldly abroad in all avenues of religion, industry, art, yes, even in the army! The Negro soldiers can only enlist in colored companies and the first regiment ordered to the front in the present war was colored. It has been graphically pictured, and most frequently reiterated, how useful the Negro soldier will be in the present campaign. If the Negro private is not allowed to enlist, if the Negro officer is not permitted to serve in white regiments, what can be the objection to placing colored men to lead their own flesh and blood to death or glory? We again respectfully call your earnest consideration to this our petition for justice.

    W. P. DABNEY,
      President of The Douglass League.

    W. L. ERVIN,
      President of The Douglass Club.

    A. S. NORRIS,
      President of The Douglass Fraternals.

    J. E. JACKSON,
      President of The Douglass I. A.

    FRANK HURDLE,
      President of The Douglass S. C.

Douglass League Assembly Rooms,
 420 McAllister Street,
  Cincinnati, Ohio.

COLORED CITIZENS

Asked Mayor and Chief of Police for Protection

A delegation of colored citizens called on Colonel Deitsch and Mayor Fleischmann yesterday and asked for protection against persecution by the police. They complained that there is prejudice on the part of the police against colored men. Speeches were made by Rev. Prowd, Mrs. Nesbitt and Prof. Dabney. The mayor and superintendent of police promised to see that colored people are protected against the police.—(*Commercial Tribune*, July, 1901.)

POLITICAL

Letter of notification to Wm. Copeland, signed by Geo. B. Cox, president, and Rud Hynicka, secretary, of the Blaine Club, at the Burnet House.

Cincinnati, Ohio, Sept. 27, 1884.

Mr. Wm. Copeland:

You have been selected by the campaign committee to act as a member of the committee and entertain the Hon. James G. Blaine, Thursday, October 2, 1884.

Geo. B. Cox,
Rud. K. Hynicka.

The sentiment expressed in this letter that we have dug from the grave of long buried years brings fragrance of roses from the garden of a manhood that has long since departed. Our political soil now brings forth only weeds.

THE FLEISCHMANN CLUB

The life of the Fleischmann Club was brief but brilliant, short but sweet. Nobly did Mayor Fleischmann and friends assist in relieving the heavy strain of its financial burdens. The trip to the Roosevelt inauguration in Washington marked the high point of its ascension as well as the beginning of its declension. The great success of the Republican party at this time had drawn to the club hundreds of members, many of whom, tempestuous as well as turbulent, sought the sceptre of rulership. In those days pre-eminence in clubs meant preferment for office. Presidents were ever in the political limelight, exposed on every side to the lightning that strikes, when the position thunders for the man, or the man thunders for the position. Attorney Abraham Lincoln Dalton, then in the hey dey of his glory, was the president when the memorable trip to Washington made the Fleischmann Club an organization of national importance. It was probably one of the biggest legitimate political clubs ever in this city. The Hamilton County League of Clubs, in a parade once when Senator John P. Green (colored) was the orator, threw into line 2200 men. The Republican organization bore the very heavy expenses of the display in an effort to dwarf the growing power of the Douglass League.

RESIGNED

The Paymaster of Cincinnati has resigned. Most people have not realized that this great and semi-southern city has for years had a Negro, W. P. Dabney, as Paymaster. Mr. Dabney has handled millions of dollars without a mistake and has the record of paying five hundred men in 65 minutes without a single error. But Mr. Dabney has resigned and the reason is interesting. He was made License Clerk in 1896 in the Auditor's office; the next year he entered the Treasury and staid three years as Assistant Paymaster. He then went out of office when the Republicans were defeated, but returned in 1907 and has virtually been Paymaster ever since. We say virtually because for years while Mr. Dabney did the work, a white man held the title and received the salary. In January, 1923, however, he was made Paymaster but no change was made in his salary. Twice, white employees in the office who were receiving the higher salary which ought to have gone to Dabney resigned and still Dabney's salary was not increased. At the second happening of this sort Mr. Dabney resigned and he did what we call a very fine piece of work.—From *The Crisis*, November, 1923, W. E. B. Dubois, Editor.

Today Negro political clubs are a thing of the past. The Republican leaders here have discouraged their formation. A club could grow sufficiently powerful to demand and to enforce its demands. In not having the colored clubs the wisdom of white politicians is shown as well as the apathy of colored voters.

"THE OLD DUMAS HOUSE"
Famous "Underground Railroad Station"

No street in this city is of more importance, historically, particularly to colored people, than McAllister Street. It adjoined the northern boundary of Fort Washington, which was built in 1789. Running north and south from Fourth to Fifth, it is one-half block east of Broadway. When that street was in its infancy and called "Eastern Row," McAllister was a part of the city's handsomest e s t a t e, known as Sargent's Square, because of the beautiful gardens and palatial frame residence of Colonel Sargent, secretary of the territory. Changes came.

In the course of years, as "Eastern Row" bloomed and blossomed into Broadway, the short cut road that grew through Sargent's Square became McAllister Street, for the frame house that upon it stood, was leveled to the earth and "not a rose of the wilderness was left on its stalk to show where the garden had been." Soon small frame houses dotted each side of the street, for lumber was plentiful. Later on bricks were born and more substantial structures proudly lifted their heads on Broadway, and finally the grandeur trickled through to McAllister and several buildings of that material arose upon that thoroughfare. Among them, higher than all, were the three houses that consolidated into "The Dumas." Four stories and a half constituted a skyscraper in those days. Negroes gradually became owners of most of that street. As the days lengthened into months and years, "our people," Nimrod-like, became mighty hunters, but money was the game. Their possessions were mainly in that vicinity, and all along east Fifth Street, upper Broadway, Sycamore, Sixth, and Seventh, Negro houses "were as plentiful as autumnal leaves in Vallombrosa." As servants, steamboat, trades, and sporting-men, they found money very abundant. The McAllister Street skyscrapers were converted from lodging houses into a hotel, and in those days, as Levi Coffin's book records, wealthy Southerners, whose descendants now are such sticklers for racial purity, were wont to bring their colored affinities to Cincinnati, and place them in the colored hotel on McAllister Street while they would go to a white hotel.

We know of no colored lodging house and hotel in the United States possessing greater antiquity than "The Old Dumas House!" In 1841 a terrible race riot began there and extended over to Sixth and Broadway. In other disturbances of that nature, for many years, McAllister Street was always more or less involved. The reason can be clearly indicated. It was the fashionable thoroughfare of the "Black 400." The center of class and culture in colored society. Every Negro with the slightest ambition to rank as a "swell" or disciple of "Beau Brummell" made it his business to glide through McAllister Street at least once every day. A failure in this regard, unless sickness was the cause, was sometimes fatal to his aspirations. "The Dumas" had porches on the second and third floors, and large dining and ball-rooms. In the rear was a two-story addition. Gentlemen of sporting proclivities found ample opportunity for indulgence of their inclinations, for the biggest poker and faro games in the West could be found in "The Old Dumas." In those days Negroes made money, and spurred by the example of their former owners or employers, they gambled like gentlemen and the sky was their limit. "The noble game of craps" had not made its appearance. In the fifties, "Sandy Shumate," my great uncle, was the owner. Well fitted was he for the role. A bachelor, handsome, debonair, bon vivant, he stood well with the boys of that period. Old Col. Harlan, reputed half brother of Chief Justice Harlan, Pinchback, who afterward became temporarily governor of Louisiana; Alex Thomas, the city's leading photographer; Duncanson, the great painter; "Col. Bob" Church, who used to come up from Memphis, and others of that class were the boon companions of "Sandy," and gay was the day when they foregathered. In '69, "Sandy" Shumate died. His sister, Mrs. Serena Webb, inherited the estate as John Shumate, the brother, was in New Zealand.

He and Sandy ran away from Virginia together, went to Canada and California before separating. Years passed. McAllister followed the example of other old streets in illustrating the song, "She may have seen better days!" The Star of the West was rising; Western Row had long been Central Avenue. In that direction the whites treked, and of course, Negroes followed suit. "The Dumas House" began its descent to Avernus. Its main revenue was now derived from its saloon and the successive proprietors, Andy Slaughter, Dan Carter and others drew great patronage, for the old charm of the street was still magnetic.

> "You may break, you may shatter,
>   The vase if you will,
> The scent of the roses
>   Will linger there still."

The house continued its downward trend. Property all through the East End depreciated in value. Slump followed slump. "The Old Dumas" became a lodging house. In the Spring of 1894, Mrs. Webb, old and worn, fell sick and soon "God touched her with His finger and she slept." The property, through will, came to my mother, Mrs. Elizabeth Dabney, of Richmond, Virginia, who was a niece of Serena Webb. There were other nieces, namely, the mother of Mrs. Florence Gant of Columbus and the mother of Mrs. Addie Johnson of Baltimore. There were four grand-daughters who received small legacies and an additional sum to quiet the title after a compromise of the law suit they inaugurated. W. P. Dabney was put in charge and the Old Dumas became "The Dabney Building." The property was in bad shape, $6,000 debt, and not worth that much. From a lodging house it now became a tenement, occupying a space 68 by 70 feet, including the yard in the rear. The lower floor at first remained, as it had been, a saloon, then became successively a club-room, headquarters of The Bohemian Club, the Douglass League, a dancing school, a dancing hall, the Pilgrim Baptist Church, a hand laundry, and clothes pressing emporium. The Pilgrim Baptist church stayed until it accumulated the thousands necessary for its new church. The rear yard was converted into a gymnasium, the first public colored establishment of the kind in the city. A big celebration marked its opening, nothing marked its closing except the check paying out the last of one thousand dollars spent in my experience or experiment of race betterment.

The passing of the gymnasium was followed by the coming of a hall for general and political purposes. Numberless were the political meetings held there under the auspices of the Republican Union and great were the feasts in those days when water was little used in Cincinnati, except for bathing purposes. For years no man became mayor of this city who had not been a guest of the club and thundered therein denunciation of the democracy. Among the eloquent orators who spoke there prior to the present administration, and among the greatest mayors we ever had, were Mayors Schwab, Puchta and Galvin. With them, and before them, figured Congressman Longworth, who was ever an idol of "our gang."

The gym became a garage. The top floor of the building was made into a hall for the True Reformers. It seated, comfortably, three hundred people. The True Reformers moved because their numbers increased beyond its capacity. (In this hall Lieutenant Jos. Moore, on his return from the Philippines, was guest at a banquet of our club that lasted from 8:00 P. M. to 7:00 A. M.)

The hall finally became flats. For the last twenty years the office of "The Union" occupied a part of the second floor next to the rooms in which my family dwelt. Mrs. Elizabeth Dabney died many years ago, and to W. P. Dabney came that building as an inheritance. He extended the property from the alley near Fourth on McAllister, 268 feet to Fifth and around the corner 39½ feet on Fifth. It has all been disposed of to The Western and Southern Life Insurance Company, which will take full possession in two years. 'Tis a long, long way from Sargent's Square that flourished in the ancient days of "ye olde towne" to the McAllister Street of today. The small houses "have gone where the woodbine twineth." From the western corner of Fourth, where stood the house in which Charles Dickens dwelt temporarily, The Western and Southern, Cincinnati's greatest life insurance company, stands, a monument of undying architectural beauty and grandeur. That corporation now owns nearly all of McAllister Street. On the east side, the Dabney property from Fifth Street has given way to a vast structure being erected for the "Sacred Heart Home," a Catholic edifice that will face its brother building known as the "Fenwick Club." Brick by brick the "Old Dumas House" is coming down to mother earth. When these lines are cold in type, there will be naught left but pictures framed on memory's wall and the sweet fragrance enshrined in the hearts of those who, in that famous place, danced, sang, or loved, "in days long years ago."

THE TERPSICHOREAN ART

Negroes are "natural born dancers." Some critic has said that God placed so much ability in their feet that there is not much energy left for cerebral activity. Be that as it may, the colored citizen has always excelled in almost every phase of dancing, except the ballet. In the early days of society here, the waltz and other round dances were greatly in vogue. We brought the two-step here from Newport, R. I., when we came in the spring of '94. It was new then. From that year, until about ten years ago, the standard of terpsichorean development was very high. The colored people could get any of the picnic grounds and almost any of the big dance halls for special balls. The smaller affairs were then at Genessee Hall, the K. of P. headquarters. The public dances generally given by various fraternities drew vast crowds and were most enjoyable. Those were the good old "wet days." The devotees of

Bacchus and Gambrinus were everywhere in evidence and yet, seemingly strange to say, good order and the utmost decorum prevailed among "those tripping the light fantastic toe." The reason can be easily given. There were excellent dancing schools. The one in "The Dabney Building," on McAllister Street, formerly "The Old Dumas House," was very popular, and soon became well patronized by people of class. Prof. William Johnson, long since gone to God, was, we may say, the father of local social dancing. The rules of strictest ball-room etiquette prevailed when and where he was in control. He taught also many pupils among the whites. He had a fine orchestra which was at times alluded to by the irreverent public as "Old Bill Johnson's Band." Quite a number of good dancing teachers trailed along in those days. Prof. Wm. (Bill) Johnson, George Rankins, George Matthews, Capt. Sneed, Allie Baxter, and a student of that coterie of artists, Will Williams, now known as Professor Williams, who is still trying to get some of the decency of the old into the mazes of some of the present modern movements, politely called "The New Dances." To men of the world, however, there is nothing new about the "One-Step," except it is now danced in reputable places instead of in the sporting resorts of twenty-five or thirty years ago. In those places, among the Demi Monde, the one-step was a classic, free from the vulgarity of "cheek to cheek" and close embrace, so commonly seen today even among our young picnic lads and lassies. There may be, to us, some consolation in the fact that our present day dancing is an imitation of that in vogue among fashionable whites and that their performance is far more risque and open to criticism than that in conservative colored society.

ATHLETICS

Apart from playing "Cat," the first form of baseball, and later real baseball, there was little time for our young people here to learn anything except fighting and dodging mobs. Since '84 we have had quite a number of good pugilists. Harry Woodson went East and attained fame as the "Black Diamond." A number of smaller constellations made their appearance, but "Kid" Ashe arose, and their brightness was dimmed. The "Kid" as a kid, wandered here from Kentucky, knew naught of parents, home or anybody. Short, fat, good-natured, black, he made friends, became a newsboy. A good seller, a good scrapper, strong as a young steer, he entered the circle of royalty as a matter of course, and soon became the reigning King of Newsboys. There were few colored, but hundreds of whites. They idolized the "Kid," and when he appeared, he was ever surrounded by a score or more of white boys. The sight was singular to say the least. He was never a fancy boxer, but a terrific fighter, and he fought anybody in ring or street who got before him. His motto was, "The bigger they are the harder they fall." He made a splendid record here, fought Joe Gans fifteen rounds, and Tom O'Rourke took him to New York, put him against a very tough scrapper in Madison Square Garden. "Kid" put his opponent to sleep in short order, received nearly $1,000, more money than he had had or seen, took the train back to Cincinnati to see his friends and a few children of which he was father. He did not return to New York. This city had too much charm. He was never knocked out and was ever a fair and square fighter. He has become a Catholic and prominent member of "The Holy Name Society." Ben Knox, a fine boxer, Jesse Shipp, Billy Teller, Wiley Evans, Jimmy Brackett, good fighters, as were Lewis Clark, a splendid trainer, "Goo-Goo Eyes" Fields, and other old-timers. George Young was a well-known promoter, and backed Larry Temple for a fight out at the Abbey against Pittsburg's champion scrapper. Across the river in Covington we have a young fighter named Moore, who shows great promise.

We can say for the prize-fight places of Cincinnati what we can't say for the churches; they never draw the color line. A colored man can buy a seat anywhere. Years ago we had a gymnasium on McAllister Street. Over one thousand dollars was lost in the effort to popularize same. A. J. Brown and Frank Hurdle were partners with me, but I bought them out and stood the loss. It was splendidly equipped for those days; had shower baths and other essentials. We talked, preached and published the advantages of such training for the coming generation. The dues were only twenty-five cents a month, but the membership dwindled from one hundred and twenty-five to twenty-five. Many of the great pugilists visiting here trained there. We have had some good baseball teams. In amateur ranks the Excelsiors, in the beginning, made a marvelous record by beating nearly every white team in this vicinity. Charlie Grant was a great ball player and for a long time was a member of an eastern team under McGraw. He was supposed to be an Indian. After making an enviable record it was discovered that in his veins flowed the blood of the noble black man instead of "the noble red man." Charlie's career ended. In late years high school athletics came to the front. From those realms, "armed and eager for the fray," came De Hart Hubbard, a dark but comely product of Walnut Hills. His rise was phenomenal. Today he stands, the world's wonder, in athletic achievements. He is a record-breaking sprinter and "all 'round" athlete.

THE WORLD'S CHAMPION! DE HART HUBBARD

Hubbard is one of the greatest broad jumpers ever developed in athletics. He was born in this city in 1903 and he was named after A. J. De Hart, the first principal of the Douglass School. Hubbard attended Douglass School, where he first showed ability in athletics.

Completing the eight years' work in the elementary schools, he entered high school, where he first began to attract attention as a promising track star. He attended Walnut Hills "Hi," from which he was graduated in 1921, with the highest scholastic record of any boy in his class. In his senior year he was honored by being elected captain of the Walnut Hills track team.

Hubbard was able to attend college when he won an Enquirer Scholarship. He decided on the University of Michigan and continued his hard work at Michigan, ranking high in his studies. Hubbard reached his greatest heights as a jumper in 1924 when he won a place on the American Olympic team. He won first place in this event and brought back to America the coveted world's championship in this event.

In June of this year Hubbard, wearing the colors of Michigan, established the world's broad-jumping record, making 25 feet $10\frac{7}{8}$ inches in his last mighty leap.

Hubbard is married and has one child. Two years ago he married Marion Monroe, of Walnut Hills.

—*The Enquirer*, December 1, 1925.

DeHart Hubbard

FIRST GYMNASIUM

Reprint from circular announcing the opening of the first public gymnasium for colored people of this city.

GRAND OPENING RECEPTION
for
LADIES AND GENTLEMEN

Afternoon and Evening, Monday, October 24, 1904

THE NATIONAL GYMNASIUM
420 McAllister Street

Exercises on Dumbbells, Horizontal Bar, Punching Bag and Trapeze
The Art of Self-Defense Illustrated
Inspection of Rain and Needle Shower Baths and Hot Room

MUSIC	ADDRESSES
Rev. Ross	Dr. Frank Johnson
Rev. Prowd	Dr. Louis Cornish
Rev. Bundy	Dr. Wm. A. B. Kerr
	Hon. Geo. W. Hays

Refreshments and Admission, only 25 Cents

REPORT OF THE OPENING

Only a few colored people came. Conspicuous among the whites was Attorney "Tom" Darby, now Judge Thos. H. Darby, famous jurist. Hon. Geo. W. Hays very kindly saw and sold a great many tickets to Senator Foraker, Congressman Longworth, Geo. B. Cox, August Herrman, Rud. K. Hynicka and others high in the political world. Mr. Mellish, very prominent in business and Masonic circles, and other white business men, contributed liberally for tickets on the opening night. One of the gentlemen said, as he bought five dollars' worth of tickets, "I hope this undertaking will succeed. It is greatly needed. I have my doubts, for the colored people are always selling tickets and starting something but afterwards they forget to support it themselves." I regret to say this enterprise followed in the footsteps of others. The opening sale of tickets amounted to $125.00, only twenty-five of which came from colored people. We had shower baths, tub baths, hot and cold water, gymnastic apparatus. Quite a number of young men started but soon stopped, though the dues were, just think of it, *only twenty-five cents a month*. Many pugilists trained and our first colored games of basket ball took place there. When the doors were finally closed Dabney was wiser and $1,000 dollars loser.

COLORED POLICEMEN

Until 1884 there were no colored policemen in this city. The democrats came in power and to spite the Republicans, put a colored man, Henry Hagerman, on the police force, and to spite Murat Halstead, editor of the Commercial Gazette, stationed him on the street in front of his office. Others were appointed. About 1899 the question of the advisability of having a Negro detective arose. "Bill" Copeland, then deputy sheriff, was offered the place. He declined, but named James Allen, who became a policeman in '86. After a desperate fight he had him appointed. A few years later, another colored detective was named, and since then there have always been two, as detectives are generally paired off, and were there only one colored, his partner would have to be white. Several Negroes were turnkeys in the early years. The standard efficiency of colored officers has always been high. With few exceptions they have been faithful, dutiful, intelligent, and courageous, but their color has ever kept them from rising, promotion never came. In other cities there are many colored men holding positions above that of sergeant, but this city has

Hagerman

not as yet been just enough to accord the Negro opportunity of being anything above the grade of patrolman. Only a few colored men are appointed on the police force. For more than ten years none were put on until this summer, when three were appointed as a political asset to the Republican organization, which now fighting for life, threw "a Sop to Cerberus," in the shape of a bribe for the Negro vote. From 1890, for about twenty years, colored policemen "ran beats" all around the town, but in late years they have generally been kept over on Walnut Hills in or near the Negro district. When the big graft exposure came this year, which shook the police department from center to circumference, a number of police were separated from their positions because of an involuntary trip to, and sojourn in, the United States penitentiary at Atlanta. There were no colored officers involved. The manner of keeping colored men off the police force has been very simple. The applicant had to pass two examinations, one mental, the other physical. He had no chance to safely journey between Scylla and Charybdis for, regardless of his brightness or fitness, if he passed the mental examination, he failed to pass the physical, and vice versa. Judging by the rapid increase of race prejudice, the chances for improvement of these conditions, in the near future, are exceedingly remote.

Names of All the Colored Policemen

Henry Hagerman, —— Morris, —— Johnson, Jas. A. Allen, Harry Jones, John Samples, Harry Spurlock, Richard Reed, *Lafayette (Bud) Coffey, John Miller, *John Thomas (Detective), John Hoskins, Craig Scott, *Frank A. B. Hall (Detective), Howard Greer, *Chas. H. Payne, *Chas. P. Miles, Roscoe Lewis, Luther Brooks, Mark Carroll.

Patrol Drivers

John White, Leff Smith.

Turnkeys and Station-house Keepers

James Clark, Henry Underwood, —— Baptiste, E. C. Berry.

Gymnasium and Station-house Keeper

Scott Calimeise.

Of the above, those with a star are still in active service. The others are dead or retired.

The following sub-patrolmen were appointed this summer, largely because of the incarceration of many white policemen, convicted of bribery and grafting, vice conditions in the black belt and to furnish campaign material for the Republican party in its contest against advocates of the new charter: Samuel W. Anderson, John E. Toney, Howard Hill, Wm. F. Fox, and Robt. A. Wilson.

Eight policemen and two detectives, colored. The regular police force of the city normally amounts to 752 men.

A summary of racial and inter-racial conditions existing in Cincinnati, November, 1925. The viewpoints of both races are in some cases given, the solution in some cases suggested.

PROFESSIONAL CITIZENS

Our professional men and women are doing well, more doctors, lawyers and teachers than ever before in the history of the city. They are rising rapidly. We have splendid teachers. They make salaries these days that would turn the old-time pedagogues green with envy. Our doctors and dentists dwell on an Olympus of opulence. The colored professions do not enjoy so much white patronage as in earlier days. The enhancement of racial prejudice naturally accentuates the color line. We belong to an easy-going race. Thousands of years ago the "Good Book" spoke concerning "those careless Ethiopians." Now that the color question reigns supreme, a vast amount of colored patronage comes because of that. In a few years the problem will have adjusted itself. Then 'twill be a case of survival of the fittest. Those who study and keep abreast of the times will forge forward regardless of color; those who do not will become submerged in the flotsam and jetsam of mediocrity.

BUSINESS

As our statistics show, we have hundreds of business houses. A multiplicity of certain kinds, a scarcity of others. Naturally, those necessitating small capital and of a type largely in demand are the most numerous. Apart from barber shops, beauty parlors, restaurants, lodging houses, and undertaking establishments, white merchants reign supreme in all realms of commercialism. A colored company owns a chain of drug stores. There are no big colored groceries or general stores. Why? Colored business men say that Negroes do not like to patronize each other; that they feel honored in dealing with white men and that in trade they will pay whites more promptly and submit to injustice that they would not tolerate from colored dealers, and that lack of patronage is the cause of failure of so many of their enterprises. Colored patrons, however, claim that, as a rule, Negro dealers charge higher prices, give less service and seem to feel that colored people should deal with them just because they are colored, regardless of the qualifications. That white dealers show by their politeness and service that they want and appreciate their trade. From the white dealers' viewpoint, colored patronage comes not because they are white, but because they understand better how to do business, know better the psychology of trade, buy in such quantities as will enable them, if necessary, to undersell competitors, advertise thoroughly, and last, but not least, show a feeling of appreciation by their courtesy to customers. There is truth on every side. In early days, though there were fewer, yet results show that our business men were better. We have, despite present prosperity and education, produced no such giants as Gordon, Wilcox, Gaines and others we could name. They all built up big business despite white competition. Now colored business men know little of advertising. Their employees are rarely as polite as they should be. Instead of living within their means and laying up a fund for times of depression or to take advantage of buying bargain goods in big quantities, the proprietors generally spend as they go, and seemingly expect customers because of their color rather than through merit of wares or efficiency of service. In the early days our merchantmen catered to everybody and they got the trade. Money speaks all languages. A Jew will buy from a Negro, Dutchman,

West Ninth Street

German, or any person from whom he can get the best bargain. Jews are the finest salesmen in the world; they study how to win purchasers and then go forth to get them. We need make no business segregation in our search for an easy road to trade. The white man will buy from anybody. Our merchants here must, in order to succeed, pull down the signal of distress, "Trade with me because I am colored," and erect the flag of victory, "Trade with me because I am best."

RESIDENTIAL SEGREGATION

In seventeen prominent cities of this country litigation is pending as a result of segregation in residential districts. In nearly every big city movements are on foot to prevent the purchase of property in certain sections by Negroes. Why? The whites claim that the property of a locality depreciates in value when Negroes become residents. That cause for such depreciation arises from the Negro's failure to keep his property up to the right standard, the neglect of its appearance, his tendency to make money by subletting his rooms to irresponsible people who lower the tone of, as well as become a nuisance to, the neighborhood. The colored people reply by saying they have the same right to buy property as any other citizens, that if white people did not sell they could not buy; that white people can have no valid excuse for objecting to purchases in select neighborhoods by wealthy, intelligent colored people. The whites reply that wherever one Negro comes, the others feel that they have the right to follow, and that while the firstcomer may be all right, those who follow will be the opening wedge for a number of undesirables, with their business signs, for hair straightening, toilet preparations, and furnished rooms, in order that they may make enough money to pay for a swell-looking place. They cite in substantiation conditions of formerly splendid streets in New York and Chicago. The problem is most difficult of solution. Candor compels the statement there is truth in the argument of both races. The Negro's entrance into fine houses on "White streets" is an evidence of his desire to rise. The wisdom of his method of attaining that desire produces the argument and friction that only the courts and Father Time can adjust. That he should drag obnoxious signs into neighborhoods occupied by people whose business is conducted elsewhere will ever be a source of trouble. Such trouble would hardly exist if the masses moved into neighborhoods in keeping financially and otherwise with their circumstances. In this city, as in others, Negroes have clustered instead of scattering. In consequence, the West End has a vast colony which has largely driven out the Jews, Germans and Italians. The central part of Walnut Hills has also a great mass of Negroes. The East End, the suburbs of Cumminsville, Madisonville, College Hill and Lockland are largely populated by them. Comparatively few live in white neighborhoods. In every locality, as Negroes increase, the whites diminish. Before the black invasion, the whites retire and disappear as snow 'neath the rays of the rising sun.

PREJUDICE IN PUBLIC PLACES

Despite the riots of early days, generally little personal prejudice prevailed. The differentiation between dark and light Negroes, from the standpoint of color, was often marked by similar difference in the treatment accorded them by the public. Mulattoes had more privileges and greater opportunities. They could go to school with the whites; they could go to the polls and vote. They often enjoyed the social advantages concomitant with inter-racial commingling. However, Negroes generally got to the point of being accommodated in saloons, restaurants and theaters. They were not allowed to ride on street cars until one day, a colored woman, a mulatto, wife of Rev. Peter Fosset, attempted to board a car. The conductor would not allow her to enter and pushing her off, started the car. She clung to the steps and was dragged over a block. The occurrence aroused a storm of indignation. Her work had endeared her to many of the wealthiest ladies. The agitation resulted in permission for colored women to ride. Finally, colered men were given the same privilege. Colored people used to go to Parker's Grove, the site of our Coney Island. All of the picnic grounds were open to them, the beer gardens, theaters, Over-the-Rhine resorts, the Zoo cafe, dining room and most of the ordinary restaurants.

In late years, however, the prejudice has grown by leaps and bounds until now, the United States constitutional amendments and civil rights law of Ohio notwithstanding, colored citizens generally receive welcome, consideration or courtesy in but very few places of public welfare or entertainment. Why? That's the question. Always a large increase in numbers of colored people has been followed by a large increase of prejudice. The whites, in vindication of their inhospitality, claim "that while Negroes, as citizens, are entitled to the civic rights of other citizens, yet Negroes as a class or in the mass are poor, ignorant, loud, noisy, devoid of refinement and are therefore offensive to white patrons. That they mistake liberty for license and know not that enjoyment of rights entails the performance of certain duties. That Negroes have not as yet classified themselves, for as a result of slave training, most of them believe and contend that all Negroes are the same and that one is just as good as another. In consequence they say they can not discriminate in favor of the educated, wealthy Negro, since the common Negro will demand the same, and make a disturbance if he does not get it, hence they solve the difficulty by admitting no one with a visible admixture of Negro blood."

Colored people claim the ostracism results from jealousy over the progress colored people are making. While they cite the fact that Negroes now are wealthier and better educated than ever, yet the fair-minded among them admit that the conduct of low class Negroes has a great deal to do with the rapid increase of prejudice. They concede also that the average Negro has no conception of class as have the whites. A low class white man studiously avoids places frequented by the upper class of his people. He seems to feel a little ashamed of his condition, whereas the lower the Negro the more apt he is to enter any place where he sees another colored person. The difference in class neither concerns nor affects him. The color being the same is all he considers. In his ignorance he can not conceive that obnoxious personal characteristics form the basis of far more prejudice than differences of race, color or religion. The solution of the problem will only come when, after many long years, Negroes will be subdivided as are the whites. Class, rather than color, will then constitute the line of demarcation. The sooner such condition comes the better, for without class there is no progress; without class there is no incentive for improvement. The harder we study, the more intelligently we labor, the higher we rise. That's the prize for which we compete. If people remained on the same level regardless of their achievements, whether mental or material, there would be no incentive to rise, no stimulus for struggle, and in a few generations such people would be as the animals of the fields, the beasts of the forest. The sooner class and inter-racial association comes, the more quickly prejudice goes.

"THE BLACK BELT"
Crime, Cause and Cure

Queen City crime runs riot as never before, and in the "Black Belt," that is, the down-town "tenderloin district," vice, naked as though in Satan's realm, rears its hideous head aloft, as did the brazen Serpent in the days of Moses. The proportion of colored criminals is appalling. To the competent student of sociological conditions, the cause is not involved in much perplexity. Thousands of Negroes, in the last few years, hailing from the most benighted of southern counties, have located in our midst. The bright red lights of down-town nights are ever most attractive to those "children of the sun," whose rearing has been in the dark atmosphere of sordid, desolate, depressive surroundings. They crowded into the tenements, already over full, that are so plentifully scattered in the West End. Walnut Hills and the suburbs, the habitat of very reputable families, had no room for these refugees. The terrible congestion brought both sexes of all ages together, under conditions most favorable for generation of immorality. Brought the vicious in contact with the virtuous. Drove the young men to the pool-room, or with some young woman to the theater, the dance hall and the saloon. The glaring poverty that has always been a feature of enforced immigration, permeated all phases of daily existence, intensifying its horrors, furnishing ever-insistent incentive to theft or harlotry. Apart from the coming of our blood brethren from the south, other causes of crime creep before us, and of them all, the giant standing aloft towering in diabolic majesty, is that poisonous fluid which insidiously steals away the brains of those

Carlisle Avenue—the Heart of the "Black Belt"

who partake of it. "Moonshine," the foul product brought into being by the mistaken zeal of a dry worshipping public, with the connivance of politicians, the dryness of whose votes affected not the wetness of their desires. The drinking of illicit liquor is the greatest cause of crime in the "Black Belt." Congestion of living ranks second in its production of immorality and ill health, and third comes political influences that foster gambling and facilitate the escape or lessen the penalty of those who violate the laws. The remedy: Transport the surplus population to small houses in the suburbs, vote for temperance rather than prohibition, crush out of existence political machines.

SCHOOLS

Public sentiment seemingly condones the violation of state laws relative to separate or segregated schools. Two are here and indications that the near future will see a third, namely a Negro high school. Later, there will probably be other primary schools and the gradual removal of colored children from "mixed" schools, and maybe, the university. The whites generally favor separate schools. Regarding Negroes as being inferior, they deplore any association with them, except upon the basis of master and man, employer and servant. They are wise enough to realize that the doctrines of subserviency can not be enforced if white children are schooled with colored, since school association and competition breed a spirit of equality, engenders a feeling of respect for those who are mentally or physically superior, regardless of their race or color. Separate schools could neither be established nor maintained under the law, were it not for the solicitation of many colored people who, through selfishness, ignorance or cowardice, submit to such conditions as the easiest method of getting colored teachers appointed. The logical solution would be to place their teachers in all public schools since, if they are capable of teaching children of colored citizens, they should be capable of teaching children of white citizens. Lack of differentiation among the young would in a few years remove the aroma of inequality and in the survival of the fittest, the best products of both races would grow to manhood having the mutual respect and regard so essential to the peace and harmony of a democracy.

SOCIETY

In and immediately after the fifties, colored society was in all its glory. Money was plentiful and its leaders found ample opportunity for imitation of the aristocratic white people with whom they came in contact. There were good houses and apart from riots engendered by the envy of the "poor whites," little prejudice. Among the big families enjoying and dispensing the amenities of high social life were the Tinsleys, who lived royally, their daughter, Ann Baltimore, Mrs. Alex Thomas and daughters Kate and Bettie, the Sheltons, the Dunlaps, the Harlans, the Troys, the Liverpools, the Roxboroughs.

In later years the wedding of Lou Easton and Kate Thomas, for gorgeous display, set the colored world on fire. It took place in an aristocratic white church. That of Mattie Fosset was also most elegant. Time is father of many changes. The high pace set by society almost brought about its dissolution, for as the river trade diminished, purses became lean. Poverty began to creep in homes that had only known prosperity. Sadly, certain families began to realize that the imitation of millionaires has pains as well as pleasures.

> "Après le plaisir
> Vient la peine,
> Après la peine
> La vertu."

"After pleasure comes pain, after pain, virtue."

Upon the ruins of the old, other social circles arose. Class began to vanish, as those who could make a showing, financially, forced themselves to the front.

Now the city has many social factions. A small group is still true to ancient conditions, but other groups, considering themselves among the elite, pay little attention to class distinction but gladly worship at the shrines of those who dress well and feed well. The church has its society, the school set and other groups, social circles based upon congeniality or more aristocratic attributes.

The grand marriage of Lillian Schooley, daughter of Dr. Chas. A. Schooley to Captain "Bob" Mallory, of Dayton, took place many years ago in St. Paul's Episcopal Church, one of

Richmond Street

the leading white places of worship in this city. Cincinnati can boast, however, of participation in the most magnificent colored wedding in the history of the United States, for the Dr. Gordon Jackson, who married Miss Mae Walker in New York, was a son of Attorney Geo. H. Jackson, of this city. That wedding was noted in newspapers throughout the world. The Easton-Thomas marriage, over fifty years ago, was featured as follows:

WEDDING EXTRAORDINARY

"The notable event among the fashionables of the colored portion of our population was the marriage, last evening, of Miss Katie Thomas, daughter of A. S. Thomas, Esq., of Fifth Street, to Mr. Louis Easton, first teacher of the colored high school. The marriage ceremony was performed at the Seventh Street Chapel by Rev. L. H. Swears, in the presence of three or four hundred invited friends of the bride and groom. The bridesmaids were Miss Alice Thomas, sister of the bride, and Miss Ella Collins, also of Cincinnati.

"Among those present were Mrs. Oscar Dunn, wife of the late Lieutenant-Governor of Louisiana, and at present keeper of the archives of that State, with her lovely and literally fair daughter; Mrs. John R. Lee, of Cleveland; Miss Mary Morris, of Cleveland; Mrs. Louisa Anderson, of Hamilton; and Mrs. Margaret Lee, of Cincinnati, with, of course, the father and mother of the bride. The bride wore white corded silk, trimmed with satin, cut low with full court train, and the traditional veil and orange flowers, a really exquisite toilette. The bridesmaids wore white tarlatan over silk, and were also admirably dressed. Following the ceremony, during which the organist performed Mendelssohn's wedding march, the bridal party adjourned to the rooms of the bride's father, No. 146 West Fifth Street, where every preparation had been made for the entertainment of the company."

The above account, taken from The Commercial Gazette, the leading daily paper of that period, relates to a marriage in high colored society which took place in July, 1874. Our citizens get neither such courtesy nor comment from the press of today.

A HANDFUL OF FLOWERS
History's Greatest Lesson

A half century ago, in a three-story brick building on Seventh Street, between Central Avenue and John Street, lived Mr. and Mrs. John Tinsley. They were owners of the house and the magnificent furniture it contained. Money was of slightest consideration, since he worked for clubs and high grade gamblers and they were in those days the salt of the earth when it came to lavish disbursements of easily gotten gains.

Mrs. Tinsley, a brilliant woman for her race and time, was society's queen. None came to dispute the sovereignty of the Tinsleys, but the

Thomases. In high society also were the stewards of steamboats and many big colored business men. One of them, Wilcox, the rich grocer on Fifth and Broadway, had a white clerk, Jas. W. Fitzgerald, who afterwards became powerful as leader of the city council and later achieved fame as police court judge. "Jimmy" Fitzgerald, the judge, attained a national celebrity. But that's another story. The colored society people lived beyond or fully up to their means. They emulated the prodigality of the whites by whom they had been owned, for whom they had worked, or of whom they heard. Years rolled on and poverty came. The star of Negroes more lowly, was in the ascendant, and as influential whites of the past had passed, so great classy colored families passed till now only the traditions of by-gone days are left to tell of their glory. Not many years ago Mrs. Tinsley, a gray-haired, tottering woman of four score and ten, impoverished, pauperized, but still cheerful, "went the way of all flesh," and this woman who had thrown away thousands of dollars, the woman at whose residence hundreds had been wined and dined, the woman who had dispensed charity with a royal hand, slept in a plain casket upon which hardly a handful of flowers found resting place. The last sad words, "Ashes to ashes, dust to dust," were heard by her poor blind daughter, once a society favorite, a few relatives and fewer friends. The tragedy of it all was not that she had outlived her contemporaries, but that she had outlived her money.

"DOWN ON THE LEVEE"

The river front from Broadway to Sycamore became known as "The Levee," after the pioneers levelled the forests and moved up-town. When the Spencer House, on lower Broadway, was in its splendor, reputable colored people were in business below, but the steamboat trade, enrolling its hundreds of roustabouts, became the main factor in the development of its undesirable elements. Soon there grew its clustering, many-roomed tenements, its saloons, its gambling dens, its dives, whose motley guests were tinted as was the sacred coat of Joseph. "Pickett's saloon" was known from Pittsburg to New Orleans, and when Chicago was but an infant, Pickett was a celebrity, the King of the Levee, 91 Front Street! Ye Gods, what memories rise before old residents and visiting aristocrats who in those days sought the slums for recreation! That region finally became known as "Rat Row," and then followed the metamorphosis of Pickett's place of pleasure into the "Silver Moon," its leading resort for residence and joy of all sorts. The inhabitants, white and black, made a beaten path to "Bucktown," and many were the daily pilgrimages to and fro, of "handkerchief"-headed, short-skirted, calico-dressed women, and "overalled" men, in various stages of inebriety. A "killing" on Rat Row evoked little comment and less criticism. The Negroes made money and they spent it. They loved much, gambled more and fought fiercely. 'Twas the ideal life of the common, ignorant roustabout and his "gal," only a few years removed from the creatures bought and sold like cattle. Only a few years from the women who were bred like beasts. Only a few years from the young girls who, lashed into gratification of the lust of the master, were passed on to the bestiality of the overseer, then to the arms of the slave! Railroads destroyed the trade of the river. Lower sank the Levee. "Rat Row" was in its decadence. "The Silver Moon" and other places of lowly pleasures went down financially as well as physically, for the frequent floods devastated the buildings, and temporarily drove to high ground, the human rats that infested them. Time passed. "Mike" Mullen came. Like the bosses of Tammany, he was the Czar of the big ward that finally became the Eighth, and included "Rat Row." The denizens of that classic suburb, "on the banks of the Beautiful River," idolized "Mike" Mullen, for he was a father when adversity came. Soup houses in winter, a coin for every beggar, assistance for every suffering family! Over and above all, however, protection from the police or succor from the courts. While he reigned, the bones (craps) freely mingled with each other regardless of the presence of the "Blue Coated Guardians of the Law." In the dance halls, beer and whisky flowed, even after the town had gone dry, but no policeman ever saw infraction of the law, unless 'twas by some enemy of "Mike" Mullen, or the Republican party. In summer the doors of the big saloon and gambling den stood wide open to admit the zephyrs, bringing from the river those balmy breezes laden with woodland odors from the hills of Kentucky. Their fragrant perfume was seemingly heavenly incense replacing the malodorous vapors, rising from feet of sleepers, who with heads on piles of rubbish, slumbered promiscuously around the floor. Ofttimes a "Rat Row dandy" would lie upon two newspapers spread under the "crap table" so that his clothes would be protected from dirt below and dust above. He dreamed of his "honey," "his gal," and in sweet fancy saw her coming, laden with wealth sufficient to afford him the luxury of bed and board. "Mike" Mullen was gathered to his fathers. This year the "Silver Moon" came down. Soon Rat Row will be but a memory, for verily its glory has long since departed.

We give below a few paragraphs, by Lafacadio Hearn, concerning some of the audience at a minstrel show down on "Rat Row" many years ago.

"The attractive novelty of theatricals at old Pickett's tavern, on the Levee, by real Negro minstrels, with amateur dancing performances by roustabouts and "their" girls, has already created considerable interest in quarters where one would perhaps least expect to find it; and the patrolmen of the Row nightly escort fashionably dressed white strangers to No. 91 Front Street. The stage curtains were made by a mild-mannered brown girl called Annie, remarkable for deep, dark eyes, light, wavy hair, and wonderful curves of mouth, chin and neck; but poor Annie is no better than she ought to be, and loves to smoke a great, black, briar root pipe.

Ere the curtain rose we found it extremely interesting to glance over the motley audience, largely made up of women less fair but not less frail than Annie.

A sharp-faced Irish girl, with long fawn-colored hair and hard grey eyes, a pretty and ruddy-faced young white woman, very neatly built and fashionably dressed, the wife of a colored barkeeper; a white brunette, with unpleasantly deep-set black eyes, and long curly hair, who feigns to have colored blood in her veins; a newly arrived white blonde, who last week followed a roustabout hither from Ironton through some strange and vain infatuation; the notorious Adams sisters; a young Cincinnati woman of evil repute, whose parents live but a few squares up-town and have not for years exchanged word or look with their daughter, though she almost daily passes by the old home; and one Gretchen faced woman, with rather regular features and fair hair, who has lately deserted a good home at Portsmouth to become the mistress of a stevedore; these comprised the white women present. Excepting the barkeeper's little white wife, they evidently preferred to sit together. The picturesqueness of the spectacle was rendered all the more striking by the contrast.

There were full-blooded black women, solidly built, who were smoking stogies, and wore handkerchiefs of divers colors twisted about their curly pates.

It was curious to observe the contrast of physical characteristics among the lighter-hued women; girls with almost fair skins frequently possessing wooly hair; dark mulattoes on the contrary often having light, floating, wavy locks. One mulatto girl present wore her own hair—frizzly and thick as the mane of a Shetland pony—flowing down to her waist in gypsy style.

At least three-fourths of the audience were women, and of these one-third, perhaps, were smoking. Several of the white girls were chewing. Of the men present, the greatest number were roustabouts, in patched attire, often of the most fantastic description."

"BUCKTOWN"—"BIG BUCK"

The four places in early Cincinnati, nationally known, were "Over the Rhine," "George Street," "Bucktown," and "The Levee." The last two places were inhabited by the very lowest class of Negroes and a sprinkling of whites. Bucktown was located east of Broadway, between Sixth and Seventh, and ranged through the bottoms to Culvert Street. Many years later another spot of similar characteristics, known as "Little Buck," to distinguish it from the original, arose in the West End near the vicinity of Sixth and Freeman. Many people have the erroneous impression that only Negroes lived in Bucktown. As a matter of fact many whites dwelt therein, and with but few exceptions, its streets were filled with people of the lowest type. Through the valley back of "Bucktown" swept Deer Creek, and that region was conspicuous for the Irish and other white types who loved brawls and fights. Often did they charge upon "Bucktown" and as often did "Bucktown" drive them back to the hills. When we came to town in '94, the mantle of civilization had almost completely overspread that unsavory section. "Jim Allen," Negro policeman, was put on the force in 1886, and his reputation for scrapping received the acid test, for "he got the 'Bucktown' beat." He and his partner, a colored "Cop" named Miller, cleaned up "Bucktown" by sending most of its tough men and women to the hospital or workhouse. It still had many dissolute women and gambling men, but gradually murder became a lost art, and sometimes several nights would pass without any one being killed around there or at Sixth and Broadway, then known as "Deadman's Corner." "Allen Chapel," located in the heart of "Buck," closed its doors, for the congregation had moved into the aristocratic Jewish Synagogue on Broadway and named it Allen Temple. There were two or three saloons in the district, and a Negro known as Webster, was called the Mayor of Bucktown. Good order was partly established. As time rolled on, the shanties and shacks, foul smelling and crumbling into decay, became a nightmare of the past, for progress was on the wing and soon great sewers took away the filth that oozed from the cesspools and gutters, eliminated the hellish odors that emanated from their ever-increasing sea of putrescence. Buildings arose as though by magic. When one now walks through "Old Bucktown," looks at the massive manufactories, listens to the ceaseless hum of machines, a conception of the hideousness of its bygone days would seem only a freak of the imagination, a foul eructation of a deranged mind, rather than a true picture of the past. The following extract from an article written by Lafcadio Hearn for "The Commercial Gazette, in the "seventies," will give a good idea of "Bucktown" and its inhabitants when this town was young in years and "wide open" in ways:

"Bucktown was once not less celebrated as a haunt of crime than the Five Points of the Metropolis. Lying in the great noisome hollow, then untraversed by a single fill, the congregation of dingy and dilapidated frames, hideous huts, and shapeless dwellings, often rotten with the moisture of a thousand petty inundations, or filthy with the dirt accumulated by vice-gotten laziness, and inhabited only by the poorest or the vilest of the vicious, impressed one with the fancy that Bucktown was striving, through conscious shame, to bury itself under the earth. Today we find much of the horrible hollow filled up and the ancient Bucktown is gradually but surely disappearing, not as though by reason of a fiat from the board of improvements, but as though the earth were devouring, swallowing, engulfing this little Gomorrah. And our modern Bucktown is thus, perhaps, partly divested of its old terrors. People can remember how, in a certain low brothel there, masked by a bar, a Negro levee hand blew a brother roustabout's brains all over the bar; and how the waiter girl related the occurrence with a smile to divers breathless policemen and reporters, at the same time wiping the blood and white brains off the counter with a cloth like so much spilt beer. It was said in those days that many a stout man had been decoyed into a Bucktown den, who disappeared forever from public view.

"The inimity ordinarily concomitant with the admixture of race ceases to exist on the confines of Bucktown; whites and blacks are forced into a species of criminal fraternization; all are Ishmaels bound together by fate, by habit, by instinct, and by the iron law and never-cooling hate of an outraged society. The harlot's bully, the pimp, the prostitute, the thief, the procuress, the highway robber, white, tawny, brown and black, constitute the mass of the population. But there are two other classes, very small indeed, yet still well worth notice. The first is composed of those who have lost caste by miscegenation; the second, that of levee hands, who live in a state of concubinage with mistresses who remain faithful to them. Of the former class it is scarcely necessary to say that white women wholly compose it, women who have conceived strange attachments for black laborers and live with them as mistresses; also, women who boast black pimps for their masters, and support them by prostitution. Of the other class referred to we may observe that it constitutes but a part of the floating population of Bucktown, in as much as the levee hands and their women are the most honest portion of this extraordinary community. Consequently, they live there only because of their poverty, not their will.

"As the violation of nature's laws begets deformity and hideousness, and as the inhabitants of Bucktown are popularly supposed to be great violators of nature's laws, they are vulgarly supposed to be all homely if not positively ugly or monstrously deformed. 'A Bucktown hag,' and 'an ugly old Bucktown wench,' are expressions commonly used. This idea is, however, for the most part fallacious. The really hideous and deformed portion of the Bucktown population is confined to a few crippled or worn-out, honest rag-pickers, and perhaps two or more ancient harlots, superannuated in their degrading profession, and compelled at last to resort to the dumps for a living. The majority of the darker colored women are muscular, well-built people, who would have sold at high prices in a Southern slave market before the war; the lighter tinted are, in some instances, remarkably well favored; and among the white girls one occasionally meets with an attractive face, bearing traces of what must have been uncommon beauty. Gigantic negresses, stronger than men, whose immense stature and phenomenal muscularity bear strong witness to the old slave custom of human stock breeding; neatly built mulatto girls, with the supple, pantherish strength peculiar to half breeds; slender octoroons, willowy and graceful of figure, with a good claim to the qualification, pretty, will all be found among the crowd of cotton-turbaned and ebon-visaged throng who talk alike and think alike and all live alike.

"Desiring to see the inner life of Bucktown, the writer, some evening since, accompanied a couple of police officers in the search for a female thief. Dens, indeed, is the only term which can with propriety be applied to many of their dwellings, whereof the roofs are level with the street, and the lower floors are thirty feet under ground, like some of those hideous haunts described in The Mysteries of Paris.

"The buildings between the corner drug-store and the first alley east of Broadway are occupied by people who claim to be respectable. We entered the house of Mary Williams. A very ordinary-looking woman is Mary—bright mulatto, with strong Irish features, slight form, apparently thirty-five years of age. This blood seems to predominate strongly in the veins of half the mulattoes of Bucktown. Mary swore 'to her just God' that no one was concealed about the premises.

"A tall, good-looking mulatto girl, with long, black, wavy hair and handsome eyes, but who smokes a very bad stogie and squirts saliva between her teeth like an old tobacco chewer, answers the patrolmen's queries. 'What are you doing here, Annie?' 'I was hiding.' 'Who are you hiding from at two o'clock in the morning?' 'Chestine Clark, Mr. Martin; for Christ's sake don't tell him I'm here; he swears he'll kill me.'

"Chestine is something of a dandy ruffian in Bucktown; a tall and sinewy mulatto, who always resists officers when opportunity offers, and is, altogether, a very unpleasant customer. Clark's father is a respectable and well-to-do old man, and has helped his son out of several very ugly scrapes." * (He was old man Jim Clark, formerly a turnkey.)

" 'I always made it a rule,' said Officer Sissman, 'to keep the greater part of these women in the workhouse during the time I ran the beat. Otherwise the life of a patrolman would not be worth a hill of blue beans here. Where the prostitutes collect the thieves always gather. There are now between one hundred and fifty and two hundred women from Bucktown in the workhouse.'

"There were two women in white dresses sitting on door-steps a little further on down the alley, one a bright quadroon with curly hair twisted into ringlets, and a plump, childish face; the other a tall white girl, with black hair and eyes and a surprisingly well-cut profile. Both are notorious; the former as a Sausage Row belle; the latter as the mistress of a black loafer whom she supports by selling herself. Her sister, once quite a pretty woman, leads a similar existence when not in the workhouse.

"Molly is the colored belle of this district. She seemed to be about eighteen years old, of lithe and slender figure, complexion a gypsy brown, hair long and dark with a slight wave, brows perfectly arched and delicately penciled; dreamy brown eyes; nose well cut; mouth admirably molded; features generally pleasing; but Molly is said to be a 'decoy' and a thief, and her apparent innocence a sham.

"It is a curious fact that business men and people of respectability get decoyed down here occasionally by girls like that and get infatuated enough to bring them presents.

"Further on was the noisome underground den of Gilbert Page, who has lived in Bucktown for twenty-two years, and has paid over five thousand dollars for fines to the clerk of the police court.

"Over Joe Kite's lives a good-looking white girl, with some outward appearance of refinement, and who still retains that feminine charm soonest lost by a life of dissipation, a sweet voice. This is Dolly West, or "Detroit Dolly" as they call her, a colored man's woman, and one of the princesses of Bucktown.

"On the south side of Seventh Street matters are equally bad. The density of the population here is proportionately greater than in any other part of the city, although it is mostly a floating population, floating between the workhouse or the penitentiary and the dens in the filthy hollow. Ten, twelve, or even twenty inhabitants in one two-story, underground den is common enough. At night even the roofs are occupied by sleepers, the balconies are crowded, and the dumps are frequently the scenes of wholesale debauchery, the most degrading. How it is that sickness is not more common among this class we confess ourselves unable to comprehend.

"It was not uncommon to find white men of respectable appearance and well dressed, sleeping in such dens. The police will seldom molest them while they 'behave themselves,' but the well known male thief, be he white or black, is allowed no place in Bucktown to hide his head. The first instance of this which came under our personal observation was in the brothel of a white woman known as 'Fatty Maria,' who keeps on Sixth, near Culvert, opposite Kirk's. A fellow named Collison was found by the officers sleeping between two women, and at once ordered to vacate the premises. He refused to depart. The women took part, and 'Fatty Maria' attacked one of the officers like a wild cat. During this episode at Fatty Maria's, a disgusting occurrence which well illustrates the brutality of the Bucktown rough, occurred almost immediately across the way. There is a young white woman now in Bucktown, who spends the greater part of her existence in the workhouse for drunkenness, and whose degradation is such that she has even ceased to be known by name. Some one had decoyed her into a low den, made her drunk and taken the most cowardly advantage of her condition, afterwards thrusting her into the street.

"While the police were expelling Collison from Fatty Maria's a crowd of ruffians, white and black, lifted the unconscious woman and carried her to a vacant lot in the Hollow in the rear of Kirk's, where they tore off part of her clothing. Before the police could reach the spot the fellows fled beyond pursuit.

"It is comforting to think that in ten years hence Bucktown will have ceased to exist."

As we have told, it has ceased to exist, thank God.

"LITTLE BUCK"—"LIL' BUCK"

"Little Buck" was not so well-known to the nation as its illustrious progenitor, the place from which it derived its patronymic, but the police, to their sorrow, sadly recognized its potentialities. "Crap shooting" Negroes, and gun "toting" Negroes, and "knife-handling" Negroes, permeated every hole and corner of "Little Buck." Also included among them were many hard-working, poverty-stricken, honest Negroes who could find no other place to go. The denizens of color fraternized well

Taylor Alley in Little Bucktown

with the whites, for "birds of a feather flock together." Years have removed nearly all of the "old-timers." I recall the night when, in 1900, down in that vicinity, while sipping a few steins and talking over old times with George Harris, Dud Tillman and Irvin Wheeler, many were the stories told of "Big Buck," "Little Buck" and the fellows who fought for sheer love of fighting. How the inhabitants of both places treated with the utmost respect the bunch of fellows, Fox Anderson, Ollie Anderson, Hiram Hendricks, Jim Chatman, Buff Garret and other great scrappers who sometimes wandered forth on warfare bent. Finally, Irvin Wheeler, half Indian and Negro, arose. He was a powerfully built man, a native of Canada. Five feet ten in height, dark yellow color, long, curly, black hair, handsome as Adonis. "Dabney," said he, "this town has gone to H———. It's too nice. They even arrest a man now for fighting; who would have thought this back in the days when we would walk, by G———, from Big Buck to Little Buck, and fight any d——— man or in any d——— place?" Then, doubling his big right fist, and looking down upon it, he sadly said, "You don't get any exercise these days, old 'Bunch of Fives,' but you have the pleasure of knowing that you hit lots of folks in your time, and you never hit a one, whether Cop, Irishman, or Nigger, that they didn't have to pour water on him to bring him back to life."

It is said that Irvin Wheeler once beat up two policemen, took their guns and clubs down to the police station with this request, "Next time sen' to Lil' Buck, men, instead of tenderfeet." He was the real cause of racial separation in the county jail, for during his incarceration, he fought so much that he made life a torture to the white prisoners as well as the keepers.

Now, "Little Buck" has gone and so has Irvin Wheeler. The one became a business center, the other a deputy sheriff of St. Louis. Last week he died, game as he lived. Popularity and prosperity never eradicated the love for "Little Buck," which continued his favorite theme until he crossed the great river.

"The heart that has truly loved,
  Never forgets, but as truly loves on to the close,
 As the sunflower turns to her God when he sets,
  The same look she gave when he rose."

THE DEMI MONDE AND "THE TENDERLOIN"

In the good old days harlotry played well its part here as in all young western towns. It is woman's oldest profession, and the only one in which man is the game and to blame. The street of streets, famed wherever Cincinnati is known, was "George Street." Three blocks, East to West, from Central Avenue to Mound, lined on both sides with pretentious houses, neatly, cleanly kept, constituted the principal realm consecrated to the worship of Venus. Red lights above the doors gave it the name of "The Red Light District," "for red is the flag of health, the banner of love." In later years it became commonly known as "The Tenderloin." The few colored sporting houses existing then were mainly for white men. Many were the colored maids, cooks and laundresses employed in the swell establishments. Strange to say, most of them were respectable, despite the fact that numerous men preferred the maid to the mistress. Longworth Street also was the habitat of "fallen angels." There were quite a number of "colored" houses on this street and the shorter thoroughfares bisecting it. Of these colored houses only a few were for colored men. Males of that race are not conspicuous for maintenance of such establishments. "They like not the fruit that grows on the high road." They love deeply, are extremely jealous natured, will risk life or gladly take life for those they love, for when they love, they worship. That's the source of their attraction for women, of all races. Love is to the average white man of today a thing apart. He worships money and likes women as children like toys. The man who will share a woman with another is considered by respectable Negroes as scum of the lowest dregs, a scoundrel of the deepest dye. The Negro "Pimp" or Paramour will take money but not give it. He will beat the woman should she fail to provide liberally. She glories in the martyrdom of brutality, considering it an evidence of love. He simply regards it as a matter of business. "Her man" will attack, maybe kill, a rival, not from jealousy, but because of the probable interference with his income. Prostitution flourished before and after the civil war. Money was plentiful. White and black women vied with each other for the common game, the white man. They were friendly, however, though rivals. Crime rarely draws the "color line," and misery loves company. Many were the assignation houses. In them, white women sought colored men, and in them white men looked for colored women, ranking above the prostitute class. A white man from the South would invariably request the proprietor to get him a good, honest, respectable, colored servant girl. He had been accustomed to that in his southern home. The proprietor would telephone to "Ollie" or to some other sporting establishment to rush over at once a girl, looking, acting, and dressed, like a servant. As years rolled on the districts became segregated, put under police and medical supervision. Soon colored race pride began to assert itself and there was less and less commerce between white men and colored women except those so ignorant as to be flattered by such attentions, or those to whom gold spoke more loudly than honor. This refers to the ones who frequented assignation houses or had white male affinities. The prostitute class, of course, remained wedded to its idols, and like Tennyson's brook, seemed destined to go on forever. The "color line" downtown began to vanish. In sporting cities people are too busy making and spending money to pay much attention to race or color. Cincinnati was no exception. White women noted how their fathers and brothers lavished every luxury upon colored women, even those of the most repulsive type. Some of them gradually started to associate with colored men. Forbidden fruit is ever the sweetest. Obstacles enhance enchantment. Hades began to diffuse itself over the Queen City. The colored woman was stirred to her profoundest depths, for no colored woman, however depraved, likes to see a colored man with a white woman, unless as a species of revenge on the white race. The white man was even more deeply affected. The law could not be used to check the relationships, but the police and judges could. A white servant girl was seen to kiss her black sweetheart "good night." She was arrested. The judge fined her twenty-five dollars for her "bad taste." A white prostitute, Clara Colville, at three o'clock in the afternoon, stood out on Longworth Street, near Vine, hugged and kissed a black Negro musician called "Pork Chops," to show the white men across the street that she preferred the black man. For this public exhibition of her preference she resided in the workhouse for six months. Negro musicians were not allowed to play any more music in the houses of prostitution. Police hounded or arrested white women whenever seen with colored men, but encouraged rather than molested white men with colored women. A "Cop" seeing a "white woman" eating down-town at a colored restaurant with a colored man, called her every variety of filthy names and arrested the couple. Police assume the right to arrest a prostitute on sight. The case was dismissed, it being proven that she was colored. It was not long before, as an alibi, white women out with colored fellows, began to claim that they were colored. Matters came to a crisis in 1900. The police dragged a dark man and light woman from the street car, beat him up and arrested them. She proved to be a well-known light colored woman of this city. A number of citizens, among them Dr. and Mrs. Prowd (she was a white woman), Mrs. Street Nesbit, Mrs. Arizona Miller, Mrs. Porter, and Mr. and Mrs. W. P. Dabney, called on Mayor Julius Fleischmann. Chief of Police Deitsch was present. Dr. Prowd gave a statement concerning conditions and the danger of a race riot. Mrs. Nesbit made a powerful speech showing what the slaveholders had done in prostitution of our race and the damnable hounding of respectable people by our police. Dabney stated that a colored man had as much right to go with a white woman as a white man had to go with a colored woman. That the colored man in such cases deserved no censure, since the desire of the women engendered the association, whereas the white man's gold and power were still freely permitted to ruin Negro girls unrestricted by law, unchecked by public sentiment. Mayor Fleischmann promised to regulate the police, and thus promote racial harmony. He knew that in the eyes of the law all citizens were equal and that the tyranny of the local officials was unjustifiable. The public oppression ceased. Privately, it was still rigid. To colored assignation housekeepers, the police said: "In your place colored man and colored woman, all right; white man and white woman, all right; white man and colored woman, all right, but if you admit a colored man and white woman we'll break up your business and drive you out of town." In this year of the Lord, 1925, that principle still holds good. A white woman "Over the Rhine," about ten years ago, maintained a very swell private establishment, almost as fine as that of Alice Duvall's, a colored woman, on Poplar Street. By request of her cook, she permitted a colored business man to bring his girl, a light mulatto. Some white men seeing them enter, thinking she was white, telephoned to the police. When the lieutenant and two men came, the couple had gone. The proprietress informed the police that she would run her place to suit herself, what difference did it make if the woman was white? She found it made a great difference. She was knocked down, arrested and when taken to the station and afterwards to the hospital, it was found that the chivalrous lieutenant of the police had broken two of her ribs! He did not even receive a reprimand for his brutality. The war came. Imperative was the order to close all sporting houses. It was done. Poor old George Street! Gone were the red lights. Gone were the brightly lettered signs of "Marie," "Lucy," "Kate," "Nellie," "May," etc. Gone was the picturesque cleanliness. Gone was the quiet of its day, the noise of its night. The weeping white denizens bartered away, gave away, threw away, the furniture for which they had sold their souls. " 'Tis an ill wind that blows nobody good." The second-hand dealers were enriched. Negro tenants came and paid double prices to rapacious landlords. The street is now a wreck. The former inhabitants scattered, entered reputable flat buildings, slept by day, and at night through the streets they roamed, "seeking whom they may devour." The Negro women fared better. They wasted no time in tears, being daughters of a race saturated with a philosophy born of centuries of oppression. They flocked into Carlisle Avenue, lower John and Smith Streets. They, still, a little more discreetly, however, followed "Mrs. Warren's profession." Few women of this class ever change, except through matrimony or death. Today there are many public places down-town, laden with colored women who reap at times rich reward from their white patrons, who have more money than brains. For this condition their colored gallants, "who toil not," are deeply grateful. The blindness of the police in those vice-haunted districts has often been attributed to the charity with which white men generally indulge the moral laxity of colored people, as well as to their suffering from the disease Shakespeare characterized as "an itching palm." The amelioration of this ailment depends upon copious and continuous applications of cold cash. At the time the edict for closing "The Tenderloin" district went forth, we wrote the article herewith appended:

"GOOD NIGHT!"

"Taps" Have Sounded for the Red Light District of this City. Orders Came from Washington. "George" and Other Internationally Known Thoroughfares Bid Farewell to Their Greatness.

"At once, Good Night;
Stand not upon the order of your going,
But go at once."

"Farewell, a long farewell to all my greatness."

"The edict has gone forth." From Washington came the mandate to wipe from the map of Cincinnati its "vice district." To the rounders and roystering males of all races "the tenderloin district" of this city has been known personally, by hearsay, or traditionally. Of George Street, probably named after King George, we can not say, "Evil be to him, who evil thinks of it," for its glamour blinded no one to the fact, that it fully lived up to its reputation. "But it is all over now" and soon its inhabitants, "those soiled doves of commerce," may be all over this, or some other city. Wise birds always scatter when shot is fired at the covey. However, " 'tis an ill wind that blows nobody good." Those palatial palaces of pleasure will now most likely become the residences of the vast floating colored population which will be undeterred from renting by recollections of the past glory of that district. We feel that the landlords will soon be glad to get any kind of tenants, regardless of race, color or previous condition of servitude. The closing brought forth varied emotions among the proletariat, patrons, patronesses and denizens of the district. Some viewed it gladly, others sadly.

"But she's gone, just let me tell,
She had her boots on when she fell."

Shall we say, vale, vice? That would be very nice, for regardless of sentiment, regardless of gold, the morals of our gallant soldier boys deserve careful consideration.

George Street—In the Olden Days

However, we should not lose sight of the lessons of history. Wherever there are soldiers, women are not far away. Even on the frozen, barren wastes of Russia, in Napoleon's disastrous retreat from Moscow, women following the soldiers, fell on the roadsides and died by the thousands. Closing the houses does not necessarily close the desires and habits. It makes attainment more difficult. "The mountain couldn't come to Mahomet and so Mahomet went to the mountain." "The Washington powers that be" have commanded. Cincinnati has obeyed.

Relative to the wisdom of the proclamation, God forbid that we should even presume an interrogation. Fair females, of easy virtue, drifted into the world in the days of Adam and Eve. They will be drifting around when Gabriel's trumpet begins the last solo. Some persons feel that 'tis far safer for a community to have its "scarlet women" segregated than to have them scattered. In segregation you know what you have and where you have it. Otherwise you know not what you have and you know not where you have it. In regard to reformation, experience teaches that in difficulty, the problem of reforming people who do not want to be reformed, ranks with the twelve labors of Hercules. About the proposition to make of them domestic servants? Wow! We can imagine how long they would last in one of our swell households should the gentleman of the family be under ninety-five years of age and his wife should observe him talking to one of the Magdalens she has brought in to reform. But that's another story. No matter what is done these facts stare us in the face. "Water seeks its level" and "Nature takes its course," regardless of the laws and enactments of man.

DABNEY.
—*From the Union, Cincinnati, O., Nov. 24, 1917.*

OUR CHURCHES

America gave the Negro Christianity to console him for the loss of his body. His ecstatic, anticipatory raptures of heavenly bliss, only exceeded his audible exuberant joyousness over escaping the fiery tortures of hell. Religion became the foundation of his fatalistic philosophy, prayer the key that un-

He was the Real Founder of Antioch Baptist Church

locked the door of his troubles. For many generations he sang: "You may have all the world, but give me Jesus." The yoke of poverty rested lightly upon him. The Bible was his panacea for every ill. The harder the road in this world the greater his glory in the next. In the past preachers "were called" by God. If this method of procedure still prevails, then judging from the vast number now flourishing in this city, our Heavenly Father has in recent years been calling continually. Their services, however, are sorely needed, for an inspection of police records shows that the Devil is by no means idle. The whites say, "There are too many incompetent Negro preachers. More time is spent raising money for lavish display in equipment and building fine churches than is spent in training the people in lessons of conduct, economy and the real principles of religion." In partial substantiation of this, a book, The Education of Negro Ministers, has just appeared, written by a colored minister for the Institute of Social and Religious Research.

The colored people say in reply: "God has called these ministers for us and we can never sacrifice too much, for God's temples should be as fine as they can be made and if white folks can have fine churches and elaborate ceremonial, then we can and we will." The young colored people now are not so wedded to the church as were their ancestors. On Sundays, many go to the parks, picture shows, theaters, auto riding and even to dances. They do not regard their preachers with the same spirit of reverence, and education generally has removed or weakened their fear of hell. The old ministerial dictum, "Don't do as I do; do as I tell you," has lost its efficacy. To regain their grasp, pastors will find it necessary to adopt modern methods. Hell has lost its terrors. Love is now a more potent magnet for getting members in the church than fear. Fewer little churches would mean more prosperity. Less wrangling over doctrines, would give more time for betterment of conditions. Our people must be taught that "Heaven helps those who help themselves." The successful preacher of the future will be a real shepherd of his flock. Instead of building a fine church for poor people, he will buy land in the suburbs, build small houses, remove his members from the slums. He will have a building association to enable his flock to buy or rent those houses. He will have aid societies to help the needy and he will either have a home for the aged as an adjunct of his church, or will unite with the pastors of his denomination in the establishment of such an institution. He will make his church a community center. He will teach the people how to behave themselves in public and thereby gain the respect of other citizens. Those "old handkerchief headed days," of whooping about the glories of the next world, no longer furnish an excuse for being a nuisance in this. The honest, loyal ministers and church members of Cincinnati must get together on a progressive, ameliorative program, or else in a few years there will be many empty churches and far greater financial stringency. They should learn a lesson from the Catholics, whose Church, the strongest in the realms of Christianity, largely rests upon the corner-stone of Charity.

AN OPEN LETTER TO A LOCAL NEWSPAPER FIFTY YEARS AGO

THE CONDITION OF THE COLORED PEOPLE

Cincinnati, Ohio, February 22, 1874.

To the Editor of the Commercial:

I admit the truthfulness of some of the statements made by "Layman" in your issue of this date. It is a fact that the moral standard in our colored churches is very low at the present time. There was a time when it was much higher, but those were the days of Liverpool, Fowler, Mount, Woodson, Nickens, etc. The fact is our "elephant" is too big, has grown fat, and is crushing us beneath its feet. And these are great "revival times," bringing in the "uncircumcized in heart," and God has a great controversy with us. All our churches are burdened with debt. Our ministers get big salaries and presents the year round. Then we have so many societies, "Daughters of Rebekah," "Sons of Ham." And it is not altogether true that the "well paid ones" furnish most of the money. Our churches are supported mainly by whitewashers, and those who do "washing and ironing." But, thank God, we have one man in our city, the pastor of a flourishing church, who has always been able to say, "Mine own hands have ministered to my necessities." "Layman" says we have too many churches; true, and our orphan asylum begging for bread, and were it not for some good "white folks" would go under. Politics has taken hold of our pulpits. Because Revels went to the senate, each of our elders thinks he must go, too. And the great effort is to preach big sermons, print them, and make the poor people pay for them.

Oh, for a freedmen's bank! Our people are growing poorer year by year. Won't some one come among us and teach us how to lay by for a rainy day? It must be said that our white friends are somewhat hard on us; they give us the oldest houses and make us pay the highest rents. And when we work for you, and prove ourselves faithful in all things, you only pay us half what others would get. Is it not time to "undo the heavy burdens and let the oppressed go free?"

Deacon.

MISCEGENATION
"They Mixed Not Wisely, But Too Well"

Before, during and immediately after the war this city was a fertile field for miscegenation and the products thereof. Close to the borders of Kentucky, strongly pro-slavery in sentiment, enjoying vast commercial relations with the South, planters and business men from that section were frequent visitors to this "the Queen City of the West." Before the war they brought their slave women. After the war, their "kept women." As before narrated, the women became guests of the Old Dumas House and many a grand supper and champagne jamboree figured in the history of that hostelry. Mulatto children and adults abounded in this vicinity, for those not born here were often sent by their white fathers. To the wealthy white man of the South, his colored children, his own flesh and blood, were sacred. Other colored children, of course, were "Niggers." He provided them liberally with money and if they were fair enough "they passed for white, married white and so in the veins of some of our most aristocratic white families here the Negro blood has added to their strength and beauty, if not to their pride. On upper John Street, before the war, there came a colored woman, Mrs. Gibbs, who brought loads of money and several children. Her old owner, like the patriarchs of Hebrew lore, had been stricken with illness. Death stared him in the face and he knew it. He had this dark but comely woman take her children and flee to Cincinnati, for he knew when God's call came where the vengeance of his wife would fall. The eldest boy stayed with him and followed his instructions to steal all the money he could from his strong box and send it, concealed in merchandise, by boat to his mother. The planter died. His wife said to the colored son, "In twenty-four hours if you are on this plantation you will be sold far south." In twenty-four hours he was in Cincinnati.

The mother bought lots of property, the children became white and departed to various cities where their offspring may now, be even members of the Ku Klux Klan. A mulatto woman came up on a boat. With her were her two sons. She passed as their nurse. Twenty-five years later they were among the leaders here in society and business. Their offspring shows the fallacy of the theory that descendants of the Negro and white are sometimes born black. Instead, they frequently become white.

The late Jacob G. Schmidlapp said to me: "Dabney, a lady came in here today, a Mrs. Gamblee. I thought all the time that she was white until she told me her son, Lieut. Gamblee, was the physical culture teacher at Douglass School."

"Mr. Schmidlapp," said I, "there are thousands of colored people who are apparently white. An octoroon crossed with the white often produces a whiter child than the product of two white persons."

"How can that be possible?" said he.

"Why, on the same principle that a whitewasher adds a little blueing to his whitewash to make it whiter." That ended the conversation.

An old white-haired aristocrat, one of whose sons climbed to topmost heights in American political history, drove from his garden several boys. To one more stubborn than the others he angrily said, "Get out, you little Nigger." The little boy ran through the gate and yelled, "My grandma say you is a Nigger yourself." The old man "folded his tent and quietly stole away." Not many years later his son, a magnificent specimen of intellectual and physical manhood, was probably kept from the presidency by the *bar sinister*, that dark strain that lost one of our presidents recently thousands of votes before the confiscation of the book, giving his family tree, that nearly ruined his chances for the White House.

A colored grandmother came from the South, who had money enough to buy most valuable property in the heart of our business section. She was finally cheated out of it, as was another old lady here, whose mother was the daughter of her owner, her father, one of the slaves. She was robbed out of an immense estate in later years.

There were the Berrys, the Flowers, the Hickeys, the Lees and many other families composed of southern white fathers and colored mothers, whose descendants are now white. They came to this city over fifty years ago, many of them with thousands of dollars and servants galore. In some cases the white owner came and remained with his colored common-law wife; in others they visited them periodically unless, as often happened, a dark cloud in the shape of some colored gentleman arose on the horizon of his affections, in which case the faithless female was left bankrupt. Not so many years ago there came from Alabama, a colored family which turned white en route, and settled in the West End. The mother, who was a splendid woman, had two beautiful girls and a son not so beautiful. The white father used to pay long visits. The mother tried to learn the Italian language but passed to a world where neither color nor language was a requisite for celestial society. The younger girl married the son of a white business man.

In the early days, as we have shown, miscegenation was not the horrible monster that has been materialized today. White men, before the war, recognized their children and, when in hard luck, often sold them. This town formerly had a number of descendants of great Americans. Even now, some of Thomas Jefferson's colored descendants live within a few blocks of where this article is being written, which is less than two blocks from where Harriet Beecher Stowe gave birth to Uncle Tom's Cabin. Soon after the war many colored men had white wives in this city. Their children generally did, when possible, as did the colored children of white men, that is, they became white. All United States citizens realize that skin, if white, affords far greater opportunities for success than brains. Today there is little racial intermixture in this city. White men who incline to Negro women, and their name is legion, generally find them only in the "tenderloin." Few colored women, apart from prostitutes or ignorant servant girls, are sufficiently credulous or mercenary to yield to the blandishments or cash of those, who not only despise the women they use, but lynch or burn their fathers, brothers and mothers. Ninety colored women have been lynched in the United States! Not many colored men form association with white women for several reasons. First, assertions to the contrary notwithstanding, Negro men prefer dark women, since their emotions and passions are greater and more steadfast than blonde types. Second, the few colored men who are tempted to eat of the fruit, forbidden, not by God, but the K. K. K., are either halted by prejudice, or butchered by police.

MUSICIANS AND SINGERS

Of colored devotees of Orpheus and Apollo who flourished here before the Civil War, contributing to the pleasures of white and black society, few traces are left behind of their brief but melodious existence. Among the great singers of that day we note Mrs. Townsend, then Miss Martha Mitchell. During the social reign of the Tinsleys, her daughter, Ann Baltimore, studied in Oberlin College, taught music, became a good pianist and was the first colored owner of a piano. In later years, Prof. Ferguson flourished and his great choral society journeyed with seventy-five members to Louisville and remained several days. Some of its survivors still tell of the pleasures of that memorable trip. Charlie Hawkins was a good pianist and all around musician, who furnished music for church and social functions. Prof. "Dave" Hamilton and his singing orchestra, sang and played its way into many homes of the city's wealthy citizens. He was greatly in demand and made a big reputation. His widow, Ella Hamilton, is well laden with reminiscences of his achievements. The Harper Sisters attained quite a reputation at home and on the concert stages as singers of jubilee songs. Our church choirs were always excellent. Prof. Harry Jackson, who died recently in Chicago, was a famous basso profundo and choir master. "Blind Hawkins," one of our best pianists, was a protege of his. Prof. Alfred Quarles was a great organist of that period, and Prof. Charles Trotter was also largely in the limelight. Prof. Wm. Johnson, known as "Bill" Johnson, had an orchestra which furnished music for quite a number of white affairs, but its reputation was based upon the dance music furnished for the big K. of P. balls, as Garnett Lodge, Excelsior Co., Polar Star, and Palestine Co. B were in all their glory, and could secure any hall or picnic ground in Cincinnati.

Mrs. Ernestine Nesbit, daughter of Peter H. Clark, and wife of Street Nesbit, Esq., now of St. Louis, was a most accomplished pianist and had a large number of pupils.

Leubrie Hill, well-known pianist, cabaret musician and stage performer, whose career was brief but brilliant, spent a large part of his life and began his theatrical career in this city.

Gussie L. Davis. Ah! thirty years ago that was a name to conjure with, for in the realm of popular songs he reigned supreme. His glorious career began in this city, and after going to New York, "the garden of the gods," he became the father of a dozen songs, the charms of whose harmony encircled the civilized world.

Clarence Jones, fine pianist and record maker.

W. P. Dabney, in 1894, had a studio in Wurlitzers, where he gave lessons on guitar, banjo, mandolin and bandurria. He taught in the very wealthiest families, had two string orchestras, one white, one colored. Their prices were of the highest for those days. Some patrons preferred white musicians, others colored. He used the colored orchestra for the receptions given Prince Hohenlohe at banker Schmidlap's, for those at the Cincinnati Womans' Club, and other swell functions and places, but at the Gibson House banquet for Bryan, and other big affairs his white orchestra was in demand. He forsook music for politics. Ragtime came. That practically changed entirely the condition of affairs. The whites wanted amusement rather than music, and so "Pork Chops" and his band became the center of attraction for those desiring that class of entertainment. In late years music has become an established feature in all of our

Masonic Parade — Hotel Sterling
Int. Conclave, Knights Templar, Imperial Council Mystic Shrine, August, 1920

churches, social and general life, and there are many proficient pianists, singers, a few organists and many choir directors. Prof. John Hoffman has had here now for several years an orchestra of high class musicians who have made an enviable reputation. Jazz and the craze for "colored" music has resulted in the formation of quite a number of small orchestras in town. Our concert music is all good and Negroes are singing and playing for radio broadcasting. Unfortunately, possibly, there is now put in our folk songs so much of the classic, that much of the real music is being eliminated by excessive refinement. This condition has generally been true of the whites, and so, music hungry, they have turned to feast upon Negro musical products, but alas, Negroes are beginning to travel the same road and therefore we may expect in the future, music that affects the mind, but leaves untouched the soul.

THE TURF

The proximity to Latonia and other great Kentucky tracks made this city a rendezvous and dwelling place during the racing season for jockeys and trainers. Old Col. Bob Harlan was known here as a horse owner and turfman over a half century ago. He even made a trip to England.

"Old Jim Scott," father of Jas. Scott, coachman for the Tafts, came from Virginia, and at Tree Hill, Fair Oaks and other great Virginia tracks won fame as a jockey. Among modern knights of the saddle, Isaac Murphy, Tony Hamilton, Lonnie and Al Clayton, Ollie Lewis, "Pike" Barnes, "Soup" Perkins, all great jockeys, great stake winners. Their fame was international. Ollie Lewis, who won the first Kentucky Derby, was in this city many years. His widow, now over eighty years of age, lives here with the Moseleys, old friends of hers. A legion of the lesser lights also flourished here. Then there was "Brown Dick," the great Kentucky trainer, and in late years, Will Perkins, of Lexington, not only a marvelous trainer, but for a time stable partner of "Mose" Moore, the great colored capitalist and horse owner of Dayton. There are no more colored jockeys in America. Their day has seemingly gone forever. They made too much money, they lived too high. When they began to be accused of "putting over" winners and pooling their interests, the newspapers made so much scandal about the "Black Racing Trust," the white jockeys showed so much jealousy and developed such a spirit of animosity, that the "color question" became acute, and the Negro was eliminated. An inglorious end, but as he made much of the history of the turf in the last hundred years, he may some day stage a comeback. Stranger things have happened.

SALOONS

"The Old Dumas House," in its golden age, long before the Civil War, had its saloon, a most creditable affair for those days. A few pool rooms existed in the East End. After the war the West End had its saloons, pool and billiard rooms. Copeland and Jones had a well-known place; Andy Slaughter and then Dan Carter ran the Dumas Hotel bar. Beginning in the nineties the Old Timers were going or gone. Long John's saloon on West Fifth Street was for a long time the center of attraction. Ollie Dempsey's Bar was always full, as he was very popular. Gaither's place on Fifth and Central Avenue gave way for his new cafe called "The Turf," located on West Fifth, where the drug store now stands. It was said to have cost $25,000 and was our finest. Harry Gardner's saloon was followed by Crittenden's. Afterwards, from Chattanooga, came Will Nunn, who soon had an immense trade. At Carlisle and John, Les Blackburn and Charlie Thomas; on Fifth, John Thomas. All popular places, where beer flowed and merriment reigned. The Douglass League had a class that consumed large quantities of champagne and a number of white business men had cards of admission. The Ruffin Club carried all of the old regulars. The best billiard players were found there; the most select and consistent worshippers of "draw poker." Among the numberless sports of the period none were greater favorites than John Stowers, "the fashion plate," and "Jack" Dillihay. The former has gone to his reward, but "Old Jack," a little disfigured, is still hale and hearty, and just as eager to bet on a tip as though horses were not as uncertain now as in the days when first from Kentucky he came. In the early days white saloons were wide open; everybody's money was good. As prejudice grew, with the exception of a few, the lines were drawn against colored customers. The growing resentment of Negroes at such conditions came to a climax when the prohibition issue was fought out at the polls. Determined, Sampson-like, to get their enemies, even though they themselves suffered, they voted dry and to the saloons said good-bye.

CATERERS

This city has had many caterers. In that field "color" caused little complication, and the achievement of the individual, regardless of race, was only limited by his capability.

FOSSETTS

The most prominent of the early caterers were the Fossetts. The parent stock came from Virginia, and its blood from the father of Democracy, Thomas Jefferson. "Jos" Fossett was the son of America's president and remained with him at Monticello until he went above to join the great galaxy of other notables. The sons of "Jos" Fossett were Peter, William and Jesse. Peter and William were famous as caterers, and royal were the receptions and banquets they served. They acquired wealth and later Peter became Rev. Peter Fossett, a famous preacher, the father of Ohio Baptists and the greatest exemplar, expounder and disciplinarian of that doctrine in this state. "He practiced what he preached." The marriage of his daughter, Miss Mattie, was the grandest matrimonial event of that time. The older Fossetts passed away, and John Miller, who had been in charge for Wilson and Reeder, the great white caterers, of this city, married Edith Fossett and became virtually the head of the Fossett catering industry. He died some years ago, and the widow, Edith Fossett Miller, still very successfully carries on catering for many of the old families who were patrons of her father and husband.

John Miller

Lloyd Johnson, a pillar of Allen Temple, and a number of smaller caterers in times long past, did quite an amount of business in the city.

CONNELLY

Mr. Robert Connelly, custodian of Christ Church, embarked in the catering business many years ago, and his acquaintanceship with the large number of wealthy members of that church caused him to obtain so many high class patrons that he finally retired from church service to devote himself exclusively to the business in which he has been ably assisted by his wife to that stage which has made them financially independent.

SIMMS

Washington Simms developed from an Avondale Club stewardship into a well-known caterer. The business that he acquired was largely due to Mrs. Simms, who worked most energetically in its development.

MERCHANT

Miss Daisy Simms married Harry Merchant. Her large experience from working with her mother engendered an efficiency that was most valuable after her separation from her husband and consequent dependence upon her own resources. She built up a splendid catering business, but unwisely associated with herself an unnecessary adjunct in the shape of a white partner. The firm thus created was known as the Mercamp Catering Company. The dissolution of that partnership, now said to have resulted, will probably greatly improve her prospects.

BERRY

For many years Ed. J. Berry has been listed among this city's leading caterers. Apart from serving receptions of all kinds he has had charge of the commissary department of some of our largest summer resorts.

OTHER CATERERS

There is a class of small caterers who go from house to house, cooking and serving for special entertainments. The profits are small but they maintain a large number of people who were formerly cooks or waiters. The big white hotels now have the cream of events which colored caterers formerly controlled.

ORIGIN AND EVOLUTION OF OUR UNDERTAKERS

Over a half century ago, when Negroes died, white undertakers buried them. Now very rarely does any white undertaker bury a colored person, for an agreement has been made by them in that regard with our colored undertakers. It is the only business in which colored men have practically a monopoly. The beginning of this gigantic industry started in a very simple manner over fifty years ago. A colored man came here from Tennessee and after some struggle, acquired enough money to buy a hack. He was a handsome yellow individual, and though his name was Wm. Porter, everybody called him "Bill." A little while and "Bill" had two hacks. A woman, Mrs. Livingston, died in the South, and relatives were notified that the body had been shipped here for burial. "Bill" borrowed a hearse and with his two hacks, went to the train, secured the body, and after a lot of trouble, managed to have it consigned to mother earth. "Bill's" friend, George Hayes, now United States court crier, advised him to go into the undertaking business. Elated by his success in his first effort at planting remains, "Bill" was not at all loth. He labored incessantly. His business grew and as his wealth increased, so did his name, until in a few years "Bill" had become Mr. Wm. M. Porter. For a long time he was one of the largest taxpayers among Cincinnati's colored citizens. His wife, a very brainy and estimable woman, went the way of all flesh; his son, "Willie," journeyed to Chicago; Arthur, the youngest, is a well known singer and actor; and Jennie, the daughter, stands prominently before the public as principal of Harriet Beecher Stowe School.

There are no more undertakers, but this city is now full of funeral directors, who are exceptionally well fitted to handle the remains of the departed in the latest and most highly approved style. 'Tis the one profession in which the Negro is most lovable and reliable, the one profession in which every atom of his energy is ever in evidence. No soul ever leaves Cincinnati so suddenly but what some hearse is ready for its body, but what some funeral director is softly singing, "I Am Waiting, My Darling, for Thee."

BARBERS

FOUNTAIN LEWIS, SR.

Back in the early forties came Fountain Lewis to Cincinnati. He soon sought and found work in a barber shop kept by Ferree, a Frenchman, famed for his accomplishments along tonsorial lines. As years rolled on

he older grew, and disposing of his shop to Lewis, went to New York. The business prospered and in the fifties Fountain Lewis became known as "Old Fountain Lewis," to distinguish him from "Young Fountain," who had made his appearance in this "vale of tears." "Old Fountain's" place was now the great resort of the bankers and aristocrats. Grant, Lincoln and other famous dignitaries were soothed into slumber by the rhythmic music of his scissors, or the magic touch of his razor. He moved into various localities as changing conditions came, but until he died, not so many years ago, his trade was still aristocratic. A noble man was he, prominent in church and conspicuous in all movements for elevation of his people. The business descended to Fountain Lewis, Jr., and until recent years his establishment was one of the most magnificent in town. Later he embarked with his son Fred in the undertaking business and that, with other investments, caused him to dispose of his interests in the enterprise that had been guided by the hands of his family for nearly three-quarters of a century.

In the early days colored men enjoyed a monopoly of the barber business.

Henry Mount, of Philadelphia, became an officer of Union Baptist Church, and in 1845 opened a barber shop on Columbia, now Second Street.

Mr. Mount died in 1865. Robert Griffin, also from Philadelphia, worked for Mount and followed him in the business. He ran the shop until 1869. Lewis Cunningham succeeded Mr. Griffin. John E. Dixon continued to work there until 1876 when he became, and still remains, its proprietor. Many of the old citizens have worked in this shop. It has never been opened for business on Sunday.

At the Burnet House, Hunt, Wm. Ross and later Warren King, had the shop before he took charge of the Cumberland Flats. About twenty-five years ago, Wm. Ross had a splendid shop on Vine near the Grand Theatre. Fountain Lewis' shops were on Race, above Sixth, and on Vine, between Fourth and Fifth. John McRoberts was the tonsorial king of Walnut Hills until Thad Bramlette appeared on McMillan, near Peebles Corner. E. L. Thomas, now the manager of Hotel Sterling, had a shop on the Broadway side of the site now occupied by the John Van Range Co., on Fifth Street. He moved into the swell new Ortiz apartment building, at Fourth and Sycamore, and held on there until that building, a few years ago, was torn down to make way for the railroad office building. "Ed" Thomas was very precise, most particular, and had a very quick temper. As a result he conveyed to a number of barbers the information that they could quit, which they did. Others realized they could, without being told, and they did also. In short, "Ed" became known as the father of Cincinnati's modern barbers, since from his shop no less than eight men graduated who became boss barbers. Among them were S. H. Alexander, who now has a commodious establishment on Main Street, and "Hutch" Ross, on Walnut Street. Louis Cunningham, long years before the war, was barber at The Old Dumas House. In his day, Governor Pinchback, as a young fellow, did odd jobs around the place and afterwards grew to be a boon companion of "Sandy" Shumate, the proprietor. "Old Man" Fortune was for years barber at the Palace Hotel. "Old Griff" Watson had a barber shop near Fifth and Vine, where Mabley and Carew's department store stands. He was the porter and proprietor. As the former, he gathered in all the tips; as the latter, he hired or fired the barbers. Major Hardy followed him in the business and had a shop near the site of the Lyceum. John Jackson used to have the swell shop on Main in Lincoln Inn Court, where the Southern Ohio Bank now handles its millions.

In the early days the journeyman barber was as temperamental as a prima donna. If he got into a little poker game (there were no craps), the customer simply had to wait if he wanted his services. On Mondays many barbers failed to show up for work and if they had enough cash on hand they did not even show up Tuesday. Barber shops were the great places for gossip and the white customers were generally quite well informed as to the doings of Negro society. The patrons and barbers were very chummy in many ways. The Negro barber, as a workman, was an artist. The razor in his hands became an instrument that made sweet melody as it charmed away the grass that grew on facial lawns, but alas, from a business standpoint the Negro journeyman barber left much to be desired. Finally white men came into the barber business. The Negro barbers laughed. More white men came. Less laughing. The white man brought business methods. He stood for the ridicule and kept working, quiet, easy, like the Boll Weevil in a crop of cotton. He gave new names to old things. Sanitary and sterilized became his great words, the open sesame for the coming generation. He was on the job from early Monday morning till late Saturday night. The inevitable happened. Old customers died and then came their sons "who knew not Joseph." Negro barber shops for white patrons melted away as snow before a July sun. White barber shops became "as thick as autumnal leaves in Valombrosa." Only a few "colored" are now remaining to remind us of the past. Skillman's, formerly Fountain Lewis's big shop on lower Vine, with its $5,000 or more a year rental, Ross on Walnut, Ross and Alexander on Main, and a few others.

THE LAST OF THE "BUTLERS"

The day of the Negro butler practically ended with the departure of "Ben" Hunter, whom God called only a few years ago. He was a "Prince," the greatest of a class that began with the aristocracy of this city. He was in the employ of Captain and Mrs. W. P. Anderson, of Grandin Road, a family of unlimited wealth. The Andersons and the Longworths were bound by ties of blood, linked by chains, fraternal and social. They all knew "Ben." He ruled the house absolutely, but with such finesse, that Old Captain Anderson was content to "pass on," knowing that with "Ben" his widow would be spared the infinitesimal annoyances that the care of such a large estate entails. For nearly forty years "Ben" was in charge. Smooth, dark complexion, medium height, corpulence that comes from a clear conscience and good food, dressed in the height of fashion, all the dainty ways and classy mannerisms of those he served, that was "Ben," the "Black Beau Brummel" of Grandin Road, the last of the butlers. In St. Mary's Hospital, eloquently talking, he glided into eternity. At the graveyard, none wept more bitterly than Mrs. W. P. Anderson, the ninety-year-old widow of Captain Anderson.

Almost a contemporary of "Ben's" was Alexander Norris, a handsome, tall, light mulatto, who for many years was the butler of the Wiggins and Skinners. They thought the world of "Alec," whose loyalty and efficiency fully merited the affection they felt and praise accorded. Finally incapacitated, the family pension maintained him until death.

Slightly preceding the days of Norris came "Charlie Banks," "Old Baltimore," who for many years was with the old Woods family. Banks was a "high liver" and though of brown com-

Lincoln Avenue, Walnut Hills

plexion, yet was hail fellow well met with the Dutch of Corryville. He wore this world as a loose garment and few cares ever clouded the sunshine of his soul. He left two daughters and a wife whose loyalty and fidelity should ever bring her the best of good fortune.

Far, far in distant days, was the beginning of Frank Jones, "black, but comely." Grave, courtly, gallant. "Old Frank" Jones, as we saw him, white whiskered, gentle, well poised, bore nobly his ninety years. He, as butler for the Bowlers, served the creme de la creme of the aristocracy and also the Prince of Wales, who was here in '48. During the Civil War, he was sent across the river with a most important message, and because of his complexion, had difficulty in escaping being shipped South as a slave. No more could he be induced to cross the Ohio until years after the Negro was firmly entrenched behind, as Lawyer Brown would say, "the bulwarks of liberty." The old aristocratic families have gone, and so have their butlers.

CHARLIE TUCKER

A most unique character was, and is, Charlie Tucker, six feet tall, yellow, handsome and happy. He was with the Fleischmanns when they lived far from the palace in Avondale that later became their home. "Charlie" was with them when they got the first carriage and remained with them as long as life lasted for the founders of the family. In spirit, in loyalty, in service, he is a Fleischmann in all but the name. He was well provided for by the generosity of that family, and his old age is being comfortably spent with his charming daughter Grace, wife of "Father" James.

THEATRES

Only in the last few years have colored citizens here been financially interested in theatres. Ollie Dempsey, well-known sporting man of this city, opened the Pekin Theatre, which was operated by his widow and her husband, Mr. Oscar Hawkins. It is located on West Fifth Street and is now owned by Mr. Wm. Gunn, a native of Cincinnati.

Major E. G. Gaither had a theatre on West Fifth Street, next to his cafe. The theatre, after being in operation a long time, was closed on the grounds of non-compliance with the laws regulating theatres and public buildings. He then operated for a time the old Lyceum Theatre.

"From little acorns mighty oaks arise." Mr. Rebhun, president of the Rebhun Last Co., had a colored cook. She often lamented over the race prejudice that fostered discrimination in local theatres. Mr. Rebhun listened to the lamentations; also to her opinion that a theatre for colored people would be so well patronized that the "standing room only" sign would be nightly in evidence. The Lincoln Theatre, at Fifth and John Streets, was the result. Mr. Rebhun had two partners, Mr. Morton and Mr. Bruner. Contrary to expectation, the "standing room only" sign was not often in evidence, although the land and building cost a great deal of money. Mr. Rebhun died. Mr. John B. Bruner bought out the interest of Mr. Morton and became the sole proprietor. He now owns, in addition, the Roosevelt Theatre. Both places received highest commendation from the Building Commissioners Office, Committee on Sanitation, and the State Examining Board. Attaches are colored, as well as the manager.

There are a number of smaller picture houses on West Fifth Street whose prejudice against admission of colored patrons has been removed by the scarcity of white patrons and consequent diminution of box office receipts.

THREE BIG MOVEMENTS

TRUE REFORMERS

The "True Reformers," mushroom like, sprang up almost in a night. It began in the Dabney Building on McAllister Street, soon attained a membership of about two thousand, bought a hall on West Sixth Street. Its failure was caused by a $200,000 defalcation at its national office in Richmond, Virginia.

N. A. A. C. P.

The Cincinnati branch of the National Association for the Advancement of Colored People in its early days had a large and loyal membership. Interest in it gradually died, since our people require constant stimulus to hold their attention for any length of time, and the fight for race rights and against race abuses generally appeals only to those who realize the value of such action.

THE U. N. I. A.

The Universal Negro Improvement Association, commonly known as the Garvey Movement, has had a large following in this city. Its headquarters on George Street are always thronged with its adherents. Its founder, incarcerated by the United States Government, is regarded as a martyr, and as desperate efforts for his relief are continually made, the zeal of the members is kept at fever heat and Sir William Ware, the president, is strongly supported.

NEWSPAPERS

The newspaper life of our group has been vast and varied. There have been many false conceptions, others that "died aborning," as Wm. L. ("Bill") Anderson so sweetly said in his toast to newspapers at the Charlie Bentley banquet concerning "The Enterprise," a paper that I published for one year and owned for a few months. We have weeklies that

Chapel Street, Walnut Hills

lasted a week and a daily that had a name though the paper itself never came. "The Colored Citizen," by Rev. Geo. Williams, and a few other periodicals had temporary existence, but Dan Rudd's paper, The Catholic Tribune, lasted several years. "The Voice of the People," by Sam B. Hill, dwelt with us a while, then "The Rostrum," by W. L. Anderson, held the boards a few years. Others by Prof. Chas. Bell, Tom Triplett and Tom Johnson came and went, their lives short but strenuous. Those were the days of violent personalities that added so much to the joys of living. "The Brotherhood," owned by Dr. Williams, had an intermittent and feverish existence for a long time. It was very strong during election times. There have been many papers of predatory proclivities, whose entrances and exits in the journalistic world occasioned much financial flurry and some political worry. Some whose editors made a special business of "grafting" through this and adjacent states. Their policy has made it quite hard for legitimate colored newspapers to secure advertising from white merchants who generally follow the American custom of blaming all Negroes for the actions of a few. Possibly the most versatile newspaper pirate we have had was Gray, whose paper, "The Bee," furnished him golden opportunity for the display of talents that would have done credit to the famous stock manipulators of Wall Street. Gray's greatest feat took place in one of our hottest political campaigns. He brought out, on the same day, a Republican edition of "The Bee" in the morning, a Democratic edition in the afternoon. He collected from candidates on both sides before they discovered the duplicity. He then departed, for the financial fertility of this field was exhausted. "The Pilot," edited by W. L. Anderson and owned by him and nine other prominent citizens, made great history and did a lot of damage to "The Union" treasury before it joined in the Cincinnati newspaper cemetery, a year later, about fifty predecessors. It was a good strong sheet, catered to the churches, and made its battle with "The Union" the most vicious newspaper war ever witnessed in this city. "In such a victory there was glory; in such defeat no disgrace." "The Union" is now about twenty years old, has never missed an issue, has never knowingly published a falsehood, has ever lived up to its obligations. "The Optimist," edited by J. W. Gray, appeared about two years ago. It was a very ambitious publication, attained quite an amount of prominence until its absorption by "The Union" last year. Several others started, one or two still in existence. The Fraternal Monitor, a monthly publication, was owned and edited by Gen. Jos. L. Jones for a number of years. Many of the churches now have weekly bulletins which leave, from the standpoint of publicity, much to be desired. All scientific advertising experts unite in declaring that the newspaper is the best medium for dissemination of news, general advertising, and such publicity as has for its object the conveyance of information to the masses.

MORAL CONDITIONS TODAY

Every indication points to an enormous increase of immorality unless some disastrous national cataclysm, some gigantic upheaval of social and economic conditions shock civilized humanity back to reason. Negroes, in contact with whites, subconsciously sense aught that affects them, and are ever ready to move along lines of least resistance. Their emulation generally follows the pathway of pleasure, for the narrow road of virtue is filled with obstacles. "The World War" brought luxury, which has developed enormously indulgence in automobiles, the vehicles of Venus; alcohol, that forbidden product of prohibition; narcotics, the soul destroying fruit of the Orient. Newspapers are filled with the notorious deeds, scandals and viciousness of prominent white people. The screens teem with pictures depicting every detail of deviltry, all phases in the sensuality of love, and the final, though long delayed, triumph of goodness. We see naked women in the "movies," and we see them on the streets. The way that the demi monde sat in the parlors of pleasure, ladies now sit in public places, their faces laden with rouge and paint. Their beautiful lips are fast learning to be repositories of cigarettes. Colored girls and women are apt pupils. They are beginning to do the same things, for they feel that what is right for high white society surely can't be wrong for high colored society. As are women, so are men. The examples enumerated are doubly demoralizing for our colored people, since they are still too far behind in the real material progress of this country to indulge in the habits and luxuries that nations only attain at the height of their greatness and which generally prelude the beginning of their descent to the bottom from which they started.

"THE GODDESS OF CHANCE"
Faro—Poker—Craps

Negro gambling in the early days was of the high class in vogue among whites. As slaves and servants, the process was easily learned, the example more easily emulated. Faro Bank, something unknown to the present generation, and Draw Poker were the great games. Fortunes came and went in a night. A sporting crowd from all over the country would come to the "Queen City" of the West. The Dumas House had, as did all hotels of that day, its place for "bucking the tiger," and in it was the biggest colored Faro game in the country. Time passed. Money became less plentiful. The high grade of Negroes gave way to the lower. Gone were Shumate, and his friends, Pinchback, Church, Langston, Troy, Fossett, Thomas, Tinsley and the high society rollers of earlier days. The West End now had the population. Cheap saloons flourished and "craps" came. From then until now that species of gambling, the lowest, yet best for the poorest, the most remunerative for the house, is the favorite among modern worshipers of the Goddess of Chance. It gives quick action. The man with the dime, if lucky, has as much chance as the man with the dollar. Several years ago I saw, for the last time, John Alexander. That name means nothing now, but once John Alexander was known from coast to coast. Nice looking, yellow, medium sized, plainly dressed, that was the great Alexander, "the Black Prince" of his legion of white associates. In dealing Faro he had few equals, no superiors. North or South, he was admitted to the biggest of white games, for his credit was unlimited and he is said to have lost, without the lift of an eyelash, as much as twenty-five thousand dollars at a sitting. Very wealthy at one time, splendid property, but alas it all had wings. Broken, old, with Faro a joy of the past, he spent much time in this city, staked often by fellow sports who knew of his ancient glory. I still see him as he appeared, sick, weak, faded, shabbily dressed, standing at the edge of a crap table down-town, jostled in a crowd of rough, common Negroes that he would not, in his good days, have permitted to touch the hem of his garments; that he would not have spat upon. But the lean years had come and though he stood a pauper, where once he reigned as king, he was as poised and calm as ever. His money was gone, but his courtesy was still as courtly as of yore. Tears came to my eyes as, in passing, I heard his gentle, "Excuse me, please," to an unheeding young roustabout into whose rough life the charm of politeness had never come.

The take-off from a good crap game should be not under $100 a night. The whites used to call it "a Nigger game," but if that cognomen was true at one time, it certainly is so no longer, for the whites have captured it, bag and baggage. White games flourish in town to which Negroes have access, but only two are owned and operated by colored men. They get only a small part of the profits of Negro gambling, for after money is paid for police and political protection, comparatively little is left. Thousands and thousands of dollars are spent by Negroes in craps, handbooks and policy. In the past the "color line" was not much in evidence in the small public gambling resorts, however, apart from betting on race horses, colored gamblers and whites now rarely enjoy inter-racial relations, since, with but few exceptions, Negroes have too little money to compete with white men who are able and ready to bet big money on the turn of card or dice.

PULLMAN PORTERS

This city has for many years been a place of residence for many Pullman porters. They have contributed greatly to the cause of good citizenship, since many of them have been prominent in every walk of church, business and fraternal life. They own a great deal of property and are noted for being listed among our most solid and law abiding people, since the sporty, spendthrift element is dead or eliminated from the service.

TWO FAMOUS CHEFS

Henry Washam had charge of the private car of M. E. Ingalls, president of the Big "4" Railroad, and Henry Clay had similar duties on the car of General Manager Stevens of the C. & O. Railroad. They were both great chefs and royal were the meals they served to the many dignitaries who were guests of their employers. They and their families were well thought of in this community. When Washam crossed the great river, Clay took his place, and a few years later joined him over there. We shall never see their like again.

MESSENGER

No railroad messenger stood higher in this section of the world than Taylor Lightfoot, the messenger of President Ingalls. Lightfoot had for years been a butler in his family, and his services indicated such loyalty and efficiency that the rise of Mr. Ingalls meant the promotion of Lightfoot. He became the private messenger of Mr. Ingalls, and as such his power was practically unlimited. Mr. Ingalls, his son George, now a prominent railroad magnate of New York, and in fact all of the family, regarded Lightfoot with the greatest esteem and affection. A few years ago he passed away. His widow resides on Walnut Hills.

GRAVEYARDS!
Our Greatest Enterprise!

We have clustered five great profitable avenues of human interest. Preachers, churches, doctors, undertakers, graveyards. The two outstanding general investments indicative of strong racial traits, are the providing of many churches for the welfare of their souls and two large graveyards for the rest of their bodies.

The Colored American Cemetery was once in a choice section of Avondale. The rapidly increasing white population soon discovered that Negro tombstones, even though white, were undesirable works of art. Their delicate nostrils seemingly scented an aroma arising from their defunct colored brethren which gave to the atmosphere a tang not redolent with fragrance. In short, the whites objected to the black burying ground. Rev. Geo. Williams, colored ex-pastor of Union Baptist Church, was in the legislature. The legislature, largely through the connivance of Williams, it is said, caused the condemnation and removal of the graveyard. It is now known as The Colored American Cemetery, is located in the vicinity of Oakley, and is a very prosperous proposition for its stockholders who, un-Negro like, are living examples of the adage, "A still tongue maketh a wise head."

The other graveyard, The Union Baptist Cemetery, is located on Cleves Pike, Covedale, now known as Price Hill. It is called "Warsaw Burying Ground." It is owned by the Union Baptist Church and "since the memory of man runneth not to the contrary," it has been a grand source of revenue to that institution. In a few of the white burying grounds some colored people are buried, notably in the Catholic Cemetery of St. Joseph and at Spring Grove, one of the most beautiful cities of the dead in America. The same criticism is made concerning colored graveyards as of residences, namely, that they are not carefully kept, that too little regard is paid to appearance. If the criticism is true, then the removal in the near future of cause for such complaint is "a consummation devoutly to be wished."

[7]

HOTELS

After "The Old Dumas House" ceased being a hotel, a number of mushroom establishments sprung up bearing the name of hotel, but they were only lodging houses. In the last thirty-five years, however, a few good ones came, such as The Sumner House, which flourished in the early nineties; the "Bee" Hotel, and then the Douglass Hotel. They were owned by colored people. About six years ago the Old St. Claire Hotel, formerly the habitat of wealthy white citizens, was made into and still is a hotel for colored people. It is called the Sterling and is a magnificent structure. Its first owner fitted it up elaborately, had all colored help, and ran it as an up-to-date establishment. He was a white business man and recently sold it to other whites, as colored men would not venture to invest in the proposition. The manager and help are colored. The Gordon Hotel on Walnut Hills is another white-owned establishment, but it has a colored manager and the help is colored. There are enough colored people to own a first-class hotel in this city, but as yet they have not gotten over the stage of talking big business instead of doing it.

"BOB AND WEBB"

No sketch of McAllister Street for the last thirty years would be complete without mention of "Bob" and Webb. The former was "Bob" Ellyson, who as a Pullman porter, lost both legs. They were finally replaced by others made of cork. "Bob" was custodian of The Douglass League Club, and as such became a great favorite with its members and citizens generally, as he was a "natchel" (natural) born sport. Webb, or rather John Webb, had charge of the Dabney Building and when, as frequently happened, the tenants departed from the straight and narrow path, morally or financially, Webb steered them back with a flow of profanity that would have done credit to the captain of a pirate ship. After a long lapse of busy years, Webb passed, and was planted in Warsaw Cemetery. Between him and Bob there was a fraternization characteristic of the customary relations of a dog and cat. "Bob" drifted to New York, ran a bootblack parlor, and by virtue of his love for "policy and poker," became afflicted with an impecuniosity that seemed destined to be chronic. But, you can never tell. A month ago "Bob" returned. He wanted to see dear old McAllister Street. In a limousine he rode with his niece and chauffeur. Our club veterans gathered, gave him a dinner in the old club rooms of the Dabney Building. The mystery of his transposition from bootblack to plutocrat was solved. A few months previously "Bob" had bought a ticket of the baseball pool. It won, and our "Bob" was richer by eight thousand dollars. He is now back in New York, owns a home, and has, we hope, forever dispensed with "policy and poker."

DUEL TO THE DEATH
ON CARLISLE AVENUE
(From "The Union" of Jan. 20, 1922.)

[Of the many fatal affrays in "The Black Belt," this duel shows most clearly the desperation of our men when swayed by the passion of love.]

Thursday morning came, Thursday, January the eleventh, and with it a tragedy that has no parallel in the history of "Colored Cincinnati," for on that fateful day two young men, talented, handsome, of good families, fought a duel that brought death to both, and a lifetime of grief to their devoted relatives.

It is a sad, sad story, redolent with the aroma of the underworld, yet our sorrow for the dead should not cause us to forget our duty to the living.

There are many young men and women today dwelling upon the brink of disaster that this story may cause to pause and retrace their steps to the narrow path that ends in honor and prosperity.

"God moves in a mysterious way His wonders to perform." The sacrifice of these two young men undoubtedly was for a purpose that may in time be unfolded to those whose hearts are now laden with suffering.

The eternal triangle is again before us. Both young men spring from reputable families. Anthony Thomas, twenty-six years of age, came here with his people from Virginia many years ago. Tall, handsome, good-natured, he, like his ancestors, loved hunting, fishing and field sports. Early in life he went into the army and on the battlefields of France, he won distinction both for bravery and marksmanship. He was in the railroad service for awhile and then became chauffeur for a well-known business firm.

Jas. W. Stewart, Jr., after leaving school, also became an attache of the railroad, and was very popular as a dining car man. His people are old residents here, well and favorably known, and so James had the best of instruction and family training.

The parents knew not of the mad infatuation of their sons. The woman in the case, the flame that drew the moths, is young, the mother of two children, and so in deference to them and her relatives, we will not call her name. Her brief career has been filled with the sensations that crowd into some lives, while others are left conspicuous by their absence.

A good-looking woman, petite, attractive, from childhood she possessed that charm which ever attracts males of similar temperament, a magnetism that needs no assistance from beauty to enhance its powers. She married early. A most estimable man. A brief sojourn in New York. The divorce court.

Some way, some how, young Stewart drifted across her path. 'Twas fate? In one brief moment he was a changed man. Madly infatuated, madly jealous. He quarreled with her. Though said to be engaged, finally life became a burden to both.

She met Anthony Thomas. From friendship to love was but a step. "She folded her tent and quietly stole away." That was the last straw for Stewart, whose mind was inflamed with anger, jealousy and the drinking to drown his sorrows. He left his room with the intention of bringing her back or to die trying. There is an old adage, "Be well off with the old love before being on with the new." She did not know that, and so to Anthony she became engaged, and to his room quickly fled for protection.

Stewart missed her, he knew not where the gods had placed her, but his love sense told him, that where his rival was, there his sweetheart was, and so he found her! Most desperate was his courage. *Think of it!* He knew the man with her was a brave soldier, a medal winner for marksmanship, and yet he went to take that girl away from him! Ye gods, he should always have, both from friend and foe, credit for gameness.

He knocked. Anthony Thomas, clad only in pajamas, threw open the door, smilingly unconscious of harm, for he was in the house of his friends. A word of anger, the scream of the woman as she threw herself upon Stewart, the flash of the revolver as a bullet ploughed its way through Anthony's leg! She tried frantically to hold Stewart, but was powerless against his frenzied strength. From under her arm he fired again! The bullet lodged in the left lung of Anthony, who had reached and fallen across the bed in a rush for his gun. He got it. An automatic. The girl, swifter than lightning, dropped out of range. Four shots! Three in the body, one *flush between the eyes! The troubles of Stewart were over.*

Lying on the floor, Anthony Thomas called the owner of the house, apologized for the trouble. He was taken to the hospital and before dying that night, told his mother he was sorry that he had not died before she found out about it.

Two bright young men, both game, both well reared, who could and should have died in a better cause. We have no blame for the young woman. We are all more or less creatures of circumstances and children of destiny. No woman starts on the downward path unassisted. We have nothing but good to say of the parents, for they did what they could in the rearing of their children, and are surely not responsible for their wandering from their training and the unfortunate result.

This sad story should be a lesson to the thousands of young men and women who are now drifting away from home and mother.

—*Dabney.*

CHISUM AS LABOR PROCURER

During the World War this city became a center or market for the importation of Negroes from the South. That species of labor was in great demand and those engaged in this business found it a most arduous undertaking, for the South has never looked kindly upon people who sought to seduce from their fields those upon whom they depended for labor as well as for festal occasions, such as lashing or lynching, mobbing or burning. Jos. L. Jones and Melvin J. Chisum established an employment agency here. Men were brought from the South and shipped all over the North for mercantile, manufacturing, and munitions of war establishments. Upon Chisum devolved "the dirty work," that is, the job of going South to get the "goods." No better character could have been selected. A product of Texas, a life-long newspaper man, short in stature, dark in complexion, aldermanic abdomen, a typical old-time Methodist preacher in appearance, but with a fluency of speech, a lightning rapidity of thought that would do honor to a 33rd Chicago lawyer, and the cheek, brass, nerve that would have made a reputation for a cowboy or a king. In addition, he was a Southern Negro, and who knows the white man better? He did an enormous business, ran a thousand risks. A price was set upon his life and liberty, but when cornered he would simulate a sweet simplicity, a servility that savored of the "good old days," as he talked with an unction and dialect that Uncle Tom would have envied. Thousands of Negroes were brought up by Chisum. That versatile genius is now located in Chicago, the representative of the Negro Press Association. He does business with the leading corporations and political interests of America, and has discarded forever the disguises and manner that enabled him so successfully to run the gauntlet in the cotton fields of the Sunny South.

THE UNION OFFICE

"The Union," our weekly newspaper, W. P. Dabney, owner and editor, was brought into existence by him twenty years ago. A small temporary allowance from the Republican organization for political advertising, a fluctuating income from advertisers and subscribers, endless hours of soul-racking labor, and the paper grew in strength and size. For years it was handicapped, since the owner, being in political position, could in consequence neither make demands for compensation nor publish material for any party other than the Republican. It has never been a big paper, but has ever commanded a good strong following because of its original portrayal of current events, well-known veracity and race loyalty. Sensationalism, crime, scandal, have never been featured. The employes have been mainly young ladies whose efficiency and fidelity have had much to do with its success. Miss Allye Taylor was one of the first regular employes. The longest in point of service was Miss Eileen Yarbrough, who assumed entire charge of the business and collection department. She remained for four years, made a most creditable record and resigned to become an attache of the Associated Charities, in which field she has had an enviable career. For two years Mrs. Maude I. Allen, nee Goodson,

Office of the Union

has been very successful as bookkeeper and business manager. Miss Thelma A. Maurea was private secretary and stenographer for one year prior to her acceptance of position in Pittsburgh, and that department is now in charge of Mrs. Freddie Bunton Walls.

COLORED PATHFINDERS AND PIONEERS OF CINCINNATI, AND ITEMS OF INTEREST

Dr. Tate, our first doctor, volunteered to fight yellow fever plague in Memphis. Died there.

Dr. Buckner, though not a graduate, yet became a very successful practitioner through ability and experience in nursing.

Dr. Frank W. Johnson, physician and surgeon, was the first of the modern school to settle here.

Peter H. Clark was the outstanding character in school and public life.

Rev. E. H. Blue was one of the most brilliant and progressive young ministers in this city. From a humble beginning, he arose to the pastorship of the Second Baptist Church in Madisonville. By his death, two years ago, this city sustained an irreparable loss.

Prof. Andrew J. De Hart, the first principal of Douglass School, a minister and a leading politician until his death.

Barney Schooley, father of Dr. Chas. A. Schooley, was owner of a pickle and preserving factory on Fifth Street.

Henry Collins owned a large second-hand store.

Robert Gordon, coal dealer and financier, succeeded in coal business by his partner, Wm. P. West.

Rev. Geo. Williams, preacher, author, politician and first member of the legislature from this county, was once protege of Chas. Fleischmann, multi-millionaire yeast manufacturer.

Ball and Thomas, famous photographers, owned first Daguerreotype gallery in town.

"Joe" Early, oldest living colored man native of Cincinnati and oldest politician, was first colored constable. Largely identified with the dominant political machine fifty years ago and the public schools.

Hon. Wm. (Bill) Copeland, politician of prominence, one of the founders of the organization from which emanated the Blaine Club. Saved the life of Cox, who became the uncrowned king of Ohio politics, the Czar absolute of Hamilton County, and a multi-millionaire. Copeland was the first gauger in U. S. Revenue Department and surveyor in waterworks.

Baker Street Baptist Church was down in Baker Street, now the rear of Sinton Hotel. It gave birth to the Union Baptist, "Mound Street Church," and Zion Baptist or "Ninth Street Baptist Church."

Sol White, great scenic painter, whose brush made the beautiful pictures on the curtains of some of our leading theatres.

R. S. Duncanson, one of the greatest of American painters. A product of this city who achieved fame in Europe. A few of his paintings are still in this city. Notable among them being the life-size picture of "Nicholas Longworth," now hanging on the wall of Ohio Mechanics' Institute.

Thomas Morgan for a short time taught music in the mixed schools.

Harry Griffin graduated from the old McMicken University.

Charley Turner, who became an eminent biologist, graduated from the University in 1891 and was student teacher or professor's assistant there.

Alice Easton was the first graduate from the Cincinnati University as now incorporated and modernized. She received her diploma in 1897.

Rev. Dangerfield Early built our first church on Walnut Hills.

Rev. Wallace Shelton was called to Lockland to establish the Mt. Zion Baptist Church.

Allen Temple, started from Allen Chapel, a little frame house near the heart of Bucktown.

"The Attucks Blues" was our first military company. At the beginning of the Civil War its offer to enlist was not accepted. Its first captain was Julius Hawkins, father of Ralph Hawkins, attache of U. S. Court for this district.

Henry Boyd became wealthy in the furniture manufacturing business. He employed large numbers of white and colored men. The members of his family married into the white race.

Wm. H. Parham worked on steamboats, studied under Peter H. Clark, became principal of Gaines High School, studied law, first graduate of Cincinnati Law School, went to the legislature, became wealthy and died.

Hugh Carr inaugurated and became leader in the window washing business. He has acquired a substantial income and valuable property.

Henry W. Forte became Governor Hoadley's messenger.

The Ninth Battalion was organized when Foraker was **governor.**

Chas. W. Fillmore became major of Ninth Battalion. He was the handsomest man, barring men of no race, in the military service of his time.

Governor Bushnell assigned Young to the Ninth Battalion. He later became a colonel in the U. S. Army. A great deal of his time was spent here.

Many market stands were owned by families of note, among them the Taylors, Slaters, Plumbs, etc. Today the race has lost that honorable and lucrative business enterprise.

Members of the legislature: Geo. W. Williams, Col. "Bob" Harlan, Wm. Copeland, Geo. H. Jackson, Sam B. Hill, Wm. H. Parham, Geo. W. Hays, three terms, A. Lee Beaty, two terms.

Edward Hawkins was the first dentist.

Dr. Chas. A. Schooley was the second dentist and still has a large practice, three-fourths of which is white.

Dr. Eugene Cox had the first large establishment of mechanical dentistry.

The first colored drug store was located on Chapel Street, Walnut Hills. It is still in existence, and now owned by Mrs. Carl Beckwith.

The Model Drug Stores Co. now has eight branches, including the one in Covington.

Harry Williams was purchasing agent and still holds executive position in one of the largest foundries in this city.

Nearly all of the many males of the Troy family were employed as bank messengers, and were the first in that branch of banking.

R. D. G. Troy, now in Philadelphia, became a bookkeeper in the Ohio Valley Bank and later assistant bookkeeper in the City Auditor's Office. He was rated as an expert accountant and took a leading part in the tabulation and computation of election returns.

Scott Berry was a very efficient bank clerk for many years. He "passed for white" except at night when he socialized with the friends. His wife was unmistakably colored.

Dr. Jared Cary had the first chiropodist establishment in this city. It was located in the Arcade, is still in existence, and always had an immense white patronage.

Dr. John Banks, nephew of Dr. Cary, became a splendid chiropodist, who founded and owned, until he died several years ago, a magnificent place on West Fourth Street. The business is now operated by Dr. Jno. Hoffman, who also has great patronage. Mrs. Patterson, the mother of Dr. Banks, is a wealthy property owner of Columbus, Ohio.

Wm. L. Anderson, proprietor of first and only large colored printing plant in the city, publisher of many newspapers, tracts, bulletins and books. First colored member of Typographical union.

Wm. Porter, first colored undertaker and prominent in that field until his death several years ago.

Ben McPherson, one of the first and finest automobile drivers in this city. He has been blind for many years.

Prof. Chas. W. Bell taught penmanship in the mixed schools of this city.

Mrs. Zenobia Cox Russel taught in the oral schools until she was released on account of her color, much to the regret of the school patrons.

Thos. J. Triplett was the first colored man in the Registry Department of the post office. He was followed by St. Julian Renfro, who has since become an undertaker.

Major Travis passed an examination at the bar of this city and became our first colored lawyer. There were admitted to practice, later, Handy, Hargo, Parham, Jackson, and the legion of today.

Drove First Street Car

James Ray, father-in-law of our veteran dentist, Chas. H. Schooley, worked for the street car company for over fifty years. He drove its bus and later was the first man to drive a street car in this city. After saving a number of the company's horses at a most disastrous fire, he received from the daily press flattering congratulations and from the street car company an equal amount of thanks. Since his day and time the only colored men who have officiated on street cars were those who "passed for white."

"Bob" Harlan and James Ray were the last colored members of the Blaine Club. "The last of the Mohicans," so to speak. The story concerning the expulsion of our brunette brethren has already been told in this volume. Suffice it to say,

> The method used
> Was most painstakin',
> And the "Colored Group"
> Was quickly shaken.

Geo. Taylor was the first deputy sheriff of this county. Herbert Clark the second. Since their time there has, in that office, always been a colored representative.

Street Nesbit, now a resident of St. Louis, was the first mail carrier of this city. Prof. Chas. W. Bell was first appointed but did not serve.

Mr. James A. Allen was the first detective in the police department.

Henry Hagerman was the first policeman.

Dr. John McLeod was the first and only U. S. veterinary surgeon of this city.

Mr. Henry M. Higgins is the first and only assistant city sealer.

Alfred Marchand, secretary of the Hospital Board, the first and only assistant librarian of the hospital and the real authority on its many volumes.

Geo. Hays, Jr., first colored clerk in U. S. Court Clerk's office.

Mrs. Jessie Slater, now Mrs. Fillmore, copied court records for many years.

Miss Gladys Willis first regularly employed clerk in County Recorder's office.

W. P. Dabney, first colored Assistant City Paymaster and later the only head paymaster the city has ever had and the only holder of such executive position in any city of similar size in the United States.

The Smiths

Albert E. Smith, church organist and for long years a mail carrier. Mrs. Georgine Kelly, University graduate, brilliant scholar, teacher of Douglass School. She became Mrs. Albert E. Smith. To Poughkeepsie, New York, they went. Into community work they entered. Now they have a school in that city whose teachings have been so salutary, whose inufluence has been so beneficient, that the fame of its excellence has not only penetrated the walls of Vassar College, but has even gained the admiration of other great Eastern institutions of learning.

John R. McLean

Nearly fifty years ago the Enquirer occasionally had writers on its staff who were much addicted to using opprobrious terms and epithets concerning the Negro. Colored citizens called on the owner, John R. McLean, and stated their grievances in regard to his publication. Mr. McLean regretted exceedingly the necessity for such a committee, and assured its members that the policy of the paper was opposed to such practices and that prejudiced reporters were the persons guilty of disseminating the anti-Negro propaganda. He promised that it would not occur again "and it didn't."

Tokens of Appreciation

Salmon P. Chase, for his labors in the interest of colored people, was presented by them in 1845 with a silver set, and about sixty years later Senator Foraker was given a loving cup by our citizens as a tribute of appreciation for his noble work in behalf of the colored soldiers.

The old colored health operator, known as Dr. Ruffin, had an enormous practice among white people. Carriages lined the street in front of his house, while aristocratic patrons awaited their turn for his treatment, which consisted of a species of massage. The electrical emanations from his hand were supposed to have vast therapeutic value.

It is noteworthy, that despite the enormous increase of over 100 per cent in charges for rent to tenants of tenements, that at the "Dabney Building," from 1894 until its evacuation and subsequent demolition in July, 1925, the rent was never raised, though many improvements had been made.

Doctors Ben and Cliff Hickman were the first graduates of the Eclectic Medical College. Dr. Kerr, who graduated third, is the only one of that trio living.

The First National Inter-racial Conference took place here this year. Dr. George E. Haynes, now of New York, was the bright particular star. It was a great success and marks a new era for the promotion of inter-racial harmony.

The health week, two years ago, was a great success and to its education along hygienic lines may be attributed the great improvement in sanitary methods of living.

Prof. Philip J. Ferguson was a school teacher and head of a big choral society in 1880. Geo. W. Hays became its president. It went to Louisville in 1882 and was royally entertained for several days. Seventy-five members made the trip. In its repertoire were the cantatas of Daniel, Esther and Belshazzar.

Several groceries were started in the last thirty years, but their death came quickly.

John Taylor, the first and only stenographer of a big white law firm, began as errand boy and porter for Kittridge and Wilby, one of the greatest law firms in this state. He took up stenography, and until his death several years ago, was their leading stenographer and occupied one of their offices.

Jos. Kelly, located out near the stock yards, became one of the greatest horse traders in this county. His word was his bond, his ability pre-eminent, his credit unlimited. He sold out several years ago and is farming in Indiana.

Conventions and Committees

Conventions of national importance were held here in 1845 and 1852. A tremendous fight was made to get Negroes to return to Africa as colonists. Peter H. Clark, Langston and the greatest colored men of the North were interested. The project was defeated. In 1913, delegates were sent to Governor Cox to secure his support in fight against inter-marriage bill. The committee that saw and discussed the matter with him was Edw. E. Minnes, Leslie Tull, Everett Spurlock, of Columbus, and W. P. Dabney. At the same session of the legislature, citizens of this city sent Attorney E. E. Minnes and W. P. Dabney, who remained in Columbus several weeks fighting proposed legislation. The bill was defeated. In 1925 an inter-marriage bill was again brought up. A committee, Rev. Samuel Brown, B. F. Smith and W. P. Dabney, was sent by the Cincinnati Branch of the National Association for the Advancement of Colored

People to appear before the Judiciary Committee in opposition to said bill. It was killed in that committee.

A pamphlet, "The Wolf and the Lamb," was brought out in 1913 by the first-named committee. It was an argument against the inter-marriage law.

Wm. Copeland was the first Negro parlor car conductor.

Old Griffin T. Watson, grandfather of Mrs. Geo. W. Hays, was sent to New Orleans to examine a man's Masonic credentials. The grand lodge was organized in this state. Cincinnati was the center of its activities. Samuel Clark wrote the first and only Masonic book here setting forth the claims of Negro Masonry.

Colored society in summer went to Tuwahwah House at Wilberforce, kept by Sampson Lewis.

Hon. Geo. W. Hays, first U. S. Court Crier, has held that position for over one-half a century.

Miss Ardenia White, our first artistic wood carver. She is now living in Boston.

Miss Delilah Beasley, a girl of this city, who went to California and has written a very creditable history of that state.

Jos. L. Jones, great secret fraternity magnate and founder of Central Regalia Company.

"Charley" Bentley, now Dr. Bentley, of Chicago, one of the greatest dentists in the United States, was famous as a singer when a young man in this city.

John Lewis, of the Union Baptist Church, was also noted as a good vocalist.

Along dramatic lines, Alexander Thomas and Powhattan Beaty achieved quite a reputation for forceful, fiery declamation. We have now many ladies who are exceptionally talented along histrionic and elocutionary lines, and the amateur plays periodically performed almost attain the grade of professionalism in the excellence of their rendition.

Prof. John Blackburn, probably the oldest and most distinguished colored educator in this state if not this country, lived next door to John R. McLean on Race Street, and they enjoyed the most friendly relations. He knew well his father, Washington McLean, and also the sister who married Admiral Dewey and whom he pictures as a most beautiful young woman. The son, Edward McLean, Esq., he knew only by reputation, but he declares that all of the McLeans were very cordially disposed towards colored people.

Dr. L. A. Cornish achieved distinction as a physician, acquired valuable property and last year returned with his wife to Washington, the city of their birth.

Rev. Jas. P. Foote, former pastor of St. John A. M. E. Zion, departed for Cleveland last year, leaving here an unsurpassed record for labor in God's service.

Rev. B. F. Smith, an eloquent speaker, now in Detroit, former pastor of Park Street Church, became a forceful factor here in the affairs, both religious and civic.

Rev. and Mrs. I. N. Cardoza, formerly of South Carolina, settled here temporarily many years ago. He did splendid work as a Presbyterian pastor and as a school teacher in Avondale. Of the family now living, Dr. F. N. Cardoza is in Baltimore, a daughter, Mrs. Rutherford, and her mother, live in Washington; another daughter, Mrs. Fred Hamilton, resides in this city.

"The Fall Festival March," played at the opening of the Fall Festival, in 1900, was composed by W. P. Dabney and published by The Rudolph Wurlitzer Co. It was the official march and was much in demand by the bands and orchestras of that period.

The Ninth Battalion, Ohio National Guards, was reorganized by Mr. Jay Wilkins and a number of citizens in April, 1924. On September 1, 1924, Company C, 372nd Infantry, O. N. G., was organized and is now in a flourishing condition. It has met with the hearty approval of Governor Donahey, under whose regime new formation was effected.

Governor Hoadley placed numbers of colored men on state boards, among the first being Peter H. Clark, on Ohio State University in Columbus, and Prof. Blackburn on the Ohio University Board at Athens, the oldest university in the West.

Our building associations, The East End Investment and Loan Co., The Industrial Savings and Loan Co., their branches on Walnut Hills, and "The Attucks," in Lockland, are doing well, as is the Creative Realty Co. of this city. There are also a Business Men's Association and a number of small mercantile companies. When confidence in each other is augmented our men will father more successful enterprises.

Among the residents of Cincinnati who became famous on the stage in recent years we note Jesse Shipp, Leubrie Hill, Cleo Mitchell, Laura Bowman, Carrie B. King and Charlie Shelton.

The social side of the K. of P.'s was well illustrated by the Owl Club and later by The Hoodlums. The old members still recall "the joys of the night, the sorrows of the morning."

The Lincoln Club, the city's most aristocratic white political club, had several colored members.

"Jim" Elliot, one of the old citizens, stately, dignified and a distinguished member of the miser class in his last days, which were passed in his house on McAllister Street. Though he would hardly buy food, yet quite an amount of money was found in his possession after death came. In the realm of recitation and declamation he was something of a celebrity.

Section VII
Institutions, Biographical Sketches and Pictures

Y. W. C. A.

"In Service for the Women and Girls of Cincinnati"

West End Branch Y. W. C. A., Miss Anna Hope, executive secretary, organized January 2, 1919. Building formally opened May 13, 1919. Its growth has been phenomenal and its contribution to the moral and ethical standards of the girls and women of Cincinnati valuable. It is one of five branches in the United States whose committee chairman is a member of the Board of Directors of Central Association, which contact has considerably assisted in the growth of mutual understanding between the two races. In the beginning the fourfold program of the Association was undertaken by three volunteer chairman and two paid workers. To date there are twenty-two volunteer women and five paid workers. The breadth and scope of the work may be better understood by the numerical summary of last year following:

The resident department shows 49 permanent residents, 76 transients, 92 placed in homes, 158 outside organizations using the building with an attendance of 5,895.

The Girl Reserves have 11 clubs, an enrollment of 269, and an attendance of 5,868 at recreational events.

In the Industrial Department are three clubs, 80 members, and an attendance of 3,509 at group meetings.

The Tea Room meets a great need among our women and girls, where a wholesome, well-balanced meal is served in attractive surroundings; 10,679 meals were served last year.

Total number of contacts made during the year, including the above, through club meetings, assemblies, conferences, vespers and committee meetings, 40,943.

Ninth Street Branch
YOUNG MEN'S CHRISTIAN ASSOCIATION
"Builders of Manhood"
636 West Ninth Street   Cincinnati, Ohio

Active interest in the Cincinnati Young Men's Christian Association has been manifested by a small group of colored people for a number of years. It was in 1912, however, that plans for the promotion of the program among the colored people began to take definite shape. Mr. Washington Simms assumed leadership of the efforts in the year mentioned, and directed a canvass to ascertain the sentiment of the community in regards to the erection of a building for the work among colored people. As a result of this canvass it was decided to have a Building Fund Campaign. The campaign was successful and the plant on Ninth Street was dedicated February 6, 1916.

The building represents, including the site and furnishings, an investment of $111,545.00, of which amount $15,248.19 was contributed by the colored people. It contains a tile-lined swimming pool, 20 feet by 60 feet, shower baths, separate lockers for men and boys, social rooms containing billiard tables and bowling alleys, a gymnasium, 44 by 70 feet, completely equipped with modern apparatus, a comfortable and inviting lobby, a cafeteria, a boys' department with special equipment for the boys of different age groups and two floors of dormitory rooms. Every colored man and boy in Cincinnati may now enjoy the privileges mentioned above.

A four-fold program calculated to develop the bodies and minds of young men and to care for their social and religious needs is carried on. Great attention is given to work with boys. The proportion of boys in the Ninth Street membership increased from twenty percent in 1917 to forty-four percent in 1925. The amount of money spent in conducting this department has increased more than three hundred percent in the past seven years. The money for operating this department is provided in part from membership fees paid by the men. Many men who do not particularly care to use the privileges of the Y. M. C. A. carry a membership in order that the work with boys might go on.

The most important factor in the Y. M. C. A. program is the relationship to the churches of the community. The Y. M. C. A. is an instrument of the church used to bring boys and young men under Christian influence.

The work of the Y. M. C. A. is conducted under the supervision of a Committee of Management; the personnel (1925) is as follows: Horace Sudduth, chairman; Jos. H. Paghe, Dr. W. T. Nelson, W. B. Young, Wm. J. Decatur, B. H. Richardson, Dr. R. E. Beamon, J. J. Woodson, Dr. R. P. McClain, Jas. H. Thompson, Chas. A. Howard, C. E. A. Hunt, Dr. E. A. Williams, Edward Brooks.

ESTABLISHED 1921

COSMOPOLITAN SCHOOL OF MUSIC
CINCINNATI, OHIO

Cosmopolitan School of Music is a modern school of Music, Expression and Language, organized on a broad art basis. It aims to develop its students artistically, mentally and physically into the highest types of useful citizens as well as thorough musicians and artists. One of its most highly prized privileges is the opportunity to share in the perpetuation and advancement of Negro music and art.

Departments of instruction and Faculty personnel:
Language—Francis Lesley and Lillian Foster.
Expression—Lillian Foster and Naomi Blackburn.
Public School Music—Helen Greer.
Theory—Artie Matthews.
Violin—Robert Partridge and N. W. Ryder.
Voice—Anna Matthews.
Piano—Helen Greer, Anna Matthews, N. W. Ryder and Artie Matthews.
Organ—Artie Matthews and N. W. Ryder.
Band, Orchestra and Ensemble—N. W. Ryder and Lucion Ramseur.
Natural Dancing—Clara Hough.

Division of courses or plan of education is as follows: Preparatory, academic, normal, advanced and general.

Examinations are conducted semi-annually, and tests are given quarterly, in all departments. Lessons are graded and records faithfully kept. Credentials, i. e., statements, certificates and diplomas are awarded upon the satisfactory completion of prescribed courses.

Artie Matthews

Mrs. Anna Matthews

Cosmopolitan School of Music

Anna Matthews, registrar, and wife of the director, was born in 1887, at Steubenville, Ohio, and received early musical training under W. E. Gossette, and later studied voice with W. S. Sterling; has been organist and choir director at Park Street M. E. Church, Cincinnati, Ohio, for more than sixteen years; has exercised great influence on the musical life of this vicinity, and shares equally with her husband in establishing and developing Cosmopolitan School of Music.

Artie Matthews, the director, is a native of Illinois, born November 15, 1888; received early training in music from his mother; studied piano, organ and theory five or six years under W. Elmer Keeton at St. Louis, Mo.; is a graduate in organ and theory (1918), Metropolitan College of Music and Dramatic Art, Cincinnati, Ohio.

WILLIAM WARE

Social Work

Son of Alfred and Jane Ware. Born October 17, 1872, in Lexington, Kentucky. Attended public schools. Married Lucy Jones. He has been at his vocation since 1914. Politically an Independent. Came to Cincinnati, May 22, 1903; was in active work in Antioch Baptist Church until 1914. Sir William Ware, as he is called in the U. N. I. A., has been for years one of our foremost advocates of race rights and opponent of vicious conditions in the down-town district of our city. As president of the Cincinnati Branch of the U. N. I. A., he is using his immense power for the betterment of the down-trodden people of this community. In his organization there is among its members a strong spirit of race pride and unity. Resides at 927 Barr Street.

William Ware has been active in social uplift among his people for the past eleven or twelve years. He was active awhile in fraternal work before coming to Cincinnati and was a member of Main Street Baptist Church, Lexington, Kentucky, and moved his membership to Antioch Baptist Church.

He founded an organization called the Welfare Association for the Colored People of Cincinnati in 1917, incorporated under the laws of the State of Ohio, in which he was president and was active in that work until August 1, 1920, when he went as a delegate to New York, representing his organization to the first International Convention of the Negro Peoples of the World, in Liberty Hall, New York, 120 West 138th Street, from August 1st to August 31st.

Sir William Ware

After the rising of that convention he then came back to Cincinnati. After reading the aims and objects of the organization he turned the Welfare Association into the Universal Negro Improvement Association and African Communities League, and organized on September 1, 1920.

From that time until the present time he has been president of said organization and has enrolled in Cincinnati 8,000 members. He has attended every International Convention of the organization since 1920.

At the Fourth International Convention, held in New York, and the Third Court Reception of the Supreme Highness, the Potentate, he was knighted on the 20th day of August, 1924, and his title now is Sir William Ware, K. C. D. S. E.

Aims and Objects of the Universal Negro Improvement Association

The objects of the Universal Negro Improvement Association and African Communities' League shall be to establish a universal confraternity among members of the race; to promote the spirit of pride and love; to reclaim the fallen; to administer to and assist the needy; to assist in civilizing the backward tribes of Africa; to assist in the development of independent Negro nations and communities; to establish commissionaries or agencies in the principal countries and cities of the world for the representation and protection of all Negroes, irrespective of nationality; to promote a conscientious spiritual worship among the native tribes of Africa; to establish universities, colleges, academies and schools for the racial education and culture of the people; to conduct a world-wide commercial and industrial intercourse for the good of the people; to work for better conditions in all Negro communities.

DR. E. A. WILLIAMS

Sir E. A. Williams, Past Supreme Chancellor, K. of P., born in Alabama, 1851; a leader in reconstruction in that state; a member of the Senate one term and of the House, two terms. In Washington City he served

the government six years, studied medicine, then went to New Orleans, La., and finished his studies. Among the first to whom Dr. Stringer gave the rank of Knights of Pythias, in 1880, he assisted in organizing lodges Nos. 2 and 3 at New Orleans. At the organization of the Grand Lodge of Louisiana, 1881, he was elected Grand Lecturer, and in one year organized eighteen lodges. At the first regular session of the Grand Lodge, 1882, he was elected Grand Chancellor and during that year organized thirty-two lodges in Louisiana. At the session of the Supreme Lodge at St. Louis, 1883, he was elected Supreme Vice Chancellor, and served until 1887, when at Richmond, Va., he was elected Supreme Chancellor and served until 1895. At St. Louis he declined to serve longer. He wrote the ritualistic ceremony of Past Chancellor's rank, also rank of P. W. C. He, with W. H. Green, L. A. Bell, Mrs. M. A. Williams and Mrs. V. C. Green, wrote the ritual of I. O. O. C. or Courts of Calanthe. He organized all the Grand Lodges in the order except the Grand Lodges of Mississippi, Arkansas and Texas, up to 1895. He served six years as Grand Secretary and five years as Grand Master of Masons of Louisiana. He assisted in organizing the Grand Chapter, Royal Arch Masons, and the Grand Commandery of Knights Templar of Louisiana and served ten years as Grand Secretary and Grand Recorder. He is a member of the Scottish Rite and has served in the Supreme Council of the Southern and Western Jurisdiction as Grand Minister of State and Grand Chancellor, serving each three years. He is a Noble of the Mystic Shrine, having served as Grand Imperial Pasha. He organized the first chapter of the Order of Eastern Star of Florida and Texas. He served as Grand Patron of Louisiana ten years. He participated with the late G. F. Bowles in his work in launching the Knights of Honor of the World, and Knights and Ladies of Honor. At the death of G. F. Bowles he was elected Supreme Dictator and Protector in 1889 and has served ever since. He has written several works for the order, also ritual of Grand Lodge and Daughters of I. B. P. O. Elks of the World.

He removed from New Orleans to Cincinnati in 1898, with the late W. T. Jones and G. F. Bowles, of Mississippi, J. F. Fielding and others and organized the Fraternal Mutual Benevolent Association, which employs an army of colored girls as clerks and stenographers. He is chairman and manager of the Knights of Honor Hall and is president of "Our Regalia House" at 1414 Chase Avenue.

Mrs. Mattie Augusta Williams, wife of Past Supreme Chancellor E. A. Williams, began her first services with secret orders soon after her union with her husband. She was a member of Esther Chapter No. 1, O. E. S. of New Orleans, La. At the formation of Electa Chapter No. 2, in 1882, she was elected its first Matron and served as such until 1888, when she declined to serve further. At the formation of the Grand Chapter in 1884, she was elected its first Grand Secretary and served as such for nine years, or until 1893. She was among the first women to confer the Degrees of the I. O. O. C. (Court of Calanthe) in 1883. She, with Mrs. W. H. Green, Sir W. H. Green, and her husband, Dr. E. A. Williams, organized the first Court of Calanthe, known as Calanthe Court No. 1, I. O. O. C., at White Hall, La., in 1883; she was elected the first Supreme Register of Deeds in 1883 and served until 1893. She received the degrees of the Knights and Ladies of Honor of the World from the late G. F. Bowles before he organized any lodges, at Chicago in 1893. At the formation of Alpha Lodge, K. & L. of H. of W. at New Orleans, she was one of its organizers, and remained as such until she moved to Cincinnati, Ohio. When Sir G. F. Bowles organized Lily of the Valley Lodge No. 84, K. & L. of H. of W., she was among its founders. She is in good standing in all of the above orders. It was to her that the late Dr. T. W. Stringer, Supreme Chancellor, appealed for aid in making collars and regalia for the order of K. of P. in 1882. She opened up "Our Regalia House" at New Orleans in 1884. When her husband moved to Cincinnati, Ohio, in 1898, she reopened it in that city. It is the oldest colored regalia house and furnishes work for many women and girls. It was indorsed by the Grand Chancellors' Convention at Cincinnati, Ohio, December 28, 1921 and 1925, as one of the official regalia houses of the order of K. of P.

Mrs. Williams has seen the Order of Calanthe, organized by her in 1883, grow from 28 members to 200,000 members in 1925. It has now over one million dollars in the treasury.

HOME FOR COLORED GIRLS

The Home for Colored Girls was established by the Cincinnati Protective and Industrial Association for Colored Women and Children, a nonsectarian organization composed of both colored and white citizens. The following persons became members of the first board of trustees: M. C. B. Mason, Dr. J. E. Erwin, Rev. T. L. Ferguson, Fountain Lewis, Geo. W. Hays, Mrs. Julia Porter, Mrs. Phoebe Allen, Mrs. J. P. Monroe, Luke A. Staley, J. G. Schmidlapp, James N. Gamble, L. H. Weir, C. M. Hubbard, Dr. John Robertson, M. L. Kirkpatrick, A. L. Copeland, Geo. H. Stearns, Mr. and Mrs. R. B. Henley, Mr. W. P. Dabney, Mr. Wm. J. Decatur, Mrs. James H. Thompson, Miss Ella Mae Talmage, Miss Ethel Ideson, H. R. Alcorn, Elma C. Leach.

J. G. Schmidlapp, James N. Gamble and Mrs. Mary Emery each gave $3,000 for the first payment on the house at 649 W. Seventh Street, in which the institution was opened on December 11, 1914. Mrs. Cora Oliver was

chosen as superintendent and has served in a highly acceptable manner in this capacity ever since the beginning of the work.

The primary object of the founders of the work was to provide a temporary home for young women who were strangers in the city. An employment bureau was opened and situations were found for those who applied. In a few months the management was requested by the Juvenile Court to accept girls of school age from broken and improper homes. This request was granted and the need proved so great that a choice had to be made between them and the young women. The decision was in favor of the former as being the more helpless.

Funds were raised by private subscription. A Big Sister's Auxiliary was formed which renders great financial and social assistance. Its thirty members are God-serving women of the highest standing and ability. Mrs. Luke Edinburg is the president and Mrs. Jas. H. Thompson the treasurer.

In 1915 the institution became a member of the Cincinnati Council of Social Agencies, and has since received its support through their central budget system. In May of that year the "Home" was moved to its present location at 816 W. Ninth Street. The capacity of the building is twenty-five girls and four resident members of the staff. The property is valued at $10,500. The playground is an attractive feature, with a wading pool and a set of swings, a gift from the Big Sister's Auxiliary. Miss Emma C.

Leach, a most efficient secretary, a product of Oberlin and abolition stock, labored many years before this institution became firmly established. It has been exceedingly fortunate in having on its staff women of marked ability and fitness. Mrs. Ella Glenn, after serving as assistant matron for seven years, was called to take charge of the Friendship Home in Buffalo, N. Y. Mrs. Lucy Lee was asked to take charge of the Shelter Home for Colored Children after serving two years in the Home for Colored Girls, and Miss Myrtle Willette left, after two years, to be superintendent of the Friendship Home of Cincinnati.

The "Home" girls have received every encouragement and assistance in getting an education. Many have worked their way through school and one is now a student in Cincinnati University. The religious life is especially emphasized, and high ideals of Christian womanhood are held up as the only legitimate goal in life.

The average length of residence is one year, but several have been compelled to remain over a period of years. Over two hundred girls of school age have passed through the "Home" during the fourteen years of its existence. It ranks as one of the best conducted institutions of its kind in this country.

EVANGELINE HOME

Salvation Army Branch, located at 712 W. Sixth Street, Cincinnati, Ohio

This institution was opened at the request of social workers and citizens of Cincinnati who were in a position to know of the great need for a place of shelter for unfortunate colored girls. Those who constituted this initial committee were Mrs. Phoebe Allen and Miss Alexine Crawford, Juvenile Court; Mrs. Mabel Feree, Social Service, Cincinnati General Hospital; Mrs. Cora Oliver and Elma C. Leach of the Home for Colored Girls, and W. P. Dabney, editor of the Union. They met with Mrs. Brigadier Dunham and through her requested the Salvation Army to open a home for unmarried colored mothers. This request was granted and Ensign Elizabeth Symmes (colored) was sent from New York to work up interest among the Negro churches and clubs.

An advisory committee was formed of prominent citizens, including J. G. Schmidlapp, James N. Gamble, Charles J. Livingood, Mr. and Mrs. D. B. Meacham, E. H. Oxley, D. D. Jennie Porter, Prof. Francis M. Russell, Mr. Clarence I. Smith, Dr. W. A. D. Kerr, Mr. Edgar A. Stark, Mr. J. O. White, Bishop Boyd Vincent.

The Cincinnati Council of Social Agencies agreed to assist with funds. Mrs. Mary Emery gave a building worth $12,000 and a fund of $13,000 was raised for remodeling, equipment, etc. The institution was formally opened on September 10, 1917. Adjutant Lillian F. Wright was placed in charge with a staff of officers, including a graduate nurse. A medical staff of seven Negro physicians agreed to serve gratuitously. They were Drs. W. A. B. Kerr, Frank Johnson, W. T. Nelson, J. C. Erwin, Wm. O. H. Ross, N. C. Vaughn and E. B. Gray, of Cincinnati, and Chas. Horner,

of Covington, Ky. G. E. Loverett and E. B. Stone have also joined the staff recently.

The capacity of the home is: Girls, 22; babies, 10; private outside patients, 4. All departments are substantially and comfortably furnished. The operating room is splendidly equipped and has been used by the best surgeons in the city with marked success. Its standard of health, sanitation, and cleanliness receives highest commendation.

Length of residence for mother and child varies from three to six months. The great majority of those received are well under twenty years of age, many of them school girls as young as twelve and thirteen years. They are well trained in housework and sewing and in the care of their children. Positions are found for them and boarding homes for their babies unless they return to relatives or marry. Adjutant Lillian F. Wright, the superintendent, and her staff, are very religious and the spiritual life in the "Home" is the outstanding feature.

During the eight years of its operation the Evangeline Home has cared for 292 girls, and 202 babies were born there. It has had 274 private outside patients and 43 legitimate births.

JAMES HATHAWAY ROBINSON

Born, Sharpsburg, Bath County, Kentucky, October 6, 1888, son of Nathaniel and Martha Robinson.

Attended public schools of Winchester and Lexington. Attended Russell High School of Lexington, the Hyde Park High School of Chicago and the preparatory school of Fisk University.

Received A.B. magna cum laude, Fisk University, 1911, with the highest average of any man in the class. Member successful debating teams against Atlanta University and Howard University. Winner of Mayhew-Merrill Oratorical Prize. Two years, class president. Received A.B., Yale University, 1912. Received M.A., Yale University, 1914, and completed residence requirements for the Ph.D. with sociology as major and economics as minor. Awarded University Scholarship, 1912. Awarded Larned Fellowship, 1913, the first fellowship ever received by a person of color in Yale University. Did special research work in African ethnography and folk lore and recommended books on these subjects to the Yale library. Studied sociology and social service in the Graduate School of Columbia University, 1914-15. Awarded a fellowship with the National Urban League.

From 1915 to 1917, teacher, Douglass School, Cincinnati, after declining calls to Fisk, Strait, Morehouse, Georgia State, Walden and later Howard Universities.

Summer 1917, teacher at Hampton Institute, instructing teachers from every state in the South.

From 1917 to 1925, Executive Secretary, Negro Civic Welfare Association, Department Community Chest and Council of Social Agencies. In this position he has been a potent factor in the development of the city's social work among colored people which today is widely recognized as the outstanding social service enterprise of any city. In this position he has advised community chests and social agencies in many cities. During the past year, for example, Brooklyn, Hartford, Los Angeles, Jacksonville, St. Louis, Atlanta and Youngstown have sought his advice.

Offices and Memberships: Alpha Phi Alpha Fraternity, American Economics Assn., American Sociological Society, American Historical Society, National Conference of Social Work, American Association of Social Workers (the only colored member of the National Council); Ohio Conference of Social Work Among Negroes, Association for the Study of Negro Life and History, National President Fisk Alumni Assn., member Greater Fisk Committee, Methodist Episcopal Church, Ninth Street Y. M. C. A., Cincinnati Yale Club, American Academy of Political and Social Science.

Mr. Robinson has contributed a number of magazine articles, has spoken before the National Conference of Social Work, University of Cincinnati, Cincinnati City Club, Peabody College and numerous other colleges, conferences and conventions over the country and is in demand annually as a commencement speaker.

The following is quoted from Dr. George E. Haynes in the proceedings of the National Conference of Social Work, Toronto, 1924:

"Perhaps the most fully worked out and best piece of social engineering in race relations in a northern community has been developed the past six years in Cincinnati, in the Inter-racial work of the Council of Social Agencies, with James H. Robinson as Executive Secretary."*

His unpublished social and sociological study of the Negro in Cincinnati to which he has devoted several years, is used as a hand-book by social agencies of the city and publication of it is now pending.

He was married in 1916 to Neola E. Woodson, daughter of Jesse J. Woodson and Cassie Guthrie Woodson, the latter deceased. There are two children, James H., Jr., 6, and Jeanne Cassie, 4. Mrs. Robinson is a graduate of the University of Cincinnati and has taught in the Douglass, Stowe and Jackson schools, and the Covington High School.

NEGRO CIVIC WELFARE ASSOCIATION

Department of Community Chest and Council of Social Agencies, representing Cincinnati's organized co-operative social, charitable and welfare work

AIMS AND PERSPECTIVE

Twelve years ago there was no organized social work among the colored people of Cincinnati. The few agencies then at work labored valiantly but without adequate moral or financial support.

About that time what is now the Community Chest and Council of Social Agencies came into existence. Four years later the war-born migration began. Thousands of people, many of them unaccustomer to urban life, came to Cincinnati and found the city unable to offer them desirable living and working conditions and unable to cope with problems in dependency, delinquency and other social ills which inevitably resulted. An appeal was made to the Council of Social Agencies. The result was the creation of the Negro Civic Welfare Association. Among its active organizers were Mr. A. G. Bookwalter, its first chairman, and Mr. C. M. Bookman, director of the Community Chest, in whose successful administration at the Chest the development of a strong Negro social service program has been a major objective.

The Association is a clearing house and co-ordinating agency sponsoring the Negro social work of the city as a whole. What the Baptist Convention does among the Baptist churches; what the Methodist Conference does for the Methodist churches, the Negro Civic Welfare Association does among the social agencies. It brings social workers and other representatives of the agencies together in council in the interest of social welfare. Together they study and discuss social problems, plan new work, advise and encourage social agencies working among colored people. They frequently enlist the interest of agencies not previously at work on the problem. Through these councils and conferences they determine policies, eliminate overlapping and duplication and from time to time secure joint action on the more serious problems of the community. During 1925, for example, twenty-five health and social agencies, the colored churches, schools, other organizations and the physicians were induced to work together in the observance of Negro Health Week. This has been done for four successive years, thus paving the way for a more effective health program as is now in progress at the Shoemaker Center.

The Association is thus the conscience and intelligence (and to some extent, the material resources) of the community organized in the interest of Negro welfare and race relations.

In this way co-operation has taken the place of competition and the few colored agencies and workers have now grown into a large organized group of colored people and white friends of the race, supporting the colored work and exhibiting a surprising degree of unanimity of thought and opinion on the most difficult issues that arise.

In addition to hundreds of colored subscribers to the Community Chest, which we hope will increase, and more than fifty trained colored social workers, the colored social work today has behind it some of the biggest subscribers to the Community Chest and the best thought of some of America's strongest white social thinkers.

CINCINNATI'S COLORED CITIZENS

More than two dozen agencies, twelve of them colored, are now actively engaged in the colored work, spending jointly more than $150,000 per year on colored work alone.

NEGRO CIVIC WELFARE ASSOCIATION
Department of
COMMUNITY CHEST AND COUNCIL OF SOCIAL AGENCIES

Office—520 West Fifth Street—Phones, Canal 4034; Canal 6950

JAMES H. ROBINSON, Executive Secretary

28 Co-operating Agencies—For Home, School, Church, Community

Studies Social Conditions—Plans New Work—Advises and Encourages Social Agencies Working Among Colored People—Holds Educational Conferences—Eliminates Duplication—Secures Joint Action on Major Problems.

Central Clearing House—Co-ordinating Agency—Bureau of Information—Medium of Co-operation

A RECORD OF SERVICE

1917—Negro Civic Welfare Association created as a department of the Community Chest, to organize and promote the social work among colored people as a whole.

1918—A survey of social conditions in Cincinnati made, and from it a city-wide social service program covering years worked out. The Better Housing League urged to begin work among colored people.

1919—Orphan Asylum, Home for Aged Colored Women, and Old Men's Home brought into the Community Chest. The Orphan Asylum remodeled.

1920—Recreational program worked out, reaching nearly every community—West End, Walnut Hills, O'Bryonville, Madisonville, Lockland, and Steele Subdivision.
Industrial Welfare work begun to help colored men and women to get into plants and factories and make good.

1921—Tennis courts established on Ashland Avenue.

1922—Two day nurseries established, the one at St. Andrew's and the other at Friendship Home.

1923—A Co-operative Summer Camp for children conducted.

1924—National Negro Health Week Prize won by Cincinnati.
Miss Edith M. Campbell completed five years' successful work as chairman of the Association. She was succeeded by Mr. John J. Emery.

1925—A West End office opened. Survey of Children's Institutions made looking forward to improvement.
National Inter-racial Conference, probably the first of its kind ever held in America, brought to Cincinnati.

CINCINNATI'S COLORED CITIZENS

SOME GENERAL AND INCIDENTAL RESULTS

1—The social service needs and problems of the colored community better understood.
2—More agencies at work than ever before.
3—Their work better organized and correlated.
4—Colored institutions better financed and thus enabled to maintain higher standards of service and comfort.
5—A growing understanding and appreciation of the service rendered by the agencies.
6—Better race relations.

The Shoemaker Health and Welfare Center opened 1925-26. One of the many social service enterprises promoted by the Negro Civic Welfare Association.

Here one finds a health center, recreation room, a housekeeping center, family welfare service and better housing work—all for the uplift of the people of the community.

In the spring of 1925 the Community Chest campaign fell short of its quota by more than $50,000. This placed in jeopardy all prospects for the Health and Welfare Center. After this was made known groups of representatives and boards of various social agencies, colored and white, met and requested the Community Chest to admit the Health Center at any

[8]

rate which meant that they themselves were willing to have their own budgets cut for the sake of this piece of work. It is doubtful that this instance of magnanimity can be equaled in the history of the social work in any city in the country. It may be doubted whether a consideration of the Negro has ever engaged the attention of an entire city as did the need of health and housing work among the colored people of Cincinnati during the Community Chest campaigns of 1924 and 1925.

AMONG THE SOCIAL AGENCIES CO-OPERATING

American Red Cross
Anti-Tuberculosis League
Associated Charities
Babies' Milk Fund Association
Better Housing League
The Boy Scouts
Bureau of Catholic Charities
Children's Home
Community Service
Old Men's Home
Evangeline Home
Federation of Churches
Friendship Home
The Girl Scouts
Home for Aged Colored Women
Home for Colored Girls
Juvenile Court
Juvenile Protective Association
Cincinnati Kindergarten Association
New Orphan Asylum for Colored Children
Ninth St. Branch Y. M. C. A.
Ohio Humane Society
St. Andrew's Day Nursery
The Shelter Home for Colored Boys
Social Hygiene Society
Valley Branch Y. M. C. A.
West End Branch Y. W. C. A.
Visiting Nurses' Association
Shoemaker Health and Welfare Center
Public Health Federation

COMMITTEES

Relief and Institutional Care
Civics:
  Citizenship
  Character-building
  Race Relations
Economics:
  Thrift
  Home Ownership
  Industrial Welfare
Child Welfare
Recreation
Housing and Health
Education
Publicity and Research
Social Service and the Church
Administration

BOARD OF DIRECTORS
(Executive Committee)

Mr. John J. Emery, Chair.
Mr. Max Hirsch, V. Chair.
Mr. F. M. Russell, 2d Vice.
Mr. B. W. Overton, Rec. Secy.
Miss M. Edith Campbell
Mr. W. P. Dabney
Miss Ethel Ideson
Mr. W. L. Anderson
Mr. Henry W. Backus
Mrs. Charles A. Blinn
Mrs. Elizabeth Branch
Miss M. P. Cheseldine
Rev. L. W. Gray
Mr. George W. Hays
Rabbi James G. Heller
Miss Elma C. Leach
Mr. Bleecker Marquette

Mrs. August Marx
Mr. Leonard R. Minster
Mrs. Josephine M. Norcom
Rev. E. H. Oxley
Miss Jennie D. Porter
Mr. P. A. Rankin
Mrs. A. J. Rankin
Miss Alice E. Richard
Mr. A. E. Roberts
Mr. Murray M. Shoemaker
Mrs. M. C. Slutes
Mr. Charles P. Taft, II
Mr. E. F. VanBuskirk
Dr. N. C. Vaughan
Mr. Morris S. Walton
Mrs. Ruth I. Workum
Adjt. Lillian F. Wright

J. H. Robinson, Executive Secretary

Dr. "Frank" W. Johnson

FRANCIS W. JOHNSON, M.D.

Francis W. Johnson, M.D., was born in Ripley, Ohio, February 24, 1866. Attended Ripley schools until 1879. In 1880 he entered Earlham College at Richmond, Indiana, and graduated in 1884. He then came to Cincinnati, railroaded until 1887. Entered Columbus Medical College at Columbus, Ohio; graduated in 1891, the second colored man to receive a diploma from that school. After practicing a short time in Chicago, he located in this city, being the first of the modern school of colored doctors established here. In 1900 he became assistant paymaster of Cincinnati and remained in office five years. He established a private hospital, was later interested in the formation of others, became trustee of Crawford's Old Men's Home, Wilberforce, and received from that college the degree of LL.D. Dr. Johnson had a charming personality, possessed boundless ambition, and was interested in many race enterprises. He married Miss Lena M. Conley, a graduate of Wilberforce. His son, Frank, is a pupil of the public schools, a natural artist, and possesses excellence of traits and characteristics that promise much for his development into a noble manhood.

HONORABLE GEORGE W. HAYS

The only colored man in the Seventy-Fifth General Assembly was Hon. George W. Hays, of Cincinnati, and by his quiet demeanor and close attention to the business of the House, where he was chairman of the Blind School Committee, made a wide circle of friends, who recognized in him a man of much moral and mental fibre, fully abreast of the times and a safe and careful legislator.

Hon. George W. Hays was the youngest son of Joshua and Anna Hays. His father was a Creole and Anna Hays was the daughter of an Indian squaw and a colored man. There were seven children, five boys and two girls, the subject of this sketch having been born in Louisiana in 1847. The mother being a slave, made all of the children slaves.

At seven years of age he was taken with the family to Franklin, Ky., where he remained until the fall of Fort Donelson, February 16, 1862, when he was pressed into the Confederate army on General Floyd's retreat, September, 1862, when he escaped and joined the Union army at Fort Negley. Being then but fourteen years of age he was assigned to duty as attendant to the officers; was with General Negley's army when it consolidated with General Sherman's and went with General Sherman's army on its march to the sea. Remained with the Union army until April, 1865, when he went to New York City in search of work and mental improvement. He secured a position as waiter and with the books at his command began at once to acquire an education which until that time he had been unable to begin. From New York he went to Cleveland, Ohio, where he entered the public schools. In August, 1867, he went to Cincinnati to work as a waiter, and during his leisure moments applied himself to study. January, 1869, he joined a surveying party in charge of Colonel Abert, U. S. Engineers, and assisted in a survey of the Grand River in Indian Territory, and the Arkansas River to Little Rock. After the completion of the field work of the survey he returned to Cincinnati, where he entered the public schools. In October, 1871, he was appointed as an attache of the United States Circuit and

District Courts. He continued his connection with the court until his nomination for Representative in 1901, nearly thirty years. During his service with the court he has served under Judges Swing, Emmons, Sage, Baxter, Jackson, Taft, Lurton, Stevens, Day and Thompson, all of whom have commended him for his faithfulness and fidelity to duty. As court crier he had the distinction of opening the first session of the Circuit Court of Appeals in Cincinnati, July 1, 1892. In April, 1890, he was appointed by Governor Jas. E. Campbell as trustee of the Ohio Institute for the Blind, and has been honored by reappointment by Governors McKinley, Bushnell and Nash. In his twelve years' connection with the board of trustees he has served as its secretary. He has also been a trustee of the Orphans' Home for Colored Children in Cincinnati for several years. Mr. Hays, on coming to Cincinnati, connected himself with the Union Baptist Church and has served as trustee of that body continuously since January, 1872. He is superintendent of the Sabbath schools of both the Union Baptist and the Calvary Baptist Church. In fraternal organizations Mr. Hays is quite prominent. He is a thirty-second degree Mason, a District Grand Director of the G. U. O. O. F., and an active member of the True Reformers.

Mr. Hays was married to Miss Mamie L. Forte, in July, 1874, five children having been born to them, three boys and two girls.

Mrs Hays was the daughter of Elijah Forte and Amy A. Watson, whose father was an original African and fine mechanic. He worked at his business at what is now Third and Elm Streets, Cincinnati, and owned all of the corn fields that now form the business block in the heart of Cincinnati, bounded by Third, Elm, Fourth and Race Streets. This was in 1820. Her grandparents were Griffin T. Watson, white, and Harriet Gregory, colored. They were married in 1838.

The above sketch was taken from Representative Men of Ohio and other publications. Mr. Hays was in the legislature three terms. He was appointed a trustee of Wilberforce by the governor and served with distinction for many years. He has been United tSates Court Crier fifty-four years; Superintendent of Union Baptist Sunday School thirty-five years, and held innumerable positions in the fraternal world. His wife has long since passed away and his two surviving children are George, married to Mada Dunlap, and Amy, wife of Ralph Hawkins.

REV. EDMUND HARRISON OXLEY, D.D.
Rector, St. Andrew's Episcopal Church

Rev. Dr. Oxley is the son of the late James Christopher and Laura O. Oxley, born in Trinidad, B. W. I., January 30, 1881; he is a graduate of the Queen's Royal College, affiliated to Cambridge University; a graduate of Howard University, Washington, D. C., College of Arts and Sciences with the degree of B. A., 1906; of King Episcopal Theological Hall in 1906; winner of Hebrew Prize and the Alpha Phi Prize Debate in Oratory, 1906 (Howard); ordained Deacon, Trinity Sunday, June 10, 1906, and priest, 1907, by the late Henry Yates Satterlee, D.D., L.L.D., first Bishop of Washington; received the degree of B.D. from Howard, 1908; and the

degree of S.T.B. from Harvard University, Cambridge, Mass., in 1909. Winner of the Billings Prize in Elocution and Pulpit Delivery at Harvard in the spring of 1909. In 1922, Howard University conferred upon Rev. Oxley the honorary degree of D.D.

Dr. Oxley is at present a graduate student in the Department of Philosophy, University of Cincinnati. From 1906-1908, he held charges on the eastern shore of Maryland in the Diocese of Washington; 1909-1912, he was rector of St. Augustine's Church, Harrisburg, Pa., and St. Barnaba's Church, Altoona, Pa. In October, 1912, he was called by Bishop Boyd Vincent to his present work in St. Andrew's, Cincinnati. The work here has flourished, the membership has increased ten-fold and the church now occupies a unique place in the religious, economic and social life of the colored people of Cincinnati. Dr. Oxley's pastorate has been marked by a new and substantial church of brick and Indiana limestone with parish hall and social center, a parish house, a free labor bureau, a nursery giving daytime care to the children of working mothers, and the St. Andrew's Branch of the Cincinnati Settlement School of Music (Miss Lillian Aldrich Thayer, founder), affording a rare opportunity for musical and aesthetic education on conservatory standards. The day nursery (now three years old) is one of the agencies of the Community Chest and participates in the benefits of the annual Community Chest drives.

Dr. Oxley has been active in civic and social movements; he is a member of the Board of Directors of the Juvenile Protective Association of Cincinnati, and of the Negro Civic Welfare Association of the Council of Social Agencies; a trustee of the Evangeline Home for Colored Girls, at one time acting chairman of its temporary Advisory Committee; chairman of the campaigns for the Howard University Medical Endowment and School of Religion Extension and Building Funds.

In fraternal circles Dr. Oxley is a member of the Cincinnati Clericus (ministers of the Episcopal Church), an Alpha Phi Alpha and a thirty-second degree Mason.

On June 17, 1911, in the Church of the Crucifixion, Philadelphia, Pa., the Rt. Rev. James H. Darlington, D.D., L.L.D., Bishop of Harrisburg, assisted by the Ven. Archdeacon Henry L. Phillips, D.D., united in Holy Matrimony the Rev. Oxley and Miss Esther Winifred Turner, daughter of Edward Walter and Lucy Turner, of Washington, D. C.

Mrs. Oxley is a graduate of Howard University, Teachers' College and has done special work in Cornell and in the University of Michigan. She has taught in the public schools of West Chester, Pa., and Atlantic City, N. J., where she established an enviable record for character and efficiency. Her artistic temperament and high idealism enable her to co-operate most effectively with her husband in the whole program of the church.

Three children bless this household: Lucy Orintha (13 years) now a first year student in the Woodward High School, having graduated from the Dyer Intermediate with honors as the Valedictorian of her class (the first colored girl to take part on the program of the graduating exercises); Edmund Harrison, Jr. (11 years) in the seventh grade A, Dyer Intermediate, and Elizabeth Turner (6 years) in the first grade in Sherman School.

A loyal vestry and a faithful congregation of some of the most outstanding citizens have done much towards making successful this long pastorate of increasing usefulness and power.

St. Andrew's Episcopal Church

The New Harriet Beecher Stowe School

THE NEW HARRIET BEECHER STOWE SCHOOL
Dedicated, Thanksgiving, 1923

This building, together with Sinton Park and Jackson Colonies, has a membership of 3,080 pupils. Besides the class rooms, the new building has two open air rooms, a kindergarten, two domestic science rooms, two domestic art rooms, a catering department, laundry, power machine sewing room, print shop, house construction room, cabinet making shop, wood-working shop, library, teachers' room, two shower rooms, swimming pool, doctor's office, pre-natal clinic, two play rooms, principal's office, assistant principal's office, lunch room with kitchen and storeroom, gymnasium and auditorium. The auditorium contains a pipe organ which serves its purpose in inspiring the children to better conduct.

The school is reorganized on a psychological basis and is now functioning (1) in providing equality of opportunity for all; (2) in providing the educational training that will be most valuable both for the individual and from the standpoint of society; (3) in providing teachers who are specialists not only of their particular subject, but also of human nature; (4) in providing classification of pupils according to their intelligence, followed up by a carefully planned program of educational guidance. This classification is a means by which problems become isolated, studied and solved psychologically for the good of the child, society and the state.

MISS JENNIE D. PORTER
Educator

Daughter of Wm. and Ethlinda Davis Porter. Her father was our first undertaker, her mother a school teacher in our public schools. Miss Porter was born in Cincinnati, Ohio. Graduate of Hughes High School, Cincinnati Normal School and the University of Cincinnati, where she received the degrees of B.S. and M.A. President of the local chapter of National Association of College Women (Negro division). Member of the Eastern Star. Has state life elementary and high school certificate; special certificate in music and art. Organizer, founder and principal of Harriet Beecher Stowe School, largest public school in Cincinnati, irrespective of race, having more than three thousand students. Besides Stowe school proper, Jackson Colony is under Miss Porter, and three assistant principals, Mr. Caliman, Mrs. Knight and Miss Hammond, who is psychological examiner.

Stowe school is the only school in the city organized on a psychological basis to prove statistically that the Negro is not mentally inferior. Theodore Berry, a product of Stowe, was the first Negro to represent Woodward High School as commencement orator. He appeared in that capacity at Music Hall in June, 1924. Miss Porter was the first grade teacher of DeHart Hubbard, the world's greatest athlete. Besides being an active member of Union Baptist Church, she has found time to take deep interest in the betterment of the thousands of school children who have been under her jurisdiction. Of her work the daily press and many magazines have given highest commendation.

MR. AND MRS. H. E. BRYANT

Mr. and Mrs. H. E. Bryant, natives of Kentucky, are now located at 117 W. Twelfth Street, where they have "The Restaurant of Quality," which is largely patronized for the excellence of food and service. They are members of the Oddfellows, Good Samaritans and First Baptist Church, and have a large circle of friends.

HORACE SUDDUTH

Horace Sudduth, born August 8, 1888, in Covington, Kentucky, son of Charles and Mattie Sudduth. Attended Covington High School, 1908. Married Miss Melina Jones. Has two daughters, one three years old, one one year old. Seventeen years at vocation. A member of the K. of P. and the M. E. Church. Chairman of the Committee of Management of the Ninth Street Branch Y. M. C. A. President of the Walnut Hills Enterprise Co. President of the Industrial Loan and Savings Co., a daylight building association. President and organizer of the Creative Realty Co. Owner of the Sudduth Real Estate Agency. Trustee of the Colored Orphan Asylum. Trustee of the Colored Industrial School.

Mr. Sudduth, who has been eminently successful in his profession, lives at 624 West Eighth Street.

HOME FOR AGED COLORED WOMEN

The Home for Aged Colored Women is a monument to the broad vision and benevolent spirit of the colored women of Cincinnati who, in July, 1896, organized the Progressive Benefit Society for the purpose of founding an institution which would take care of the aged women of our group in their declining years. Membership in the society was open to all and many of the charter members are still active in the society.

Incorporation papers were secured August, 1897, and the society purchased property at 2918 Park Avenue, the corporate name being "The Home for Aged Colored Women." In November of the same year the Home was opened and one of those who first entered is still a member of the aged family. This Home is the only charitable institution in the city which was founded by women and paid for by funds raised in small sums through voluntary contributions of our group. The work was maintained in this way for twenty years.

In 1919 they became members of the Community Chest and by that means the monthly maintenance is paid which assures the best care to the aged charges and the Home being operated on a high standard of efficiency.

Increasing numbers of applicants for admission compelled expansion and in 1918 the present site, 1334½ Lincoln Avenue, was purchased at a cost of $10,500. It is a modern brick structure with room to accommodate twenty-two persons.

The present family number twenty women whose ages range from 69 to 98 years.

Vesper services are held in the Home, and parties, picnics and auto rides are given by friends in the community for pleasure.

In the early years of the institution men were on the advisory board, but for nineteen years the women have had complete charge. As the Community Chest does not contribute to purchasing property, the Progressive Benefit Society faces the entire property indebtedness and all contributions received are applied to this debt. The Home has no endowment but the trustees look forward to the day when this worthy institution may be endowed through the generosity of charitable citizens of the community. The present official staff: Mrs. Elizabeth Branch, president, Progressive Benefit Society; Mrs. B. Frye, chairman of the trustee board; Mrs. Estella B. Davis, secretary; Mrs. Lucy White, treasurer; Mrs. Anna Lowe, Mrs. Jane Randolph and Mrs. M. Sneed.

Too much can not be said in praise of these self-sacrificing women who are so generously giving of their time and talent to add comfort and cheer to the lives of their aged charges. They always appreciate the co-operation of the public.

CAMMACK

The life of Richard Cammack, of Wyoming, Ohio, shows what a man can accomplish by honesty, industry and perseverance though deprived of the assistance of school education. Born in Louisiana, his mother and family came to Cincinnati in 1859. A brief stop at "The Dumas House," on to New Richmond, and finally located for about eight years on a farm bought at Mt. Healthy. Negro schooling was very scarce in those days. Young Cammack got a little of it. The schools for "colored" were only open a few months. The school board would say, "You Negroes don't pay enough taxes to have schools like white folks." Some old cast-off shack, a pine table, an old leaky stove, green wood for fuel that the pupils would chop, then in the cold, shiveringly they sat, studying, reciting, and wiping away

the tears that flowed so freely from the pungent smoke. Richard and his two brothers did all the farming. He arose at 2:00 A. M., the produce hauled to market, sold, and back again to work by 11:00 A. M. The mother died. The family scattered. For several years he "Steamboated." The drowning of his two brothers brought him back to land work. Employed in a restaurant on Western Row, now Central Avenue. From there he went to Cumminsville. Married in 1867 to Miss Ellen Ripley, of Wyoming, Ohio, formerly of Richmond, Indiana. Her brother, Jackson Hunter, the tailor, learned his trade in Tennessee on the same bench with Andrew Jackson, who became president of the United States. Ellen, the wife, was a jewel. The two planned, worked and saved. The day after marriage he had only fifty cents. She said, "We will get along," and they did. He still preserves as keepsakes, two "shin plasters," that is, three-cent pieces. One he earned, the other she found. Worked at many things, but they always saved. Learned the carpenter trade. When fifty dollars were accumulated, a lot was bought on Vine Street, Wyoming. Two rooms were built, and for forty years there they lived, gradually increasing the size of the house, buying other lots and building upon them until now there are thirty-three lots, twenty-four houses and forty-eight families renting them. His financial resources are worth thousands of dollars and his reputation for integrity amounts to a great deal more. Forty years in church work, over thirty as trustee of the A. M. E. Bethel in Lockland. Of twelve men who bought the Beech Grove Cemetery in North Wyoming, he, the only survivor, assumed all responsibility, paid off all claims, made improvements and money for the enterprise. He was a founder and was president of The Crispus Attucks B. & L. Association in Lockland until illness of his wife forced him to resign. Two years ago his devoted wife was called above. His advice to young men is, "Be true to God and man, work hard, use horse sense and mother wit; never say die, but keep on trying; success will come."

WALTER SCOTT HOUSTON

Mr. Walter Scott Houston, born near Owensboro, Davis County, Kentucky, in 1888. His father, Robert Houston, died in 1907, and his mother, Mrs. Maggie Houston, now lives in Evansville, Indiana. Industrious, energetic, economical, at an early age he began working and saving. At eighteen, though his earnings were small, yet he saved $2.50 a week, later increasing that amount to four dollars. He soon began paying on a house, and in six years had finished that and started with another, which was paid for on the same instalment plan. He married Miss Grace Harding, of Owensboro, who passed away in five years. Moving to Lockland, his work with the Phillip Carey Company made him quite a reputation for efficiency. With his savings he started a cigar booth in a prominent locality, but afterwards bought property near the corner of Wayne and Wyoming Streets, where he opened a grocery store which, under his skillful manipulation, became one of the best in the city and enjoys the patronage of both races. He married Miss Annie Mae Lee, of Hartwell, a most charming and excellent young woman, a graduate of Fiske, and now a teacher in the public schools of this city. The son, Walter Scott, Jr., has exhibited great mental brilliancy. Mr. Houston belongs to the Masons, U. B. F. and the Mt. Zion Baptist Church. He recently embarked in the undertaking business and has a thoroughly modern equipment. His property is valued at $50,000, a grand testimonial to his judgment, thrift and economy.

GEORGE W. B. CONRAD

One of Cincinnati's honored citizens is George W. B. Conrad, who holds the important position of Assistant in the Bureau of Claims, Legal Department, of the Pennsylvania Railroad Company. Mr. Conrad is probably the only colored man holding such a position with a large corporation in this country.

He was born in Xenia, Ohio, and entered the railroad service when fifteen years old. He received his preliminary education at Xenia, Ohio, and Richmond, Indiana, and in 1895, by the consent of his superiors, he was given a leave of absence to better equip himself for railroad service and spent three years at Oberlin College, after which he entered the University of Michigan and graduated from the law class of 1902, being selected as the alternate class orator by a class of 256. He has been admitted to the bar in Michigan, Indiana and Ohio.

During his many years of service with the Pennsylvania Railroad, Mr. Conrad served as messenger, clerk, stenographer and telegraph operator, and is said to have been the first telegraph operator on the railroad to "take" matter over the wires directly on the typewriter.

During his service he was associated as Secretary with many prominent railroad men, namely, Col. J. F. Miller, formerly vice-president of the Pennsylvania Railroad and United States Commissioner of Louisiana Purchase Exposition at St. Louis; J. J. Turner, who became first vice-president, Pennsylvania Railroad; W. B. Leeds, afterwards designated as Tin-Plate King; G. W. Davies, general freight agent, and others. In fact, Mr. Conrad has served with distinction in every line of the railroad service and is considered a thorough railroad man.

In 1903 he was given the position of Assistant in the Bureau of Claims, Law Department, and has represented the railroad company a number of times in court in friendly suits. He enjoys the respect and confidence of men high in the councils of the railroad company and has been highly commended for the results he has achieved as an adjuster and investigator.

In 1910 he married one of Cincinnati's most beautiful and accomplished young ladies, Miss Beatrice Cox, a member of one of Cincinnati's oldest and most highly respected families. Mrs. Conrad for a long time was a teacher in the high school of Wheeling, West Virginia, and is now a successful teacher in the Cincinnati schools. Mr. and Mrs. Conrad have one child, Elizabeth, who has seemingly inherited the best attributes of her parents. They reside at 3220 Beresford Avenue, Walnut Hills.

It is interesting to note that Mr. Conrad's father, Thomas A. Conrad, deceased, formerly resided, with his wife and three children, at Xenia, Ohio. He was a contractor and builder, Grand High Priest, Royal Arch Masons, State of Ohio, a veteran of the Civil War, and his grandfather, Scipio Conrad, was a member of the Revolutionary army.

ELIZABETH JONES EASTON

Elizabeth Jones Easton, nee Elizabeth Moore, daughter of Mrs. Richard Connelly, was a young woman of most charming personality. Born in Cincinnati, but of Kentucky stock, she was an exemplification of the graces of both places. In her high school days she belonged to the Wit and Wisdom Club, and when from Woodward she graduated, none of her classmates were more popular. Thanks to her complexion, she was able to enter and graduate from the Cincinnati College of Music. A period of teaching at West Virginia Institute, and she became the bride of its president, J. McHenry Jones, whose fame as an educator, orator, Oddfellow, was national. After his passage to the great beyond, Madame Jones increased her culture and musical knowledge by a journey to Europe. On her return, a love of school girl days was revived and she became the wife of L. D. Easton, Jr., of Detroit, a scion of the well-known Easton family, prominent in this  city for half a century. Some travel, as accompanist for Madame Mitchell, then God called, and she left behind a weeping mother and thousands of friends. Her life was an inspiration to the race of which she was never ashamed, and it is to be hoped that the perusal of this sketch may serve as a beacon light to teach other girls that virtue, learning and industry are in the reach of all and ever bring their devotees to the glorious harbor of prosperity and happiness.

F. M. RUSSELL
Principal of Douglass School

Born March 31, 1879, at Knoxville, Tennessee, the son of Thomas and Elizabeth Russell. Attended the University of Cincinnati, receiving his A.B. Degree in 1904 and the M.A. Degree in 1906. Married Miss Zenobia Cox. A member of the A. M. E. Church, the Masons and the Alpha Phi Alpha fraternity. Teacher in Covington High School, 1904-05. Principal, Newport, Ky., 1905-09. Principal, Douglass School, 1909-22. Supervisor, Baltimore Schools, 1922-24. Principal, Douglass School, 1924. Member of first Board of Trustees of the Colored Industrial School, member of first Committee of Management of Y. M. C. A. and Executive Board of Negro Civic Welfare League.

DOUGLASS—*School Edifice, Alms Place and Chapel Street.*—Completed in 1910; cost $167,871. Lot, 200 by 200 feet; cost $63,300. Building has nineteen classrooms, two kindergarten rooms, auditorium, household and industrial arts rooms, laundry, model flat, sewing room, library, gymnasium, lunch room, open air room, neighborhood club room, boys' and girls' shower baths, nurse and doctor's office, principal's office, two indoor play rooms, home school and community house in six-room, modern, furnished house on school playground; also school garden; seats 800 pupils. In addition the school has three portable buildings containing six rooms and seats for 180 children.

BENJAMIN H. BAKER
Insurance Manager

Born March 21, 1870, at Beaufort, South Carolina. Son of Rev. Benjamin and Emily Baker. Attended public schools in Beaufort. Graduate of Beaufort High School; graduate of Lincoln University with degree of A.B. Student in Howard Medical School. Interne in Freedom's Hospital, 1904-05. With Columbian Fraternal Association as manager for thirty years, having charge of offices at Washington, Philadelphia, Augusta, New Orleans, Pennsylvania. Opened present office in Cincinnati in 1923. For twenty years superintendent of Sunday School, also choir master. Now located at 636 W. Ninth Street.

JEANETTE LUELLA HENDRICKS

Daughter of Josephine and Frank Mitchell. Born March 8, 1875, at Lexington, Kentucky. Attended public schools of Lexington. Her husband, J. F. Hendricks, died September 26, 1924. She has been 23 years in the business and fraternal field. H. P. of Crystal Fount Tabernacle No. 473. Member of the Calvary Baptist Church and a Republican. Arrived in Cincinnati thirty-three years ago; became active in fraternal world. Owner of the Southern restaurant for seven years. High Priestess for twenty-two years. Past G. H. P., Ohio Jurisdiction, Knights and Daughters of Tabor for six years. Treasurer of Etowah Temple, Daughters of Elks, seven years. P. M. N. Governors Household of Ruth; P. Presiding Daughter of Good Samaritans. Worthy Princess St. Cecelia Temple No. 15. Sister of Mysterious Ten. Grand Queen Mother, Wilson Court, Court of Calanthe No. 45. A. U. K. & D. of A, Golden Rule Council. Grand organizer of The Sisters of the Mysterious Ten. Past G. C. Elks of World.

JOHN S. FIELDING
Business and Fraternity Man

Born January 26, 1872, at Lancaster, Ohio. Son of Wm. and Eliza J. Fielding, successful business people. Graduate of Lancaster Grammar and Lancaster High School, 1884-77. Twenty years at vocation. Nine years notary public. Organizer of Garnet Lodge, K. of P., No. 32. Organizer of Excelsior Co. E.; Zenith Court of Calanthe; Lebanon Guiding Star; Lockland Links of Friendship; Columbus Pride of West; Queen Etta Court No. 1. Member Eva Lodge of Oddfellows No. 8218. Member Eva Household. Past Grand Chancellor of Ohio. Past Supreme Worthy Counsellor. Past Grand Worthy Counsellor. Organizer of Ohio Grand Court. Organizer of Alpha Lodge of Elks. State Grand Chief of the Ohio Good Samaritans. Major General in command of Good Samaritans. Supreme Protector of K. P.'s since 1903. Organizer of present Fraternal League, 1909. Organizer and manager Famous Fraternal League Band. A member of the Episcopal Church and of the Republican party. A founder of St. Andrew Episcopal Church Sunday School. Superintendent thirty years. Scoutmaster of Troop No. 53, Boy Scouts. Member of Co. E. Secretary of Insurance Department of O. O. C. Engrossing and Calendar Clerk in the House of Representatives. Organizer and member of Galilean Fishermen. Formerly undertaker. Business place, 510 West Sixth Street. Residence, 728 Barr Street, Cincinnati, Ohio.

MR. ANDREW SHARP

Mr. Andrew Sharp, a slave of the Adair family, Carlisle, Kentucky. Sergeant in the 177th Regiment during the Civil War. Died one year ago, aged ninety-three. After the war he located in Lockland, his family being the third to settle there. He became one of our leading contractors and did most of the work for the wealthy Hosea family. Two of Clifton's finest avenues, Brookline and Hosea, were made by him. He was ever on the best of terms with the Adairs, his former owners in Kentucky, and they made him splendid inducements to return there to live. His second wife was Miss Georgia Elizabeth Minnegan, of Xenia. Her grandfather was Sir Wm. Minnegan, a noble of Scotland. He had three colored sons, all light mulattoes. One he took back to Europe, another he made a sea captain, the third married and remained in this country. The daughter of Mrs. Minnegan, Mrs. Consuelo Sharp Holloway, is a very intelligent and highly respected citizen of this community and resides at 806 Hopkins Street.

JOHN W. HUFFMAN

John W. Huffman, born in Springfield, Ohio, in 1884. His parents, Mr. and Mrs. Samuel E. Huffman, were well-known residents of that city. After attending high school he went to Chicago and finished the study of Chiropody. In 1914 he came to this city, opened an office and later became leader of Huffman's Dansant Orchestra, which furnished music for the principal parks, hotels and dancing academies. Since 1917 he has been located at 122 W. Fourth Street, the well-known offices of chiropody established by the late Dr. John Banks.

NED HARRIS GILLARD
Tonsorial Artist

Born November 23, 1873, at Huntsville, Alabama. Son of Moses and Sallie Gillard, prosperous farmers. Married Miss Ella Kendrich, February 6, 1924. One child, Louise, by former marriage. Seven years at vocation. A member of the Masons, Oddfellows, Woodmen, U. N. I. A., and of the Presbyterian Church and the Republican party. Came to Cincinnati in 1903. In butcher business in Huntsville, Alabama, 1903. Melter of Cincinnati Abatoir for fifteen years. Opened present place of business in 1918. Now located at 756 Barr Street, and is now very well and prominently known in business circles.

JOHN E. DIXON
Barber

Son of Mr. and Mrs. Stokes. Born at St. Joseph, Missouri, April 4, 1844. Attended public schools in Cincinnati. Married Miss Harriet Werles. He has been working at his vocation fifty-nine years. An Oddfellow, a member of Allen Temple, and politically a Republican. Born a slave, taken from parents and sold South when very young; ran away and came North. Resident here since the war, prominent in church, a model of sobriety and propriety. Owner of the only barber shop in the lower downtown business district for nearly sixty years. Resides at 834 Barr Street with his wife and his daughter who is zealous in work of church and social betterment.

E. B. GRAY, M.D.
Physician and Surgeon

Born Lincoln, Pennsylvania, 1888. Son of Mr. and Mrs. Samuel Gray. Graduate of M. St. High, Washington, D. C., 1908. Attended Amherst, 1908-09. Graduate of Howard University, 1913, Degree M.D. Interne Kansas General Hospital, 1913-14. Began practice in Cincinnati, 1915. Married Miss Corolynne Wilson, employed as school teacher in Atlantic City, N. J., Public schools, 1917. One child, Corolynne, born November 10, 1918. Chief of Staff, Mercy Hospital. Member of Alpha Phi Alpha. Methodist Episcopal. President of Model Drug Co. Thirty-second Degree Mason. Star all-American athlete; was physical training coach of Wilberforce. Office, 542 West Fifth Street. Residence, 878 Buena Vista Place, Walnut Hills.

WM. A. JACKSON

Son of Eliza and Augustus Jackson. Born October 7, 1870, at Lebanon, Illinois. Attended public and high schools of Illinois, and Cincinnati business college. Married Carrie Glenn of Ohio. He has spent ten years at his vocation. Captain of Co. F, K. of P., and also an Elk. Member of Park Street M. E. Church. A Republican. Came to Cincinnati in 1890. Associated with the Arcade Barber Shop for twenty-seven years. Opened first class shoe shining shop, 1915, at 8 West Twelfth Street, having for sale cigars and periodicals. Resides at 530 Richmond Street.

MRS. MARTHA B. WILLIAMS
Beauty Culturist

Born at Lexington, Kentucky, March 10, 1892. Daughter of Mr. and Mrs. Simon Engleman. Graduated from Cincinnati public schools 1911; graduated from E. Burnham's School of Beauty Culture, Chicago, Ill., June, 1920. Pursued and specialized in the beauty profession in Cincinnati and opened a first class beauty shoppe, March 27, 1924, at present business place. A member of Park Street M. E. Church. She has, in the last year, built up an immense trade. Her place of business is at 506 West Fifth Street. Residence, 634 West Fourth Street.

WM. JOS. DOUGLASS
Proprietor of Restaurant

Son of Benjamin and Hattie Douglass. Born December 20, 1872, at Madison County, Kentucky. Attended public schools in Louisville. Married Mary Banks, 1900. Has spent two years at vocation. He is a Mason and K. of P. and a member of the Independent party. Associated with Liberian haberdashers as director, formerly vice-president. A man of thorough business qualifications and experience. Proprietor of Palace Grill restaurant, which is located at 2966 Gilbert Avenue.

T. L. BERRY, M.D.
Physician and Surgeon

Born October 17, 1892, at Hopkinsville, Kentucky. Son of Louis and Josephine Berry. Graduate of M. & F. College, Hopkinsville, 1910, with degree of A.B.; Meharry Medical College, 1911-15, graduating with degree of M.D.; graduate of Meharry with Ph.D. in 1915. Now en-engaged in general practice of medicine and surgery. Ten years at vocation. A member of the Independent party. Practiced in Frankfort, 1915-24. Surgeon in Chief at Winnie Scott Hospital. On staff of Mercy Hospital, and a member of the Cincinnati Medical Association. Is located at 530 Mound Street, Cincinnati, Ohio.

CLAY E. HUNTER
Attorney at Law

Born, Union City, Tennessee, January 14, 1895. Son of Mr. and Mrs. J. C. Hunter, prosperous farmers of Yellow Springs, Ohio. Graduate Bath Tp. Public School, Ohio, 1909; of Bath Tp. High School, 1913; of Wilberforce University, A.B., 1917. Served as second lieutenant, U. S. Army, in World War, 1918-19, 92nd Division. Engaged in Metz drive on Marbache sector. Graduate of Ohio State University, '23, Degree L.L.B. Associate attorney with W. E. King, Columbus, Ohio, 1923-24. Came to Cincinnati, 1924. Associated with law firm of Hunter & Blythe. Independent Republican, Baptist, Kappa Alpha Psi fraternity, and an Elk. Located at 605 Smith Street, Cincinnati.

WM. H. BUCKNER
Proprietor Shoe Shining Parlor

Born September 19, 1890, at Fayette County, Kentucky. Son of Mr. and Mrs. Wm. Buckner. Attended public schools in Cincinnati, Ohio. Married. Five years at vocation. A member of the Independent Republican party. Came to Cincinnati in 1900. Opened up first class billiard and pool-room the spring of 1920. Now located at 517 West Fifth Street, Cincinnati, Ohio.

MACK WALLS
Contract Cleaning

Son of Elijah and Sallie Baufman. Born June 5, 1884, at Owensboro, Kentucky. Attended public schools in Owensboro. Married to Ada Delaney, 1922. Three children by former marriage. He has been at his vocation for eight years. A member of the K. of P. and formerly U. B. F. Deacon of the First Baptist Church and a Republican. Carpet maker and cement finisher, at which trades he worked in Owensboro and Covington. Opened first class cleaning establishment (window washing and contract cleaning) in 1918. Now resides at 116 East Ninth Street, Covington, Kentucky.

CHAS. A. SCHOOLEY
Dentist

Son of Barney and Sarah Schooley. Born December 18, 1861, at Wilberforce, Ohio. Attended public and high schools in Cincinnati. Married Mary Ray, deceased ten years, to whom one child was born, Mrs. Robt. Mallory, of Dayton, Ohio. He has practiced dentistry for twenty-seven years. An Episcopalian and politically a Republican. Captain of Co. E formerly, a K. of P., and a member of the Crescent Club. Moved to Cincinnati when one year old, schooled and reared here. Has been engaged in the practice of dentistry since the early eighties. Associated with the Ohio Dental Co. for thirteen years. Opened present place of business at 757 West Court Street, in 1898. He is one of our most substantial citizens and has a large white practice.

M. T. SWEENEY
Custom Tailor

Born at Casey County, Kentucky, 1889. Son of Mr. and Mrs. James Sweeney. Graduate of Bates High School, Danville, Kentucky, 1908. Came to Cincinnati, 1913. Served in World War as Post Tailor, 1916-17, at Fort Thomas, Kentucky; 1918-19, Fort Sheridan, Illinois. Opened complete tailoring establishment, 1923. Married Miss Goldie Dalton, graduate Ohio University, 1924, employed as teacher in Cincinnati public schools. One son, Moss T. Jr., a child by former marriage. Baptist. Business place located at 525 West Fifth Street. Residence, San Rafael Building.

MADAM CORA E. WALKER
Beauty Culturist and Musician

Born June 27, 1892, at Cincinnati, Ohio, the daughter of Rev. and Mrs. J. G. Orr. She attended public schools in Cincinnati. Married Mr. J. A. Walker in 1924. One child, Edith, by a former marriage. She has been at her vocation five years; church organist four years. A member of Mt. Zion Baptist Church and a Republican. A member of the Eastern Star, A. U. K. and D. of A., and a Good Samaritan, being secretary of the three. Reared in Cincinnati. A graduate of Poro College of St. Louis in 1920. Opened modern beauty shop in 1923. Now located at 702 Maple Street, Lockland, Ohio.

H. I. WILSON
D. D. S.

Son of Mr. and Mrs. James R. Wilson. Father real estate agent and mother a school teacher. Was born September 15, 1893, at Danville, Virginia. Graduate of Danville public schools, Howard Academy, Howard University, B.S., 1918, and Howard College of Dentistry, 1921. A member of the Episcopal Church and politically a Republican (Independent). Associated in dentistry with Dr. I. O. Mitchell, of Washington, D. C., from 1921-1922. Came to Cincinnati, September, 1922. A member of the Alpha Phi Alpha fraternity. Located at S. E. Cor. Sixth and Mound Streets. Has a rapidly growing business.

JAMES A. WALKER
Policeman and Business Man

Born May 24, 1892, in Warsaw, Kentucky, the son of Wallace and Sarah Walker. Attended public school in Warsaw and Lockland. He married Cora Orr of Cincinnati in 1924. He has been ten years on the police force and two years in business. A member of Mt. Zion Baptist Church and a Republican. A member of the Corinthian Lodge No. 1, F. A. M.-K. of P., Anthony Lodge No. 30 of U. B. F., and the A. U. K. and D. of A. Came to Cincinnati in 1905. Opened tonsorial shop in 1923. One of the leaders of the community, also a property owner. Resides at 729 Mulberry Street, Lockland, Ohio.

STEPHEN H. WATERS
Assistant Librarian, Circuit Court of Appeals (Notary Public)

Son of Jacob and Julia Waters. Born August 14, 1860, at Paris, Kentucky. Attended public schools in Lebanon, Ohio, and at Wilberforce. Married Minnie M. Moore, of Cincinnati, June 29, 1899. He has been at his vocation thirty-five years. Trustee of Allen Temple, A. M. E. Church, and a Republican. Formerly an Oddfellow and K. of P. Associated with dry goods store in Lebanon, Ohio, six years. Messenger for the Lebanon National Bank six years. Served also as guard. Associated with law office of Runyan Diltusch for about six years. Crier of Circuit Court of Appeals and personal messenger for Wm. H. Taft for nine years, serving as night librarian the same time. Was appointed assistant librarian in 1900. A property owner and a valuable citizen. Member of the Board of Trustees of Colored Orphan Asylum. Resides at 2813 Lincoln Avenue.

MORRIS S. WALTON

Born in 1887 at Camp Dennison, Ohio, the son of Louis S. and Fannie L. Walton. Attended Howard University and the University of Cincinnati. A member of the Baptist Church, Alpha Phi Alpha, K. of P. and Masons. He taught at the Tuskegee Institute in Alabama, Douglass School, Principal of the public school in Lockland. Ex-Secretary of the Y. M. C. A. in Lockland. At present manager for the Art Print Shop owned by W. L. Anderson. Trustee of the Colored Industrial School of Cincinnati. First lieutenant of the 372nd Infantry, O. N. G. Mr. Walton is located at 636 West Ninth Street.

JOHN B. BUSHILLON
Professional Barber

Son of Sarah and Woody Bushillon. Born January 19, 1884, in Clinton, Alabama. Attended public schools in Alabama. In 1924, he married Minnie Roberts of Kentucky. He has one child, Benjamin, by a former marriage. He has spent fifteen years at his vocation. A Baptist, Republican, Mason, K. of P. and an American Woodman. Came to Cincinnati, 1916, where he was associated with the Charlie Williams barbering establishment. His business is located at 1130 Lincoln Avenue and his residence at 2829 Ashland Avenue.

DR. J. H. WALLACE
Surgeon and Physician

Born at Bessemer, Alabama, March 12, 1896, the son of Mr. and Mrs. Eugene and Nannie B. Wallace. Graduate Anniston Normal and Industrial High School, 1913; Selma University, 1914; Meharry Medical College, 1914-18. Interne Hubbard Hospital, Nashville, Tenn. Began practicing in Lockland, 1920. Staff surgeon Mercy Hospital. An Oddfellow, K. of P., Elk, Baptist and Republican. Married Miss Lygia Kaufman, R. N., employed as public health nurse in City of Cincinnati, December 5, 1923. One child, J. H. Wallace, Jr., born March 8, 1925. May be found at 622 Maple Street, Lockland, Ohio.

ROBERT AUGUSTUS FOWLER
Pullman Porter

Son of William and Luella Fowler. Born April 22, 1875, at Georgetown, Kentucky. Attended the public schools of Georgetown. Married Miss Laura Bell Watson. He has been at his vocation twenty-two years. Member of the K. of P., U. B. F. and F. A. M. Member of the Methodist Episcopal Church and politically a Republican. Founder and organizer of the Colored Railway Employees' Beneficial Association of America, incorporated in Ohio. Now residing at 3015 Kerper Avenue.

REV. SAM ALBERT BROWN
Clergyman

Son of Rev. Albert and Sarah Brown. Born November 9, 1870, at Kingston, Tennessee. Married Geneva Shorter of Mt. Washington, to whom five children were born, S. Albert, Jr., Edith G., Robert H., Howard S., and David Anderson Brown. Attended Rochester Academy, Howard University and Boston Latin School of Theology. Twenty-six years at his vocation. Presbyterian, an Independent, and an Oddfellow. Pastor of Congregational Church, Boston, Mass., for ten years. Member of the N. A. A. C. P., on executive committee for seven years. President of the Board of Trustees of Harriet Tubman House. Worked as secretary of Y. M. C. A. at Camp Dix during World War. Appointed Chaplain in U. S. Army day of armistice. Accepted call to Carmel Presbyterian Church, Cincinnati, 1923, of which he is now pastor. Member of the Board of Directors of Mercy Hospital. Property owner and resides at 655 Melish Avenue.

Carmel Presbyterian Church

CHAS. E. A. HUNT
Pullman Porter Instructor

Son of Jeremiah and Frances Hunt. Born August 15, 1867, at Middleport, Ohio. Attended public schools. Married Clara B. Dudley. At his vocation thirty years. Member of the Metropolitan Baptist Church and politically Independent. Member of the G. U. O. of O. F., K. of P., G. U. O. of G. F., P. P. B. A. of A., A. U. K. & D. of A., and Vice-President of the N. A. A. C. P. He is one of the most efficient, active and loyal men in the railway service. Resides at 1056 Baymiller Street.

REV. C. W. WRIGHT
Business Man and Clergyman

Born Upson County, Georgia, February 7, 1878. Attended school in Upson County, Georgia. Son of Mr. and Mrs. Green and Sarah Wright. Pastor St. Timothy Baptist Church, Birmingham, 1910-1916. Came to Cincinnati, November 19, 1916. Pastor of Second Southern Baptist Church, 925 West Fifth Street, 1917-25. Opened present place of business 1922. Married Mrs. Mattie Miller, Birmingham, Alabama, 1908. One boy, Corneil W., Jr., by former marriage. Now located at 816 West Fourth Street, Cincinnati, Ohio.

ALBERT C. TEDFORD

Born September 19, 1892, at Knoxville, Tennessee, the son of Walter and Lula Tedford. His father was a successful roofer. Attended public schools in Cincinnati. Married Mary Ellison in 1919. They have one child,

Juanita Tedford. He has been at his vocation four years. A Republican and an Elk. Associated with Hubig's pie plant for four years. Served in U. S. Army for two years; engaged in Meuse-Argonne offensive for four months. Entered present business as associate, 1921, becoming proprietor in 1923, where a modern shoe shining business is conducted with the agency. Located at 331 West Fifth Street.

MISS BELZORA J. MATTHEWS
Teacher

Born May 14, 1898, at Akron, Ohio. Daughter of James and Jennie Matthews, the father a mechanic. Attended public schools in Youngstown, Ohio. Attended Selma University; graduate of Normal and College Prep., 1914. Ten years at vocation. A member of the Baptist Church and the Republican party. Began teaching school in Dothan, Alabama, in 1915. Teacher of Troy public school, Alabama, 1917-19; teacher at Memphis, Tennessee, 1914-24. From 1924 to the present, matron and teacher at Colored Girls' Home. Located at 816 West Ninth Street.

MADAM L. J. REED
Beauty Culturist and Manufacturess

Born November 15, 1885, at Tuscumbia, Alabama. Daughter of Dr. and Mrs. Frank Hubbard. Attended public schools in Alabama and Ohio, Clifts College at East Lake, Alabama, and graduate of Wyoming High, 1917. Beauty Culturist eight years. Proprietor of notion store seven years. A member of the American Woodmen, Spiritualist Church and of the Republican party. Came to Cincinnati in 1911. Graduated from Twin Beauty System in Indianapolis. Specialized in French system and established own manufacturing of hair and toilet preparations, 1918. A teacher of modern methods in beauty culture. Located at 713 Cutter Street, Cincinnati, Ohio.

CHARLES O. TURNER
Grocery Store

Born at Lockland, Ohio, the son of John and Eliza Turner, who were among the earliest pioneers. His father was a dentist. He attended the public schools of Lockland and has been at his vocation seventeen years. A member of the A. M. E. Church and a Republican. He has been generally employed as a grocery clerk in the vicinity; also as a man in private family. Opened the present place of business in 1908. Located at 634 Maple Street, Lockland, Ohio.

CARRIE L. JAMES
Civic and Social Worker

Daughter of Edward and Anna Gillock. Born March 2, 1885, at New Albany, Indiana. Attended grade and high school. Married Wm. James. They have one child. She has been at her vocation ten years. A member of the Zion Baptist Church and politically Independent. A member of the Eastern Star, Daughters of Isis, and the Ladies Auxiliary of the Railway Association. A Christian for twenty-five years and a missionary worker in Zion Baptist Church for twenty years. At present engaged in civic work in her community. Resides at 803 Richmond Street.

MRS. RICHIE KYLES SMITH
Pharmacist

Daughter of Richard A. and Claudie B. Kyles. Born December 24, 1897, in Sanford, Florida. Attended grammar and high school in Birmingham, Alabama. Student at Talladega College. Received professional training and Ph.C. degree from Meharry Medical School in 1916. Member of the Congregational Church. In charge of Andrew's Hospital, Tuskegee, Alabama, for two years. Hay's Drug Store, Richmond, Virginia, for two years. With Ferguson's Drug Store, Tulsa, Oklahoma, for one year, during which time the Tulsa riot took place, from which Miss Kyles escaped with many bruises and great loss of personal property. Associated with Bright's Pharmacy, Louisville, Kentucky, two years. Accepted position with Model Drug Co. of this city, 1923; now in charge of the branch store in Covington. She has held positions of responsibility in Detroit and Chicago.

MR. AND MRS. HAMLIN

Mr. Nash Hamlin and Mrs. Ruth Hamlin came from Leaksville, North Carolina. They were married there and have lived here many years. In 1913 they started in the coal, ice and express business. The success of that enterprise prompted the entrance of Mr. and Mrs. Hamlin in the grocery business in 1925. They are located at 620 John Street. Though Mr. Hamlin has had only three months' schooling he has been very successful.

MRS. ANNA BECKWITH
Pharmacist

Daughter of Elijah and Amanda Logan. Born August 12, 1888, in Berea, Kentucky. Attended Berea public schools and Berea College. Married Carl Beckwith, post office clerk of Cincinnati. They have two children, Alice and Juanita. Has spent two years at her vocation. She is a member of the M. E. Church and the Independent party. Came to Cincinnati in 1903; purchased the Peerless Pharmacy, Alms and Chapel Street, in 1923. Mrs. Beckwith ranks as a most efficient pharmacist and since her purchase in 1923, of the Peerless Pharmacy, she has done wonders in reestablishing the business it formerly enjoyed.

WM. ARTHUR CARTER, Esq.

Wm. Arthur Carter, Esq., was a graduate of the Law Department of Howard University, honored member of the Hamilton County Bar, a highly respected citizen of Cincinnati. He was responsible for initiating the movement which allows colored men in Cincinnati to take the firemen's examination. On November 21, 1917, Attorney Carter departed this life, leaving a devoted wife, Mrs. M. Q. Carter, and a dear mother. During the brief span of his existence he made every effort to improve living conditions in this city and render more fraternal the relations between his fellowmen.

JAMES W. QUINCY
Real Estate

Born October 24, 1864, at Shelby County, Kentucky, the son of John and Sarah Quincy. Attended public school in Louisville, Kentucky. Married his second wife, Miss Mary Frances Walker, in September, 1915. At eight years of age, began work in a tobacco factory; at sixteen, rough railorad work; at twenty, went into the Pullman service. Two years in Monarch Company sleeping cars. Seventeen and a half years with the C. & O. R. R. About eight years in private family. Four and a half years with the Times-Star. Two years as shipping clerk of Book Shelf, No. 15 Doctors' Bldg. Seller of nursery stock and real estate agent for twelve years. A member of the Methodist Church and politically a Republican. At this writing, acting master of the Masonic Club, which will be known as the Euclid Lodge of F. & A. M. of College Hill. Now organizing The Ideal Subdivision Company on College Hill, to secure better homes and better people for the suburb.

JOSEPH AMOS
Proprietor of Restaurant

Born March 1, 1872, in Sumpter County, Georgia, son of Mr. and Mrs. Chas. Amos. Attended public schools of Georgia. Married Miss Isabelle Messenger of Alabama in 1915. Ten years at vocation. A member of the Masons, Baptist Church and of the Republican party. In Birmingham, Alabama, owned barber shop and restaurant, 1910-15. Professional fireman till 1910. Opened present place of business, 1915. Located at 654 West Fifth Street.

FERGUSON-McLEOD CO.

The Lincoln Oil and Supply Co. is owned and operated by The Ferguson-McLeod Co., Inc., at Alms and Lincoln Avenue. It is the first and only oiling and supply station of such magnitude in this city owned by colored people. It marks their entrance into what is destined to be a most lucrative financial field.

DENNIE JONES

Dennie Jones, born in Columbus, Ohio, has made a specialty of the express business and contracts for hauling of all kinds. In three years he has acquired many patrons. He is a Mason, Corinthian Lodge No. 1, and is located at 734 West Seventh Street.

THE HALE SISTERS

The Hale Sisters came to this city many years ago from Kentucky. Being well versed in the art of cooking and serving, they opened a restaurant at 506 Carlisle Avenue about ten years ago. They have built up a splendid business, achieved great success, and made many friends.

REV. RICHARD H. DAVIS
Clergyman

Son of Rev. Isaiah and Elizabeth Davis. Born October 10, 1881, at Jamaica, B. W. I. Attended public schools in Jamaica; Southern Christian Ins., Edwards, Mississippi; Eureka College, Eureka, Illinois; and U. of C. In 1920 he married Mabel B. Isle, of Cincinnati. He has spent twelve years at his profession. He is a Mason, K. of P., Good Samaritan, Pastor of the Disciples of Christ Church. Came to Cincinnati, December, 1916. Pastored in Edwards, Mississippi, and Bloomington, Illinois. Called to Kenyon Avenue Christian Church, 1916, of which church he is now pastor. Membership increased from sixty-five to four hundred and seventy-five. Additions to the church at an approximate cost of $15,000. He is president of National Bible Department of Christian Church, associated with Supreme Life and Casualty Co. for seven years, chairman of Committee of Juvenile Delinquency under Federation of Churches (colored department). Residence, 2037 Edison Street.

IRENE J. KIRKE
Accountant and Notary Public

Born at Milford, Ohio, September 18, 1887. Daughter of William and Margaret Anderson. Attended Cincinnati public schools and Wilberforce University. Sixteen years spent at present vocation. A member of the A. U. K. and D. of A.; Eastern Star, United Daughters of America; a member of First Baptist Church, Walnut Hills, and a Republican. Also Olive Leaf. Kowalige Acad. & Indus., Alabama, 1909-1912; secretary to Pres. Benson; bookkeeper for Dixie Industrial Co., Benson, Alabama, 1912; cashier of Brown's Savings Bank, Norfolk, 1912-1913; bookkeeper, Americus Institute, Americus, Georgia, 1914. Since 1915, accountant and manager of Horace Sudduth Real Estate establishment. Secretary, Industrial Savings & Loan Co. Secretary, Creative Realty Co. Secretary, Walnut Hills Enterprise Co. Lives at 2008 Freeland Avenue.

J. C. STEELE
Proprietor of Pressing and Cleaning Establishment

Son of Frissby and Ollie Steele. Born November 15, 1887, at Cincinnati. Attended public schools. Graduate of West Virginia Collegiate Institute, 1906. In 1912 he married Pearl Dickson, of Portsmouth, Ohio, who is a competent business partner. Has spent four years at vocation. He is a Mason, a member of the Mt. Zion M. E. Church, and the Republican party. Pursued painting, 1908-1915. Taught school, West Virginia, 1906-1908. Opened present place of business in 1921. Has contributed several works of art. Two shops, 766 West Fifth Street and 3063 Kerper Avenue.

HENRY M. HIGGINS
Assistant City Sealer

Born April 14, 1864, at Louisville, Kentucky, the son of Monroe and Sarah Higgins. He attended school in Indianapolis. First marriage was to Miss Susie Johnson, of which union one son was born, Dr. Henry M. Higgins, Jr., of Chicago, Ill. Second marriage June 21, 1924, to Miss Ida Liverpool, member of pioneer family and teacher of art. He is a member of Brown Chapel A. M. E. Church and politically a Republican. A member of the Knights of Pythias, Oddfellows, and the Independent Order of Elks; trustee of the Colored Orphan Asylum for twenty-seven years; secretary of our First Building and Loan Company in Hamilton County; secretary of the Civil Rights League, one of the first organizations formed in Hamilton County for the purpose of securing civil rights. Prominent member Pythian Home Board. Now resides at 2807 Park Avenue.

GEORGE W. SMITH
Proprietor of Shoe Shining Parlor and Confectionery

Born February 28, 1894, at Rutherford County, Tennessee. Son of Joe and Mary Smith, prosperous farmers. Attended public schools in Tennessee. Married Miss Della McPherson in 1923, of Cincinnati, Ohio. One year at vocation. A member of the Elks, Antioch Baptist Church, and of the Republican party. Came to Cincinnati in 1918. Served in World War, entering at Camp Sherman, six months. Now located at 710 Linn Street.

CAPTAIN ELIZABETH MOORE
Organizer

Daughter of Rev. P. H. and Fannie Smith. Born January 2, 1878, at South Charleston, Ohio. Attended school at New Richmond, Ohio. Married James B. Moore. She has been at her vocation as a fraternal organizer four years. The only lady that stood on Major General Jackson's staff of K. of P., August, 1917, in St. Louis, Mo., representing the State of Ohio. Now residing at 3041 O'Bryon Street.

EUGENE F. LACEY
Proprietor of Gene Bess Store

Son of Samuel and Emma Lacey, one of oldest families. Born March 19, 1888, at Covington, Kentucky. Attended public schools in Covington. Married Bessie Meritt of Falmouth, Kentucky. Seven years at his vocation. 32nd Degree Mason, Oddfellow, past officer and secretary in Consistory and Shrine. Member Ninth Street M. E. Church and politically non-partisan. Messenger in the German National Bank six years. Associated with Duncan's Drug Store two years. Opened first class grocery and general store in 1918. Property owner of Covington. Now residing at 205 E. Robins Street, Covington, Kentucky.

JESSE D. LOCKER
Attorney

Born May 31, 1891, at College Hill, Cincinnati, Ohio. Son of Rev. L. S. and Elizabeth Morgan Locker. Graduate of the College Hill High School, 1911; Law School, Howard University, degree LL.B., 1915. Married in 1915 to Anna French-Locker. Three children by this marriage, Mary, Vivian and Cleo Ann. Six years at vocation. Member of Masons, Christian Church, and of the Independent Republican party. Now resides at 730 West Sixth Street.

ALBERT PARKS
Confectioner and Shoe Repairer

Son of John W. and Laura Parks. Born February 21, 1888, at Carlisle, Kentucky. Attended public schools in Ohio. Graduate of Wilberforce trade school 1921. Has spent three years at vocation. He is a member of the Christian Church, American Legion, and the Republican party. Came to Cincinnati after being honorably discharged from U. S. Army. Has seen active service with 365th Infantry engaged in Meuse-Argonne drive. Opened present business in 1922. Now located at 1106 Foraker Avenue.

DR. B. JAY LOCKLEY
Physician and Surgeon

Born December 24, 1894. Son of Victoria and B. J. Lockley. Graduate of grammar school. Gilbert Academy, Baldwin, Louisiana. B.S. from New Orleans University, 1916. M.D. from Meharry Medical College, 1917-1921. Married Miss Viola Grant, of Paris, Kentucky, a teacher in the Cincinnati public schools and who is a B.A. graduate of Fiske University and author of Standard Test devised while a special Psychology student at Ohio State University (1921). One child, Geraldine, born August 6, 1925, at Cincinnati, Ohio. Member of Park Street M. E. Church, Oddfellows and also a Mason. Interne, Mercy Hospital, Philadelphia, Pennsylvania. Practiced in Philadelphia, Pennsylvania, one year, 1922. Began practice in Cincinnati, May, 1923. Member of Alpha Phi Alpha fraternity. Staff surgeon at Mercy Hospital. Resides at 408 West Fifth Street.

EDWARD JAMES ROSS, M.D.
Physician and Surgeon

Born July 3, 1896, Lockland, Ohio. Son of Anderson and Ann Ross. Graduate high school, 1915; Premed. U. of C., 1916; Howard University, 1917; Meharry Med., 1917-21, M.D. Married Miss Mary Roan, Cincinnati school teacher, May 31, 1924. Engaged for three years in general practice of medicine. Fraternities: Kappa Alpha Psi and Masons. Church, Baptist. Politics, Republican. Member of staff of Mercy Hospital. Member Cincinnati Medical Association. Member of Committee of Management, Lockland Y. M. C. A., 1922-23. Instrumental in organizing Kappa Chapter of Kappa Alpha Psi at Meharry. Now located at 621 Cutter Street. Residence, 615 Walnut Street, Lockland, Ohio.

GEORGE NELSON
Dry Cleaner

Born July 24, 1894, at Chicago, Illinois, the son of Edward and Emma Nelson. The father, a clergyman, died in 1911. Attended public schools in Chicago. Married Miss Thelma Ousley of Frankfort, Kentucky, in 1921. A Methodist and a Republican. With David Weber, dry cleaners, nine years. Came to Cincinnati in 1920. An employe of the C. & O. Worked with Fenton's for one year. Opened modern establishment for cleaning, dyeing and pressing in 1924. Resides at 107½ Wayne Avenue, Lockland, Ohio.

G. E. LOVERETTE, M.D.
Physician and Surgeon

Son of George and Rebecca Loverette. Born March 8, 1870, in Richmond, Virginia. Attended Richmond public school, Hampton Institute and Leonard Medical schools. Married Miss Mary B. Rogers, daughter of Mr. and Mrs. Clayton, of Bristol, Virginia. He has been engaged at his vocation since 1905. He is a member of Zion Baptist Church, a Mason, K. of P. and an Elk. Grand Medical Registrar, second term, of K. of P. of Ohio. Now located at 906 Clark Street.

WM. F. REED
Tailor

Son of Fannie and Redley Reed. Born May 13, 1893, at Lexington, Kentucky. Attended public schools in Lexington and a graduate of St. Paul Normal and Industrial School, Lawrenceville, Virginia, 1914. He has spent fifteen years at his vocation. He is a member of the A. M. E. Church, the Independent party, a Mason and K. of P. Came to Cincinnati in 1913. Opened present place for first class tailoring, cleaning and pressing. Now located at 1225 Chapel Street.

MARTIN V. ROBERTS
Foreman of Supplies in Post Office

Son of Mitchell and Martha Roberts. Born August 21, 1864, at Overton County, Tennessee. Attended public schools of Lockland and Cincinnati high school. Married Ella Taylor, of Cincinnati, 1887, to whom three children were born, Cora B., Edith M., and Nadyne E. He has been at his vocation twenty-five years. Deacon of Christian Church and politically a Republican. A Mason and a K. of P. Formerly Grand Keeper of Records and Seals; at present Supreme Representative U. B. F. Director of Crispus Attuck Building Association; Director of Mill Creek Valley Realty Co.; on Board of Directors of Y. M. C. A. of Lockland, Ohio. Only Negro foreman in Cincinnati mail service. Now residing at 627 Vine Street, Wyoming, Ohio.

L. E. HANCOCK, D.C.
Manufacturer of Medicine

Born in Mississippi. Parents, Isaiah and Amanda Hancock. His father was a successful clergyman. He attended the grammar school at Little Rock, Arkansas, and the American University of Chicago. Twenty years were devoted to his vocation. He is a member of the American Woodmen, Masons, and is connected with the Baptist Church. A Republican. Came to Cincinnati in May, 1918. Started, in 1921, "The Seven Wonder Remedy Co." It is now on a substantial financial basis. Located at 550 West Sixth Street.

RICHARD H. BAILEY
Clergyman

Born December 10, 1881, in Lafayette, Chamber County, Alabama. Son of Randle and Betsey E. Bailey, prosperous farmers. Attended public schools in Lafayette, Alabama; Tuskegee Academy, from which he graduated. Pursued post-graduate work with Princeton Seminary, Princeton, Indiana. Married Luvada Gray in 1903. Three surviving children, Alcavis, Ozelle and Abobbie. Thirty-five years at vocation. A member of the Baptist Church and Republican party. First pastor of Hosanna Baptist Church, 1904, Chambers County, Alabama; pastor, Baptist Cluster Church, Tuskegee, Alabama, 1904-08; pastor, Camp Hill, Alabama, Popular Springs Church, 1908-13; First Baptist Church erected Crawford, Alabama, 1913-18. Principal of Sanford District School, Society Hill, Alabama, four years. Erection of school building completed at this time. Taught four years in Chambers County. Principal of Titonic Institute one year. Pastor,  Union Baptist Church, Titus, Alabama, 1918-19. Pastor, Mt. Canaan Baptist Church, Talladega, 1919-23; Hall Street Baptist Church, 1923. Pastor of New Hope Baptist Church of Cincinnati, Ohio. He resides at 723 West Eighth Street.

RICHARD CONNELLY
Caterer

Born March 25, 1858, in Verona, Kentucky, the son of Susan Connelly. Attended public schools in Covington, Kentucky. Married forty-four years. One son, Robert E. Twenty-three years at vocation. A member of Allen Temple A. M. E. Church and a Republican. Page at M. E. Conference, 1871, in Covington, Kentucky. Associated with Holden Brothers, grocers, Fourth and Greenup Streets, three years. Nine years as coachman and houseman for J. O. Erntz. Established retail vegetable business three years. Employed by Thomas Emery Estate as janitor in charge, nine years. Sexton at Christ Episcopal Church fifteen years. Began catering while employed by Christ Church, and in that profession he still remains. Attributes success of his business to encouragement received from Rector F. H. Nelson and vestrymen of Christ Episcopal Church. Property owner.

Helped to found Ninth Street Branch of Y. M. C. A. and received the title of captain for efficient work in this undertaking. He resides at 414 Richmond Street with his second wife, Mrs. Eliza Connelly, to whom he has been happily married for many years.

THE STERLING BARBER SHOP

Simmons and Randall are joint proprietors of The Sterling Barber Shop at 575 West Sixth Street. They began business in that location in 1918 and 1919 and have built up a splendid trade. They have availed themselves of the services of Mr. C. Spivey, manager, and Mrs. Margaret Spivey, an expert manicurist.

DR. R. P. McCLAIN
Physician and Surgeon

Born January 3, 1890, at Nicholasville, Kentucky. Son of Meredith and Ellen McClain. He attended public and high schools in Cincinnati, 1908; Howard University, 1913; interne at Freedman's Hospital, Washington, D. C., 1913-14. Married, 1918, to Alice E. Martin, graduate nurse of Freedmen's Hospital, '16. He is a K. of P., Elk, 32nd Degree Mason, and a member of the Alpha Phi Alpha fraternity. He belongs to the Independent political party and is chairman of the Trustee Board of Antioch Baptist Church. Manager Mercy Hospital, secretary Model Drug Co., member Committee of Management, Ninth Street "Y", and president of the Buckeye Medical Association. Now located at 912 West Seventh Street, Cincinnati, Ohio.

REV. S. O. SHINNAULT
Tonsorial Artist

Born November 14, 1865, in Augusta, Georgia, the son of Edmond and Pollie Shinnault, successful farmers. Attended public schools in Georgia. Married Miss Louisa Dunn of Kentucky in 1892. Three surviving children, Clara, Mary and Martha. Thirty years at vocation. A member of the Masons, Oddfellows, Good Samaritans, the U. N. I. A., the Baptist Church and the Republican party. Came to Cincinnati in 1895. Was proprietor of a barber shop in Lexington, Kentucky, one year. Opened present place of business in 1913. He has been very successful in the ministerial field as well as in the business world. He is located at 660 West Fifth Street.

JAMES E. RANDOLPH, M.D.
Physician and Surgeon

Son of Frank and Lizzie Randolph, prosperous farmers. Born January 17, 1888, at Frankfort, Missouri. Attended grammar and high school in Hannibal, Missouri, Jefferson City Normal, pre-medic course, Lincoln University, Missouri, 1910-1913. Entered Meharry Medical College, 1913, graduating in 1917 with the degree of M.D. Married Sarah Temple, graduate of

Turner College, in 1918. He has been at his vocation eight years. Member of the A. M. E. Church and politically a Republican. He began in Shelbyville, Tennessee, where he enjoyed successful practice for four years. Opened office in Covington, Kentucky, in 1922, where he is now engaged in the general practice of medicine and surgery. Received commission of first lieutenant of Medical Officers' Reserve Corps. Commission renewed in 1923. Member of the Kentucky State Medical Association. Member of the staff of Mercy Hospital, Cincinnati. Now resides at 1014 Greenup Street, Covington, Kentucky.

GEORGE A. JOHNSON
Tailoring, Cleaning and Pressing Establishment

Born December 28, 1891, in Kingston, Jamaica. Attended public schools in Jamaica and the Department of Agriculture at Howard University. Married Miss Carolyn Cushenberry, March 19, 1924, at Pembrook, Kentucky. A member of the Episcopal Church and politically at Republican. A member of the Masons, K. of P., Elks, A. U. K. and D. of A., and U. N. I. A. For many years he served as entertainer in Jamaica and the United States. He has a well trained tenor voice. Served in the U. S. Army in the Argonne and Meuse drive nineteen months. Opened place of business in 1924 with equipment for cleaning, pressing, tailoring and dyeing. He was the first among the colored citizens of Lockland to have such a complete establishment for all the branches of clothes renovation.

MRS. FANNIE COLLINS
Music Teacher

Daughter of Mr. and Mrs. James Shepherd. Born March 28, 1861, in Memphis, Tennessee. Attended Le Moyne Commercial and Normal School. Married Geo. W. Collins. She has been at her vocation since 1879. Her mother gave her and her brother an education. She is the oldest colored music teacher in Cincinnati, and many of her scholars have made a record worthy of praise. In 1881 she played at the Arlington, now the Dennison Hotel. Mrs. Collins still performs upon the piano and teaches. Her son, Norman, is a prosperous dentist in West Virginia. She resides at 665 Linn Street.

S. J. WATKINS, M.D.
Physician, Surgeon and Dentist

Son of Anderson and Mary Watkins. His father, Anderson Watkins, was a slave, but acquired higher education without the advantages of an instructor. Dr. Watkins was born in Courtland, Alabama. Attended public schools of Courtland; Lane College, Jackson, Tennessee; Waldon University, Nashville, Tennessee; entered Meharry Medical and Dental School, finishing dentistry in 1891 and medicine, 1892. Married Rosa A. Moore, January 12, 1893, to whom one child, Anna May, was born. Thirty years at his vocation. Member of the M. E. Church and politically a Republican. A member of the Oddfellows and Medical Association. Appointed by

Governor of the State of Kentucky as member of Interracial Committee. Appointed by State Medical Board as sanitary officer of Covington, the appointment being confirmed by the health board who presented him with a sanitary police badge, which he now wears. Came to Covington in 1892, where he began the practice of medicine, surgery and dentistry. Delegate to C. M. E. general conference for three consecutive years. Now resides at 115 East Ninth Street, Covington, Kentucky.

LENINE R. BREEDLOVE, M.D.
Physician and Surgeon

Born February 9, 1896, in Tennessee, the son of Mr. and Mrs. A. J. Breedlove. His mother, Mrs. Alice B. Breedlove, was a famous cateress. Dr. Breedlove graduated from Champaign public schools in 1910; high school in 1914. Pursued course of agriculture at University of Illinois in 1915. Attended Fiske University, Nashville, Tennessee, from 1915 to 1916; Meharry Medical College from 1916 to 1920; graduated with degree of M.D. Internship, Kansas City, Missouri, General Hospital, 1920-22. Came to Cincinnati in the fall of 1922. A member of the Kappa Alpha Psi staff. Surgeon of Mercy Hospital. Member of Cincinnati Medical Association. Belongs to the Oddfellows. Literary contributor to various publications and periodicals. Takes a leading part in the Annual Benefit given for Mercy Hospital by the doctors. His office is at Fifth and Mill Streets.

BENJAMIN W. HALL
Tonsorial Artist

Born September 2, 1856, Bourbon County, Kentucky, the son of Mr. and Mrs. B. W. Hall, prosperous farmers. Attended public schools in Kentucky. Married Miss Anna Hawker, of Danville, Kentucky, in 1905. Forty years at the trade. Republican in politics. A member of the Masons, K. of P. and Elks. Prominent in secret fraternities and is identified with many business enterprises. First officer of local Elks, outside guard. One of the oldest barbers in the city with a record of twenty-two years at present business place. Now located at 508 John Street.

ADAM DAVID KELLY, M.D.
Physician and Surgeon

Son of Julia and John B. Kelly, a former slave, who, after gaining his freedom, became a successful millwright. He was born July 19, 1860, at Carthage, North Carolina. Attended public schools; Bennett College, Greensboro, North Carolina, receiving his A.B. degree in 1892. Graduated from Meharry Medical School in the year of 1896. Married Miss Mary Wendell, of Nashville, Tennessee, to whom four children were born, Wendell, Adam D. Jr., Ichler, and Coleman. He has been at his vocation thirty years. Trustee of the M. E. Church and politically a Republican. Thirty-Second Degree Mason and High Priest of Consistory; Judge Advocate of Oddfellows; District Deputy, Grand Chancellor of Knights of Pythias; Eastern Star Past Patron, first Past Patron of local lodge. Came to Covington in 1896, after successfully passing the state board; opened office in Covington, where he is now engaged in the general practice of medicine and surgery. Resides at 514 Scott Street, Covington, Kentucky.

G. W. GAMBLE
Business Man

Born in Williamsburg County, South Carolina, August 15, 1892. Son of Mr. and Mrs. Ezekiel Gamble. Went to Florida as lumber mill laborer in 1912. Came to Cincinnati in 1917. Married Miss Frances Lee Winder, of Florida, April 1, 1916. Opened present business, ice, coal and express, 1920. A member of New Hope Baptist Church, Oddfellows, K. of P. and a Republican. Located at 652 West Fourth Street.

GEORGE W. GOSSETT

George W. Gossett, proprietor of a confectionery and shoe shining parlor at 731 West Fourth Street, was born at Mt. Sterling, Kentucky. He married Miss Beulah Ewing of that city in 1910. He came to Cincinnati and about six years ago started the business which he now successfully operates.

VANGIE HILLIARD CLINTON
Federal Employe

Son of Rev. T. H. and Mary Clinton. Born December 19, 1869, at Shelby County, Ohio, near Lima. Attended Ripley Union schools at Ripley, Ohio. Married Anna Rollins in 1905, to whom five children were born, three boys and two girls, all living. Taught school eight years and in the Federal post office service twenty. Member of the Methodist Episcopal Church and politically a Republican. Resides at 923 Churchill Avenue.

MR. AND MRS. CHAS. H. KELLY
Home and Studio, 740 West Ninth Street

Mr. Kelly is a teacher of singing. Studied music at Fiske University, Nashville, Tennessee, and Metropolitan College of Music, Cincinnati, Ohio. He is now head of the Orpheus S. M., a prominent Mason, Presbyterian, U. S. Government employe. Mrs. Kelly is a business woman and a product of South Carolina, while Mr. Kelly is from Nashville, Tennessee. They have been in Cincinnati sixteen years and are property owners.

St. John's A. M. E. Zion Church

REV. JAS. L. BLACK
Clergyman

Born in Charlotte, North Carolina. Son of Isaac and Hariett Black. Attended public schools in Mecklinburg, South Carolina, and received professional training at Johnson C. Smith, formerly Biddle University, Charlotte, North Carolina. Married Miss Lillie Twitty, of North Carolina, in 1902. Parent of four children, Trent, James Jr., Emma, and Fanny. Twenty-five years at vocation. A member of the Masons, Oddfellows, American Woodmen and of the A. M. E. Z. Church. Republican. Pastored five years in North Carolina; ten and one-half years in South Carolina; District Superintendent one and one-half years; pastored seven years in Knoxville, Tennessee; four years in Akron, Ohio. Degree of D.D. conferred by Livingston College in 1918. At present pastor of St. John A. M. E. Z. Church. Built parsonage at Rock Hill, South Carolina. Bought parsonage at Knoxville, Tennessee. Added $20,000 to church property at Akron, Ohio. Resides at 628 West Eighth Street.

WORFORD SIMPSON
Restaurant Proprietor

Born April 11, 1894, at Clark County, Mississippi. Son of George and Mahalie Simpson, prosperous farmers. Attended public schools in Mississippi. Married Miss Ada Buhrl in 1919. Parent of two children, Edward and Henry. Eight months at vocation. A member of the Republican party. Came to Cincinnati in 1912. Opened present business establishment in 1925. Now located at 526 West Sixth Street.

MRS. MAZIE EARHART
Poetess, Beauty Culturist and Chiropodist

Born in Glendale, Ohio, daughter of David and Fannie Earhart. Attended public schools in Glendale. Studied chiropody in Cincinnati and opened first class establishment twenty years ago in connection with a "Shoppe" of beauty culture. A writer of songs, author of creditable poems, and a member of the Union Baptist Church. Located in the Arcade.

MRS. MATTIE SIMMONS

Mrs. Mattie Simmons is operating very successfully The J. K. Sherman Beauty Shop at 535 West Fifth Street, founded by her daughter, Mrs. Jennie Sherman, a specialist in that line, having been a product of the Moler Beauty College of this city, an associate of Madam Thomas, of Court Street, and a dispenser of high grade beautifiers. She was born June 12, 1884; attended the high school in this city and passed away in 1917, much to the regret of many patrons and friends.

JESSE J. WOODSON
Mail Carrier

Son of Jesse and Patsy Ann Woodson. Born June 13, 1861, in Cincinnati, Ohio. Attended public school and Gaines High. Married Miss Cassie Guthrie, to whom two children were born, Neola Woodson Robinson and Wilbur Woodson. She died early and he then married Mrs. Emily Hawkins. Member of Brown Chapel A. M. E. Church. Member of the K. of P. Lodge No. 32, F. & A. M. St. John Lodge No. 3. Was a member of the Trustee Board of our Orphan Asylum for twelve years. Chairman of the committee of one hundred which gave a six-day bazaar at Music Hall, where the largest sum of money ever made for this institution was realized. A trustee of the Old Woman's Home and trustee for the Shelter Home for Colored Children. Grand Chancellor of the State for the Knights of Pythias for two terms and during his term of office the endowment insurance department was placed upon a firm foundation. At present Supreme Representative of the State. Trustee of Brown Chapel A. M. E. Church; a member of the Board of Committee of Management of the Y. M. C. A.; member of the N. A. A. C. P. and a member of various other clubs, civic and social. Mr. Woodson has been employed in the post office as a letter carrier for a period of forty years and is the third oldest man from point of service. He will be retired on an annuity in June, 1926. Now residing at 2717 Ashland Avenue.

WILLIE HARRIS
Custom Tailor

Son of Mr. and Mrs. William Harris. Born March 16, 1894, at Birmingham, Alabama. Graduate of the public and high schools of Birmingham. Member of Garnet Lodge, K. of P. Served apprenticement in the approved tailor shops of Birmingham. Came to Cincinnati in 1917 and opened first class tailoring establishment March 10, 1917. Place of business located at 611 West Fifth Street.

"JACK" ROBINSON
Deputy County Treasurer

Son of John and Rachel Robinson. Born August 20, 1874, at Cincinnati, Ohio. Attended public schools in Cincinnati. Widower; one child, Leroy Robinson. Politically a Republican. Member of the K. of P. and Masons. Assistant Assessor of Eighteenth Ward two terms. Was appointed clerk in Treasury Department under Charles Cooper in 1917, which position he occupies at present. Executive of Precinct R, Eighteenth Ward. Loves baseball and general sports. Throughout his life he has been very active in politics for the Republican party. He now resides at 423 Central Avenue.

L. L. HUBBARD, JR., D.D.S.

Born at Columbia, Missouri, June 20, 1899. Son of Mr. and Mrs. L. L. Hubbard. Graduate of grammar and high school of Columbia, Missouri. Graduate of University of California, degree B.S., 1919. Married Miss Tommie Smith, linotype operator, September 7, 1922. Graduate of Meharry Dental College, D.D.S., 1924. Came to Cincinnati, December, 1924. A member of Alpha Phi Alpha. Episcopalian, Republican, Mason and Elk. A baseball and football player. Member of Cincinnati Medical Association. Served in World War, first lieutenant, infantry, 92nd Division. Office, 538 West Fifth Street. Residence, 2819 Park Avenue, Walnut Hills.

ALBERT G. WILSON, JR.
Proprietor and Manager of Garage

Born March 25, 1888, at Wilberton, North Carolina. Son of Lee and Sarah Wilson. Received private tutorship. Came to Cincinnati in 1922. Operating manager of service ice plant, Brooklyn, New York, for six months. Installer of The Frick Ice Refrigeration Co., fifteen years. In sales department of June Bruening Co. for two years. Opened present place of business in 1925. Located at 736 West Seventh Street.

J. C. ERWIN, M.D.
Physician and Surgeon

Born in Savannah, Georgia, December 22, 1863. Son of William and Roberta Erwin. Graduate of Beech Institute, Savannah, Georgia, 1880. Attended Atlanta University, 1880-1884. Graduate Howard University Medical Department, 1894, degree M.D. Interneship Freedom's Hospital, 1895. Practiced, Washington, D. C., 1894-1896. Came to Cincinnati, summer of 1896. Member of Cincinnati Academy of Medicine. Staff of Evangeline Home and Hospital, Clinician St. Andrew's Day Nursery. A Mason, Oddfellow, U. B. F., vestryman of St. Andrew's Episcopal Church. Now located at 603 West Eighth Street.

HENRY H. GRANDISON
Insurance Agent

Son of Henry H. and Elizabeth Grandison. His father was Chairman of Deacon Board and was employed by Fries and Fries Chemical Co. thirty-three years. He was born April 24, 1881, in Cincinnati, Ohio. Attended public schools and Woodward High; graduated night high school 1899. Married Myrtle Nunn, of Louisville, Kentucky, 1905. Four years at his vocation. Member of the Union Baptist Church and politically Independent. Mason, Keeper of Records of K. of P., Master of Finance of U. B. F., Treasurer for thirteen years of the Union Baptist Church;

president of the Union Baptist Church Sinking Fund. Member of Construction Committee for Annex of church. Associated with the firm of Fries and Fries for twenty years. Established business of fire, tornado and automobile insurance in 1921, and has served an immense number of patrons.

FRANK ATKINSON

Born October 22, 1881, at Montgomery, Alabama. Son of Alex and Minnie Atkinson, prosperous farmers. Attended public schools in Alabama. Married Miss Belle Jones, of Verbena, Alabama, May 4, 1902. Five years at vocation. A member of the Masons, K. of P., the A. M. E. Church, and of the Republican party. Came to Cincinnati in 1916. Molder from 1916 to 1920. Opened an ice, coal and express business in 1920. Three living children. Now located at 425 Smith Street. Residence, 754 Betts Street.

THOMAS B. RICHMOND
Attorney at Law

Born November 24, 1884, at British Guiana, South America. He is the son of Frederick Alex. and Platina Richmond. He attended public high school, British Guiana, New York Prep. School, 1910 (N. Y.), and 1913, New York University, LL.B. He married, first, Christine Annie Andrews of Georgetown, British Guiana. One child was born of this union, Christine Louise, now seven years of age. Later, Mary B. Thomas, December 5, 1921. He has spent ten years at his profession. He is a member of the I. B. O. E., a Methodist Episcopalian, and a Republican. Formerly telegraph operator and post office clerk, 1901-1905; later assistant postmaster, Ancon, Canal Zone. Studied in law offices of Wilson M. Powell, 29 Wall Street, New York, 1907-1910. Now located in Temple Court Building. Residence, 938 West Seventh Street. Practiced law for one year in Indianapolis, Indiana, from which place he came to Cincinnati.

JOHN R. PATTERSON
District Manager, National Benefit Insurance Co.

Son of Wm. R. and Mamie E. Patterson. His father was founder and principal of first colored high school in Texas. Born March 5, 1895, in Calvert, Texas. He attended and graduated from Armstrong High School, 1912; Prairie View, 1913-14; student of New Orleans University, 1915-16; student of U. C., 1924. He married Miss Bessie L. Stevenson of Cincinnati, October 29, 1924. He has spent two years at his vocation. Member of Kappa Alpha Psi fraternity; Mason and Republican. Came to Cincinnati, 1924. Traveling representative for National Insurance Co., 1921-24. Began with company as agent in 1920. Located in Temple Court Building, Cincinnati. Residence, 3068 Kerper Avenue.

AUGUSTUS G. BEAM, M.D.
Physician and Surgeon

Son of Hines and Maria Beam. His father was a slave, but became United States gauger, which position he held for thirty-two years, becoming wealthy. He was born January 16, 1884, in Nelson County, Kentucky. Attended public schools of Nelson County; Normal High School and College in Vincennes, Indiana; post course on literature in Lawrence University, Wisconsin. Graduated Louisville Medical School with degree of M.D. Married, having two children, Arnetta and Earl. Nineteen years at his vocation. Member of the Baptist Church and politically a Republican. Formerly a member of the Masons, Elks, and K. of P. Practiced in Lima, Ohio, two years. Enjoyed successful practice in Henderson, Kentucky, twelve years. Came to Covington in 1919. Now engaged in the general practice of medicine and surgery. Resides at 220 East Eleventh Street, Covington, Kentucky.

HARRY H. FRIASON
Assistant Paymaster

Son of Augustus and Elizabeth Friason, successful fireman. Born July 28, 1866, in Cincinnati, Ohio. Attended public school and Gaines High. Married Lucy Armstrong, of Ohio, to whom three children were born, Camille, Lawrence and Laverne. Treasurer and Steward Brown's Chapel A. M. E. Politically a Republican. Member of the Masons, Assistant Secretary of the K. of P. Was engineer in the Arctic Ice Factory ten years. Machinist associated with S. T. Holmes, four years. Guard in the Ohio penitentiary two and a half years. Associated with the Crane-Holley Co. ten years. Clerk, County Recorder's office for two years. Inspector in the Improvement Department of Waterworks, two years. Inspector in Engineer's Department, nine years. Appointed Assistant City Paymaster, 1923, which position he still holds. The family has for a long time been well-to-do financially and the children have married well.

CHARLES EDWARD JONES
Undertaker

Son of E. L. and Amanda Jones. Born August 25, 1880, in Covington, Kentucky. His parents were devout Christians, who inspired their son to take up his present profession. He attended school in Covington and the Cincinnati College of Embalming. Married Miss Julia E. Delaney, Covington school teacher. He has been at his profession twenty-nine years. Thirty-second Degree Mason, Oddfellow, K. of P. and an Elk; member of Mosaics and True Reformer; Deputy Grand Commander of State of Kentucky Masons; Past Royal Grand Patron of Eastern Star of Kentucky; also a member of the U. B. F. Treasurer of the Ninth Street M. E. Church and politically a Republican. A man who, being reared in this city, availed himself of the educational facilities and has stuck to the embalming and funeral business since his graduation. Mr. Jones is one of the most popular business men in the city of Covington and is almost equally as well known in Cincinnati and in the large cities of Kentucky. He is located at 638 Scott Street, Covington, Kentucky.

CAPT. JAY W. WILKINS
Road Construction Foreman

Son of Dr. J. H. and Cornelia Wilkins. Born December 30, 1883, at Houston, Texas. Attended Galveston public schools; New York High, Meharry Medical School, Morrison Sanitarium. Married Myrtle S. Douglass in 1908, to whom one child was born, John, age sixteen, who is a student at Stowe Junior High. Five years at his vocation. Member of the Baptist Church and politically a Democrat. Member of the K. of P., Oddfellows and Good Shepherds. Reorganized the old Ninth Battalion, Ohio National Guards, in April, 1924. Organized the Cincinnati Company as Co. C, September 1, now Co. G, 372nd Infantry. Was appointed captain April, 1924, and is senior captain of the Second Battalion. He was appointed by Governor Donahey as the first colored foreman of the State Highway

Captain J. W. Wilkins, Mrs. Myrtle S. Wilkins and their son John W. Wilkins

Department, handling a crew of men. He was chairman of the committee of the Cincinnati branch, National Negro Business League, that caused the appointment of five colored policemen to the Cincinnati force after a period of seventeen years. Through his activity in Democratic circles colored employes are drawing more than one hundred thousand dollars annually from public work. He spent over $5,000 of his and his wife's personal funds in organizing the Cincinnati company of the National Guard and repairing the armory at Fourth and John Streets. He has always been a loyal race man. He has a beautiful suburban residence at Mt. Healthy.

THOMAS O'BANION
Chiropodist

Born November 9, 1859, at New Richmond, Ohio. Attended public schools of New Richmond. Married Miss Ernestine Jackson, October, 1888, who died October, 1906. Later married to Mrs. Eldona Carey, July, 1911, who died March, 1924. He has been at his vocation fifteen years. Mr. O'Banion has the distinction of being proprietor of the oldest establishment of the kind in this city, if not in this state. It has kept pace with all modern requirements, both in equipment and efficiency. Resides at 1541 Blair Aenue.

REV. PLEASANT S. HILL
Clergyman

Son of Evelene and Alex. Hill, successful clergyman. Born August 17, 1877, at Marshall County, Tennessee. Attended public schools in Arkansas. Graduate of Branch Normal College (Arkansas University), L.I. Graduate of Wilberforce University, theological department, B.D. Post-graduate work, University of Chicago. Private course in German and French in Arkansas. Valedictorian of class at graduation in Wilberforce, 1904. Married (first) Jennie J. Hill, to whom three children, Lloyd, Evelene, Eunice, were born. Later married to Etta J. Hill, by which union Arthur J. was born. He has spent twenty-three years at his vocation. He is pastor of the A. M. E. Church, a Republican, Mason and Oddfellow. Pastored in Cowden, Arkansas, five years; Hot Springs, Arkansas, two years. Laid foundation for new church. Professor of Historical Theology and Hebrew, Payne Seminary, Wilberforce, twelve years. Came to Cincinnati, to Brown's Chapel, 1923.

MRS. M. B. BROOKS
Beauty Culturist

Born June 2, 1880, at Washington, Georgia. Daughter of Mr. and Mrs. Thomas Simpson: Graduated from public schools in Georgia, 1900. Attended public schools in Cincinnati. Married Mr. Alonzo Brooks, of Kansas City, Missouri, 1907; one adopted child, Hattie Belle. Eight years at vocation. A member of the following fraternities: Household of Ruth, Woodmen, Samaritans, Past officer Knights and Daughters of Honor, and Park Street M. E. Church. Has agents in fourteen states. Manufactures own goods. Pursued course of Beauty Culture under Madam Duncan, 1917. Graduate Moler College, 1908. Opened present place of business, 1919, at 615 West Fifth Street.

G. R. BRYANT, D.D.
Theologian

Born in Colorado County, Texas, June 10, 1869. Son of Mr. and Mrs. Gloster Bryant. Early education in public schools in Texas. Graduated from Los Angeles Bible Institute; University of Southern California, 1905-07-08. Law Student, Central Law School, Louisville, Kentucky, 1910. Degree D.D. conferred by Lane College, Jackson, Tennessee. Pastor, Flatonia, Luling, Waco, Austin, San Antonio, Texas, 1901-02. Pastor Wesley M. E. Church, Los Angeles, 1902-09. Pastor, Paris, Kentucky, 1909-11. Pastor, Louisville, Kentucky, 1911-12. District Superintendent, Indiana District and Chicago District, 1912-19. Pastor So. Park M. E. Church, Chicago, Illinois, 1919-23. Pastor of Scott M. E. Church, Detroit, 1923-24. Pastor of Park Street (now Calvary) M. E. Church. Married and has three children. Lives at 626 West Fourth Street.

DR. CHAS. E. HORNER
Physician and Surgeon

Born August 1, 1882, at Cumminsville, Cincinnati, Ohio, the son of Rebecca Day Horner, nee Minnes, and Charles D. Horner. Attended public schools to eighth grade and the Eclectic Medical College. Married Emma Kelly, nee Walker, in May, 1911. He has been at his vocation fifteen years. A member of St. Andrew's Episcopal Church. A member of Kenton Lodge No. 16, Masons; Scottish Rite Masons, King Solomon's Consistory No. 20, and the Licking Valley United Brothers of Friendship. A 32nd Degree Mason of Cincinnati.

At seventeen, moved from Ohio to Newport, Kentucky. Was employed as a janitor, and during his college career, was the principal support of mother, three brothers and three sisters.

Left school at fifteen, did chores of all kinds. At sixteen, went to work in restaurant as second cook and pantryman; at seventeen, became janitor of school, waiting table at night parties; at nineteen, became janitor of two churches, Baptist and Christian, and until twenty-one years of age, was janitor and window washer; porter in stores and waiter at night poker parties.

At twenty-one years of age, had three hundred dollars in the building association. Entered Eclectic Medical College, Cincinnati, Ohio, going to college during the day and waiting parties at night. During the summer vacations, was a waiter at the Coney Island resort. Graduated in 1907 at the age of twenty-five, with total capital of fifty cents. In 1908, entered Pullman service in Chicago; traveled all over the United States, Canada, and part of Mexico. In 1910, took the Kentucky State Medical Board examination, passing with an average of seventy-nine. Started practice in Newport, Kentucky, where he now enjoys a practice bringing an income of $10,000 a year. Nine-tenths of his Newport patients are white. He lives at Newport, Kentucky. As a political leader in that city he is strictly independent and supports candidates of any party who seem likely to be of greatest benefit to colored citizens.

STANLEY E. GRANNUM
Clergyman

Son of Wm. H. and Sarah Grannum. Born October 17, 1891, at New York City. Graduate of De Witt Clinton High School, Wesleyan University, Middletown, Connecticut, with degree A.B. Was the only colored member; Phi Beta Kappa; Camp Prize, English Literature Junior exhibition prize in Oratory; Rich Commencement prize in Oratory; Boston University School of Theology, S.T.B.; Boston University Graduate School; Harvard University Graduate School. He has spent fourteen years at his vocation. Married Gertrude Harper, 1920, a teacher (at that time) in Houston, Texas, public schools. He is pastor of the M. E. Church, member of the Independent party, Commons Club, Masons, K. of P. Assistant Pastor of St. Mark's, New York City, two years. Pastored Church of All Nations, Boston, three years. Mt. Zion Methodist Episcopal Church, Cincinnati, erected the church edifice with a complete community house connected, at a cost of $110,000. Secretary-Treasurer of Covington Area Council M. E. Church. Promotional Secretary for Methodist Centenary Movement. Dr. Grannum is the representative colored member of a prominent inter-racial connection of this city. His church, the Mt. Zion M. E., is located at Walter and Altoona Avenues, Walnut Hills.

FRANCIS P. GREEN
Clergyman

Son of George and Julia Green. Born April 17, 1859, at Henry County, Kentucky. Attended public schools in Indiana. Married Miss Katie Simms, of Kentucky, in 1904, and has, by that union, two children, Francis P. Jr. and Naomi E. He has spent thirty-nine years at his vocation. He is pastor of the Baptist Church, a member of the Republican party, a Mason and formerly an Oddfellow. Reared in Indiana. Began ministry with pastoring in Rushville, Indiana, Second Baptist, 1886, seven years. Erected church, Connersville, Indiana, the Mt. Zion Baptist. Property owner and race welfare promoter. Rising Sun, Indiana, Shiloh Baptist, five years; Bloomington, Indiana, Second Baptist, three and one-half years; Muncie, Indiana, Second Baptist, two years; Franklin, Indiana, Second Baptist, six months; Benton Harbor, Michigan, Second Baptist, three years; South Bend, Indiana, Mt. Zion, four years. Called to First Baptist Church of Cincinnati, 1902, at which place he has manifested his qualities as a Christian leader. The membership has increased from 300 to approximately 1000, as about 500 have been dropped. Bought a new church home and an annex is being made. Now located at 1321 Lincoln Avenue.

First Baptist Church, Walnut Hills

MRS. MARY E. BECKLEY TAYLOR

Mrs. Mary E. Beckley Taylor (deceased), was born November 8, 1845, in the City of Cincinnati. She was the eldest daughter of William and Amelia Beckley, who were pioneer citizens of this city. Educated in the public schools of Cincinnati. Married James A. Taylor, of Lexington, Kentucky. Mrs. Taylor was one of the oldest members of the M. E. Church and attended its conference annually. She was president of the Ladies' Aid Society, Home Missionary Society, and the Lincoln Lyceum of Union Chapel Church. At her death she was a member of Park Street Church. For twelve years she was president of the Board of Lady Managers of the Colored Orphan Asylum. Four of her daughters were prominent teachers in the Cincinnati schools. Misses Amelia C. and Hettie G. retired last June. A granddaughter, Miss Mary K. Holloway, is at present a teacher in the Harriet Beecher Stowe School. The family is now located in a beautiful home in the beautiful suburb of Avondale, 3252 Delaware Avenue.

Bethel Baptist Church

REV. LEE WM. GRAY, D.D.
Clergyman

Son of Lewis and Mary Gray. Born September 18, 1854, at Nicholasville, Kentucky. Attended public schools in Nicholasville. Course in Berea College and for two years in Medical School, Eclectic College of Physicians and Surgeons, Indianapolis. Study of Theology under Professor Harrison, of Moore's Hill College. D.D. conferred by Simons University, Louisville, Kentucky, in 1920. Married Katie Williams, of Indianapolis, 1886. He has spent thirty-nine years at his vocation. He is a member of the Baptist Church, the Republican party, the Masons, the Oddfellows and U. B. F.'s. Taught school seven years in Nicholasville and Harrodsburg, Kentucky. Pastored Second Baptist, Franklin, Ohio, and Harveysburg, Ohio, two and one-half years. Pastored Second Baptist, Shelbyville, Indiana, ten years. Built parsonage and remodeled church. Called to Bethel Baptist, Cincinnati, 1898 (April), for which church he secured property and built church from ground, having increased membership from 130 to 1000. Total property valued at $80,000. Now located at 1226 Myrtle Avenue.

MR. JOHN H. AYRES

Born in Paris, Kentucky, 1860. Forty-three years ago married Miss Maggie L. Frazier in and of Winchester, Kentucky. The wife and his

daughter are still living. He was business manager for many years of the National Chronicle, one of the leading weeklies in Kentucky. Came to this city in 1891. For fourteen years he was in charge of flat buildings, and several on Walnut Hills, named after colored people, were put under his exclusive jurisdiction by Mr. E. M. Benham, the owner. Mr. Ayres had a Colored Police Popularity Contest in 1899 and was the only one ever given by the police commissioners' permission for such an event. Mr. Ayres has always been a pillar of the church, distinguished for his choral work and singing ability. He has rendered great service for the U. B. F.'s and the Wehrman Ave. Christian Church. He lives at 879 Wehrman Avenue.

AMOS MAHON
Proprietor of the Puritan Cafe

Born September 9, 1889, at Springfield, Arkansas. Son of Mr. and Mrs. Lee Mahon. Attended public schools in Arkansas. Completed course in the cotton plant, Industrial Academy. Three years at vocation. A member of the Elks, A. M. E. Z. Church and of the Republican party. Formerly proprietor of the "Red Front" and "DeLuxe" restaurants of Cincinnati. Came to Cincinnati in 1921 and opened present business at 524 Mound Street.

MRS. MAMIE BACON

Only daughter of John and Belle Howard, was born at Shelbyville, Kentucky. Reared and educated in the public schools of Kentucky and Indiana, completing a business course at Benton College in 1898, which has so ably fitted her for the many vocations in which she is now engaged. She was married to the late H. Leonard Bacon, December, 1917. She has two daughters, Leota K. Dixon and Carrie B. King, by a former marriage. She is prominent in church, social and fraternal affairs; member of the H. H. of Ruth, Good Samaritans and Daughters of Samaria. Past Grand Master Council G. U. O. O. F. Organizer and founder of the Independent Sons and Daughters of America. Past Grand Worthy Inspectrix and Grand Worthy Lecturer of Ohio Grand Court of Calanthe. Supreme Representative to biennial session Supreme Court of Calanthe, Louisville, Kentucky, August 16-22, 1925. Member and secretary of the Official Board of Park Street M. E. for eighteen consecutive years. Member of Executive Committee of Five in the reception of the historic St. Paul, now Calvary, M. E. Church, Seventh and Smith Streets, their future home. Charitable worker of the Woman's H. M. S. of M. E. Church, and many other organizations. She is owner of her residence at 826 West Eighth Street.

RESIDENCE OF MRS. W. I. BRYANT

Mrs. William I. Bryant was born in Kentucky, "the Blue Grass State." In early life she traveled extensively as a maid and became most efficient in the performance of her duties. At twelve years of age, she made many sacrifices in order to learn the art of sewing. She became a splendid seamstress and has won many prizes for expert needle work. As Annie Miller, she came to this city in 1895, but in the same year her name was changed to Bryant by her marriage to Mr. Wm. Bryant. Through hard work and saving they accumulated a great deal of property, so that at his death in April of this year, she became owner of nineteen pieces of property and the beautiful residence at 608 West Seventh Street. Mr. Bryant was a prominent member of Union Baptist Church, vice-president of the Men's Forum and patron of Good Cheer Xmas Club, an organization formed to help children. Mrs. Bryant will continue his charitable labors in the vineyard of the Lord. For twenty-six years she has been an active worker in the Union Baptist Church, and is a loyal member of "The Hayes' Club," "The Lutie Club," and Missionary Societies. She has always devoted one day of the week to relieving the condition of our poor people, furnishing them food, shelter or clothing, as a free-will offering to our Heavenly Father. As an administrator of the Bryant estate, she has been most successful since, from childhood, she has been trained in progressive business methods. Though quiet and modest she ranks as one of our most valuable citizens. She expects to settle her business as soon as possible and devote the remainder of her life to missionary work.

MRS. LAURA TROY KNIGHT AND MISS LAURA KNIGHT

Daughter of Theodore and Alphia Troy. Her mother (still living), was a school teacher in New Richmond, Ohio, and the father, a messenger for the Merchant's National Bank. She was born in Cincinnati, Ohio. Attended public school, Gaines High, and the University of Cincinnati, obtaining the degree of B.S. Now in pursuit of M.A. Married James Knight, engineer, in 1905. Has three children, Laura, James and Mamie. Mrs. Knight has been following her profession twelve years. Member of the Episcopal Church. Treasurer of the College Women's Club. For seven years co-operative teacher of the University of Cincinnati, engaged in training students for teaching. Was appointed principal of Jackson school in 1924, which position she is efficiently filling.

Her daughter, Miss Laura Knight, eighteen years of age, graduated from the University of Cincinnati this year with the degree of B.A. She enjoys the enviable distinction of being the youngest graduate of that great institution of learning. When but a child her precocity and intellectuality ranked her with girls several years her senior. Her future school days are destined to add to the scholastic pre-eminence which she has so long enjoyed. Mrs. Knight and family reside at 1076 Liberty Street.

October 10, 1918

RECORD OF LAURA KNIGHT (Colored)
1076 West Liberty Street

Born April 8, 1907. Age, 11 years, 6 months.
Grade Seventh, Bloom School.
Examined at the request of the principal. Examiners, Charlotte R. Fischer and Frances A. Foster.
Recommendation: Rapidly moving class.

Laura Knight, colored, was examined October 10, 1918, to see if she were a suitable candidate for the Rapidly Moving Class at Bloom in which she is enrolled. She was given both the Stanford Revision of the Binet Scale and a Supplementary series, and in each she proved to be a gifted and able child. On the Stanford Scale she easily made a mental age of fourteen years and ten months and since her real age is only eleven years and six months, this gives her an intelligence quotient of 129, that of a very superior child. The only measurement of that scale in which the examiner thought she perhaps was simply normal for her years was that relating to sense of form. In the use of language and logic she excelled.

In the Supplementary Tests she was above the average fourteen-year-old school girl. In the tests of language she proved most able, succeeding in the Trabue Scale, in passing a fourth year high school or first year college test.

Altogether, Laura is an admirable member of the Rapidly Moving Class and she possesses to a high degree, in addition to her mental qualifications, pretty manners and pleasing, appealing ways.

Laboratory Assistant.

ROLAND BUTLER

Proprietor of Shoe Shining Parlor and Cigar Store

Born December 3, 1888, at Atlanta, Georgia. Son of Abraham and Nina Butler. Attended schools in Atlanta, Georgia. Married Miss Lula Cobb in 1913, of Waycross, Georgia. Eight years at vocation. A member of the Elks, Financial Secretary, Past Exalted Ruler of Council No. 26. A member of the Baptist Church and the Republican party. Came to Cincinnati in 1918 and opened present place of business at 517 John Street. It is thoroughly modern in all respects and, thanks to his business ability, enjoys splendid patronage.

MRS. SINA STILL
Beauty Culturist

Daughter of Henry and Mary Williams. Was Born at Midway, Kentucky. Attended public schools in Kentucky. Pursued course in beauty culture at Louisville, Kentucky. Widow of Louis Still. For nine years has been engaged in profession of beauty culturist. A member of the Union Baptist Church and politically a Republican. A member of the Household of Ruth; president of the Poro Club. Came to Cincinnati about 1900. Opened the present place of business, using the Poro system, in 1916. Madam Still is deeply interested in all movements for racial improvement and is a Lady Manager of the Orphan Asylum. She is located at 520 West Fifth Street.

MAJOR LEE ZIEGLER
President of Ziegler-Schaffer Co.

Son of Lucinda and Frank Ziegler. He was born October 14, 1871, at Sandy Ridge, North Carolina. Attended public schools in Virginia. He married Ella Bays, of Kentucky, in 1894. He has spent twenty-six years at his vocation. He is a member of the Baptist Church, the Republican party, the Masons and was formerly a K. of P. His father died when he was three years old. Mother and family of eleven moved to Virginia, where as a boy, the youngest, he stripped tobacco to pay for his schooling and to assist in family expenses. Came to Cincinnati in 1894. Associated with East End gas plant for five years. In 1899, entered vegetable retail business. In 1902, started business establishment of moving and general express. A year later storage facilities were added and since then has been president of Ziegler-Schaffer Storage and Transfer Co. President of the East End Investment and Loan Co. President, Arcady Realty Co. A member of Crescent Club. Office, 2010 Elm Street. Residence, 4214 Eastern Avenue.

W. B. BRENT
Barber

Born October 6, 1892, at Fayette County, Alabama. Son of James and Mollie Brent. Attended public schools in Alabama. Married. Twenty years at vocation. A member of the Masons, Baptist Church, and a Republican. Pursued profession in Alabama fourteen years. Came to Cincinnati, August 11, 1919, and opened present place of business. Proprietor since 1921. Now located at 634 West Fifth Street. Residence, 756 West Seventh Street.

J. C. LANGLEY
Shoe Merchant and Repairer

Born October 4, 1887, at Piedmont, South Carolina. Son of T. C. and Charlotte Langley. Attended public schools in South Carolina. Married Miss Susie Anderson of Cincinnati, June 8, 1922. A member of Park Street M. E. Church. Came to Cincinnati in 1904. Completed shoe repairing trade in Cincinnati Trade School, 1919, and opened present place of business. Served in the World War in the 365th infantry and engaged in the Meuse-Argonne drive and other big battles of the war. A property owner and taxpayer. Located at 724 Kenyon Avenue.

BYNUM GLENN
Proprietor of Glenn Taxi Co.

Born August 8, 1886, at Winston-Salem, North Carolina. Son of John and Lucy Glenn. Attended public schools in Winston-Salem and Cincinnati. Three years at vocation. A member of Park Street M. E. Church. Independent in politics. Proprietor of notion store, 1912-14. Came to Cincinnati in 1895. Opened first class taxi business in 1922. Modern car service for public. Owner of modern eight-room house located in Madisonville. Business, 516 West Fifth Street, Cincinnati.

Home of Bynum Glenn

CHARLES P. FRAZIER
Clergyman and Tonsorial Artist

Son of Charles and Sarah Frazier. Born July 25, 1858, at Lexington, Kentucky. Attended public schools in Kentucky and received private tutorship. His first wife was Laura Wilson; thirty years of happy life. His second wife is Della Cherries, of Tennessee, 1913. He has been a barber eighteen years and a minister six years. He is a member of the A. M. E. Zion Church, a Republican and an Oddfellow. Came to Cincinnati in 1878. Head waiter, Grand Hotel, six years. Then opened present place of business, barber shop. Salesman for May-Stern's Furniture Co. Place of business, 540 West Sixth Street. Residence, 4671 Cresap Street.

JOHN H. ALLEN, JR.
Professional Barber

Born May 25, 1887, at Lebanon, Tennessee. Son of Mr. and Mrs. John W. Allen, successful business man. Attended public school in Tennessee.  Married Miss Carrie Simms, of Cincinnati, October 29, 1919. One son by former marriage, Robert Allen. Twenty-one years at vocation. A member of the Elks, K. of P., Commander of the American Legion, Earl Stewart Post No. 127, three years. Member of Allen Temple A. M. E. Church and a Republican. Served in World War one year, 1918-19, Meuse-Argonne drive, 813th Pioneer Infantry, Corporal, Sr. Former Trustee, Polar Star Lodge. For twenty-one years manager The Carlisle Avenue Barber Shop, located at John and Carlisle Avenue.

MADAM J. H. REIDER
Hair Dresser

Daughter of Horace and Mary Jane Nelson. Born at Danville, Kentucky. Attended public schools in Danville. Married John H. Reider. She has worked at her vocation for eighteen years. Member of Household of Ruth No. 93. Member of Bethel Baptist Church. She first learned the scalp treatment from Madam C. J. Walker, and used that system for six years. Then began making her own grower which is known as "Reider's Wonderful Hair Restorer." It is now well established on the market, through efforts of agents in various cities and active cooperation of her husband. A very comfortable home at 2707 Alms Place is owned by the Reiders.

ALBERT HATCHER
Herbalist

Born, Washington, District of Columbia, September 6, 1892. Son of Mr. and Mrs. Allen Hatcher. Attended public schools, New Orleans, Louisiana, 1910-1919. Came to Cincinnati in 1919. Opened present business establishment (Hatcher's Medicine Co.). Married Miss Maggie Bennett, of California, 1919. Thirty-second Degree Mason, K. of P., Law Student and a Baptist. Republican. Now located at 333 Smith Street, Cincinnati, Ohio.

R. EUGENE CLARK, M.D.
Physician and Surgeon

Son of Mr. and Mrs. J. M. Clark (Merchants). Born July 12, 1897, at Giddings, Texas. Graduated as valedictorian of Giddings High School, 1913. Honor, graduate of Prairie View Normal and Industrial College, 1915. Pre-medical course at Langston University (Langston, Oklahoma), 1915-1916. Student professor of Meharry, pharmacology. Graduated from Meharry Medical College with the degree of M.D. in 1920. Youngest graduate with the highest general average for four years' attendance. Member of the Baptist Church and editor of the Union Baptist Gleaner. A Mason, K. of P and U. B. F. Interne Kansas City General Hospital, 1920-1921. House physician and Roentgenologist, Kansas City General Hospital, 1921-1922. Came to Cinncinnati, April, 1922. Polemarch, Cincinnati Alumni Chapter of the Kappa Alpha Psi fraternity. President the Cincinnati Medical Association, 1925. Secretary of staff, Mercy Hospital. May be found at 623 Cutter Street.

Rosemary Hester

Richard Pelton Hester

RICHARD PELTON HESTER
Barber

Born in 1894, in Clarksville, Tennessee, the son of Tom and Mattie Hester. Attended public schools of Clarksville. Married, his wife being Anna L. Hester. Their beautiful, bright little girl, pictured on this page, is Rosemary. A member of Allen Temple A. M. E. Church, and politically a Republican. A member of Corinthian Lodge No. 1, F. & A. M.; King Solomon's Consistory No. 20, 32nd Degree; Corinthian Chapter O. E. S. No. 34; Sinia Temple No. 59, A. E. A. O. N. M. S.; Elk's Lodge, Alpha No. 1, B. P. O. E. of W. He owns property and has a fine barber shop. He is a self-made man and always in many positions of responsibility gained a reputation for efficiency and reliability.

JOHN R. BLACKBURN
Teacher

Son of William Blackburn and Fanny Randle. Born April 1, 1841, at Essex County, Virginia. Attended public schools in Cincinnati and Dartmouth College, from which he received the degree A.M. Married (first) Charlotte J. Needham, 1870. Later married Stella E. Yates in 1880. He has worked at his vocation for sixty-four years. Principal at Xenia, Ohio, twenty-six years; at Evansville, Indiana, fifteen years; at Lockland, Ohio, eleven years; at Cincinnati and Indiana schools, ten years. Professor of Mathematics, Alcorn University, Mississippi, for two years, from 1871 to 1873. Now Professor of Mathematics at McCall's Industrial School. Member of Masons and politically a Republican. Baptist. Former trustee of Wilberforce twenty years. Trustee of Ohio University, eight years. Grand Secretary of Grand Lodge, F. A. M., fourteen years. Grand High Priest of Grand Chapter of Royal Arch Masons, one year. One of the organizers. Became a Mason in 1864. Oldest teacher in the State of Ohio. Teacher in Sunday School for sixty years. He resides with the family of one of his sons at 1117 Yale Avenue.

EARL STEWART POST

The Earl Stewart Post No. 127, American Legion, was named in honor of Earl Stewart, a Cincinnati boy, corporal of Company K, 365th Infantry. He was killed in action October 29, 1918. Much has been done by the American Legion for the care of disabled veterans, now in hospitals, and Earl Stewart Post No. 127 has gone very far in this relief work. The aim in this organization is to promote the welfare of those who gave their services in the World War. The Earl Stewart Post of the American Legion was organized in 1920. Since that time its members have most loyally kept the pledge they so nobly made.

PROF. ALFRED NELSON QUARLES

Professor Alfred Nelson Quarles, born, Frankfort, Kentucky; parents, Charleston and Mary E. Quarles. Came to Cincinnati when about one and one-half years old. Attended grammar and high school in Cincinnati. Studied music under the leading professors teaching in the College of Music. He studied harmony and pipe organ, voice and technique. Taught music in the public schools of Covington for a number of years. Was organist and choir director of Allen Temple a quarter of a century. At present is director of St. John A. M. E. Zion choir. Among his pupils were Madam Langley and daughters, Julia Friason, Ozetta Wallace and Laura Bowman-Kirkpatrick, who has been on the stage for years, and several others. Professor Quarles has bought two valuable pieces of property on prominent streets and has also accumulated a substantial bank account. He has traveled extensively. His residence is 1034 Linn Street.

REV. W. HENRY WILLIAMS, D.D.

The subject of this sketch, the Rev. W. Henry Williams, D.D., was born in Lexington, Kentucky, September 9, 1876. His parents were Timothy and Harriett Williams, who were among the leading citizens of their day.

He attended the public school in the little town of Nicholasville. He entered State University (now Simmons) and enjoyed the rare opportunity of the tutorship of the late Dr. C. L. Purse. He was set apart to the work of the gospel ministry, September, 1900, and was called to the pastorate of the First Baptist Church of Somerset, Kentucky, the same month. His work there as a young minister soon attracted the attention of prominent citizens of both races. Studious and industrious, he was looked upon as a coming leader of his race and opportunities were given him to study in the best libraries among the white people of the city. Dr. O. M. Huey, the pastor of the First Baptist Church (white), took a most fatherly interest in him and gave him the privilege to use the library in his residence at all times. There were others equally interested in him. Among them was Mr. Edwin P. Morrow, a young and very brilliant attorney, the son of the Hon. T. Z. Morrow, who was Circuit Judge of that district for twelve years, and during all these years, it is said, not a single opinion of his was reversed by a higher court. Young Morrow formed a very strong attachment for the young minister and never lost an opportunity to help him, often speaking in his church and encouraging the members and citizens to support and encourage him. It was in his library young Williams spent a great deal of his time. It was during his memorable campaign for governor of Kentucky that Mr. Morrow would refer his Owensboro, Kentucky, audience to Rev. Williams, whom he said could tell you all about him. It is needless to say that until this day a warm friendship exists between the ex-governor of Kentucky and Rev. Williams. For nearly ten years young Williams labored in the little city of Somerset, his first charge, and his life and work made a powerful impression upon the citizens of that city and county.

In March, 1910, he received a unanimous call to the pastorate of the Fourth Street Baptist Church of Owensboro, Kentucky. Here his labor was blessed with extraordinary success for more than thirteen years. In 1916, March 4th, at high noon, he married Miss Arabella Smith, the only daughter of Captain J. W. and Clara E. Smith, of Xenia, Ohio. She, a very able and capable young woman, already engaged in teaching and supervising the music of the city high school of Owensboro, Kentucky, brought to his aid her splendid ability and willing co-operation, which was immediately manifested and felt through the entire program of that great church and community.

In 1923, April 3rd, the Antioch Baptist Church of Cincinnati, Ohio, extended a unanimous call to the Rev. Williams to become its pastor. After a careful consideration of several months, he accepted the call. His deciding to leave the church at Owensboro was the occasion for great regret on the part of the church people and the citizens who were interested in the progress of religion and the welfare of the people generally. The white newspapers of the city spoke in commendable terms of his ability and service to the community. He came to Cincinnati and was installed into the pastorate of the Antioch Baptist Church, July 8, 1923, with elaborate and appropriate ceremony, many of the leading citizens participating in the program. This church, which is the largest in the city, and one of the largest in the denomination, was very anxious to build a house of worship adequate to the needs of an ever-growing congregation, and the activities of modern church life. He soon set about the task of helping the church to realize its long and fondest hope, a new building, and in April, 1924, he submitted his plan for the new building, this having been sketched by a Mr. Rayfield, colored architect of Birmingham, Alabama, which was readily accepted by the congregation.

At this writing, November, 1925, the building, a beautiful Gothic style of architecture, is nearing completion. It is built of beautiful gray pressed brick, stone and concrete. It will consist of one large auditorium, with balcony running around the entire room, which will have a seating capacity of two thousand. In addition to this, the Sunday School department, with its individual class rooms and assembly room seating more than five hundred. It is also equipped with a large gymnasium, social hall, library, shower baths, offices, dining room and kitchen. As to its exterior appearance, the five sets of double doors, marking the front entrances, with beautiful white steps, its highly ornamented front, make it a thing of beauty and a joy forever. It is not only a beautiful church, but a costly one, representing an outlay of more than two hundred thousand dollars. It is by far the most elaborate and costly plant ever attempted by race people in the middlewest. Shortly after Rev. Williams came to Cincinnati there was occasioned quite a little stir, both in Kentucky and in the church, when it was announced that the First Baptist Church of Somerset had again extended a unanimous call to Rev. Williams and that the leading white citizens of that city had signed their names to an indorsement of the call. This is remarkable and seldom happens, that a church calls a minister who had previously served them for a period of nearly ten years, and this, too, after a lapse of fifteen years. It shows the caliber of the man as well as the character of his service. Antioch Church is now in the midst of its greatest progress and prosperity, and the citizens, regardless of color or denomination, are extending congratulations to it and wishing the pastor and his better half many years of useful service in this city. In May, 1922, Selma University conferred the honorary degree of Doctor of Divinity upon Rev. Williams, and he has and does hold many positions of honor and trust. Trustee of Simmons University; member of Federation Council of Churches of Christ in America; member of the Board of Education of the National Baptist Convention of America; president of the City Baptist Ministerial Alliance; Vice-moderator of the General Association of Colored Baptists of Kentucky; Ex-Moderator of Green River Valley District Association; Ex-Vice-President of National Baptist Convention of America for Kentucky; Ex-musical director of State Grand Lodge of Masons of Kentucky. The Doctor and Madam Williams are splendidly situated at 735 West Ninth Street.

MRS. ARABELLA WILLIAMS
Music Teacher

Daughter of Captain and Mrs. James W. Smith. Her father was a prosperous farmer and formerly captain U. S. V. I. of 48th Infantry.

She was born September 7, 1886, at Xenia, Ohio. Attended public and high schools of Xenia from which she graduated. Graduate University Extension Conservatory in 1905, then studied under private tutorship. Married Dr. W. H. Williams, of Kentucky, March 4, 1916. She has been at her vocation fifteen years. Member of Antioch Baptist Church and politically a Republican. Formerly a member of the Eastern Star. Began teaching music lessons in Xenia, 1905. Was instrumental in formulating music course and taught in public schools of Owensboro, Kentucky, for six years. Came to Cincinnati in 1923; taught nine years as a public school teacher. She has rendered most valuable assistance to her distinguished husband in his church work.

MRS. FLORA HECTOR
Beauty Culturist

Born, Knoxville, Tennessee, February 17, 1888. Daughter of Mark and Martha Henderson. Attended grammar schools of Knoxville, Tennessee. Came to Cincinnati, 1919. Pursued special course in Poro in Cincinnati, 1919. Opened present beauty parlor in 1919. Proprietor of first class rooming house since 1923. Married Mr. Tee Hector, Cincinnati, 1923. A member of St. John A. M. A. Z. Now located at 630 West Fourth Street, Cincinnati, Ohio.

REV. HENRY WISTER TATE, D.D.

Born in Hayesville, North Carolina, December 6, 1855. His mother, a slave, his father a prominent white physician. With mother and stepfather he settled in Troy, Ohio, in 1866. Completing the colored school course, his promotion to the Edwards school, white, made a sensation, he being the first colored student. At eighteen, he graduated from the National Normal University of Lebanon. Called to the ministry, he attended the Wittenberg Theological Seminary at Springfield, Ohio, and later graduated from the Theological department of Central Tennessee College, Nashville, Tennessee, in 1889. Taught in the Ohio public schools for seven years. Began preaching in 1878 and has held for many years, with signal distinction, most important and honorable positions in the M. E. Church Conferences. Since 1893 he and his charming family have almost

continuously resided on Walnut Hills. An eloquent speaker, a forceful lecturer, he has been remarkably successful with the many churches so fortunate as to secure his services.

MRS. ESTELLE RICKMAN DAVIS
Organizer and Social Worker

Daughter of Edward and Rebecca Rickman, teacher and purchasing agent for steamboat lines. She was born at New Albany, Indiana. Attended public schools in New Albany and high school. She completed her education as the youngest graduate. Married C. R. Davis of Kentucky. She has spent twenty-five years at her vocation. She is a member of the Baptist Church and the Republican party. Taught school in New Albany, Indiana, and Henderson, Kentucky. State Federation of Women's Club president for past four years. President of the West End Branch of the Y. W. C. A. Secretary of Trustee Board of Home for Aged Colored Women. President of Missionary Society of Union Baptist Church and teacher in Sunday School. A member of the inter-racial Council of Federation of Churches. A woman whose experience renders her invaluable in affairs of civic and social welfare.

Home of C. R. Davis

CHARLES R. DAVIS
Contractor and Builder

Born in Louisville, Kentucky. Attended Louisville, Kentucky, High School. Married Estella I. Rickman. Has spent fifteen years at his vocation. He served nineteen years as head clerk at the John D. Park's Wholesale Drug Store; since then contractor and builder. He is now in the insurance business. He resides at 3046 Gilbert Avenue. Mr. Davis is a member of the Union Baptist Church and the Republican party.

ILLUSTRIOUS EDWARD SAMUEL TOWNSEND, 33°

One of Cincinnati's representative and most efficient race men, Masonically speaking, for where Masonry is concerned he has no peer. Besides belonging to all branches of Masonry he has been crowned a Sovereign Grand Inspector General of the Supreme Council, Thirty-third and last Degree, as a result of meritorious services. He is the hub of the huge wheel that rolled the Masons of True American Lodge No. 2 and St. John's Lodge No. 3, F. & A. M., into a home of their own, for the first time in the history of Negro Masonry in Cincinnati. He is at present Worshipful Master of St. John's Lodge No. 3, F. & A. M.; Illustrious Potentate of Sinai Temple No. 59, A. E. A. Order Nobles of the Mystic Shrine; Most Excellent King in Prince White Chapter, Royal Arch Masonry. Mr. Townsend is also Deputy County Recorder of Hamilton County, Ohio, having held that position for nineteen consecutive years. He is a son of the late David Cornelius and Martha Townsend (nee Mitchell), who came to Cincinnati when it was a border town. Mr. Townsend resides with his mother, who is one of America's foremost Bible students.

IMPERIAL DEPUTY ANDREW L. INGRAM, JR., 32°

Son of Andrew L. Ingram, Sr., and Lila Ingram (nee Gill). Mr. Ingram is a native born Cincinnatian, having received his education in the public schools of Cincinnati, Ohio; attended the Cincinnati University. Mr. Ingram is now taking a special course in law, preparatory to opening an office. He is one of the few men whose character is above reproach. His affable disposition has won to him friends by the legion. As a speaker he is very eloquent. Mr. Ingram is the Imperial Deputy of the Oasis of Cincinnati, Desert of Ohio, having been appointed to that high office as the personal representative of the Imperial Potentate (of Shriners) of North and South America and jurisdiction. He is Past Master of True American Lodge No. 2, F. & A. M. He resides at 3139 Gaff Avenue.

MRS. IVANORA B. COPELAND
Funeral Director

Born in Mason County, Kentucky. Daughter of Joseph and Maria Lindsey, who later became Mrs. Ferguson. Attended public schools in Cincinnati and Berea College of Kentucky. Married Wm. Copeland thirty-five years ago. Ten years at vocation. Organizer and Past Matron of St. John's Chapter of O. E. S. Past Grand Officer of O. E. S. Organizer of the First Golden Circle in State of Ohio. First Daughter of Isis in State of Ohio. A member of the Episcopal Church and of the Republican party. Past G. A. C. and P. W. International O. E. S. Her ambition and ability have been great factors in the business success of herself and husband.

WILLIAM COPELAND
Funeral Director

Born July 30, 1848, at Columbus, Ohio. Son of Wm. and Mary Copeland. His father was a painting contractor. Attended public schools in Columbus. Married Miss Ivanora Lindsey, of Kentucky, thirty-five years ago. Ten years at vocation. Thirty-third degree Mason, Past Commander of S. of Ohio K. T., and member of the Episcopal Church and of the Republican party. During the Civil War in the quartermaster department at Camp Chase, Ohio. Messenger for G. A. R. to Grant at Vicksburg. Porter and brakeman in O. & M. R. R. for fifteen years. Formerly proprietor of cafe in Cincinnati. Assistant Market Master for two years. First colored U. S. Gauger under President Arthur. Surveyor in city waterworks for two years. Member of the Ohio Legislature, 1888-1889. Deputy Sheriff for twenty years till 1911. One of the four organizers of Young Men's Blaine Club. Opened first class undertaking establishment in 1915. Residence and business, 748 Barr Street, Cincinnati, Ohio.

E. L. SHEDD
Tonsorial Artist

Born in Nashville, Tennessee, January 19, 1860. Son of Mr. and Mrs. Samuel Shedd. Rural school, Taladega, Ala., 1875-1876. Married Miss Iola Barefield, of Florida, November 5, 1895. Children, Alonzo and Cleola. Forty years at present occupation. A member of Knights of Tabor and a Mason. Republican. A successful farmer in Alabama, 1876-1884. Musician, waiter and barber shop in Knoxville, Tennessee, 1886-87. Saloon business, 1888, Knoxville. Musician and barber shop in Chattanooga, 1888-91. In 1892, came to Cincinnati and opened place of business in 1911. Now located at 422 West Fifth Street.

WM. F. LEE
Plaster Contractor.

Born June 30, 1868, at Lockland, Ohio, the son of Edward and Amanda Lee, the father a successful grocer. Attended the schools of Lockland. Married Miss Blanche Armstrong of Lockland, Ohio, to whom five children were born, Winston, James, Roberta, Edward F., William Jr. He has been at his vocation for thirty-eight years. A member of the A. M. E. Church. A member of the K. of P., and the Masons. Now residing at 631 Mulberry Street, Lockland, Ohio.

DR. JOHN C. McLEOD

Born in Covington, Kentucky, September 27, 1877. He went to the public schools of Cincinnati and graduated from Hughes High School. At the Phoenix Grain and Stock Exchange he became assistant bookkeeper and was most successful in the performance of his duties. October 5, 1901, he married Miss Elvira Cox, the charming daughter of Doctor Eugene Cox. Studied Veterinary Surgery at the Cincinnati Veterinary College. After graduation he was appointed U. S. Veterinary Inspector in the Bureau of Animal Industry and served in the stock yards of Chicago. He is the only colored veterinarian ever in Cincinnati. There were only three colored listed in the United States Stock Bureau. He is prominent in Masonic circles, has attained the 32nd degree, is a Shriner and Past Master of St. John's Lodge. His son has distinguished himself in school and the daughter is very popular in her social set.

CLINTON GIBBS

Clinton Gibbs, born in Petersburg, Kentucky, August 8, 1891, son of Francis and James Gibbs, who soon moved to Cincinnati. This afforded opportunities for the public schools and University. Interested in music, he studied piano under the most competent teachers; theory at the Holderbach College, and organ under Mr. Prower Symon, formerly of the Cincinnati College of Music. His piano studies are now under a member of the faculty of the Cincinnati Conservatory of Music. For fifteen years he has given piano lessons. After seven years' service as organist of Carmel Presbyterian Church, in December, 1918, he became organist and choirmaster of St. Andrew's Episcopal Church. He is director of the Queen City Glee Club, the leading organization of its kind during the eight years of its existence. From 1924 he has conducted the classes in piano at Douglass school and is one of the faculty of the Lillian Aldrich Thayer Settlement School of Music at St. Andrew's. Mr. Gibbs, ever actively engaged in club and fraternal work, is now vice-president of Cincinnati branch of N. A. N. M., secretary of True American Lodge No. 2, F. & A. M., a member of King Solomon Consistory No. 20, Scottish Rite, and a faithful member of First Baptist Church, Walnut Hills. He resides at 2819 Preston Street.

ENOCH N. METTS
Deputy Sheriff

Son of Houston and Sarah Metts, wheelwright and carpenter. Was born November 10, 1871, at Newberry, South Carolina. Attended public schools and Allen University, graduating at the head of the class in 1891. Married Evelyn Duckett, 1893, to whom four children were born, Hubbard, Thomas, Henry and Sarah. For four years he has been engaged as deputy sheriff. A member of Jones Tabernacle A. M. E. Steward and trustee of same. Republican. General inspector for N. C. Insurance Co. for ten years. Manager State Metropolitan Mutual Benefit Association for five years. Taught in South Carolina and Georgia for thirteen years. Master carpenter and contractor, Columbia, South Carolina. Elected deputy sheriff of Hamilton in 1922. Representative of the Southern Ohio A. M. E. Conference at Louisville, Kentucky, 1924. In general conference two sessions. Resides at 1023 Clark Street.

MRS. INEZ L. RENFRO

Mrs. Inez L. Renfro (nee Inez Hamilton), was born in Woodville, Mississippi, October 10, 1885. She went to New Orleans at six and after a preliminary education, became a student of New Orleans University and Southern University. She taught school one year and was principal of Glencoe public school for two years. In 1904 she married St. Julian Renfro and moved to his residence in Shreveport, Louisiana. Within a few years they went to Jackson, Mississippi, and she taught at Campbell College. Later was principal of the kindergarten at St. Andrew's in Jackson, Mississippi. Arriving in this city in 1913, she began a commercial course at Woodward High night school from which she graduated with honor, having attained one hundred percent. in the examination. The year 1922 saw the entrance of herself and husband in the undertaking business. Their rise in it has been phenomenal. Mrs. Renfro is an accomplished pianist and formerly taught music. She is a member of nearly every benevolent fraternity in the city. Her charming daughter Marietta, fifteen, is a brilliant pupil in the third year of Woodward High School. Jenifer, her son, nine years of age, is in the fourth grade.

ST. JULIAN RENFRO

St. Julian Renfro, born in Shreveport, Louisiana, August 30, 1882, was a product of the public schools and an attache of the largest drug store in that city for many years. During vacations he served as night clerk, entered New Orleans University; left there to become steward of Gilbert Industrial College, Baldwin, Louisiana. He thus paid his way through school and graduated. He lived in Chicago several years as shipping clerk of its largest saddle factory. Returned home and entered the holy bonds of matrimony. He again became night clerk in the drug store. Moving to Jackson, Mississippi, he became a mail carrier and remained until transferred here to a clerkship in our post office. He was the second colored man to be appointed in the Registry Division. While there he trained several white clerks, took a commercial course at Woodward, a course at the embalming college, and then entered the business world as Funeral Director, and with his wife, famed for capability, is now recognized as one of the leaders in that exacting field of human endeavor. He stands well in many organizations.

MR. AND MRS. WALTON

Louis S. Walton, born at Hillsboro, Ohio, November 20, 1864. His parents moved to Camp Dennison in 1865 and the family has resided there and in Cincinnati ever since. In 1884 he married Fannie L. Cisco. Five children were born to them. In 1904 he was elected a member of the

School Board of Hamilton County, Special District No. 1, succeeding his brother, who in turn had succeeded their father. He served as clerk of the board until 1909. He was appointed Superintendent and his wife Matron of the New Orphan Home for Colored Children in 1917, which position they now hold. He has been a member of the Baptist Church since 1877, thirty years of which he has served on the Deacon Board. He is now a member of the First Baptist Church, Walnut Hills. Mr. and Mrs. Walton and family rank among our most capable and progressive citizens.

BISHOP MARY MACK

Born December 4, 1888, at Nicholasville, Kentucky. Came to Cincinnati in the year 1903. Founded the Spiritualist Church of the Soul. Eight churches have been set up under her jurisdiction: St. Mary's Spiritualist Church, 730 West Sixth Street, Cincinnati; St. Joseph's Spiritualist Church, (White), West Clinton Street, Cincinnati; St. Luke's Spiritualist Church, Washington Terrace, Walnut Hills, Cincinnati; St. Paul's Spiritualist Church, Newport, Kentucky; St. Matthew's Spiritualist Church, Lexington Kentucky; St. Peter's Spiritualist Church, Detroit, Michigan; St. John's Second Spiritualist Church, Detroit, Michigan; St. John's First Spiritualist Church, Chicago, Illinois. There are three presiding elders, twenty-seven preachers, seventeen ministers, eighteen messenger bearers and six auxiliaries serving the various churches. Proprietor of confectionery and grocery store. Daughter of Loris Bell, of Kentucky.

GEORGE RYAN HICKS

Born, Loveland, Ohio, November 25, 1889. Son of Mr. and Mrs. George R. Hicks. Mrs. Carrie Hicks, his mother, was a school teacher; his father, in railway mail service. Dr. Hicks graduated from Chillicothe grammar school, 1904; graduated from Chillicothe high school, 1908; graduated from Ohio State College of Pharmacy, Ph.C., 1910. Associate Pharmacist with Palace Drug Co., Kansas City, Missouri, 1910-1912. Associate Pharmacist with Harris Drug Co., St. Louis, Missouri, 1913. Came to Cincinnati, 1916. Became member of firm of Model Drug Co. at its organization, 1916. Married Ida L. Jones, November 16, 1918. One child, George Jr. Kappa Alpha Psi fraternity. Independent Republican, a Mason, and Episcopalian. Now located at Model Drug Store, Fifth and Smith Streets.

FRANK KELLAR, SR.

Frank Kellar, Sr., reared an estimable family, three girls and one son, Adah Chappel, social worker and teacher in this city; Louise Kellar-Stewart, one of the outstanding Sunday School teachers; Gladys Kellar-Harrison; Frank Kellar, Jr., one of the A. E. F. soldiers who fought in the World War. Mr. Kellar was one of the pioneer citizens; one of the organizers of Bethel Baptist Church, Walnut Hills, the first and only treasurer until his death in 1923; one of the organizers of the Benjamin Lundy Lodge G. U. O. of O. F. Property owned by Mr. Kellar estimated at sixteen thousand dollars. He died March 29, 1923, at the age of sixty-five.

WM. SULZER

Born September 20, 1884, at Cincinnati, Ohio. The following sketch from "The Optimist" is of interest: One of the outstanding concert singers of the day is a young Cincinnati man, William D. Sulzer, a dramatic baritone. Mr. Sulzer has studied with some of the best teachers. He began with Pelazie Blair, who discovered that he possessed the voice and musical ability and talent that creates a singer. He next studied under the famous Italian, Mariano Miana, who had sung in grand opera for fourteen years. Mr. Sulzer studied with this master for four years, at the same time singing with the Catholic choir where Mr. Blair was organist, the famous Umbrian Glee Club and the Great Choral Study Society, of which the late Professor Pedro Tinsley was director. Then Mr. Sulzer studied with the great Herman DeVries, grand opera singer of Chicago, for two years. Mr. DeVries coached him in operatic arias and prepared him for the concert stage. He made his debut west with Buckner's Concert Company, and studied with Kirk Towns and David, of Seattle.

Mr. Sulzer, being poor but independent, worked hard in the hotel world for the money necessary for his tuition. He, in collaboration with Mr. Artie Matthews, founded the Cincinnati branch of The Negro Musical Association and is a charter member of the Musical Association of Chicago. He devotes quite an amount of time to improvement of the choir of his church, the Union Baptist. Upright, industrious, his merits bespeak a brilliant future.

JOHN H. COLEMAN
Real Estate

Son of David and Mary C. Coleman. His father was church fireman for thirty years. He was born January 31, 1868, at Covington, Kentucky. Attended public schools. Married Sabina Richardson, of Kentucky. Three children were born, John H. Jr., Russell C. and Regina. At his vocation fourteen years. Member of Mt. Zion M. E choir, second tenor, and politically a Republican. Thirty-second degree Mason. President, United Order of Good Shepherd. Formerly president of Queen City Fountain 853 (seven years). President of Walnut Hills Welfare Association. Came to Cincinnati in 1882; head bellman, Palace Hotel, Sixth and Vine Streets, for twelve years. Second cook for John Brizolara, seven years. Methodist Book Concern elevator operator for thirty years. Pursued real estate while employed for the Methodist Book Concern. Established independent real estate office, 1919. Formerly president for ten years of the Negro Protective Association. Formerly member of Park Street M. E. Church. Instrumental in getting church on financial basis as chairman of special committee which secured and beautified the edifice. Now residing at 1214 Lincoln Avenue.

GARLAND YANCY THOMPSON

Garland Yancy Thompson, son of John Henry and Clara Jane Thompson, who came to Cincinnati from Virginia directly after the Civil War and settled in Rossmoyne.

The death of his mother, the departure of his older brothers, gave him the care of the children. His ability as a wood carver caused his introduction to Benjamin Pittman, the noted wood carver, and pioneer expert of stenography of Cincinnati, who encouraged him in the art, and presented him a set of carving tools, which he still owns. The illness and death of his father forced him to decline the opportunity of living with and studying under Mr. Pittman. His genius is demonstrated in a rare collection of his handiwork, specimens of which won splendid prizes in the Hamilton County Fair Art Exhibit. Mr. Thompson attended the public schools of Rossmoyne and is a cementer and molder by trade. He is a brother of, and resides with, the Thompson sisters, poets, of Rossmoyne. His brother, Aaron Bedford Thompson, is the poet of Indianapolis, Indiana.

THOMAS J. HOWARD
Attorney

Son of Thomas A. and Rachel J. Howard. Born in 1880, at Hamilton, Ohio. Attended Hamilton High School, Howard University. Married Miss Elizabeth Wells. Has spent twenty-two years at his profession. Belongs to K. of P. and Elks. Member of A. M. E. Church and Republican party. Was the first Negro boy to graduate from Hamilton High School. Though the only colored student of his class, yet he was chosen as speaker at commencement. Youngest Negro admitted to bar of Ohio at time of admission.

MRS. LIZZIE BRANCH

Mrs. Lizzie Branch, born in Georgetown, Kentucky, March 22, 1869, came to this city when seven years old and found employment at the home of Mrs. Douchman on East Seventh Street. After serving there five years as a maid she was in similar employment with Mrs. Dorty on Mt. Auburn for many years. In 1889 she joined the Avondale Baptist Church, married Mr. J. H. Branch, and later joined the First Baptist Church, Walnut Hills, and worked so zealously that she raised over $6,000 to help build the church. Nineteen years ago she bought a home at 2918 Monfort Street and became an expert in the renovation of lace curtains. She was instrumental in locating and securing the Old Women's Home and the Women's Federation Clubhouse. She is prominent in the Y. W. C. A., N. A. A. C. P., U. N. I. A., and every movement for racial uplift. An expert in flower designing and needlework, she won the prize, of an embroidered luncheon cloth, at the Lincoln Exhibition in Chicago. Young in years, possessed of a beautiful home and loyal husband, her life sets a beautiful example for coming generations. She resides at 2918 Monfort Street.

AARON BEDFORD THOMPSON
Poet

Born in Rossmoyne, Ohio. Educated in the public schools. Wrote poetry. Meeting with little encouragement from various book publishers,  he purchased a small printing outfit and became his own publisher. His first publications, "Morning Songs" and "Echoes of Spring," won Mr. Thompson fame. He was married in 1902 and moved to Indianapolis, where he still lives. Here he was discovered by the late James Whitcomb Riley, who highly commended his third volume of poems, "Harvest of Thoughts." Mr. Thompson, though greatly handicapped, has met with much success as a poet. He owns a cozy cottage with a well equipped printshop in the rear, at 2109 Howard Street. He is a reciter, a gifted humorist and the brother of Misses Clara and Priscilla Thompson, our well known poets.

GEO. W. HAYS, JR.
Deputy County Auditor

Son of Geo. W. and Mamie Hays. Born December 22, 1876, at Cincinnati, Ohio. Attended public school in Cincinnati. Married Maida Dunlap, of Cincinnati, 1913. Eleven years at his vocation. Politically a Republican. Secretary of St. John's Lodge No. 3, F. & A. M. Member of the K. of P. Member of the auditing committee for the last five years. Formerly keeper of records and seals. Representative of Garnet Lodge to Grand Lodge for the past four years. Clerk in the office of Clerk of District Court of Southern Ohio District for fifteen years. Clerk in City Engineer's office for three years. Appointed Deputy County Auditor in 1914, which position he holds at present. Resides at 626 West Fourth Street.

MISS PRISCILLA JANE THOMPSON
Poet and Public Reader

Daughter of John Henry and Clara Jane Thompson. Born at Rossmoyne, Ohio. In public schools and under private instructors she was educated for a school teacher, but owing to ill health she never taught but has devoted her life to literature and public recitals of her poems. Miss Thompson is the author of two books of verses, Ethiope Lays and Gleanings of Quiet Hours. Her poems show elevation of thought and sincerity of purpose, while the rhythm is smooth and pleasing. Her representative poems are: "An Afternoon Gossip," "Freedom at McNealy's," "David and Goliath," "The Old Freedman," etc. Miss Thompson's recitals are entrancing and sparkling with wit and wisdom. Her poems have received attention from foreign countries, England, France and Australia being in the number. Notwithstanding her literary efforts, Miss Thompson is an ardent worker in her church, being the oldest Sunday School teacher from the point of continuous service in her church, Zion Baptist, Cincinnati, Ohio. She resides at Rossmoyne, Ohio.

MRS. PEARL LOUISE GRINAGE TULL

Owns Pearl Louise Beauty Parlor and School of Beauty Culture. She was born December 3, 1910, at McKeesport, Pennsylvania. Daughter of Joseph and Francis Grinage. Attended public schools and Hughes High School. Studied her profession at Roubay Beauty College and the Dollie Dickman's School. Has first class beauty parlor at 702 West Ninth Street. Secretary of the B. Y. P. U. State Convention six years. Member of Ebenezer Baptist Church.

CLARA ANN THOMPSON
Writing and Elocution

Daughter of John Henry and Clara Jane Thompson. Born at Rossmoyne, Ohio. Attended public school and studied under private tutorage.

A member of the Baptist Church, N. A. A. C. P. and the Y. W. C. A. Educated for a teacher but gave up that field for writing, elocution and public readings. Her first book, "Songs from the Wayside," was published in 1908. In 1921, her book containing a single poem, entitled "What Means This Bleating of the Sheep." Another publication, in 1923, was entitled "There Came Wise Men." A new book entitled "A Garland of Poems," will soon be off the press. She has been written up in anthologies and has received requests from anthologists to use her poems, among them Carl Kjersmeier, a Danish anthologist, who praised her poems very highly. She is considered a fine elocutionist and often gives readings of her poems. She has resided in Rossmoyne all her life with the exception of the year spent in teaching.

FRED COPENING
United States Mail Clerk

Son of James and Ella Copening, was born June 5, 1895. Attended Cincinnati public schools and night high. He has been at his vocation for six years. Ardent supporter and member of Zion Baptist Church. Politically a Republican. A member of Garnet Lodge and the Y. M. C. A. Honorably discharged after three years of service in United States Army. Resides at 1211 Lincoln Avenue.

HATTIE BROWN WALKER
Librarian

Daughter of Robert and Anna Brown. She was born in Philadelphia, Pennsylvania, and her father not only spent twenty-seven years on the police force, but was the first colored policeman of Philadelphia. She attended public and high school at Philadelphia, Temple University, special student of U. of C. She married Rev. J. Franklin Walker of Virginia, and has two daughters, Helen and Breta. She has spent five years at her vocation. She is a member of the Baptist Church and the Independent party. Attendant officer for school board. Only colored Librarian appointed at main library. Organizer of Interdenominational Ministers' Wives Association. Chairman of Ed. Religious Committee of Y. W. C. A. At present a librarian of Stowe Branch. Resides at 3240 Beresford Avenue.

COLONEL LOUIS WHARTON
Catering Department, Hotel Gibson

Son of Louis and Amelia Wharton. Born May 28, 1865, in Louisville, Kentucky. Attended Central High and Baptist Normal School of Louisville. Married December 10, 1883, to Miss Mary Pierce. Twenty-seven years with the C. H. & D. R. R. Member of St. John's Lodge No. 3, F. A. M.; King Solomon's Consistory No. 20, 32nd degree Mason. Member Union Baptist Church and politically a Republican. A representative of the National Life Insurance Co. Chairman for fourteen years of the Christmas and Easter Committee for the children of Union Baptist Church Sunday School. Member of Ninth Street branch, Y. M. C. A. Residing at present at 618 Carlisle Avenue.

MR. AND MRS. LEROY J. WALKER
Funeral Directors and Embalmers

They are natives of Charlotte, North Carolina, have lived in Cincinnati for twelve years, and have been engaged in the funeral business for four years. They are the first colored undertakers to open a funeral home and they have kept pace with the progress of the profession ever since. Mr. Walker was married seventeen years ago to Miss Ruth Hendricks and they have two children, LeRoy Jr. and Mary Elizabeth. Both of the children are attending Walnut Hills High School. It was at the suggestion of Mrs. Walker that they entered Cincinnati College of Embalming in 1919. February, 1920, they passed the State Board as Class A embalmers. They are members of the Pythians, Elks, Tabors, A. U. K. & D. of A. Mr. Walker belongs to St. John's A. M. E. Zion Church, his wife and children belong to St. Andrew's. Their equipment is fully up to the standard. They reside at 714 West Ninth Street.

WILBUR A. PAGE
Clergyman

Born August 27, 1895, Cincinnati, Ohio. Attended Woodward High School and University of Cincinnati. In 1917, after returning from the war, he again entered the University. On September 5, 1919, became regular pastor of the Union Baptist Church. During the brief period, Union Baptist Church has been completely remodeled, new property purchased, an annex erected, a pipe organ with chimes installed. Total expenditure over $50,000. Membership increased five hundred. Rev. Page acted as chaplain of the American Legion, Ohio National Guards, Company C.

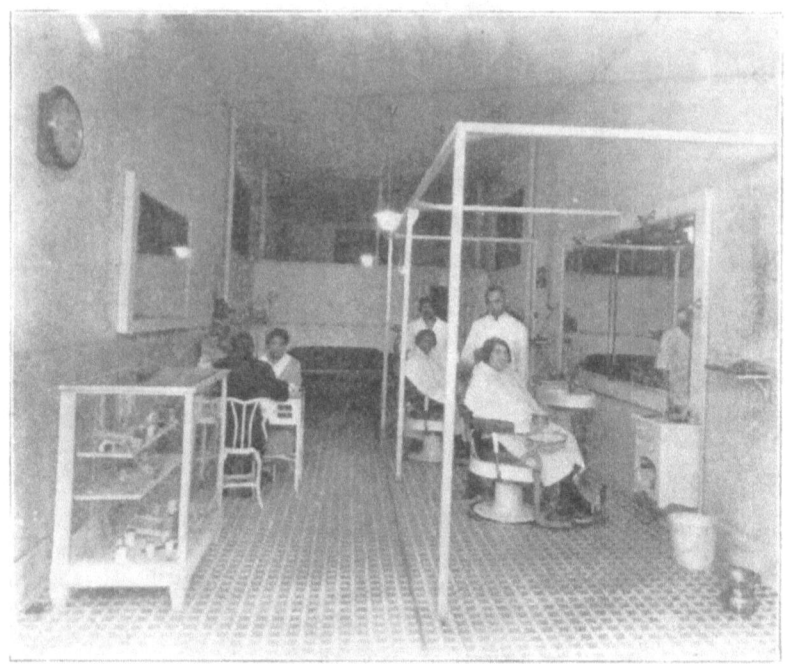

Clara B. Scott's Beauty Shoppe

CLARA BELLE SCOTT
Beauty Culturist

Born August 12, 1881, at Hasburg, Kentucky. Daughter of Mr. and Mrs. Simon Engleman. Attended public schools in Lexington, Kentucky. Married Mr. Clenny Scott, of Lexington, Kentucky, in 1904. One year at vocation. A member of the Antioch Baptist Church. Opened most modern beauty parlor of the midwest May 15, 1925. Also proprietress of the DeLuxe Tea Room. Her place of business is located at **532 West Fifth Street.**

REV. PLEASANT WHITFIELD EIDSON

Born in 1862, Iredell County, North Carolina. Was one of fourteen children. First a pupil of his sister who was school teacher of Siloam, North Carolina, then to high school, afterward to college at Salisbury, North Carolina. Early called to the ministry, he was licensed about forty years ago and took charge of the Second Baptist Church in Ypsilanti, Michigan. Converted one hundred and forty-four, twenty-eight joined, baptized fifty-seven, married twenty-four couples, preached seven funerals. Took a church in Canada in 1904. Had three hundred and eighty-seven converts, baptized fifty-four, added to the church four hundred and ninety-nine, married fourteen couples, preached seventeen funerals. Rev. P. N. Eidson, D.D., is the only living child of his first wife, who was Miss Rhoda Gilreese. His second wife was Miss Carrie Bradford. He married his present wife, who was Martha Henry Bolden, in 1911. She has been of immense value to him in the performance of his ministerial duties. He was called to the Zion Baptist Church here in 1913. The debt of $2,000 on it has been paid, added about two thousand two hundred and sixty members, baptized one thousand and eighty, married eighty-three couples, preached two hundred and sixty-seven funerals. The church is in a flourishing condition and Rev. Eidson enjoys the respect of the community.

MARY M. STREETS MOSS
Grocery Business

Born July 4, 1869, at Camp Nelson, Kentucky, the daughter of Edward and Tempa Jones. Attended elementary school. A member of Antioch Baptist Church. She has been at her vocation eight months. A member of the Good Samaritans and D. of S., Knights of Honor of the World, Royal House, Past M. N. G. Chamber, Household of Ruth, S. M. T., Elks, A. U. K. & D. of A., Daughter of Tabor's Masons Court. First president of the American Legion Auxiliary. A member of the Eighteenth Ward Republican Club. She has been in Cincinnati since 1883. Married Cornelius Streets, who became the father of nineteen children, and died in 1910. Married John Miles in 1913. In 1923, was married to Allen S. Moss. She resides at 525 Richmond Street.

DR. WILLIAM O. H. ROSS
Physician and Surgeon

Born November 10, 1879, at South Plymouth, Ohio, the son of Bishop Isaac Nelson and Mary R. Ross. Attended and graduated from the Eclectic Medical College, Cincinnati, Ohio. He has been at his profession twenty-one years. A member of the A. M. E. Church and politically a Republican. The fourth highest in class of twenty-seven in college. Average of ninety-one percent. in medical state board examination, with a class of two hundred and twelve in 1904. Thirty-second degree Mason, Shriner, Oddfellow, Medical Examiner for several lodges, physician of the Orphan Asylum. His death, December 6, 1925, followed a brief illness.

THOMAS J. BANKS
Dentist

Born at Chillicothe, Missouri, March 3, 1895. Son of Mr. and Mrs. Thomas J. Banks. Graduate of grammar and high school, 1905-09. Attended Lincoln University of Missouri, 1911-14; Howard University, 1914-18. Degree D.D.S. (College of Dentistry). Special at Ohio State University, 1920. Six years as dentist. A member of the Kappa Alpha Psi, Chi Delta Mu, Masons, Union Baptist Church and the Republican party. He opened dental offices, new and thoroughly modern in equipment, May, 1921, at Hotel Sterling.

Dr. N. E. Dunham   Mrs. Dunham

NORMAN EARLE DUNHAM M. D.
Physician and Surgeon

Son of Levi and Lula Dunham. Was born April 4, 1890, at Lexington, Kentucky. Attended and graduated from Fayette County schools; graduate of the academy of Clark University; pre-medic course at Fiske, 1914-1917. Entered Meharry, 1917, receiving the degree of M.D. in 1921. Married Miss Sadie Lyerson, of Nashville, Tennessee, November 23, 1921, who is now employed as a school teacher in Cincinnati. He has been at his vocation four years. A member of the Baptist Church and politically a Republican. A Mason and member of the Kappa Alpha Psi fraternity. Began practice of medicine and general surgery September 9, 1921, in Covington, Kentucky, at which place and profession he is now employed. Medical Examiner for the U. B. F. A member of the Tri-City Medical Association. Member of the staff of Mercy Hospital. Member of the executive committee of Kappa Alpha Psi fraternity. A property owner. He and his wife reside at 1222 Russell Street, Covington, Kentucky.

S. T. SNEED
Deputy Sheriff, Hamilton County, State of Ohio

Born at Pendleton, Kentucky, January 2, 1861, the son of Mrs. Amy Sneed and Mr. Sothy Sneed. Graduate public schools, New Richmond, Ohio, 1872. Came to Covington, Kentucky, 1876; to Cincinnati, April 9, 1890. Active in politics under Louis Kraft, a great Republican organizer. Watchman Cincinnati waterworks, 1909-11. Appointed deputy sheriff November 19, 1911. Married Miss Mary Paterson, July, 1907. Three children by former wife, Carrie Agnes, Ada May, Bessie Bell. Proprietor of a barber shop, 1904. Manager and owner of Fraternal Regalia Co., organized in 1905. Member of United Brothers and Sisters of the Mysterious Ten, Good Samaritans and Daughters of Sinai. Past Grand Chancellor and Supreme Representative, Knights of Pythias. Major General, uniform rank department, numbering seven thousand. Member of Court of Calanthe, an Elk, Past Exalted Ruler. Member of True American Lodge No. 2, 32nd degree; King Solomon's Temple of Mystic Shrine; Esther Lodge of Oddfellows. Commander of World's Champion Drill Team, Palestine Co. B, undefeated and retired in 1911. Member of St. John's A. M. E. Church. Executive of Eighteenth Ward, Precinct K. Resides at 627 West Eighth Street.

JOHN HENRY JOHNSON
Attorney at Law

Born May 1, 1878, in Hillsboro, Highland County, Ohio. Son of Charles and Nannie Johnson. Attended public schools in Hillsboro, Ohio. Married Anna L. Davidson, teacher of public schools, of Cincinnati, August 21, 1915. Deputy Grand High Priest, Royal Arch Masons of State of Ohio. Past Master of True American Lodge No. 2, F. A. M., Past High Priest of Prince White Chapter No. 1, F. A. M., Recorder of Simon Commandery No. 1, Knights Templar, Grand Secretary of King Solomon's Consistory No. 20, and attorney for the Order of Good Shepherds (insurance department) of the State of Ohio. Member of St. Andrew's Episcopal Church and of the Republican party. Six years he has spent in the practice of law but previously he was for many years clerk at the magnificent new waterworks plant of this city. In that position he attained a great reputation for excellent deportment as well as for a proficiency that has never been excelled. Mr. and Mrs. Johnson reside at 1014 Chapel Street.

CHAS. E. TROTTER
Musician

Son of George and Emma Trotter, charter members of Allen Temple. Born and attended public schools in Cincinnati. Married Miss Mamie E. Johnson in 1894. Forty years at his vocation. Member of the Union Baptist Church. A Republican; member of the Oddfellows. Official organist of Stowe School, and for thirty years organist of the Union Baptist Church. Has the distinction of being the first pipe organist in a colored church in this city. Mr. Trotter is a natural and self-taught musician. He is noted for his liberality in gratuitously playing for many charitable entertainments. He had the honor of being one of the first colored men to play the great organ in the Music Hall and has toured the state in organ recitals. The Union Baptist now has its second pipe organ.

MRS. MAMIE TROTTER
Organizer and Social Worker

Daughter of Louisa and Andrew Johnson. Born in Cincinnati. Was reared by aunt, Mrs. Ellen Higgins. Attended public school and Gaines High. Married Prof. Charles Trotter in 1894; one child, Harry Trotter. A member of the Union Baptist Church and politically a Republican. Worthy Recorder of Household of Ruth No. 566; held position for twenty-seven years. Formerly presiding officer of Ohio State District Grand Lodge, six years. Secretary, Oddfellows Building Association, six years. Secretary of the Eighteenth Ward Republican Ladies' Club. Lady manager of the Colored Orphan Asylum for twenty-five years. Vice-president of sewing circle, Union Baptist Church, for twenty-five years. Supervisor of juvenile department of Grand United Order of Oddfellows. One of the first colored women to serve on jury. Parliamentarian of City Federation of Women's Clubs. President of the Ideal Art Embroidery Club. Now residing at 610 West Seventh Street.

REV. JAMES E. ZELLARS

Rev. James E. Zellars, son of Mary Ann and Anthony Zellars, was born in Georgia, December 5, 1876. He attended the public schools of that state. Married Lavinia Pollard and has two children. He made a grand record in the religious life of Georgia and Alabama. Thirty-three years in the pulpit, pastored many prominent churches and came to this city in 1923 as pastor of People's Missionary Baptist Church, which he built. He is treasurer of Shiloh Association, president of Church Aid and Convention and was chairman of the Ministerial Educational Alliance. He lives at 3007 Kerper Avenue.

J. M. TADLOCK
Maintenance Man, Bell Telephone Company

Son of Joshua and Susie A. Tadlock. Father a clergyman. Born February 2, 1863, in Danville, Kentucky. Attended public schools of Danville. Married, first wife being Miss Anna Grey. Later married Miss Lena Fishburn. He has spent seventeen years at his vocation. Member of the Negro Working People's Conference. Member of the Union Baptist Chruch and politically an Independent. Was body servant of Erkenbrecher, founder of the Zoo, whose last words, as he lay dying in his arms, were, "How long the night is, Joshua; what time is it?" In unveiling the statue to his memory Mr. Tadlock played the leading part, as he drew aside the curtain showing the features that Cincinnatians loved so well. Mr. Joshua M. Tadlock has for years fought against vice in the Black Belt of this city. He resides at 734 Kenyon Avenue.

MADAM M. E. THOMAS

Madam M. E. Thomas, daughter of Augustus and Anna Alexander, was born February 4, 1870, in Tuskegee, Alabama. Attended Tuskegee Normal and Talladega College. Married Jesse Thomas, of Georgia, in 1914. Member of Park St. M. E. Church. Came to Cincinnati in 1897. Became active in the fraternal world and has advanced to positions of honor. High Priestess of St. Ann's Tabernacle, International Order of Twelve. Taught school in Alabama 11 years. Resides at 717 Barr Street.

MR. WILLIAM GUNN
Owner of Pekin Theatre

Mr. William Gunn, native of this city, reared in Madisonville. Attended high school, but an attack of rheumatism, which lingered for years, caused him regretfully to give up school. He has been in business in the Eighteenth Ward for many years, is well to do financially, always commanded a large political following, and in his ward had great influence with members of both races. He married Miss Ida Mae Symmes, of New Richmond, Ohio. A firm believer in the benefits of education, remarkably well read, he encouraged his only child, Miss Wilda Gunn, to persevere in her studies. After her graduation he sent her to school in the East. She won many prizes here, having made an average of 94¾ for her entire school days. She is very versatile, being a splendid artist, a fine musician, and is remarkably talented in many ways. She is now a pupil of Pratt's great School of Art Designing and Costuming, which is located in Brooklyn, New York. She gives promise of rare eminence in the life she has chosen.

AARON CHAMBERS
Proprietor of Confectionery

Born November 24, 1893, at Winchester, Kentucky. Son of Mr. and Mrs. Moses Chambers, prosperous farmers. Attended public schools in Kentucky. Married and parent of four children, Willie Warren, Mary Allen, Aaron Jr. and Charles Henry. Eight years at vocation. 32nd degree Mason. A member of Antioch Baptist Church, and an Independent. Came to Cincinnati in 1910. Owns first class confectionery store. It is located at 522 Mound Street.

ROBERT McWHORTER
Clerk in the Traction Company

Son of Sallie and Robert McWhorter (mail clerk), was born March 10, 1870, at Atlanta, Georgia. Attended public schools in Georgia. Married Pearl Johnson, of Illinois. He has been at his vocation twenty years.

Deacon of Bethel Baptist Church. Came to Cincinnati in 1895. Associated with Tennessee University two years. Associated with Conservatory of Music as houseman, three years. Accepted position as butler to J. E. Bell, nine years. Valet for L. D. Druitt, one year. Chef on private car with Big Four, six years. Accepted position with the Cincinnati Traction Company as messenger in 1905. Later appointed clerk. A man who has accumulated valuable real estate and personal property. His wife has been a source of great inspiration in the achievement of his aspirations. He dwells in a beautiful residence at 860 Buena Vista Place.

MARTIN F. FRAZIER
Clergyman

Born June 19, 1864, at Winchester, Kentucky. Son of Alfred and Sallie Frazier, pioneers of early Christian Church. Attended public schools at Winchester. Married Elizabeth Webb, of Kentucky. One child, Sallie, teacher of Douglass School. Thirty-five years at his vocation. One of the Disciples of Christ, and politically a Republican. Pastor of Christian Church, Corinth, Kentucky; three years, Richmond, Kentucky; three years pastor of Maple Street Church (Christian), Lockland, Ohio; two years, College Hill, Cedar Avenue Christian Church, improved church and increased membership; five years pastor of Oxford Christian Church, Oxford, Ohio; seven years John Street Christian Church, Cincinnati, Ohio; bought edifice on Hopkins Street; called to Wehrman Avenue Christian Church, building a congregation from twelve to one hundred and fifty; also built annex. Recently added another one hundred members to church. A Christian exemplary pastor whose untiring work has placed him in first rank of pulpiteers. At present pastor of Wehrman Avenue Christian Church. Owner of most modern flat apartment in city. Resides at 1241 Lincoln Avenue.

Rev. C. W. Williams

Mrs. C. W. Williams

Rev. Williams' Daughter

REV. CHAS. WILLIAMS
Clergyman

Born in Monroe County, Louisiana, March 12, 1877, son of Henry and Amanda Williams. Converted and joined the Baptist Church at the age of nine. His mother died, father being dead a year. Began preaching at the age of ten; ordained to Christian ministry at the age of nineteen in Harlinville, Louisiana. Served as missionary and organized eight churches in Louisiana. Organized the Mobile District Association. Accepted call to Emwell Baptist Church, Scranton, Mississippi; organized the Shiloh Missionary Baptist Association. Served as missionary fourteen years. Organized fifty-three Baptist churches in the State of Mississippi. Ordained thirty ministers to gospel ministry; ordained seventy-five deacons,, and baptized nine hundred and eight persons. Built five churches. Served as corresponding secretary to the East Mississippi State Convention five years. Married Miss Lillie Speight, March 8, 1909, daughter of Mr. and Mrs. Haywood Speight. One child by this union, Inez Williams, born February 14, 1911. Moved to Cincinnati, April, 1917. Has organized sixteen churches in Cincinnati. Organized Southern Baptist Church with eleven members who accompanied him from South June 6, 1918. In 1919, organized Southern Baptist Educational Association, with Mrs. L. I.. Williams secretary to the auxiliary of this association. In 1921, organized the Shiloh Missionary Baptist Association, serving as Moderator. Mrs. L. L. Williams, president of the auxiliary. Elected third vice-president, 1923, to the National Baptist Convention, unincorporated. In 1925, organized the Ohio Educational Baptist State Convention under direction of said national convention, with Mrs. L. L. Williams, recording secretary of the auxiliary department. Church membership of twenty-one hundred. Owner of property in three states. Also proprietor of barber shop and pressing club.

Mrs. Lillie L. Williams has held many offices. She was elected in 1920, Cincinnati, Ohio, president of the Shiloh Womans' Convention. 1925, in Springfield, Ohio, recording secretary of the Ohio Woman's Educational State Convention. In Kansas City, Missouri, September 13, 1925, recording secretary of the Ministers' Wives' Conference. Auxiliary to the National Baptist Convention, not incorporated. Served five years as secretary of Woman's Convention of Mississippi. Inez Williams, her daughter, was a church member at nine, elected pianist of the Southern Baptist Church when eleven, became a singer in the Gospel Band at twelve. She is also a member of the N. B. Sunday School Congress.

MRS. MARY M. BUSH

Born July 15, 1897, at Danville, Kentucky, the daughter of Mr. and Mrs. Madison. Graduate of the Pearl Louise School of Beauty Culture. Finished in 1925, manicuring, facial massage, hair dying, marcelling, and scientific hair dressing. Accomplished violinist, having completed her studies at the Cutaiar School of Music. Her husband, Vernon Bush, is a cello student of the same school. Mr. and Mrs. Bush are both members of the American Syncopators' Orchestra. Mrs. Bush manufactures her own hair preparations, namely, Mary's Marvel Hair Grower and Mary's Marvel Pressing Oil. Located at 722 West Seventh Street.

E. SHERMAN SMITH

Attorney at Law

Born September 22, 1891, at Clarksville, Tennessee, son of Henry and Mary F. Smith. Attended public school in Xenia, Ohio. Graduate Xenia High School, 1911. Attended College department of Howard University, 1911-12. Graduate of Howard Law School, degree LL.B., 1915. Married Effie V. Snowden, of Washington, D. C. Has spent seven years at his vocation. Is a member of Bethel Baptist Church and the Independent political party. Came to Cincinnati in 1922. Practiced civil law in Washington, D. C., 1918-22. Associate lawyer with W. B. Bush from 1922. Now located at Temple Court Building, Cincinnati. Residence, 1106 Foraker Avenue.

JOHN WESLEY ALLEN
Tonsorial Artist

Born April 5, 1862, at Wilson County, Tennessee. Son of Jesse and Cynthe Allen. Attended public schools in Tennessee. Married Miss Sarah Mitchell, April 29, 1917. One child, John H. Jr., by former marriage. Twenty years at vocation. A member of the Oddfellows. Treasurer of Eva Lodge No. 8218; Steward of A. M. E. Church and an Independent Republican. Proprietor barber shop at John and Carlisle Avenue since 1905. Proprietor of barber shop at Kenyon Avenue, three years. A property owner. Came to Cincinnati in 1886. Engaged for sixteen years as porter in Old Burnet Hotel. Store-room porter in charge for seven years at University Club, Fourth and Broadway. Now located at 752 Kenyon Avenue.

PROSSETT AND HARDIN

Messrs. Abraham Prossett and Andrew Hardin began business as proprietors of a grocery store in 1910. From a small beginning it has become a prosperous enterprise known as Prossetts and Hardin's grocery. Mr. Prossett belongs to the Masons, Good Shepherds, U. B. F.'s, while Mr. Hardin is a 32nd degree Mason. They have made many friends and built up a good trade.

LEW W. HENRY

Lew W. Henry, born in Leavenworth, Kansas, in 1870. After a few years in the public schools, he joined Scott's Minstrels when only ten years of age. In a year he left the stage, worked as a bellman in Kansas City and Chicago, then joined Campbell's Minstrels, next Hicks and Sawyers. Discovered "Bob Cole," who was then a bell hop. They worked together as Cole and Henry. He later doubled with Billy Caldwell. He was a member of the leading companies of his time, Sam T. Jack's Creoles, Florence Hines, many others, and later the vaudeville circuit. Throughout this country and Europe, Henry performed with great distinction. He was for a long time with the Howard Amusement Company in Washington. When with J. Leubrie Hill, they organized the Colored Theatrical Agency, the first in existence. Mr. Henry interested Mr. S. H. Dudley of the Smart Set Company in the project which has now become the greatest booking agency in America for colored artists. Lew Henry, besides ranking as one of the leading masters of stagecraft in the world, is also rated high in the ranks of managers, for during the last five years he has had charge of the Lincoln and Roosevelt Theatres. Those great centers of classy pictures and vaudeville are owned by J. B. Bruner, whose eminence in the theatrical world and philanthropical consideration of our people are well attested by his influence in the Theatre Owners' Association, his judgment in the selection of "Lew" Henry, his employment of only colored people and the noble fight he made for colored operators of his moving picture machines. Mr. Henry is an Elk, F. & A. M., and the husband of a very harmonious wife, who was formerly Miss Birdie Gibson.

A. L. DALTON

Attorney A. L. Dalton was born in Tennessee in 1863. Attended the public schools, and later college at Knoxville. After teaching school a number of years in his home state, he went to Washington, D. C., where he was appointed copyist in the United States Patent Office. He worked hard and was able to pay his way as student in the Flynn Scientific College and then through the law course of Howard University. His determination to become a lawyer came from his being robbed by a white lawyer, who caused him to buy a piece of property in which he found that he had only a life interest instead of a title in fee simple. Dalton swore that no lawyer would ever again cause him to lose property through a faulty title and so he studied law. In 1893, Mr. A. L. Dalton located in this city and speedily built up a good practice. In the great convention in which the interests of Taft and Foraker were antagonistic, he was elected a delegate and was made chairman of his delegation on Committee on Rules and Order of Business. He was a strong Roosevelt man. Several times he was appointed by Judge Lueders to act as prosecuting attorney and when Chief of Police Deitsch died, the court made him a member of the committee to draw up suitable resolutions. Mr. Dalton married when only eighteen years of age, Miss Cecilia Brewer, one of the belles of his city. They have a son and two daughters, all doing nicely. Attorney Dalton has a beautiful home, a fine car, and is proud of the fact that when he ran for legislature, though defeated, he received over 50,000 votes, the greatest number ever polled by a colored candidate in this county up to that time, which was before women could vote.

WM. L. ANDERSON

Mr. Wm. L. Anderson has been very prominent in the political, fraternal and business life of this city for many years. He comes of Kentucky stock and still bears a most striking resemblance to blue-blooded relatives of that famous state. He attended the public schools here, and as a Times-Star newsboy, became a protege of Chas. P. Taft, its editor and owner. 'Twas his mother who, as the widow, brought suit in 1906 for the wealth of Lafcadio Hearn, world renowned writer, who died in Japan. Nina H. Kennard states in her book of his life, page 83: "The courts decided against her on the ground that the law of the State of Ohio, in which state they both resided, did not recognize marriage between the races;" but the court added, "There was no doubt he had gone through the ceremony of marriage with the woman, Althea Foley, a mulatto." Young Will Anderson, or "Bill," as the boys later called him, was a great pet of the distinguished writer, and probably the association largely influenced him in his selection of the printing business. He became a writer and poet of no mean ability and was the first and only colored member of Typographical Union No. 3. For twenty-eight years he has had a large modern plant located in Temple Court where he has edited or published a number of newspapers, pamphlets, reports, and books. He has been a conspicuous member of numberless committees, and a leading figure in political movements and conventions. As Grand Chancellor of the K. of P., he made quite a record in this state. His wife, Mrs. Sallie Anderson, foster daughter of Rev. and Mrs. Peter Fossett, and near relation of the latter, has been a true helpmate, a real partner of his joys and sorrows. He went to France during the World War as a representative of the Y. M. C. A.

A. LEE BEATY

Attorney A. Lee Beaty, son of Mary C. and Powhatan Beaty, was born September 2, 1869, in this city. He was a pupil of the old Eastern District School, Gaines High School, and Law Department of Cincinnati University. He resided in the East End, near Broadway, then the aristocratic section for high class colored people of the early days. His mother was born on McAllister Street, under the shadow of the Old Dumas House. His father, Powhatan Beaty, a veteran of the Civil War, was employed at the Lincoln and Blaine Clubs and so young Beaty, even then conspicuously intelligent, came in close touch with the bright stars of the political firmament. As a boy he clerked for Old Man Gordon, later went to Washington as an attache of the government, came back to Cincinnati as a result of change in the administration, got into the post office, studied law, went to the Ohio Legislature twice, and now has distinguished himself as Assistant United States Attorney for the Southern District of this state. His ability was most clearly manifested in the recent wholesale conviction of police officials. He married Miss Bessie Buckner, who has rendered him every encouragement in the career he has so successfully followed and they have accumulated large holdings of very valuable real estate.

POWHATAN BEATY

Powhatan Beaty, born in Richmond, Virginia, October 8, 1837. Died December 6, 1916. Mr. Beatty came to Cincinnati in 1849. Enlisted in Company G, 5th U. S. Colored Infantry, and for gallantry at Chaffin's Farm, Virginia, he was awarded a congressional medal of honor. On September 29, 1864, the color-bearer was killed and Mr. Beatty's company was in retreat. Noticing the absence of the flag he went back a distance of 600 feet, recaptured the flag under fire, and the officers being killed, took charge of the remnants of his company. General Benjamin F. Butler witnessed the incident and at the same time when the above medal was presented, he also presented him with a silver medal. There were only twenty-six congressional medals awarded during the Civil War and two were won by colored men of Ohio, Mr. M. M. Howland, of Columbus, Ohio, being the other one.

WILLIE HARRIS
Custom Tailor

Born at Birmingham, Alabama, March 16, 1894. Son of Mr. and Mrs. William Harris. Served apprenticeships in approved tailor shops in Birmingham. Graduate of Slater Public School, 1907; Birmingham High School, 1910. Came to Cincinnati in 1917. Opened tailoring establishment, March 10, 1917. Member of Garnet Lodge, K. of P. Business located at 611 West Fifth Street.

JAS. A. ALLEN

Jas. A. Allen was born in the State of Kentucky. His boyhood was filled with the usual duties incidental to farm life. When quite a young man, ambition prompted his departure from home and steamboating, the most profitable pursuit for young colored men of his time, became his first real occupation. For many years he worked on the river. Tiring of that, he came to Cincinnati and was employed alternately as houseman, butler, and coachman for Robt. Morgan, the head of the United States Playing Card Co., and later Police Commissioner. As soon as colored men were eligible for police service, Allen, through the influence of Mr. Morgan was, in the '80's, made a member of the force. He soon achieved great renown since he was the main factor in "cleaning out Bucktown," that notoriously unsavory district in which murder and robbery were a pastime and a pleasure. In 1899 he won the prize in the first and only colored policemen's popularity contest. Several years afterwards he became the first colored detective of this city through the efforts of Wm. Copeland. His picture still hangs on the walls of the City Hall in the police department. Allen was pensioned after many years of meritorious service and died only a few years ago. He was married twice, his first wife being Miss Lugusta Adams, a native of Kentucky, and his second, Miss Maude Goodson, of Mississippi. The latter and son, James Allen, Jr., reside in the old homestead on Richmond Street.

JAS. E. JACKSON

Jas. E. Jackson was a great mechanic, carpenter and contractor who flourished here years ago. He was for a long time a partner of Mr. Chas. R. Davis. In his day he was prominent in church, lodge and politics. At the outbreak of the World War, he left this city, entered the Government service, secured a splendid position in its ship building department. He and his wife now reside in West Virginia.

EDGAR WATSON

Edgar Watson, one of the pioneer citizens, stood well in church, fraternal and financial circles. He was for a long time in the grocery business and was connected for many years before his death with the leading bathing emporium of this city.

MRS. MARY ROGERS WILKERSON

Mrs. Mary Rogers Wilkerson, who came to Cincinnati from Virginia when quite a girl, was a child of free-born parents who were owners of much land. She first lived on Seventh Street, opposite the Dental College. Later she married Stephen Wilkerson, son of Logan and Armelia Wilkerson, of Kentucky. He came to Cincinnati when a boy eight years old. They have a comfortable home and their lives furnish a good example of Christian happiness.

HARRIET BEECHER STOWE'S PLAYMATE

In Cleveland there lives a charming old colored lady, Mrs. Anna Bodie, nearly ninety years of age, who as a girl played and studied with Harriet Beecher Stowe. Her mother was the Beechers' cook. She tells, most realistically, stories of incidents occurring at the family residence on Gilbert Avenue and Beecher Street. Many a slave did the Beechers hide in her mother's apartment. On one occasion Mr. Beecher, while cutting wood in the yard on a cold, frosty morning, took off his coat and gave it to a poor, almost naked slave, who had just run away from the South. When the Beechers left Cincinnati, Mrs. Bodie accompanied them as their maid.

CAPT. JULIUS HAWKINS

Capt. Julius Hawkins married Miss Mary Hamilton in this city June 30, 1853. Seven children blessed the union. Edwin, graduated from Cincinnati College of Dentistry in 1880, was the first Negro dentist in Ohio. Charles became principal of the Lockland school and edited the Colored Social Column in The Commercial Gazette. Mary Emily married Philip Ferguson and was one of our leading vocalists. Eugene, society leader and dental laboratory expert. Walter, once Cincinnati's best second baseman, now property owner of Newport, Kentucky. Ralph R. Hawkins, attache United States District Court under several United States judges for twelve years. Married Amy L., daughter of Hon. Geo. W. Hays, court crier. Of four children those surviving are Geo. Hays Hawkins III and Virginia Ada.

SAMUEL E. EWING

Samuel E. Ewing was born and reared on Observatory Road, Mt. Adams, when it had only two colored families, his father and mother, Archie and Lottie Ewing, and Mr. and Mrs. Charles Wright. His father and the six children were natives of this city. "Sam" attended the old Eastern District School on Seventh Street, east of Broadway, with A. Lee Beatty, now Assistant United States District Attorney when Wm. H. Parhan was principal. He married Ida, oldest daughter of Louis and Susan Cunningham, pioneers of this city. Cunningham was formerly barber of the Old Dumas House and left there to take the shop on Second Street, then Columbia Street, which is still being operated by John Dixon. Mr. Ewing began working for the Batsche and Western Avenue Sanitary Cleaning Co. in 1890. That firm is now the largest of its kind in the state, and Mr. Ewing, who lives at 507 Hopkins Street, is its general manager.

A UNIQUE LUNCH-ROOM.

"Bud" Coffey and other old residents often recall the business place of Will Foster and Pat Williams on Front Street, near Elm. It was largely frequented by laborers. Their lunch, a cabbage sandwich and a schooner of beer, cost only five cents. The sandwich consisted of a slice of raw cabbage, sprinkled with salt, and encased in two slices of rye bread. In very cold weather, chunks of tallow were thrown in the stove. Then the habitues thought of hades.

PETER FARLEY FOSSETT

Peter Farley Fossett, son of Joseph and Edith Fossett, born at Monticello, Virginia, June 6, 1816, died January 4, 1901. His father, who was manumitted by the legislature of Virginia at the request of Mr. Jefferson, purchased the freedom of his wife and the younger children and made arrangements for securing the liberty of Peter. The family came to Cincinnati in 1833. When the money was forthwith coming, Peter's new owner refused to sell him. Later he ran away, was captured and sold supposedly south. His buyer, however, was his brother-in-law, who sent him to Cincinnati.

Here he connected himself with the catering establishment of Mrs. Kate Jonas, who in her day was par excellence in this art. On her retirement from business Mr. Fossett purchased her wonderful collection of china, linen and silver, much of which could not be duplicated in America. He continued in this business until within a few years of his death. His clientele being among Cincinnati's most wealthy and aristocratic families, and he one of the city's leading caterers.

Mr. Fossett connected himself with Baker Street Church, now Union Baptist, and served in the capacity of clerk and trustee and from this church, in 1870, he was ordained to the Christian ministry. He served as pastor of the First Baptist Church, Cumminsville, without pay, for thirty-two consecutive years. During this period he and his wife paid off the entire indebtedness of the church and an accumulated interest of twenty years.

Mr. Fossett stood for all things uplifting for his people. His own education was secured by stealth from the sons of his master, who were students in the University of Virginia. He was a member of the former colored school board of this city, the National Prison Reform Congress and University Extension Society, and also one of the leading Baptist ministers of the state.

In 1854 Mr. Fossett was united in marriage to Mrs. Sarah Mayrant Walker. One daughter, Mrs. Martha E. Kelley, and her two daughters, Mrs. Bessie Curtis and Mrs. Isabelle Butler, are surviving members of this union.

MRS. SARAH WALKER FOSSETT

Mrs. Sarah Walker Fossett, wife of Peter Walker Fossett, was born the daughter of Rufus and Judith Mayrant, in Charleston, South Carolina, June 26, 1826. At an early age she was sent to New Orleans and there studied under a French specialist the care and treatment of the scalp and hair. The manufacture of hair goods and the dressing of same was also mastered. She came to Cincinnati in care of the family of Captain Gwynne, a prominent family of Cincinnati's early period. Through their influence she secured entry in its exclusive group and had no superior in her profession.

Mrs. Fossett was noted for her philanthropic work. In the early days she was closely associated with Levi Coffin and the Underground Railroad. Her special interest was centered in the colored orphan asylum, and it was through her energetic work that the asylum secured its new building.

She served this institution continuously as lady manager for over a quarter century.

She was a constant aid and inspiration to her husband in both his secular and church work.

Surviving members of Mrs. Fossett's family, besides her daughter and grandchildren, are two foster daughters, Mrs. Sarah Anderson and Mrs. Clara Nelson, great nieces, and their brothers, Peter, Charles and John Sidney Porter.

WM. H. HILL

Wm. H. Hill, son of Daniel and Nettie Hill, of Warsaw, Kentucky. He attended the schools of that city. When he was twelve years of age his father died. Thrown out of school and with the burdens of the family on his youthful shoulders, he went to work like a man, and when able, brought to this city his mother, sisters and brothers. As prosperity dawned upon him he bought for his family the old homestead in Warsaw, Kentucky. Mr. Hill married Miss Gladys Gill, of Clarkesville, Tennessee, who has stood by him nobly in his battles for success. For seven years he has been in the undertaking business in this city, and his progress shows what energy and business ability will do to overcome obstacles and misfortunes. He belongs to the Masons, Tabors, Pythians and ranks with the leading Elks in the United States, being now president of the Ohio State Association. His office is located at 630 West Fifth Street.

MRS. PHOEBE ALLEN

Mrs. Phoebe Allen, pioneer social worker of the State of Ohio, Deaconess of Allen Temple A. M. E. Church, and State worker for the Woman's Christian Temperance Union.

Mrs. Allen was born in Flemingsburg, Kentucky; married to Thomas M. Lewis; later moved to Covington, Kentucky, where she lived until the death of her husband.

Having a lineage of ministers, she inherited those qualifications which rendered her capable of serving in the capacity of an evangelist. She worked in that field for a number of years, both in Northern and Southern Ohio, and in the mountain districts of Kentucky. She was later married to Jeremiah Allen, who assisted her in her religious campaigns until his death. In prohibition work she holds a county office of the W. C. T. U. and has charge of Ohio's children's department. In 1905, in the juvenile court of Hamilton County, she was appointed a regular officer. In 1916 she resigned, but still retains her commission as an officer. Mrs. Allen has given fifty years of service for the welfare of humanity.

R. D. G. TROY

R. D. G. Troy, son of Robert Troy, a product of that branch of the family that came from New Richmond, Ohio. He attended the public schools of Cincinnati and received every encouragement from his parents, his father being a bank messenger and his mother a very brainy, enterprising, ambitious woman. As a lad he entered the Ohio Valley Bank. Brilliant in school, the brightness of his mind endeared him to the bank officials and he worked his way up to being a bookkeeper of that bank. In

1897, though he had taken no part in politics, yet he was selected as assistant bookkeeper of the city, and remained until the party went out of power three years later. He then became secretary for Duhme, a very wealthy capitalist, and after his death, managed the estate for his widow until her departure for Europe several years later. Mr. Troy was for a long time president of our Orphan Asylum and was ever a prominent layman of the Baptist Church. He and his wife, a most estimable and accomplished woman, are located in Philadelphia, where their daughter Irma has attained distinction as a social worker.

REV. I. GARLAND PENN

Rev. I. Garland Penn, from the famous old town of Lynchburg, Virginia, a product of the schools there and later of the Baptist Theological Seminary in Richmond, Va., matured early, published a book when little more than a lad, and for his journey through life, selected "the straight and narrow path." He was for years secretary of the Epworth League, then became secretary of Freedman's Aid Society with offices in the Methodist Book Concern building in this city. He is now field secretary of the Methodist Board of Education for Negroes, a gigantic labor of philanthropy. Dr. Penn married Miss Anna B. Rhodes, also of Lynchburg. They have six interesting and accomplished daughters, and a son who has already attained enviable distinction as a minister of the Gospel.

[12]

"SAM" JONES

Samuel Jones, born October 30, 1832, son of Hester and Ann Jones, who brought him to Madison, Indiana, as a babe. He began shaving in a barber shop when only ten years of age. His shortness in height rendered necessary the use of a specially constructed stand on which he stood while shaving. He was stolen once and ran away from home many times. Once, having beaten a white boy, a mob formed to kill him, but he escaped, dressed in girl's clothing. At nineteen he married Cornelia Frances Coffey of this city, who was eighteen years of age. She, as well as he, is still strong and hearty. They had ten children. One died when two days old, the others are living and so are numerous grand and great grandchildren. "Sam" Jones has owned shops in Madison, Indiana, Indianapolis, Kansas City, New Mexico and California. His son "Sam" has now one of the best shops in San Francisco, while Richard is employed in Porto Rico by the government. During the Civil War, while in the army as an attache of a Union general, "Sam" Jones was captured and confined in Libby prison in Richmond, Virginia, for the "rebel" soldiers thought he was white. Many years ago, despite the prejudice in Madison, Indiana, Gorgas, the leading photographer there, admired his appearance so much that he kept on display in his gallery, until he died, an immense picture of him. His mother, Hester Ann Jones, had also a very romantic life. She was the child of a slave and her owner's daughter. As a stewardess on river steamers, she was the victim of several shipwrecks and burning vessels, but after leaping into the water some log or mattress saved her from drowning. She died a few years ago about the age of ninety-five. Her daughter, Para Lee Foster, eighty-one years of age, died last spring ar the residence of Mrs. W. P. Dabney, the grand-daughter of Mrs. Jones.

THE COLORED INDUSTRIAL SCHOOL OF CINCINNATI, OHIO
(Under Sallie Peters McCall Endowment)

The Colored Industrial School of Cincinnati was established in 1914 through the splendid benefaction of Sallie Peters McCall, daughter of Jeremiah and Joanna Peters of this city. Its management is vested in twelve trustees who are annually elected by the Colored Industrial School corporation membership. The endowment is estimated at $400,000 and a large part of the property is in valuable real estate and stocks, the entire proceeds to be used for the maintenance of the school.

The school has a large four-story building on a large city lot. The superintendent and nine teachers form the present teaching staff for trade and academic studies. Instruction is given in the regular grade studies through the tenth year and a three-year trade course is designed especially for those students who find it necessary to quit school early to earn a livelihood. The graduates to date number 597. School organizations: Alumni Association for men's group, Alumni Association for women's group, Chauffeur-Mechanics' Association, Neighborhood Club.

Mr. Wm. J. Decatur, of Atlanta University has, for seven years, made a most successful superintendent.

Orphan Asylum

THE NEW ORPHAN ASYLUM

Our Orphan Asylum for colored children was organized in 1844 by an association of ladies and gentlemen consisting of the following:

White

Mrs. Lydia P. Mott, of the Society of Friends, who lived in Philadelphia; Mr. Christian Donaldson, James Pullen, William Donaldson, Mr. Earnst, Robert Buchanon, Salmon P. Chase, Mrs. Sarah B. McLain, Mrs. Eustes, Mrs. Stanton, wife of Dr. Stanton; Mrs. Hannah Cooper and Mrs. Mary Jane Gordon.

Colored

John Liverpool, Richard Phillips, John Woodson, Chas. Satchell, Susan Miller, Rebecca Gaines, Charlotte Armstrong, Mrs. Hannah Cooper, Mrs. Ruthelton Watson and others.

The charter was drawn up by Salmon P. Chase in 1845, presented by him to the legislature, and its passage was successfully achieved. The first home was located on Ninth Street, between Elm and Plum. In 1852-3-4, Levi Coffin and his wife took charge of the asylum to save it from ruin, and during those years, as steward and matron, made no charge for their services. The asylum was moved to Avondale in 1866, to a site that was once used as a station for the Underground Railroad. Thanks to the generosity of the Emerys and other devoted friends, colored and white, the new Orphan Asylum, a monument to the charity, intelligence and zeal of Cincinnati citizens, enjoys the reputation of being one of the most efficiently managed eleemosynary institutions in this country.

Crescent Club

"THE CRESCENT CLUB"

There are now, and have been, many social organizations of men, called "clubs," that hardly deserve, in the strictest sense, such appellation, since they have neither club building, rooms nor equipment. The members meet at each others homes or have an entertainment monthly or yearly. The most notable of that class in recent years has been the "Argus Club." It is most regrettable that Cincinnati has no club building for colored men. They can well afford such an establishment. The Crescent Club was organized over five years ago, when the Sterling Hotel was purchased by Mr. Nathan A. Michelson, who furnished it elaborataly, bath and telephone in each room. The Crescent Club leased a suite of rooms. It was purely a social organization to which any citizen in good standing was eligible. No gambling was allowed, no drinks sold, no women admitted except at some social function. The initiation fee was twenty-five dollars and the monthly assessments approximated five dollars, since many distinguished strangers were entertained and many courtesies extended to various visitors who would otherwise have found Cincinnati absolutely lacking in hospitality except such as its Y. M. C. A. affords. A most unique feature, at least among "our folks," is the fact that the Club has never had but one election of officers, and that occurred when it was first organized. The amount necessary for its maintenance has militated against the acquirement of a large membership, and the original number of fourteen has dwindled, through death or non-payment of dues, down to seven. When the picture was taken the members were: Edw. L. Thomas, manager, Hotel Sterling; Major L. Zeigler, president, Zeigler-Schaefer Co.; Dr. W. A. B. Kerr; H. M. Higgins, Deputy City Sealer; Dr. W. O. H. Ross, Dr. Chas. A. Schooley, W. P. Dabney. Ross, Secretary; Schooley, Treasurer; Dabney, President. Thomas, Zeigler, Kerr, Higgins, members of the Board of Directors. Dr. Ross died recently. The membership is six. Mr. Henry M. Higgins was chosen Secretary.

Wendell P. Dabney   Mrs. W. P. Dabney

Wendell P. Dabney, born November 4, 1865, at Richmond, Virginia. Son of John Dabney, caterer, and Elizabeth Foster Dabney. The fifth of nine children. Graduate of high school, teacher for several years and later student of Oberlin College, Ohio. Married Mrs. Nellie Foster Jackson in 1897. City paymaster; resigned in 1923. Editor of The Union for twenty years. The loyalty and courage of his wife through twenty-five years of storm and stress engendered that domestic harmony and inspiration to which whatever success he may have attained is indebted.

MRS. RACHEL JOHNSON

Mrs. Rachel Johnson, who departed this life November 27, 1925, has a most interesting history. She was born five miles from Staunton, Virginia. When a young woman she was taken to the cotton fields of Mississippi, where she became acquainted with every phase of slave life. During the war she came in contact with hundreds of dead and dying on many a bloood-swept battlefield and saw indescribable scenes of horror at Helena, Arkansas, and other southern places. She came to Cincinnati and in the first emancipation parade proudly walked, bearing aloft a aflg, that beautiful emblem of freedom. For twenty-nine years she was a property owner in Norwood, and was the grandmother of our Gold Star soldier, Adolphus D. Saunders. A Christian for seventy-five years and member of Union Baptist Church for sixty years. When she passed away she was eighty-three years of age. Her daughter, Miss Nettie Johnson, lives at the old homestead, Norwood, a suburb of Cincinnati, 1730 Lincoln Avenue.

WILLIAM E. SMITH

William E. Smith, for many years well known in the social and business circles of Cincinnati and Covington, was born September 10, 1878, in

Flemingsburg, Ky., his parents being Walter and Nannie Smith. He married Miss Mabel Leake, a prominent school teacher, and they reside at 528 Scott Street, Covington, Kentucky. Mr. Smith has achieved signal success as the representative of The Domestic Life Insurance Company.

COLORED WOMEN'S CLUB

The City Federation of Colored Women's Clubs bought a beautiful pressed brick, stone-trimmed building in the early spring of 1925. It is located on Chapel Street, near Gilbert Avenue. Splendidly equipped, admirably adapted to club programs, it is an imperishable monument to the women whose brains and energy transformed their dreams into a building of such magnificence.

Section VIII
Sociological and Statistical Business—Postal

ALLEN TEMPLE A. M. E. CHURCH

RETROSPECT

(*From Centennial Guide, February 24, 1824—September 14, 1924.*)

In presenting this Centennial Guide to the reading public, the Committee on Historical Data finds it advisable to deal briefly with the early life of the Christian Church in Cincinnati as far as the colored race is concerned. When the city was in its infancy we find the spirit of independent church life imbibed in the colored man. As early as 1789, when Cincinnati was a hamlet, a flat-boat came into Yeatman Cave, at the foot of Sycamore Street, with its cargo, and five colored men escaped to the woods and camped near Mt. Washington. Three of these men, Joe, John and Bard, made friends with the Indians and married in the friendly tribe that inhabited that region. General St. Claire, in his exploration of the Mid-west and Northwest, took with him one Ephriam Johnson, the first colored man to enter the Northwest. They must have visited this section in their travel for after the defeat of General St. Claire, Ephraim Johnson returned to this place. He brought his wife with him and they built a hut in the woods on the present site of the Eighth District School.

Johnson was industrious and somewhat intelligent and soon got in touch with his fellow citizens and began the organization of social Cincinnati, where they could meet and converse freely and frankly. Joe, who had added Williams to his name; John, who had added Snipes to his name, and Bard, who was now Bard James, Mose Tandy and wife, Hannah Clay and daughter, with several of the friendly Indians, met with Johnson and held the first service May 3, 1790. Ephraim Johnson is said to have bought all the ground between Center Western Road, now Central Avenue, and the Indian path, later known as Cutter's Farm, and from the Indian Mound at the head of Mound Street, out as far as Court Street. All this was purchased for $175, a part to be paid in gold and the balance in timber.

In 1793, one Jake Moses came West and moved near Johnson and later on several other families came from Virginia, and on June 6, 1804, the records showed a population of 278 colored people in Cincinnati. In spite of the friendliness of the Indians, the colored populace prepared for any disaster that might arise and prepared means of escape for the women and themselves in the event. The meetings prospered until the effect was being felt over the entire vicinity and on one occasion the Indians invaded the meeting and after the women had been cared for in the cellar of the home the door was opened and in rushed a band of Indians, not hostile, but pleading to know the Lord that they were serving. The house-to-house service continued until 1808, when one Rev. Newton Wilson, a circuit rider, came into Cincinnati and preached the first sermon to a colored audience in the Northwest. After the sermon Newton called the men together and instructed them how to organize a church. The organization was finally perfected and one William (Bill) Allen became its first preacher. In 1809-1810, the first church of color was erected up the creek which ran from Mill Creek east between Seventh and Eighth Streets on toward Florence Avenue. This church was used as a station of the Underground Railroad and from 1812 to 1815 it was burned three times but rebuilt each time and the work of saving souls and protecting the fleeing slaves was continued until Rev. Allen lost his health.

Mr. Lyman Beecher, Mrs. Beecher, Mrs. Kemper and a Miss Hicks, all white, were very much interested in the colored people and during the illness of the preacher Mr. Beecher would preach and the good white women taught them to read and write. The burning of the church and the illness of the leader had a tendency to discourage them and the kindness of the white Methodists found many of them worshipping at the white churches.

Religious Oppression

Shortly after the colored Christians began to worship in the white churches the caste system began to unfold itself and express itself in such acts as inviting the colored people to the dusty galleries and pulling them from their knees while at the Communion table. Matters progressed somewhat smoothly until 1823, when a new spirit took hold of the colored members of the M. E. Church.

Sister Sarah A. Williams, who joined the A. M. E. Church in 1832, says that she has heard Father King say the immediate cause of his withdrawing from the M. E. Church was in this wise: There was a camp-meeting held by the M. E. Church, and Father King and Philip Brodie (who was also a local preacher) went to the meeting. The preaching was good, and all went on lively until the time came to take the Sacrament, when the officiating minister invited all ministers, traveling and local, to come forward and take the Sacrament to their comfort. These two ministers of the Lord Jesus went forward and knelt down at the table; but just as they bowed their heads, one of the elders came and put his hand on the shoulder of each of them and told them that they must wait until the next table, and that they must get up. They got up before the whole congregation. Father King said all the spirit left him when he got up, for he thought the Bible said God was no respecter of persons, and if that was true he had the same right at the table as the others. When all the whites had partaken of the Holy Eucharist, then the minister, with a long face, invited the colored brethren and sisters to come forward and commemorate the death and suffering of their Savior, as though there were two Saviors, one for the white and one for the black. But the spirit of soul freedom was too strong in the old fathers and Christians—they would not go forward and partake of the supper, not because they loved their Master any the less, but because they were conscious that those who made the distinctions were wrong, and were encouraging the spirit of caste and feeding the prejudices of the times. They came home and told the brethren and sisters that they were not satisfied. They said that the Methodists in the free states were just as bad as the Methodists in the South. Feeling that something must be done, they met in the house of Adam Brown, who became a local preacher in our church. The following are the persons who met at that preliminary meeting, namely, James King, Hester King (who was called Mother King), and their children; Philip Brodie and his wife, Martha Brodie; Adam Brown, who was afterwards called Uncle Adam Brown; Isaac Crosby and family, and Isaac Jones, who then was single.

A. M. E. Church Organized

In this meeting they talked over many things and prayed that God might blaze out a way for them. Uncle Isaac Jones, who went to Baltimore, Md., to select himself a helpmate, brought back the joyful news (as well as a bride) that a colored church had been organized some few years ago in Philadelphia, the City of Brotherly Love, and that said church had a colored bishop, colored ministers, and was composed entirely of colored men and women. Father King, after hearing this good news, called the little band of Christian believers to his home in order that Uncle Isaac Jones might fully tell them of the church, its doctrines and officers. After hearing him patiently this little band resolved to join the A. M. E. Church and did so immediately. Father Freeman, who was pastoring probably in Chillicothe, Ohio, came to Cincinnati and received said band into the A. M. E. Church and organized on the fourth day of February, 1824, the first A. M. E. Church in the city. Rev. Philip Brodie was given the pastoral charge of the church. They met sometimes in Father King's house and at other times in private houses and sometimes in the cellar of Brother Brodie's house, which they called Jerico. They afterwards moved into the blacksmith shop or the Little Red Church on the Green. So says Dr. B. W. Arnett, in his Semi-Centennial address. Much also that follows is from the same address.

The Little Red Church on the Green

This church was situated on North Street, near New. It was made of rough boards set on end; the floor was of clap-boards; the seats were of the same, with the legs nailed on and no backs. The front was painted red and therefore was called by some, "The Little Red Church on the Green." Sister Williams says that the first time she ever attended church was in this house; that the preacher had his head tied up in a bandanna handkerchief, and that it came off of his head and then his hair stood on end; that he went up and down the church crying that the devil was loose; and then she cried and hollered so that they had to take her out of church.

The congregation stayed in the little red church for some time, and its numbers increased daily; it was known as the anti-slavery church. When the people learned that there was not a slaveholder in the church, and that a man could not belong to the church and hold slaves, the colored people flocked to it. The ministers preached against slavery and the institution in all of its forms, and told the people how God had delivered the children of Israel, and informed them that God would hear their cries by reason of their bondage. They, on account of their anti-slavery principles, were called, by way of reproach, "King's niggers," "black abolitionists," etc. But feeling that their object was the elevation of the race, they were willing to suffer and bear the reproach for a season, knowing that God would bring them out safe in the end. As fast as fugitives from the South came across the river, the members of the church would hide them away and convey them to places of safety on the Underground Railway to Canada. Thus the good work went on, and when a free man or woman came from the South, he or she found an asylum in the little red church on the green.

The Old Lime House

The next place I find this society is in the old lime house, or carpenter shop, on Seventh Street, east of Broadway. In this house they worshiped for a number of years. It was two stories high, the lower part was used for a lime house and the upper part for a carpenter shop; so some call it the carpenter shop and others the lime house. It was both. Sister Charlotte McDonald says that she lived upstairs in one room and a Mr. Schooly, a school teacher, in the other. But they finally turned the whole into a church and stopped the holes in the sides and put an addition on it, for the congregation continued to increase by accessions from the free men and women who came to the city from different parts of the East, and those who came from the South. The preachers of this church were anti-slavery men, and they were in sympathy with the congregation, some of whom had friends in the South. Husbands had left their wives, and wives their husbands; children without parents were there. Oh, the broken hearts! the broken hearts that were in that congregation! And only one of their own race could bind up those hearts without pain. Wyle Reynolds, John Boggs, and Noah Webster would encourage the congregation to trust in God, while Austin Jones, Jeremiah Miller and others, gave them comfort. I am told that every prayer that went up in this old lime house was laden with the wants and woes of the oppressed in every land, and many were the appeals to Jehovah to come in his own way and deliver his people from worse than Egyptian bondage. Thus the fire of liberty continued to burn, and the ministers fanned the coals and raised the fire to flames. Peter H. Clark says that Job Dundy was one of the most intelligent ministers that were ever in this charge.

The Old Bethel.

The congregation continued in the old lime house for several years, until 1834, when it outgrew the shop. The officers of the church looked out for a place in which to move. After some time was spent in selecting a spot to erect a house for the Lord, they concluded to purchase a lot on Sixth Street, east of Broadway. This they did in 1834, and when the time came to lay the foundation of the new church every heart was full of joy at the thought of having a new house. Uncle Isaac Jones went to Mr. Griffity, who kept a lumber yard on Hunt Street, and bought the sills and the first lumber for the church. Peter Harbeson, a member of the congregation, was the architect and carpenter. Dr. C. F. Buckner says that he remembers when they were building the church, for he carried brick to the masons, and remembered the building. The congregation was still in the old lime house, working to raise money to pay for the new house; they continued for some time. When it was sufficiently finished for occupancy they went in and everybody was glad, for the Lord had done a great thing for them, whereof they were glad; so when they went into the house they called it "Bethel," and from that time forward the congregation was generally known as Bethel Church, instead of King's Church, as in other days. These people looked back to the time when a few of them met in the old red church and praised God; but now their numbers had increased and the congregation was large, so they continued to work and pray for the spread of the Redeemer's kingdom.

In 1839, the Lord sent a man by the name of Henry Aderisson. He was followed by Rev. Charles H. Peters, who labored with much acceptance to the congregation during the year 1841-42. Rev. Claybourne Yancy succeeded him.

In 1843, the conference sent that polished scholar and Christian gentleman, Rev. M. M. Clark, who came in November, 1843, and during the year he was elected general agent of the Book Concern. In the winter of 1843-44, there was a very large revival and many were added to the church, among them Brother George Peterson.

While the congregation was in the old Bethel, the first annual conference was held in this city. This was in 1846. There was great curiosity to see a colored bishop; such a person had never been in the city and every person was on the lookout for the conference. For months you could have seen new carpets, chairs, beds, knives and forks, etc., going to the homes of the members of Bethel. The conference came, the ministers were well entertained, and they also made a good impression for African Methodism in this city. Many of them were old warriors; their locks betokened many years of war, toil and strife in the irrepressible conflict for eternal life. Bishop John M. Brown was ordained deacon at this conference. In this church the first meeting to celebrate the emancipation of the slaves of the West Indies was held, so says Elder Shelton, who was one of the speakers, and the Rev. John Boggs was the other.

The congregation at old Bethel was very large, the population of colored people was increasing, and the congregation kept pace with the population.

Allen Chapel

During the administration of Elder Gross in this city, the cornerstone of old Allen Chapel was laid by Rev. John M. Brown.

Thomas Lawrence succeeded Father Gross. The chapel was unfinished and the people met in the basement, but wanted to get upstairs, so the trustees empowered Elder Lawrence to collect money for them. He went to Pittsburgh and called on Rev. Charles Avry, a noble philanthropist, and laid the case before him. He went to his desk and wrote a check for $1,500. When the new chapel was thrown open the congregation was larger than ever before, and the little band looked back to the Little Red Church on the Green and said: "The Lord is my strength and my reward, in Him will I trust."

This was quite a change, some who went to meetings in the Red Church, Lime House and Bethel, while some were still there who met at Adam Brown's and Father King's and as they looked back and saw the march of the church—it was one of triumphs and victories—they could enjoy themselves, for now they had a church with a basement, a main auditorium and an office for their minister.

Rev. A. R. Green succeeded the Rev. Thomas Lawrence, and remained in charge for three years. He did much good during his stay. He was one of the progressive men of his time. I find the following resolution in the minutes of the official board: "Resolved, that instrumental music does not tend to the glory of God." After some discussion, the resolution was passed. Thus the board did not favor an instrument in the church. Things continued during the time he was here to prosper in the church, both financially and spiritually.

Rev. John Tibbs met the official board on the 11th of September, 1855. His appointment was read and a motion made to raise his support by subscription. October 11, 1855, the official board had a meeting to make arrangements for the accommodation of members of the general conference. Bishop D. A. Payne was at that meeting and spoke of the duty of the board and church to entertain the conference honorably and respectably. He was sustained in this by Brothers Jos. Fowler, P. Harbeson, Reuben Fowler, George Peterson and D. Cooper, and all agreed to do their utmost to sustain the conference.

Rev. Grafton H. Graham was appointed to the Cincinnati station in 1860, just at the time when the country was in convulsions and internal strife seemed imminent, and signs of a threatening storm were everywhere visible, he entered on the discharge of his duties as pastor and watchman. He soon drew a large congregation around him but the influence of slavery was felt in the city and it was dangerous for colored men to walk on the streets. He counseled the people to be patient and trust in the Lord. The treatment of colored people grew worse. Public speakers were mobbed, and many of the poor colored people were compelled to flee for shelter to out-of-the-way places. The mob, on one occasion, beat and bruised one of Elder Graham's boys in a shocking and disgraceful manner. Many were the conflicts during the administration of this man with the friends of slavery; but God brought them out. The church, though for some time thinly attended, was filled up after the proclamation of freedom. After leaving this church, Elder Graham went to Kentucky and has been in that state ever since, working for the freed men and the cause of Christ. He is now at Harrodsburg station, working earnestly for Christ and man.

Rev. James A. Shorter was appointed here in 1863. A great many came from Kentucky with their families and stayed and joined the church. It was during his administration that the congregation voted to put an organ in the church. It created quite a stir, and some of the members would not come to church. Charges were preferred, and they were tried for the neglect of duty and found guilty and were expelled. But the administration, on the whole, was a good one, and the church still feels the effect of the work done by Bishop Shorter. During his administration, the noble women of the church formed a society called the Freedmen's Aid Society. Mrs. Eliza Gordon was president, and Lottie Step, secretary. The object of the association was to help the freed men from the South to find homes and shelter all who had no place to go. The house back of the old chapel was used for a hospital and many of the poor men and women died there. There has been as high as four in the room dead at one time. The government gave this society rations to distribute to the needy and much good did they do.

Elder Shorter was elected Bishop by the general conference in 1868.

Rev. Henry J. Young, D.D., was appointed pastor of Allen Chapel from the conference which met in Lexington, Ky., April 7, 1867. Many were added to the church. He bought a lot on North Street, and started a parsonage on it. The house has since been finished, and the property has increased in value. He repainted the chapel and made a complete change in the whole pulpit.

Rev. Robert A. Johnson was appointed by the Ohio Annual Conference, which met in Xenia in May, 1870. With the trustees he went to work to negotiate the sale of the old Allen Chapel. They were finally successful in arranging for the purchase of the Jewish Synagogue, the old Chapel being taken as part of the consideration. The sale being finally accomplished, preparations for the removal to the temple were at once made. The new place of meeting was renovated from top to bottom. The day of entering arrived, the arrangements were complete, and the opening was one of the greatest ever witnessed in this city.

Allen Temple

Elder Johnson was noted for his financial ability; he is the most successful financier in the Ohio Conference and one of the best in the connection.

Rev. Benjamin William Arnett was appointed here by the Ohio Annual Conference which assembled in Zanesville, May 17, 1873. He arrived in the city May 24th and took charge May 25th."

In concluding the early history of Allen Temple, we may say that the roof decorations are said to be representative and symbolical of a very essential part of the Jewish ceremonial. Three Allen Temple pastors became bishops, Shorter, Arnett, Ross. Rev. J. O. Haithcox has been pastor five years.

Mound Street Union Baptist Church

SKETCH OF THE UNION BAPTIST CHURCH
Revision of Report made by G. W. Hays, Sr., in 1879

The Union Baptist Church in Cincinnati is the second oldest colored Baptist church in the State of Ohio, its existence dating from Thursday, July 21, 1831, when in accordance to a notice to the people of color of the regular Baptist order to meet and take into consideration the propriety of forming themselves into a church, the following fourteen (14) persons were present: Brethren George Jones, Elijah Forte, Reuben Hawkins, Prince Austin, Thomas Arnold, Robert Lawson, Henry Williams, Richard Lunsford, Joseph Moore, and John Webb; Sisters Hannah Moore, Ann Fleming, Mila Banks and Polly Geist. The question after due deliberation was answered in the affirmative. The above had been members of the Enon Baptist Church (white), and the committee appointed to prepare a covenant and articles of faith reported in favor of remaining a branch of the Enon Church, to be known as "The Colored Branch of the Enon Baptist Church," "until such time as it may seem fit in the providence of God that we become a separate church," which was unanimously adopted.

Brother Elijah Forte was appointed to act as leader, which he did until February 3, 1835. The membership increased until at the meeting held December 25, 1834, it was moved that the church organize the second Sunday in February, 1835; for this purpose a council was called, with the consent of the Enon Church, Rev. S. W. Lynd, of the Sixth Street Baptist Church—now Ninth Street Baptist Church—moderator. The council resolved unanimously "that we recognize these, our colored brethren, in their church capacity as a regular and independent church of Christ and extend to them as such the hand of fellowship, to be known as the African Union Baptist Church of Cincinnati. The number who had subscribed to these articles and were recognized as members was forty-five (45), twenty-one (21) males, twenty-four (24) females." Their first place of worship was a brick house built by them at a cost of $600.00, situated on the east side of Western Row—now Central Avenue, between Second and Third Streets. The church chose as her first pastor Elder David Nickens, of Chillicothe, Ohio, who served faithfully until his death, which occurred August 14, 1838. His age was forty-four (44) years.

Elder Charles Satchell succeeded to the pastorate, serving a period of seven years. The church distinguished itself under his leadership in missionary and anti-slavery work. He entered heartily into Sabbath school work, and was ably assisted by Brothers W. W. Watson, Wilson Bates and others. He was also intensely interested in the secular education of the youth.

In 1840, the church moved from Western Row to Baker Street, having accepted the offer of the Enon Church for their property, valued at $12,000 for $9,000 and a donation of $3,000.

April, 1841, a discussion arose as to whether Elder Charles Satchel or Elder Wallace Shelton should be elected pastor, which resulted in forty (40) members withdrawing, receiving their letters and organizing the Zion Baptist Church of this city, with Elder Shelton as pastor. There was no split.

In 1845, by an act of the General Assembly of the state, the church was incorporated under the name of The Union Baptist Church of Cincinnati. Elder Allen Graham was elected December 2, 1845, and served the church for nearly three years. The church elected, November 27, 1848, the Rev. William P. Newman. He served until September 23, 1850. The fugitive slave law becoming disagreeable to him he decided to accept a call to Chatham, Canada. He was recalled in 1864, during which time the church moved from Baker Street to its present location, having sold their house on Baker Street for $20,000 and buying the building on Mound and Richmond Streets for $12,000, the remaining $8,000 on repairs and the purchasing of a parsonage and a tract of sixteen acres of land for a cemetery. He died August 3, 1866, the first victim of cholera; his remains were interred in our cemetery and a monument was erected by the church. The church also purchased a homestead for the widow and family in Appleton, Wisconsin, valued at $1,000.

Many distinguished men have served as pastor since then and Union Baptist continues its march onward and upward.

PARK STREET M. E. CHURCH
Now Calvary M. E. Church

First began as mission in early seventies on New Street, known as New Street Mission. Moved to Seventh Street site now occupied by French Company, and became Union Chapel M. E. Split under Rev. J. F. Mooreland in March, 1892. In December, 1893, moved to Ninth Street near Freeman, the present site of Antioch Baptist. Here known as Ninth Street M. E. Moved to Carlisle and Park in 1901 and since then known as Park Street M. E. Mrs. Hattie Grant, only surviving founder. On Sunday, November 22, 1925, the Park Street Church moved into the famous old St. Paul Church (white), and the name was changed to Calvary M. E. Church.

LUTHERAN IMMANUEL'S CHURCH

The Colored Lutheran Immanuel's Church is located at Cutter and Betts Streets. This church is backed and sanctioned by The Lutheran Synodical Conference of America. The church was started in the fall of 1922. Its pastor, Rev. Geo. Kase, is a white clergyman whose labor of love is largely responsible for the rapid growth of its congregation.

MT. ZION M. E. CHURCH

Organized Sunday, February 6, 1887. Six members met at the home of Richard Haun for organization purposes. Local minister, Rev. W. H. Croop, first chosen leader, followed by Rev. Baily. The sixteen members, known then as Walnut Hills Church, had various meeting houses until 1893. Rev. H. Payne laid cornerstone at 1119 Lincoln Avenue. Remained there until 1925, when Rev. S. E. Granum built present palatial modern edifice on Gilbert Avenue, and the only surviving original member is Mr. Wm. Buchanan.

ST. ANN'S CHURCH

St. Ann's Church, the oldest colored Catholic Church in this city, was organized in 1865. May the 10th, 1866, a lot was purchased on Longworth Street; 1873, moved to New Street; 1908 to John Street, between Richmond and Court, which site is its present place of worship.

NEW HOPE BAPTIST CHURCH

New Hope Baptist Church, organized in December, 1922, moved from George Street under the able administration of Rev. R. H. Bailey. Its membership, which started with sixteen, has increased to five hundred and eighty.

ZION BAPTIST CHURCH

Zion Baptist was formed by forty persons who received their letters from Union Baptist Church, then known as Baker Street Baptist Church. It was organized in 1840 by Rev. Wallace Shelton, the first pastor. Location, Third and Baker Street, served as headquarters for Underground Railroad. Moved to present site on West Ninth Street. Shelton, Fuller and Harrod were the first three pastors. Rev. Eidson, the present pastor, is doing grand work there.

DIRR AVENUE M. E. CHURCH

Was organized on Clifton Avenue, Cumminsville, in 1873, by Rev. Henry Steen, in the home of Mrs. Jane Boone. There were eleven original members. The first place of worship was erected on "Methodist Hill." From there they went to "Old Turner Hall," on Spring Grove Avenue, thence to the White Oddfellows' Hall, on Blue Rock Street, and finally to Dirr Avenue, its present location. The church has been recently renovated by Rev. Fred H. Bunton, its present pastor.

BROWN CHAPEL

The regular organization of Brown Chapel, with twenty-six members, was effected February 8, 1862, by Rev. Grafton H. Graham, pastor of Allen Temple. Rev. Phillip, the first pastor, appointed 1863, remained three years and built the first church which is now a dwelling on Whitlow Street. The foundation for the present place of worship, 2908 Park Avenue, was made in 1879 by Rev. R. J. Johnson. The cornerstone was laid and building erected about 1884 by Rev. Chas. Bundy, who held the pastorate three years. The present pastor, Rev. P. S. Hill, a most capable man, has greatly increased the strength and influence of Brown Chapel. The congregation is striving to build a new edifice on Alms Place, opposite Douglass School, as it already owns the ground.

FIRST BAPTIST CHURCH, CUMMINSVILLE

Was organized in 1870 by eight members from the Lockland, Ohio, Baptist Church. Rev. Peter F. Fossett was its first pastor and continued as same for thirty-two years up to the time of his death. The church owns property valued at ten thousand dollars. The church, though small, has played an important part in the affairs of the community and state.

MT. CARMEL BAPTIST CHURCH

Was started in 1894 on Corbin Street. The first pastor was Rev. Andrew Jackson. The church is now located at 3101 Eastern Avenue, and Rev. J. T. Moore is its present pastor.

ANTIOCH BAPTIST CHURCH

Originated in 1884, in Taylor Alley, by Rev. G. W. Wyatt. It is now located at 956 West Ninth Street, and Rev. W. H. Williams is its pastor.

CATHOLIC ACTIVITIES, 1925

In 1819 the first Catholic Church in Southern Ohio was erected at what is now Liberty and Vine Streets. When the Negro had become a freedman, no time was lost in endeavoring to establish a congregation in Cincinnati, and in 1865, Rev. Francis X. Weninger, S. J., a noted preacher of the Jesuit Society, raised $4,000 for that purpose. On May 10, 1866, a lot was purchased on the north side of Longworth Street, between Race and Elm Streets.

In 1873 the church was transferred to a site on New Street, and again, in 1908, to John Street, the present location.

In 1914, Rev. Edward T. Cleary, then pastor of St. Ann Church, and a friend of the author of this book, brought to Cincinnati five Sisters of the Blessed Sacrament, the congregation of religious women organized at Philadelphia twenty-one years previous by Miss Catherine Drexel, who devoted her own great fortune for work among Indian and Negro children.

The Sisters of the Blessed Sacrament have since been in charge of St. Ann school, which has an enrollment of 200 children. Rev. Henry J. Richter has been pastor of St. Ann Church since 1918. This church has two authenticated relics of St. Ann, mother of the Blessed Virgin, which are venerated during the annual Novena preceding her feast-day in July, when thousands of people of all classes visit the shrine.

A notable pronouncement with reference to the attitude of the Catholic Church towards the Negro was made on October 4, 1925, by Archbishop J. T. McNicholas, when the 91-year old Holy Trinity Church on West Fifth Street, near Smith, opened its doors to the colored race. The following extract from his letter is valuable as well as most interesting:

Archbishop's Letter

"To the Colored People of the Archdiocese of Cincinnati:

"I wish to assure the colored people of the Archdiocese of Cincinnati that the Catholic Church is their friend under all circumstances. To those who are good, she speaks words of encouragement and urges them to become better. Those of evil ways she entreats to repent and to seek the mercy of God.

* * * * *

"Not Proselytizing

"No informed judgment will accuse the Catholic Church of proselytizing practices. No one can be received into her fold unless convinced of her divine teaching, her divine constitution and her divine character. * * * It would be most gratifying if knowledge of and good will toward the Catholic Church should become general among the colored people, and thus wipe out all misunderstanding and prejudice.

* * * * *

"Against the race prejudice which has been the cause of so much injustice to the colored people in the United States, the Catholic Church protests. The only direct mission of the Church is the sanctification of souls, regardless of race, color, clime or time. The real and highest value of a soul is the value which God puts upon it, and this value is measured by the soul's love of God. Wealth, position, education, color, race, of themselves add nothing to the value of a soul.

"To the colored people in the vicinity of Holy Trinity Church we extend a cordial invitation to attend divine services there. Many not of our faith feel a certain hesitancy about entering a Catholic Church. There should be none. All should know that they are cordially welcome.

Faithfully yours in Christ,

JOHN T. MCNICHOLAS,
Archbishop of Cincinnati."

CLERGYMEN

Doc Rue	S. H. Brown	R. H. Hall
C. W. Wright	W. H. Williams	L. H. Ingraham
A. Davis	P. W. Eidson	R. W. Jackson
C. A. Jones	W. A. Page	W. J. Jackson
J. T. Jones	R. A. Moody	O. J. Jackson
S. O. Shinault	R. D. Murdock	R. T. James
James Bruce	F. P. Green	F. C. Johnson
J. S. Scott	L. W. Gray	Samuel Knox
O. J. Jackson	Wm. Taylor	C. T. McCall
M. L. Gibson	Charles Kelley	Harvey Miller
J. Hayes	J. A. G. Grant	James Montgomery
M. Ross	C. E. Ball	J. S. Mundy
G. R. Bryant	L. H. Hughes	J. Tolliver
Bishop Mary Mack	Fountain Floyd	D. Phelps
J. W. Abrams	F. C. Locust	M. S. Richardson
C. P. Frazier	S. E. Grannum	D. S. Ross
W. M. Jackson	P. S. Hill	J. I. Sanders
R. H. Davis	R. S. Adams	W. W. Smith
W. C. Thompson	C. S. Banks	S. Woodward
C. W. Williams	Mack Berry	W. H. Thomas
Madame S. Best	C. C. Cartwright	M. F. Frazier
J. F. Walker	W. P. Chapman	M. L. Bellinger
R. H. Bailey	C. C. Crum	Henry Meyers
E. H. Oxley	A. Davis	J. O. Haithcox
J. L. Black	J. L. Francis	

CHURCHES

Beulah Baptist
Churches of the Living God
King Solomon Baptist Church
Christian Mission
Shiloh Cumberland Presbyterian
First Liberty Baptist Church
Holiness Assembly Church
St. Mary Baptist
Macedonia Fire Baptist
Triumph
Revelation Baptist Church
Spiritualist
New Kenyon Ave. Christian
Mt. Tabor Baptist
Southern Baptist
Metropolitan
Brown Chapel A. M. E.
New Hope Baptist
Spiritualist Church of God
St. Andrew Episcopal
St. John A. M. E. Zion
Carmel Presbyterian
Antioch Baptist
Zion Baptist
Union Baptist
Calvary Baptist
Corinthian Baptist
Seventh Day Adventist
First Baptist
Bethel Baptist
Seventh Street Baptist
Ninth Street M. E.
Lane Chapel A. M. E.
Allen Temple
Dirr Street M. E.
Derrick Chapel
Cleaves Temple C. M. E.
Colored Lutheran
Wehrman Avenue Christian
Shiloh Baptist
Second Baptist
St. Luke Baptist

Provident Baptist
Pilgrim Rest Baptist
Pilgrim Baptist
Mt. Sinai Baptist
Mt. Olive Baptist
People's Miss. Baptist
Ebenezer Baptist
Mt. Lebanon Baptist

Jerusalem Baptist
First Masonic Baptist
First Liberty Baptist
Gaines Chapel M. E.
Gee Chapel
Zion A. M. E.
Ramah Baptist
Rock Spiritualists

NEGRO HEALTH AND RACE RELATIONS

From the *Cincinnati Sanitary Bulletin*, edited by Dr. W. H. Peters, Health Commissioner, October 14, 1925

The Negro health problem is one of the big pressing problems of the day. While the colored rate is declining, and this is a hopeful sign, the Negro contributes more than his quota to the annual death toll of Cincinnati from practically every important cause of death.

Cincinnati's white death rate was 14.3 per 1,000 inhabitants in 1924, while the colored rate was 26.0 or almost double. In 1923 the white rate was 15.1 and the colored rate 26.3. In 1922 the rates were 14.2 and 22.5 in favor of the white race.

Our colored people, who constitute about nine per cent of the population, contribute twenty-eight per cent of the deaths from tuberculosis in Cincinnati. Approximatly one-fifth of all Negro deaths are due to tuberculosis. As compared to the white race, over four times as many colored people die of tuberculosis per 1,000 of the population. "The condition is not purely local. The tuberculosis death rate in Ohio among Negroes for 1923 was 350 per 100,000 population as compared with a rate of 75.2 for whites. Tuberculosis is the leading cause of death among Negroes." Wonderful strides have been made in the Queen City in combating the great white plague, notably in the last five years. In 1910, one thousand and twenty-five people succumbed to tuberculosis. Last year the number was reduced to five hundred and twenty-four. The recession has been constant but the mortality rate among the Negroes is much too high.

Of the colored children born alive almost three times as many of them per 1,000 births recorded, perish during the first year of life.

The Negroes contributed over 70 per cent of the 218 smallpox cases reported last year in Cincinnati, and yet in the Harriet Beecher Stowe School, which is exclusively for colored children, located in the down-town center of the colored population, there were no cases of smallpox because all the children had been vaccinated. Smallpox would disappear to the vanishing point if this requirement prevailed in our industries.

Social diseases, the pneumonias and Bright's disease, claim a heavy toll among the colored people.

The excess in the colored deaths from preventable causes is responsible for more than one point in the crude death rate of the city.

Over one-half of Cincinnati's Negro population live in four down-town contiguous wards under conditions which make the Negro the victim of causes which lower resistance to disease. Among the most important may be mentioned bad housing, ignorance, race prejudice, lack of opportunity and dissipation. We list bad housing first because it is the chief predisposing factor, conspiring to keep up the army of susceptibles to disease at full strength.

Interest Manifested by the Health Authorities of Cincinnati in the Health of the Negro Population

On June 27, 1919, the Cincinnati Board of Health met in extraordinary session to consider the Negro health problem—a most significant meeting attended by many prominent citizens, leaders in civic development and social workers.

One of the remedies suggested by the health commissioner was a community health center housing bureaus for the prevention of tuberculosis and the control of venereal diseases, a dental department, general medical clinics for adults and children, a division of public health nursing and a social service department. The unanimous opinion was that the project should be carried out for the sake of the Negro and the city, but unfortunately the money never became available.

A modest beginning has been made, and we call attention now to the Michael W. Shoemaker Health Center, 667 West Fourth Street, conducted under the auspices of the Public Health Federation and the Negro Civic Welfare Association. General clinics will be established as the work gets under way in the remodeled homestead which was donated to the Community Chest. The direction of the health activities has been placed in the hands of a special committee which will co-operate closely with the College of Medicine and the Department of Health.

When the Sheppard-Towner grants became available for the protection of infancy and maternity in 1923, instead of spreading the service all over the city, we decided to intensify our work among the colored people. A full report will be found in this issue.

Thursday, April 9, 1925, marked the close of a very successful Tuberculosis Institute which was planned by the Health Department in co-operation with the Negro Civic Welfare Association, The Public Health Federation, the Anti-Tuberculosis League and District No. 8 Graduate Nurses' Association. Never before have our colored physicians had such a splendid opportunity for post-graduate study under men who are eminently qualified. Most of the lectures were illustrated by slides or by what the X-ray plate revealed. The film, "Diagnosis of Pulmonary Tuberculosis," prepared for the Army Medical School and shown through the courtesy of the Anti-Tuberculosis League was a recapitulation of the entire subject.

All of the resources in the different bureaus of the Health Department are at the disposal of the colored population. They are always welcome at our Health Center.

What Share Do Negro Citizens Have in the Public Health Nursing Service?

The public health nursing service in Cincinnati is not centralized. In addition to the Bureau of Public Health Nursing in the Health Department many public health nurses are employed by organizations affiliated with the Council of Social Agencies.

We have a complement of twenty-seven women who are working under the plan of general nursing. Instead of having highly specialized nurses for the prevention of tuberculosis, control of venereal diseases, prenatal care, infant welfare, school hygiene, etc., one nurse combines all of these functions in a circumscribed area. We make the family instead of the individual, the unit of nursing service.

Of the twenty-seven public health nurses in our bureau, four are colored. Putting it another way we have one colored nurse for every 10,000 of the colored population. Our average for the white race is one for every 17,000 of the population.

In the two schools for colored children we have special nursing service.

All children are weighed and measured three times a year, and those who are found to be 10 per cent under weight for their height at a given age are examined carefully. In addition to these we examine all other children in the first, second and third grades, and children who are referred to the doctor by the teacher or nurse.

In both schools, as was pointed out before, we have clinics once each week for children of pre-school age.

The open air children receive a warm cleansing bath each morning, and before they go to their classroom, milk and crackers are served. The children are weighed regularly, their temperatures are recorded, they are examined frquently, and a special effort is made to correct physical defects that may be found.

By making the family the unit for nursing service, many hitherto unrecognized cases among the colored people are brought to light, as a result of which many colored individuals are under observation at our Health Center, located at 209 West Twelfth Street.

In the summer time child welfare stations are established, and it has always been our custom to provide such service in the centers of colored population with the understanding, of course, that the colored people are free to go wherever they please.

What Are the Facilities for the Handling of Health Conditions of Colored People in Our Community?

We have in our community seventeen colored physicians and a halfdozen dentists. The number is a little bit below the average per thousand of the population, and it has been estimated that approximately fifty per cent of the colored people call upon the colored physicians. Among the indigent, many of the colored people call upon the district physicians of the Health Department.

Obstetric cases are accepted by the Maternity Society and the Cincinnati General Hospital. Over fifty per cent of the colored maternity cases last year were delivered in hospitals. Our colored people have access to all of the wards of the Cincinnati General Hospital and to the Out-Patient Department. Not many beds, however, are available in the private hospitals, and the Mercy Hospital, which was established a few years ago exclusively for colored people, and which is staffed by colored physicians and nurses, is struggling along under conditions that are not at all encouraging.

It is rather unfortunate for the physician, patient and community that the colored physician does not have the opportunity here in Cincinnati to acquire more knowledge and skill to deal with the medical problems in the solution of which he is the chief factor.

We have no training school for colored nurses and the colored physicians have no opportunity for post-graduate medical work or bedside instruction in the wards of any hospitals.

We have stated our problem and its causes impartially and as Mr. Jas. H. Robinson, executive secretary of the Negro Civic Welfare Association, pointed out, this analysis places the responsibility where it properly belongs, on both races.

Let us not forget that the Negro is an American citizen, and the demands for citizenship today are the same for all. The Negro can not measure up to expectancy in a bad environment, and if his health is not good.

MORTALITY FROM ALL CAUSES

Colored and White Population Compared

Rate Per 1,000 Population

Deaths:
1924.........6,218   15.2
1923.........6,528   16.0
1922.........6,041   14.9

Colored Deaths:
1924......... 911   26.0
1923......... 921   26.3
1922......... 764   22.5

White Deaths:
1924.........5,307   14.3
1923.........5,601   15.1
1922.........5,277   14.2

Colored People, 1924 (9% population), contribute 14.6 total deaths.

Colored People, 1923 (9% population), contribute 14.2 total deaths.

Colored People, 1922 (9% population), contribute 12.6 total deaths.

Population

	1924	1923	1922
White	372,835	371,312	370,862
Black	35,000	35,000	*34,000
Census Bureau	407,835	406,312	404,862

*Estimated.

Conservative judges claim that the exodus from the South has added probably 5,000 to the colored population.

Deaths—Tuberculosis—All Forms

	1924	1923	1922
White	363	388	439
Black	161	153	165
Total	524	541	604

Colored Population, 1924 (9% of the total), contribute 30.7% TBC deaths.

Colored Population, 1923 (9% of the total), contribute 28% TBC deaths.

Colored Population, 1922 (9% of the total), contribute 27.3% TBC deaths.

Over 60% of deaths from tuberculosis in three contiguous downtown wards—16, 17, 18.

Infant mortality, three times white.

Syphil's, 1924

White	63	68.0%
Black	30	32.0%
Total	93	

All Forms Pneumonia, 1924

White	373	74.6%
Black	127	25.4%
Total	500	

FROM STATISTICS OF CINCINNATI HEALTH DEPARTMENT

	Deaths				Births		
Year	White	Colored	Total	Year	White	Colored	Total
1920	5392	674	6076	1920	7213	623	7836
1921	4952	748	5700	1921	7429	721	8150
1922	5276	764	6040	1922	7202	672	7874
1923	5601	921	6522	1923	7507	846	8353
1924	5307	911	6218	1924	7747	1067	8814

THE NEGRO HOUSING PROBLEM

(From information furnished by Bleecker Marquette, Executive Secretary, Cincinnati Better Housing League.)

A large part of the Negro housing problem in Cincinnati is identical with the industrial housing problem. Builders have not found it as profitable to build the low cost house, either for rent or for sale, as the higher priced house. Building costs seem to make it almost prohibitive to build a satisfactory type of single family house for less than $6,000. There have been an exceedingly small number of new tenement houses built during the last ten years. So as far as new housing goes nothing has been done for the colored population except the houses built by the Model Homes Company.

Negroes live either in the basin of the city near the river or in small communities in the suburbs. It is estimated that 30,000 out of 38,000 population live in the West End in a highly congested area built up with tenement and business houses, factories and railroads. The houses in the suburbs are not so congested and are of a better type, including many more single family houses with yards and fairly good conveniences.

The Better Housing League does not have accurate information as to the number of houses in the West End occupied by colored families. Our facts with regard to that district have not been kept separate from data on white families. A complete survey of all houses in the sixteenth, seventeenth and eighteenth wards occupied by Negro tenants is now under way, which will give all the facts including home ownership, the number of colored people managing properties for owners, etc.

We have the following facts gathered in 1921 as to the other parts of the city where colored families live, except for Walnut Hills, which is perhaps the best colored home district in the city.

Mt. Auburn—Streets: North Main, Cottage Terrace, Mulberry, Hughes, Milton. Buildings, brick and frame. Number stories, 1 and 2. Number homes, 30-40.

College Hill—Streets: Steele Subdivision, North Bend Road, Betts, Second, Third, Fourth Avenues, Weatherby Street, Cedar Avenue, Argus Avenue. Buildings, frame (dilapidated). Number homes, 300-400.

Cumminsville—Streets: Dreman, Spaeth, Dirr, Follet, Elmo, Streng, O'Bannon, Kelley, Spring Grove Avenue. Buildings, frame, few bricks. Number homes, 300.

Northside—Streets: Chase Avenue, Mad Anthony, Fergus, Beechhill Avenue. Buildings, brick and frame, good. Number homes, 8-10.

Price Hill—Streets: Chateau and Grand. Buildings, frame. Number homes, 6-8.

Lockland—Streets: Steward Avenue, Mulberry, Maple, Walnut, Wayne, Elm and Locust. Buildings, frame (dilapidated). Number homes, 400.

Wyoming—Streets: Oak and Vine Streets. Buildings, frame (dilapidated). Number homes, 100.

Madisonville—Streets: Dunbar Place, Corsica Place, Eastford Road, Amy Street, Douglas Park Subdivision (houses not in good condition), Whetzel Avenue, Ravenna, Chandler, Ward, Walton and Desmond Streets (houses in good condition). Buildings, frame. Number homes, 300-400.

O'Bryonville—Streets: O'Brien, Lavinia, Pogue Avenue, Cinnamon, Fredonia. Number homes, 100.

Norwood—Streets: Hopkins, Webster. Buildings, frame. Number homes, 7-8.

Avondale—Streets: Wehrman, Whittier, Fredonia, Omaha, VanBuren, May Street, Rockdale Avenue, Greenwood Avenue (good houses); District back of Zoo: Forest Avenue, Irvin Street, Perdue, Dix, Tallant and Dury. Buildings, frame (dilapidated). Number homes, 400.

The lack of new building for Negroes, combined with the migration from the South and the fact that some of the old tenements have been condemned and torn down by the demands of business houses for more space, has created the shortage of homes. The shortage has resulted in greater congestion and increased rents. Our figures indicate that whereas in 1918 the average rental for tenement flats occupied by colored families was about $4.00 per room per month, in 1925 the average is something over $7.00 per room per month. The excess of demand over supply is probably the chief cause of the higher rent. The increase in rents for white tenants has been about the same although Negro tenants pay higher rent for similar accommodations.

The following efforts are being made to improve the housing conditions for Negroes:

1—The Better Housing League employs four colored visiting housekeepers who visit the homes and use persuasive methods in urging landlords to repair and remodel their property as well as instructing and advising tenants in housekeeping. The following report for 1924 shows what has been accomplished in one year by the method used.

    I—Families—Family visits, 7,800.
    II—Houses—Visits of inspection, 1,039; visits of supervision, 1,539; interviews with owners, 935.

2—The Housing Bureau of the Building Department requires owners to make necessary repairs and alterations in existing tenements. This department has done excellent work in bringing about needed improvements.

3—The Model Homes Company, formed for the purpose of providing good standard homes at reasonable rents for workers, has built homes that provide for 600 persons. The annual report, 1924, states that the death rate among the colored tenants occupying Model Homes Company houses averages for nine years 12.22 per 1,000 population, which is less than one-half the Negro death rate in Cincinnati as a whole.

Washington Terrace
Built and owned by Model Homes Co., a white corporation

LOW PRICED HOUSING FOR WAGE EARNERS
By Jacob G. Schmidlapp

Some years ago I was invited to act as a trustee of the Industrial School for Negroes. My attention was called to the appalling condition in which this part of our population was housed in our city—you will find conditions in your city little better—and learned that we could in no way help the Negroes as quickly as by offering them better housing facilities. Even without any experience, I felt it my duty to do what I could to improve this condition.

General Sternberg's Example

Upon making inquiry I was advised to examine into the sanitary housing of the Negroes in Washington started by the late General Sternberg. He called his plan "Philanthropy and Five Per Cent." He succeeded in getting together a fund of $25,000. After that he was able to get additional capital, and had up to the time of his death succeeded in building houses to accommodate over six hundred families, white and black. His work has now been in successful operation for twenty years. It is his plan of financing that we have adopted in Cincinnati. Upon this plan we charge 10% upon the total cost of the building, allowing 3% for taxes and repairs, and 2% for depreciation, leaving 5% for the capital. We find now with the advance in taxes and cost of repairs it requires 11% gross in order to net 5%.

Our second operation (the Chapel Street houses) was in the three and four room houses with bath—for we decided not to build an apartment without a bath—containing four families each. Here we succeeded in keeping the cost down to $250 per room and were able to accommodate the tenant at a rental of 50 cents per room per week. In fact, we rent apartments of four rooms—that is, three rooms and a bath—as low as $1.75 per week, we paying the water rent, which is more expensive in the houses we rent to colored than those we rent to white.

Houses For Colored People

This was our first effort for the colored people, and so far as tenancy is concerned the most successful; for, with houses accommodating twelve families we have lost only six days' rent in three years. Here we learned that the colored people appreciated better housing and improved rapidly under such conditions.

The Extent of the Work

Up to the present time we have built 102 houses accommodating 402 families or approximately 1,400 persons. The first houses were started in 1911.

Of this total, 34 are single family houses built in rows or terraces on the style of the "Philadelphia house." The others are 42 houses of the semi-detached type with four families in each; 8 semi-detached houses with two families in each, and 18 multiple dwellings accommodating 191 families. The multiple dwellings are all low and small in area. None of our buildings is over two stories high. Each apartment has a separate entrance.

The buildings are all of brick with inside plastering and concrete foundations. Every family has both hot and cold water inside their apartment, *with a private bath and toilet*, set wash tubs in the cellars or in the kitchen, and gas.

Financing and Returns

The company has a "capital and surplus" of $500,000, most of which has been expended. Our land has cost us $35,000 and our construction work in round figures $530,000. Dividends are limited to 5%.

The average weekly rental ranges from 50 cents per week per room to 74 cents per room, counting the bath-room as a room. If the bath-room is not counted, the average weekly rentals range from 57½ cents per week per room to 92 cents. The average in the first case is 62½ cents per week per room, in the latter case 80½ cents per week.

Class of People Housed

The people housed are distinctly workingmen, the colored earning on an average $16 a week. The white wage-earners earn 10 to 20 per cent more than the colored. They pay on an average one-fifth of their weekly earnings in rent. Of the heads of our families 203 are unskilled laborers, 165 mechanics, 17 clerks, 3 superintendents or foremen and 5 professionals. Forty-three per cent are white, 57 per cent colored.

No rent collectors are employed. The tenants instead bring their rent to local branch banks and offices. Only in case of delinquency do we have to go after it.

Social Features

Small play-grounds for children were provided wherever it was possible.

In the community plan which we have developed, we are making an effort beyond anything that has heretofore been tried for Negroes by the landlord in this country, in giving to our tenants social and civic opportunity and a stronger economic position.

We have a co-operative store, wherein we hope to centralize their interest. We have an assembly room large enough to accommodate 250 people, the only respectable room for such purposes, outside of church, offered to colored people in our city. We have a billiard room operated by the Community Club where dues are ten cents a week, and no other charges. We have play-grounds for children, covered sand pits, also a shelter house, and every possible precaution has been taken as to sanitary conditions. This extends down to the children's drinking fountain. I make weekly visits to this community, which are a great encouragement to the tenants as well as to myself.

Recently I told my Negro tenants that in 1916 one out of sixteen of their race in our city was in the workhouse, and that in proportion to the whites they had over four to one in the hospital, and out of a probable population of 30,000, 6,257, or 26.4% of the total number of arrests were made in 1918. In our community, comprising 188 families and operating on an average for 3 years, we have had but 11 arrests, in 1918 we had but 1 arrest. For the same period we had in the same community nineteen deaths out of an approximate population of six hundred, or 10.6 per thousand, while the death rate of the Negro in Cincinnati was 29 per thousand. I call particular attention to this as it shows what can be done.

The co-operative store is the only experiment of its kind that I know of that is being made for colored people in this country.

I am hoping to save them about 10% on their purchases. That is, we expect to make a profit of 20%, and to do business for one-half of this amount. We are gradually adding to the supplies, and the business is now on a paying basis. Last January we paid to our tenants the fifth dividend of 3% on their purchases.

The Enterprise Organized

I began this work by myself. In order to have it continued, about four years ago I invited some friends to join me, and we have incorporated under the name of the Cincinnati Model Homes Company, with a capital and surplus of $500,000, although it has not all been subscribed. I have not allowed the work to delay, and our balance sheet shows that we have exceeded that amount.

The Wage-Earner's Budget

The average wage of our colored tenants is about $3 per day. My budget for the wage-earner's family is:

One day's wage for one week's rent.
Two days' wage for one week's food.
One day's wage for one week's clothing.
One day's wage for all extras, including fuel, and
One day's wage for profit and pleasure.

It depends on the use of the latter whether or not he is to make a success in life. With frugality he can not remain poor. He has really less control over his rent than over any other of his expenses, and herein we can help him, as it is difficult for some of our Negro tenants to command a daily wage to meet the weekly rent. We hope to make up the difference in his dividend from the co-operative store.

The Gordon Hotel

As early as 1914 some of the local colored leaders impressed upon me the necessity of hotel accommodations for colored. The position of the self-respecting Negro stranger, who has no friends to recommend him to a private family, is pitiable indeed. In 1916 we commenced construction of the Gordon Hotel for colored, with baths, steam heat and electric lights. Because of the uncertainty of the undertaking we were cautious to construct the rooms so that they can easily be converted into four-room apartments. The basement of the hotel and the adjacent apartments is arranged in a spacious lobby, dining room, dressing room and two halls for meeting and amusement purposes. The Gordon has been in operation since 1917 and has proven a moral and financial success. It has become a useful institution in our community.

Good housing for the wage-earner will always be a problem. You can help to solve it if you will but make an effort.

Model Homes Company Report
February 3, 1925

These figures, supported by the number of applicants that come to our office, induce us to believe that the housing situation for the white workingman must have been somewhat relieved, while with the Negro the situation is getting more acute. There is hardly an application coming from a Negro without a letter, telephone or personal call from an employer, minister or some influential white friend.

The health and conduct records of the colored group remain the outstanding achievement of our housing experiment. During the last year only seven deaths occurred in that group, bringing up the total to 66 cases for nine years, averaging 12.22 per thousand population, less than one-half of the Negro death rate of this city as a whole.

The conduct record is yet more encouraging—one arrest on record for 1924, making a total of 36 arrests for the same period, or four arrests a year for a population of 600 souls. Indeed an enviable record for any community of the same social strata.

The Washington Terrace Grocery was incorporated during the past year under the name of The Model Homes Sales Co. The parent company owning all the stock. Your president reported the net value of the grocery, the total sales for the past year amounted close to $29,000, the largest since the establishment of the grocery. $1,385.44 were rebated to tenant-customers, or 8% on their purchases, bringing up the total of all rebates to $4,462.

At the present time, November, 1925, while Negroes are paying from eight to ten dollars per month for single rooms, unfurnished, in houses that often have little in the way of conveniences, the colored tenants of the Model Homes Company (a white corporation), are paying for modern apartments, gas, electricity and private bath included, only $15 a month for three-room flats, $18.50 a month for four-room flats. Their waiting list is so large that they could fill 1,000 rooms.

THE HOSPITALIZATION OF THE NEGRO
From Hospital Survey by Mary L. Hicks

In 1920, according to the United States Census, the Negro population of Hamilton County was 33,747, and of this number 30,079 were residents of Cincinnati. Since that time there has been considerable migration from the South, and the total number in the county has increased to approximately 40,000 according to the estimates of Mr. James H. Robinson, Executive Secretary of the Negro Civic Welfare Association. The estimate of the Negro population of Cincinnati, made by the Bureau of Census, July 1, 1924, places the number at 33,242 or 8.39 per cent of the total population of the city.

While the Negroes form less than 10 per cent of the population of our city, they constitute a grave health problem. The wretched housing conditions which they are forced to accept, the bad influences that abound in their environment, their unfamiliarity with the services offered at the clinics and dispensaries, all tend to keep their health at a low level. The death rate among Negroes in Cincinnati is much higher than that among the white population.

Approximately 10 per cent of the total patients cared for in the hospitals annually are Negroes. It is estimated that about 85 per cent of the Negro patients are cared for in the Cincinnati General Hospital. The actual number cared for in the other hospitals is not available, but it probably does not exceed 400 or 500. Negro patients in the Cincinnati General Hospital number approximately 2,500 annually or 25 per cent of the total patients.

On Census day there were 2,391 patients in the thirty hospitals from which census information was available. Of this number, 302 were Negroes or 12.6 per cent of the total. Negroes constituted 14.6 per cent of the total population of the general hospitals and 10 per cent of the population of the special hospitals. A large percentage of the Negro patients were in the General Hospital, there being 176 listed or 34.5 per cent of the total population. There were 4 in one of the Cincinnati private hospitals and 7 in another, while in the two general hospitals in Kentucky there were 4 Negroes on Census day. In the Children's Hospital there were 3, or 6.1 per cent of the population. There were 46 Negro patients at the Cincinnati Tuberculosis Sanatorium, or 22.5 per cent of the total number of patients. Of the 173 old people confined in the Hospital Department of the Hamilton County Home 47 were Negroes.

There are two institutions in the city caring exclusively for Negro patients, Mercy Hospital and the Evangeline Home. According to the accepted usage of the term hospital, neither of the above institutions qualify as hospitals.*

Evangeline Booth Home, under the auspices of the Salvation Army has, as its major work, the care of the unmarried mother. Some years ago it opened a ward of four beds for private surgical patients of the Negro physicians who did not have access to the other hospitals.

Mercy Hospital was opened to serve the pay group in the Negro population, and at the same time give the Negro physicians the opportunity for hospital experience and provide an opportunity for training Negro nurses. A group of Negro physicians actively supported the movement to open the hospital and pledged themselves to aid it by contributions towards its upkeep. The physicians have no staff organization as it exists in other hospitals; they are, instead, directors of the policy of the institution. There are no free wards, hence the physicians are not called on to give free service to patients.

The limited bed capacity (33 beds) is not used to the extent to which it should be to operate efficiently. The lack of income

---

* "A modern hospital may be defined as an institution in which there is joint use of medical equipment and co-operative organization of medical skill for diagnosis, treatment and prevention of disease."

has seriously crippled the institution from the very beginning of its work. With the present bed capacity, the hospital can not qualify as an accredited nursing training school under the regulations of the State of Ohio and this limits the number of nurses applying for admission.

With seventeen Negro physicians in the city, caring for approximately 50 per cent of the Negro population in sickness, it is evident that hospital accommodations for the private patients of the Negro physicians are essential.* There has been a gradual increase in the number of Negro patients admitted to the General Hospital and there is a definite feeling on the part of the administration of the institution that if the number continues to increase, increased accommodations for that group must be provided by assigning additional wards. Ample accommodations have been available in this hospital up to the present time for the care and treatment of the indigent Negro in need of hospital care.

It is very evident that proper accommodations for the care of the Negro who is able to pay for a part or all of his care are not available in this city. The lack of such accommodations works a hardship not only on the patients, but on the development of medical experience and advancement in medical science among Negro physicians and nurses. In numerous instances, Negro physicians failing to obtain accommodations for their patients in the hospitals, have kept those patients in their homes to the definite disadvantage of the patients. The present day practice of medicine demands in many instances that patients be hospitalized in order that modern methods of diagnosis and treatment be instituted, for it is only in the hospital that all the scientific aids can be brought into service for the patients' benefit. It is through the use of modern diagnostic methods that physicians are enabled to keep abreast of the times and increase their knowledge in medical science.

The foregoing facts, together with statements that have been made relative to Negro problems, indicate a definite need for a comprehensive health program. Such a program must include not only facilities for the hospitalization of the sick, but facilities for dispensary treatment and for the introduction of health measures.

Chronics

One hundred and seventy, or 12 per cent of the 1,417 chronics, incurables and convalescents were Negroes, and were divided as follows: 84 chronics, 81 incurables, and 5 convalescents.

Despite the lack of facilities that would warrant the name of "hospital," there is a so-called hospital building at the Infirmary devoted to the care of the acutely ill, and the incurable cases that can not be cared for in the institution proper. In addition to this building, there is one in which Negro men are housed, the physician of the institution stating that the inmates are of the same type as those in the hospital building. The hospital building has 125 beds and the one set aside for Negro men has approximately 50 beds.

EXTRACT FROM SURVEY MADE FEBRUARY, 1925, OF
ORPHAN ASYLUM, SHELTER HOME AND COLORED GIRLS' HOME
By Request of the Negro Civic Welfare League

For facilitation of consideration as to advisability of consolidation of boys and girls in separate institutions.

RESOURCES

	New Orphan Asylum for Colored Youth	Shelter Home for Colored Children	Home for Colored Girls
Value on tax duplicates:			
Land	$ 7,690	$2,450.00	$ 4,070.00
Buildings	55,000	3,400.00	6,250.00
Other property acquired 1922:			
Land	2,860	....	....
Buildings	3,500	....	....
Total	$69,050	$5,850.00	$10,320.00
Mortgages:			
First		$3,500.00	@ 6% $4,000.00
Second		@ 7% 800.00	
1924—			
Received from Community Chest	$ 6,926	6,764.00	8,600.00
Received for board of children	696	1,396.00	1,948.63
Received from other sources	7,275	1,559.16	
Total income, 1924	$14,897	$9,716.16	$10,548.63

EXPENSES

Salaries and Wages, 1924	$ 4,967	$2,467.00	$ 4,419.12
Food, 1924	4,330	3,071.39	2,940.72
Medical, 1924	75	4.00	37.73
All other expenses	4,725	3,734.81	3,506.18
Total expenses	$14,097	$9,277.20	$10,803.75

PHYSICAL CONDITIONS

	New Orphan Asylum for Colored Youth	Shelter Home for Colored Children	Home for Colored Girls
Capacity	58	23	25
Number children, Feb., 1925	55	25	25
Sex admitted	Boys & Girls	Boys only	Girls only
Ages of present inmates	5—17	5—15	5—22
Admission age	3—14	4—12	8—16

A BRIEF HISTORY AND DESCRIPTION OF THE THREE INSTITUTIONS.

NEW ORPHAN ASYLUM FOR COLORED YOUTH

This institution was incorporated in 1845. It is managed by a board of trustees of nine members, all colored, with the assistance of a board of lady managers of fourteen members. Its primary purpose is to give free care to colored dependent children from three to eighteen years of age. It receives approximately forty per cent of its expenses from the Community Chest.

THE SHELTER HOME FOR COLORED CHILDREN

This institution began as a day nursery in 1918. It moved to its present quarters and confined its new admissions to boys from "broken homes," although until 1924 it had two little girls who had been in the institution nearly all of their lives. It has a board of fourteen members, both colored and white, and depends upon the Community Chest to supplement the income it derives from the care of children placed by parents or the Juvenile Court.

THE HOME FOR COLORED GIRLS

This institution began its work as the Cincinnati Protective and Industrial Association for Colored Children and Women, caring for women and babies as well as children and operating a day nursery in connection. These activities were abandoned as they were found to hamper all of the work and the new admissions were confined to girls from "broken homes." The Home moved to its present quarters in 1915. Its board is composed of both white and colored members.

EDUCATION

Children from all three Homes attend public school, those from the New Orphan Asylum and Shelter Home at Douglass, and from the Home for Colored Girls at Sherman and Dyer Schools.

CHARITIES AND SOCIAL CENTERS

Negro Community Activities. The Negroes' schools of the city serve more completely than other schools as social centers for their respective neighborhoods. In addition to the community center activities and classes which are listed for each school, St. Ann Schools, a colored parochial school, has a number of community center activities. The tenants of Washington Terrace conduct unique community activities. St. Andrews was a pioneer in church community service, but now many of our churches have departments for this phase of social betterment. Playgrounds, bathing and gymnasiums are well established features.

Washington Terrace Community Center. Consists of a number of clubs and kindred activities for colored men and women. Most of the persons are tenants of the Cincinnati Model Homes Company's apartments in Washington Terrace. There are five women's clubs of civic, social, and literary nature (Ladies' Improvement Club, Treble Clef Club, Phyllis Wheatley Club, Carnation Embroidery Club, and Kindergarten Mother's Club). There is also the Washington Terrace Welfare Association, and a boys' band. The clubs meet in quarters provided by the Model Homes Company in the Terrace. These rooms are well equipped for social and recreational gatherings. The Washington Terrace Center also has, during the school year, a branch of the night school and community center activities of the Douglass School. A pre-school age kindergarten is conducted during the school term by the Cincinnati Kindergarten Association.

St. Ann's School and Social Center for Colored. (Estab. 1865), 937 John Street, Cincinnati. A free elementary school for colored children, in charge of the Sisters of the Blessed Sacrament, which serves also as a social center for Catholic colored persons. Open to colored children of good character, irrespective of creed. Embraces the eight primary grades, also domestic science and art classes for girls, and domestic science for boys.

Y. M. C. A., Lockland Branch (Colored). Lockland, Ohio. A small two-story brick building and a new hut type of building are used for conducting this work. The new building provides reading and social room, billiards, cue roque tables and other tables for small games such as checkers and chess. Gymnasium, shower baths, dressing room, general office. Brick building contains rooms for class and club purposes.

Ninth Street Branch (Colored). 686 West Ninth Street. A very excellent, modern building, contains general offices, gymnasium with running track, men's lobby, billiards and bowling alleys, educational class rooms, swimming pool, boys' game and club rooms, dormitory with capacity of 80 beds, and a cafeteria. Standard program of gymnasium classes, indoor baseball, basket ball, volley ball, group games. Also conducts outdoor baseball league, Bible study classes and religious meetings, personal interviews, noon-day religious meetings in the factories.

Home for Incurables. (Estab. 1890, incorp. 1892.) East Walnut Hills. A home for residents of Hamilton County afflicted with any disease pronounced incurable by the medical staff of the home, with the exception of mental and contagious cases. No limitation as to age, sex, color, religion. Admission fee, $500. Five endowed rooms.

Court of Domestic Relations. (Estab. 1915.) Hamilton County Court House, Juvenile Detention Home. A division of the Court of Common

Pleas of Hamilton County, Ohio. This court has exclusive jurisdiction over all divorce and alimony matters, and all matters arising under the Juvenile Code, which includes cases of delinquency, dependency, mothers' pensions, neglected children, crippled children, failure to provide and desertion, contributing to delinquency, contributing to dependency. Maintains a colored worker who handles colored delinquency cases and cooperates with all departments of the court in their handling of colored cases.

Home for Aged Colored Women. (Estab. 1891, incorp. 1897.) 1334½ Lincoln Avenue, Walnut Hills, Cincinnati. Conducted by the Progressive Benefit Society as a non-sectarian home for colored women. Open to residents of Hamilton County and vicinity over 60 years of age. Admission fee, $250. Capacity, 20. Support: Community Chest and C. of S. A.

Home for Colored Girls. (Estab. 1911.) 811 West Ninth Street. Provides temporary or prolonged care for colored girls from 8 to 16 years of age from broken homes. Gives household training, and either returns the girls to their families or places them in employment (usually domestic service). Girls attend public schools and various denominational churches.

Crawford Old Men's Home. (Estab. 1888; not incorporated). Under management of executors and trustees of John T. Crawford, deceased. Lantana and North Bend Road, College Hill, Cincinnati. A home for colored old men, with preference to ex-slaves. Has 18 acres of ground, a part of which is cultivated by the inmates. Open to dependent, but respectable men who have reached the age of 60 years. Capacity 12. Admission fee, $150. Support: Community Chest and C. of S. A., and rents.

Visiting Nurse Association of Cincinnati. (Estab. 1909, incorp. 1917.) 220 West Seventh Street, Cincinnati. Renders bed-side and nursing care in homes of moderate means and of the poor, both white and colored. Teaches the proper care of the sick and gives prenatal and postnatal instruction and nursing care to mothers in the homes visited. Homes where there are contagious diseases are visited and the families instructed, but no direct care is given the patient by the nurses. Territory limited to those sections of the city accessible by street cars. Care given patient regardless of age, sex, color or religion. Only graduate nurses of recognized hospitals and schools of nursing are employed.

Provincial Convent of the Good Shepherd. (Estab. 1871.) Carthage, Ohio. A home for girls, conducted by the Sisters of the Good Shepherd. Has four separate departments: white dependent, Negro dependent, white delinquent, and Negro delinquent. Admits girls from 4 to 18 years of age from any territory, without regard to creed. Visiting hours: white dependents, second Sunday and Thursday; Negro dependents, fourth Sunday and Thursday; white delinquents, first Sunday and Thursday; Negro delinquents, third Sunday and Thursday. Parents or guardians pay according to their ability. Total capacity, 450.

Needlework Guild of America, Cincinnati Branch of. (Branch of national organization.) (Estab. 1891.) The object of the Guild is to collect and distribute new, plain garments to hospitals, homes, and other charities of Cincinnati. The Guild is non-sectarian and gives to Protestant, Catholic, Jewish, and colored charities.

Evangeline Home. (Estab. 1912.) 712 West Sixth Street. Office hours, 8:00 A. M. to 9:00 P. M. A home for unmarried colored mothers, and also a boarding home for children born in the institution up to the age of six years. Babies placed for adoption through the New Orphan Asylum for Colored Youth. Girls are trained in house work and sewing. Free or according to ability to pay. Capacity, 30 adults and 10 children.

Shelter Home for Colored Children (formerly Walnut Hills Day Nursery for Colored Children). (Estab. and incorp. 1910.) 1234 Chapel Street, Cincinnati. A boarding home for colored boys from 4 to 12 years of age, who require temporary or prolonged care. Free care, or board in accordance with means. Children attend Douglass Public School and the Baptist Church. Capacity, 30. Visiting hours, Thursday and Sunday from 2 to 4 P. M. Support: Community Chest and C. of S. A., and board of children.

The activities of the Blue Triangle Branch, Y. W. C. A., West Eighth Street, are explained in connection with the brief history of that institution.

Friendship Home for Colored Girls. (Estab. 1918.) 641 West Fourth Street. A home for colored working girls over 16 years of age. Without maximum age limit so long as girl is employed. Reference required. Rate, $1.50 a week per bed. Takes care of transients sent by Travelers' Aid, Associated Charities, or Police, the expense for which is borne by the Associated Charities. Conducts a kindergarten department for the pre-kindergarten children of the neighborhood, and a Daily Vacation Bible School. Support: Women's Home Missionary Society and earnings.

St. Mary's Hospital (Betts Street Hospital). (Estab. 1858, incorp. 1859.) Betts and Linn Streets. Conducted by the Sisters of the Poor of St. Francis. Admit no social diseases, nor tubercular, contagious, maternity, or chronic cases. Patients admitted without regard to color, creed, or nationality. Free or according to ability to pay; $10.50 to $15 per week for wards; $20 to $35 per week for private rooms. Capacity, 250 beds (175 free, 28 part pay). Support: Fees and donations.

St. Francis Hospital for Incurables. (Estab. and incorp. 1888.) Queen City and Westwood Avenues, Cincinnati. Conducted by Sisters of the Poor of St. Francis for the care of incurables without distinctions of color, race, or creed. No contagious or venereal cases taken. Takes persons having any of the following diseases: tuberculosis, dropsy, rheumatism, cancer. Patients admitted at any time. Emergency cases at any hour. Free or according to ability to pay. Capacity, 357. Support: Earnings and donations from membership of St. Anthony Aid Society.

St. Joseph's Home for the Aged Poor. (Estab. 1868, incorp. 1869.) Florence Avenue, Cincinnati. A home for aged poor men and women, conducted by the Little Sisters of the Poor. Applicants must be over 60 years of age, destitute, and of good moral character. No distinction made as to creed or nationality. Capacity, 200. Support: Donations that are solicited.

CRIMINAL STATISTICS

June, 1924, to June, 1925, sentenced to jail, total 3,300, of which 1,564 were colored; includes city, county and Federal jails.

Criminally Insane—
   Total 8—6 white and 2 colored.

State Reformatory—
   Total 97—55 colored and 42 white.

State Penitentiary—
   Total 116—41 white and 75 colored.

Female Reformatory (Marysville)—
   Total 7—5 white and 2 colored.

Juvenile Delinquents—
   1923—Total boys, 1,480—1,162 white and 318 colored.
   1924—Total boys, 1,407—1,062 white and 345 colored.
   1923—Total girls,   456— 284 white and 172 colored.
   1924—Total girls,   488— 309 white and 179 colored.

Dependent Children—
   1923—Total 727—658 white and 69 colored.
   1924—Total 598—529 white and 69 colored.

Active Mothers' Pension Cases—
   1923—Total 473—447 white and 26 colored.
   1924—Total 429—408 white and 21 colored.

Complaints in Domestic Relations—
   1924—Total 340—318 white and 22 colored.

Detention Home—
   1923—Total 1,356—1,012 white and 344 colored.
   1924—Total 1,357—1,037 white and 320 colored.
   Only two or three colored sent to correctional institution per year.

NUMBER OF ARRESTS
1920 to October 1, 1925
(Statistics furnished by Police Department)

Year	Total Arrests	By Sex and Color		
1920	15,944	White, Male	10,871	
		White, Female	1,355	12,226
		Colored, Male	2,798	
		Colored, Female	920	3,718
		Total		15,944
1921	24,181	White, Male	17,808	
		White, Female	3,296	21,104
		Colored, Male	2,296	
		Colored, Female	781	3,077
		Total		24,181
1922	30,935	White, Male	23,451	
		White, Female	2,705	26,156
		Colored, Male	3,622	
		Colored, Female	1,157	4,779
		Total		30,935
1923	39,152	White, Male	29,802	
		White, Female	2,817	32,619
		Colored, Male	5,216	
		Colored, Female	1,317	6,533
		Total		39,152
1924	46,686	White, Male	35,732	
		White, Female	3,494	39,226
		Colored, Male	6,078	
		Colored, Female	1,382	7,460
		Total		46,686
(To October 1)				
1925	41,851	White, Male	32,142	
		White, Female	3,093	35,235
		Colored, Male	5,360	
		Colored, Female	1,256	6,616
		Total		41,851

Poverty, Ignorance, Race Prejudice, contribute greatly to the high percentage of Negro patrons of courts and penal institutions.

MARRIAGES

Total number of marriages in the last five years, 1920-1924, inclusive, 30,000. Among them the following were colored:

```
1920 ..............................  816
1921 ..............................  540
1922 ..............................  593
1923 ..............................  741
1924 ..............................  669
                                     ----
       Total ......................  3359
```

COLORED FAMILIES ASSISTED BY ASSOCIATED CHARITIES

1922, 1324 families needed assistance.
1923, 1639 families needed assistance.
1924, 2032 famlies needed assistance.

Of 9777 individuals who came for assistance, 434 men were married but their families were not in this city.

There were only 55 old people, they were over 65 years of age, who were absolutely alone and for whom complete provision was necessary.

THE CITY HOSPITAL

Our public hospital, a five million dollar establishment, is one of the very finest in the United States. It has no colored attaches above the rank of meniality. Many years ago at the old city hospital, Albert Marchand rose from elevator boy to secretary of the board, and to the position of assistant librarian, although he was really, from the standpoint of merit, the head librarian. His salary was pitifully inadequate for a man of his brilliant attainments. Since he passed away there has been no colored representative. Unfortunately, Negroes, through possibly an inherited slothfulness or passivity, generally incline to traverse the roads of least resistance. That trend is largely in evidence here, for instead of contending unceasingly for their rights as citizens and taxpayers, they devote their efforts to the formation and maintenance of a small private hospital, instead of fighting for colored internes, doctors, nurses, at an institution maintained from public revenues. The patients, black or white, get about the same treatment, but the colored are segregated and the segregation is received by colored citizens here with the complacence usually accorded by them to such indignities. It is used frequently as an argument for the support of a colored hospital.

COLORED HOSPITALS

The Peter Fossett Hospital made quite a name during the few years it was in existence. One or two of our doctors have had private hospitals, but they lasted only a short time. The Mercy Hospital, a purely colored institution, has been in existence several years. It has a large staff of colored doctors, nearly all of whom belong to the young school of doctors. They have formed a medical association which has shown a great deal of progressiveness and their spirit is also indicated by their patronage of the chain of drug stores in which some of them are interested.

WAR WORK

During the progress of this titanic struggle known as the World War many avenues of employment were opened, particularly in the various local United States departments. Owing to the scarcity of men, the opportunities in the field of labor were abundant for colored women in numberless private enterprises. Since the war the whites have gradually retaken their old positions. Colored women, however, remain as maids at all of the theatres and colored bootblacks are still working side by side with the whites in bootblacking shops which are so freely scattered through the business district of the city. That Negro patrons are not welcomed in such places shows that the color line in Cincinnati not only penetrates to the very soul of the colored citizen, but goes down even to his soles.

COAL, EXPRESS AND ICE

G. W. Gamble
Frank Atkinson
E. Thurman
R. Jones
I. Tolliver
George Greene
G. Wiley
Tom Bruntz
D. Jones
Nash Hamlin
Isaac Fine
Taylor Blair

E. G. Braxton
Arizona McCoy
N. Freeman
John Wilson
Jeff Doler
W. H. Wharton
Sam McGraven
C. Knighton
Hill & Son
Jennings Harris
R. H. Moore

BEAUTY CULTURISTS

Flora Hector
Mamie Jackson
Martha Williams
Clara B. Scott
Jennie Simmons
M. B. Brooks
Callie Parrish
M. Easley
L. A. Gough
S. J. Reed
Mrs. E. L. Johnson

Pearl L. G. Tull
C. Jones
R. S. Mitchell
C. N. Reeder
Pearl Christian
Mrs. M. Brown
Sina Still
Madame Butler
Mary E. Johnson
C. K. Harris

CLEANING AND PRESSING

- H. Bruce
- M. T. Sweeney
- G. W. Moore
- Willie Harris
- H. Ford
- W. Whitley
- W. H. Underwood
- Willis Filo
- M. Davis
- K. Heath
- J. C. Steele
- Wm. Givens
- Alva J. Weaver
- M. Payton
- P. French
- Chas. McCoy
- Ed Parks
- J. Morris
- I. Moran
- J. T. Ward
- H. Robinson
- S. Garland
- Ollie Wofford
- J. W. Greenwood
- E. Lumpkins
- D. Colvard
- W. H. Pepper
- R. B. Horton
- Robert McBride
- Lee Poole
- Wm. F. Reed
- C. J. Henry
- Wm. Martin

REGALIA MANUFACTURERS

- S. T. Sneed
- E. A. Williams
- J. L. Jones, Jr.

JEWELRY VENDERS

- Blackstone Rankin
- Thos. Edwards
- Frank Spillen

CARPENTER CONTRACTORS AND BUILDERS

- P. Haggard
- D. W. Stokes
- C. R. Davis
- Coleman Bros.
- A. Cabinail
- J. D. Berry
- B. R. Gates
- Jas. Smith
- E. A. Erwin
- Wm. Friason
- Wm. Lee
- T. Patten
- Kidd Bros.
- Elliott Bros.

SECOND-HAND STORES

- Wm. Grant
- G. Morris
- Bill Satchel
- Frank Battles

CATERERS

- Mrs. Edith Fossett Miller
- Richard Connelly
- W. E. Smith
- Mattie Gibbs
- Daisy Merchant

LIBRARIANS

- Mrs. Hattie Walker
- Wenwick Hargraves
- Theo. Berry
- Ella Craft
- Bush Wright

EMPLOYMENT BUREAUS

Mrs. W. A. Johnson
Y. M. C. A.
Y. W. C. A.
St. Andrew's
H. Woodfolk

PATENT MEDICINES

J. F. Walker
Albert Hatcher
G. C. Henderson
C. B. Miller
L. E. Hancock
S. W. Davis
D. Davis
S. J. Reed

HABERDASHERIES

W. S. Wright
John Hillerman
The Liberian (has two stores)

TAILORS

H. Bruce
M. T. Sweeney
W. Harris
Irwin Moran
W. H. Pepper
Wm. F. Reed
C. J. Henry
Wm. Martin

DRUG STORES

Model
Peerless
Howard
The Community Pharmacy

TAXI OWNERS

Bynum Glenn
Oliver Wilson

NEWS AGENCIES

Morton Francis
J. Buchanan
E. H. Blaney
R. Gossett
L. L. Stone
Leslie Towles
J. W. Savage

POOL ROOMS

J. T. Hill
L. Sinclair
Chas. Haggett
Geo. Holston
M. C. Finney
Jack Henderson
Harris Frazier
Lewis & Greer

UNDERTAKERS

W. H. Hill
W. M. Copeland
I. Copeland
H. G. Saunders
J. H. Thompson
Mr. & Mrs. R. J. Walker
F. D. McCoy
B. East
Walter S. Houston
C. E. Jones
Mrs. E. Delaney
Rankin Bros.
E. W. Smith
St. Julian & Inez Renfro

OPTOMETRISTS

S. B. Niles

SHOE REPAIRERS

W. H. Wheeler
J. C. Langley
A. Parks

R. D. Murdock
H. S. Speights, Jr.

PRINTERS AND PUBLISHERS

W. H. G. Carter
W. L. Anderson

A. W. Braxton

CIGARS AND NOTIONS

G. H. McMickey
B. F. Hatcher

Wm. Floyd

SOFT DRINK EMPORIUMS

Ottis Baker

Johnston Frissby

INSURANCE

Mid-Western Mutual Benefit Assn.
Columbia Fraternal Assn.
Domestic Life
American Woodmen

National Benefit Assn.
Supreme Life & Casualty
Hope Aid & Anchor Life

HOSPITALS

The Mercy

Evangeline Booth Home

REAL ESTATE

Horace Sudduth
Wm. Upshaw

J. H. Coleman

SHOE SHINING PARLORS

Washington Gossett
Henry Little
H. Bruce
W. H. Buckner
J. B. Buchanan
Lawrence Sinclair
J. H. Jones
Richard Gossett
L. L. Stone
Aaron Chambers

John Laucy
R. Butler
J. H. Willis
Charles Weaver
P. Haggard
David Fuller
Leslie Towles
G. W. Smith
W. M. Rogers
F. G. Harris

BARBERSHOP PROPRIETORS

James Franklin
I. W. Newberry
E. L. Shedd
H. Boone
Porterfield Clark
D. L. Smith
Chas. Humphrey
Wm. Dillard
J. T. Jones
W. B. Brent
C. C. Thompson
S. D. Shinault
J. M. Burnside
Wesley Shavers
G. W. Hellard
George Powell
L. Cornett
John H. Allen
John W. Allen
B. W. Hall
G. W. Ulman

W. E. Smith
W. Randall
S. Simmons
W. M. H. Wrenn
Wm. Johnson
B. F. Smith
S. T. Sneed
C. H. Rhodes
John S. Fielding
Charles P. Frazier
W. M. Jackson
Harding Beasley
C. W. Williams
Mrs. O. L. Fitzpatrick
J. T. Ward
N. H. Gilliard
David Fuller
L. Thomas
J. H. Smith
James Ponds
Tommie Thomas

R. S. Mitchell
James Johnson
John Bushillon
J. V. Garrett
J. Collins
J. W. Swanns
J. H. Ross
John Dixon
Henry Skillman
Douglass Finley
Chas. McLeod
J. McKinney
M. Shaeffer
R. J. Hester
N. Brooks
N. Jones
James Starks
Wm. Ross
Siton Alexander
Williams and Whitson

CONFECTIONERY

W. Gossett
J. C. Boler
H. Murphy
E. H. Blaney
G. Scheller
Eva Dudley
L. B. Allen
Aaron Chambers
M. C. Finney
Mrs. Mattie Jackson

Isaac Fine
G. W. Smith
J. W. Savage
L. Jordon
I. Jones
W. M. Rogers
A. Parks
F. G. Harris
Lewis & Greer
S. J. Reed

DOCTORS

B. J. Lockley
E. B. Stone
W. T. Nelson
E. D. Colley
E. B. Gray
L. R. Breedlove
J. H. Wallace
E. A. Williams
R. E. Clarke
E. J. Ross
R. P. McClain
J. C. Erwin

M. F. Leland
N. C. Vaughan
W. O. H. Ross
W. A. Kerr
G. E. Loverette
A. D. Kelley
J. E. Randolph
N. E. Denham
S. J. Watkins
A. D. Beam
T. L. Berry

CHIROPODISTS

M. E. Clarke
W. L. Harris
H. Ferguson
John Hoffman
Tomas O'Banon

ARCHITECTS

E. E. Birch
A. Townsend

MUSIC TEACHERS

Leslie Towles
Artie Matthews
Anna Matthews
G. A. Hilliard
A. Jones Hilliard
C. H. Kelley
Fred Armstrong
Charles Trotter
Shirley Hawkins
A. Tibbs
H. Ryder
Mrs. A. Williams
Mrs. Merry
Fannie Collins

WHITE HOTELS AND CLUBS EMPLOYING COLORED HELP

Gibson
Burnet House
Vernon Manor
Kemper Lane
Broadway
Coney Island Club
Latonia Jockey Club
Yellow Hen Club

NURSERIES

Friendship Home
St. Andrew's Day Nursery

PLUMBERS

Harry Friason
John Lutie
George Johnson

PAPER HANGERS

Harry Smith
George Logan
C. H. Duval
Clarence Brown
Bryant Bros.
Ernest Germany
Julius Moping

MECHANICS' REPAIR SHOPS

H. Jennings
J. W. Taylor
C. W. Hall
George Conner
G. Wilson
H. Ewing
J. W. Billings
W. H. Ferguson
H. Jameison
E. Slummault
——— Broadus
McCall Industrial

HOD CARRIERS

There are several hundred hod carriers in this city.

GROCERIES

C. W. Wright
Florence Crew
Bishop Mary Mack
M. F. Steele
I. Tolliver
J. C. Conyard
F. H. Hall
Virgil Harris
E. P. Rogers
C. Luidell
A. Johnson & Son
C. H. Turner
B. Bonner

S. C. Carter
Wm. Grant
Mrs. N. Hamilin
Prosset & Harding
A. Kalfer
S. H. Colquit
M. Jackson
John Hill
C. F. Lacey
Mrs. Allen Moss
H. Battle
W. A. Houston

BANK MESSENGERS AND BANK CLERKS

W. B. Young
Joe Arnold
Harry Brill
Harry Jordan
Charles Maxburry
James Jones
Fred Hilleman
Robt. Belringer
Frank Garner
A. Williams
Walter Griggs
Shirley Hawkins
George Baltimore

Bertram Roots
Louis Wilson
Wm. Hughes
Wm. Gaines
Frank Oats
Herman Swering
McKinley Newby
M. Warfield Hocker
Chas. Lobert
Horace Allen
Melvin Travis
Clifford Gaston

STORAGE WAREHOUSE

The Ziegler-Shafer Co.—The president, M. L. Ziegler, is colored.

FRATERNITIES

Alpha Phi Alpha, Alpha Chapter   Alumni Chapter
Kappa Alpha Psi, Cincinnati

ATTORNEYS AT LAW

Fred J. Hamilton
Thos. J. Howard
C. E. Hunter
A. L. Beaty
Thos. B. Richmond
E. S. Smith

Jesse D. Locker
O. K. Blythe
A. L. Dalton
J. H. Johnson
W. L. Ricks
R. G. Brown

RESTAURANT PROPRIETORS

Mrs. L. Cook
Mrs. Anna Miller
Ida Miller
Mrs. J. Buchanan
Joe Amos
E. H. Blaney
Mattie Pail
James Bruce
George Schelley
Helen Casey
Wm. H. Hoffman
A. Crew
H. P. Speights
A. Paris
R. L. Cooper
Edward Saunders
L. H. Harris
Mrs. Beatie Fearce
Hale Sisters

Wm. Miller
P. L. Allen
L. B. Allen
Amos Mahon
Mrs. C. Davis
Davis Sisters
Mrs. G. Oliver
Mrs. James Harris
James H. Stokes
L. Morgan
S. Gross
Walford Simpson
A. Gaither
O. Taylor
Mrs. B. Anderson
J. McNeese
Mrs. Elizabeth Caldwell
Y. W. C. A.

Y. M. C. A.
L. Givens
George Jefferson
L. Graham
Mrs. Ardailyer Arnold
W. M. Palmer
Mrs. L. E. Austin
Mrs. B. Cummings
W. J. Douglass
Richard Suggs
Floyd Suggs
Albert Glass
Lottie Friason
H. Anderson
E. Toles
Mrs. G. Stewart
Mrs. R. Kidd
Mrs. C. Foster

SORORITIES

Alpha Kappa Alpha   Delta Sigma Theta   Zeta Phi Beta

COLORED MEMBERS OF CINCINNATI POLICE DEPARTMENT

In Active Service

Frank A. B. Hall, Detective
John Thomas, Detective
Lafayette Coffey, Patrolman
Charles H. Payne, Patrolman
Charles P. Miles, Patrolman

Sam'l W. Anderson, Sub-Patrolman
William F. Cox, Sub-Patrolman
Howard N. Hill, Sub-Patrolman
John E. Toney, Sub-Patrolman
Robt. A. Wilson, Sub-Patrolman

PHARMACISTS

George Hicks
Amos Goode
Mrs. A. Young
Mrs. B. L. Patterson
Mrs. Anna Beckwith
C. A. Anderson

R. D. Russell
Mrs. F. L. Berry
Mrs. R. Kyles
J. Jones
A. N. Giles
Joe Courtney

Have Not Passed State Board

Wm. Johnson
J. Carlisle
H. Piersawl
M. T. Garrett
W. S. Averett

Miss Ruby Anderson
——— Evans
John Lacey
Mrs. W. T. Nelson

DENTISTS

Reginald E. Beaman
T. J. Banks
L. E. Payne
E. H. Green

L. L. Hubbard
Chas. A. Schooley
E. C. Cox

RESIDENT NURSES

Mrs. L. Wallace
Mrs. Stella Teaters
G. Wheeler
C. Stoner
J. M. McConico
A. M. Johnson

L. B. Hurley
Mrs. F. W. Helvey
———— Evans
Mrs. Howard
H. N. Littlejohn

HOTEL GIBSON WAITERS

W. Sulzer
L. Smith
H. Matthews
J. Goodman
J. Fry
S. Graves
F. Ward
B. Campbell
W. Harris
E. Maxwell
J. Reeves
R. Shirley
H. Thompson
G. Stark
W. Brown
R. Cook
A. McMurry
J. Roland

S. Johnson
J. Lipsey
H. Foots
J. Goss
T. McCauley
H. E. McRae
H. McCauley
G. Pryor
F. G. Peterson
Oscar Carter
R. Benifield
A. Allen
J. Hundley
E. Edwards
Fred Sweeney
W. Chambers
L. Randell
J. Tribue

Wm. Johnson
F. Steele
H. Johnson
Frank Sweeney
Chas. Bell
A. Pulliam
C. J. Turnell
Capt. J. W. Wilkins
G. B. Peterson
Capt. J. W. Gray
Vernon Manior
Sherrell
Ellison
Lewis
Birch
Stokes
Jamerson
Hinkins

POST-OFFICE CLERKS

Alexander, Clark A.
Banks, Louis E.
Baynes, Cample D.
Bryant, Clarence A.
Burr, Foster K.
Butler, Chester R.
Coffey, Paul (sub)
Cromwell, Elwood L.
Cromwell, Eugene E.
Brosby, James H. (sub)
Deal, Chas. H. (sub)
Dixon, Stanley
Doran, Chas.
East, Thomas G. (sub)

Ewing, Cecil
Foster, Frank B.
Friason, Lawrence H.
Fullman, Louis E.
Gallagher, John W. (sub)
Gentry, Jefferson E.
Greer, Robt. C.
Gross, Hugh C. (sub)
Hamilton, Fred J.
Harris, Richard H.
Hood, John P.
Howard, Chas. A.
Johnson, Elmer
Johnson, Joseph

410 CINCINNATI'S COLORED CITIZENS

Jones, Lesley W. (sub)
Kalfus, Louis
Kinney, Roland D. (sub)
Lewis, Courtland
Liggins, Lloyd (sub)
McConnell, Wm. A. (sub)
McLean, James P.
McLeod, Donald W.
McPheeters, Winston
Miller, James B.
Moore, Dana L. (sub)
Owens, Clarence N.
Paghe, Jos. H.
Parks, Warfield
Payne, Frank
Penn, Ambrose D.

Pierce, Chas. H.
Plumb, Chas. H.
Roberts, Edw. E.
Roberts, Martin V.
Sandipher, Aaron H.
Sandusky, Garret B.
Seymour, Fred D.
Shannon, James W.
Simms, Eugene H.
Smith, James W. (sub)
Spencer, Chas. A. (sub)
Tate, Henry E.
Turner, Houston
Watson, Wm. E.
Woodford, Richard B.
Wrenn, Louis W.

CARRIERS

Anderson, James H.
Armstrong, Chas. E.
Beckwith, Carl
Blackburn, Robt. L.
Bradley, Wm., Jr.
Bray, Russell
Burrus, Otto W.
Butler, Wm. T.
Childs, Norman J.
Clinton, Van
Coleman, John H.
Craig, Wm.
Fox, John R.
Franklin, Wm. M.
Goode, Chas. E.
Goode, L. P.
Graham, Hamilton D.
Greer, James S.
Hall, Wm. H.
Hall, Wm. H., Jr.
Hatfield, Chas. W.
Hopson, John
Houston, Chas.
Hull, Arthur F.
Hunter, Wm. F.
Ingram, Andrew L., Jr.
Jackson, Eugene H.
Jackson, Samuel E.

Jackson, Walter A.
Jackson, Wm.
Johnson, Clarence
Johnson, Wm. A.
Jones, Geo. J.
Kelly, Lewis V.
Lee, Andrew W.
Lewis, Walter
McCaleb, Wm. R.
Mack, Tonny
Marshall, Oscar T.
Mason, Edw. T.
Menifee, Wm. L.
Morris, Clarence W.
Noel, Melvin C.
Ozier, Geo. W.
Parker, Alonzo
Renfro, Golden E.
Ross, Albert
Stewart, Walter H.
Thompson, Wm. H.
Tivis, Richmond E.
Wallace, Alfred
Ward, Dennis H.
West, Harry B.
White, Fred
Woodson, Jesse J.
Zeigler, Penn W.

FEDERAL EMPLOYEES

Ayres, J. H.
Jones, Alonzo
Monroe, T. J.
Guthrie, Jerry

Williams, John
Yarbrough, D. S.
Bullock, Samuel

ASSOCIATION OF NEGRO FEDERAL EMPLOYEES

Baynes, Decatur
Childs, Norman J.
Clinton, V. H.
Cromwell, Elwood
Dudley, Grant
Gentry, Amos
Greer, James
Hall, Wm. H. Sr.
Hall, Wm. H. Jr.
Howard, Chas. A.
Ingram, Andrew L. Jr.
Johnson, Clarence N.
Kalfus, Lewis T.
Lewis, Courtland
McLeod, Donald W.
Owens, Clarence
Paghe, Jos. H.
Parks, Warfield
Penn, A. D.
Reed, John
Roberts, M. V.
Shannon, J. W.
Simms, Eugene
Tate, Henry E.
Turner, Huston
Watkins, Wm.
Woodson, J. J.

Wrenn, Louis
Goode, L. P.
Jackson, Samuel E.
Burr, Foster K.
Payne, Frank
Madison, Likel L.
Bryant, C. A.
Fullman, L. E.
Ewing, Cecil
Renfro, St. Julian
Foster, F. B.
Seymour, Fred D.
Sandusky, G. B.
Johnson, Elmer
Cromwell, Eugene
Spencer, C. A.
Ward, Honshell
Hawkins, Ralph
Ward, D. H.
Willis, A. L.
Gentry, Jefferson
Hood, J. P.
Hamilton, Fred J.
Pierce, Chas.
Gross, H. C.
McPheeters, Winston
Harris, Richard
Dixon, Stanley

COLORED SOCIAL WORKERS

Associated Charities, 304 Broadway
1—Mrs. Verna P. Greene
2—Mrs. Martha F. Howard
3—Miss Eileen Yarbrough
4—Mrs. Verna P. Roberts
5—Mr. Cleveland Turnell

Better Housing League, 25 East 9th St.
6—Mrs. Drucilla Clay
7—Mrs. Myrtle N. Grandison
8—Mrs. M. E. Wilson
9—Mrs. J. P. Monroe

Catholic Charities, 125 East 9th St.
10—Miss Theresa Lee

Children's Home, 312 West 9th St.
11—Miss Mary E. Hargrave
12—Mrs. Adgelee Reeder

Cincinnati Community Service, Southern Ohio Bank Bldg.
13—Mr. E. P. Robinson
14—Mrs. Clara Hough

Cincinnati Social Hygiene Society, 25 East 9th St.
15—Mrs. Leila Davis

Crawford's Old Men's Home, North Bend Rd., College Hill
16—Mrs. Martha Botts

DAY NURSERIES

Friendship Home Day Nursery, 641 West 4th St.
17—Mrs. Etta Smith   20—Miss Louise Battle
18—Mrs. Mary Henry   21—Miss Lyra Benton
19—Miss Goldie Dalton

St. Andrew's Day Nursery, 8th & Mound Sts.
22—Mrs. E. H. Oxley

Evangeline Home, 712 West 6th St.
Commissioned Officers:
23—Lillian F. Wright, Com-   25—Evelyn Richards, Ensign
   mandant (white)   26—Louise Armstrong, Ensign
24—Lillian Jacobs, Adjutant   27—Mary Davis, Captain
   (white)   28—Hazel Snow, Captain

Non-Commissioned Officers
29—Marie Brown, Envoy   30—Sue Hargrave, Envoy

Friendship Home, 641 West 4th St.
31—Miss Myrtle Willette   33—Mrs. Anna Lewis
32—Miss Delia Charles

Home for Aged Colored Women, 1334½ Lincoln Ave.
34—Mrs. Olive Shorter

Home for Colored Girls, 816 W. 9th St.
35—Miss Elma E. Leach,   37—Mrs. Ella Glenn
   (white)   38—Miss Talitha Sanford
36—Mrs. Cora Oliver   39—Mrs. Nellie Williams

Juvenile Court, Hamilton County Courthouse
40—Miss Alexine Crawford   41—Rev. A. W. Jackson

Lockland Branch, Y. M. C. A., 310 North Wayne Ave.
42—Mr. W. V. Eagleson   43—Mr. J. O. Collins

Negro Civic Welfare Association, 25 East 9th St.
44—Mr. Jas. H. Robinson   46—Miss M. W. Swanson
45—Miss Boggs Hargrave

New Orphan Asylum for Colored Youth,
Van Buren & Melish Aves.
47—Mr. L. S. Walton   49—Mrs. M. Q. Carter
48—Mrs. L. D. Walton

Ninth St. Branch, Y. M. C. A., 630 West 9th St.
50—Mr. B. W. Overton   53—Mr. R. O'Blennis
51—Mr. W. N. Lovelace   54—Mr. Wilson Berry
52—Mr. H. T. Miller

NURSES

Department of Health, City Hall, 8th & Plum Sts.
55—Miss Amelia Johnson   57—Miss Gladys Wheeler
56—Mrs. Estella Teeters

Shelter Home for Colored Children, 1234 Chapel St.
58—Mrs. Lucy Lee   60—Mrs. Hannah Tate
59—Mrs. Hettie Parsons

West End Branch, Y. W. C. A., 704 West 8th St.
61—Miss Isobel Lawson   63—Mrs. Etta Forte
62—Mrs. Eliz. N. Elliott   64—Mrs. Anna H. Turnell

PULLMAN PORTERS LOCATED IN CINCINNATI

Abernathy, O.
Akins, J.
Andrews, J.
Alexander, P.
Anderson, E. (1)
Allen, B. J.
Anderson, E. (2)
Abernathy, W. A.
Anderson, W. S.
Adair, C.
Boler, J. C.
Blaney, J. A.
Baker, F.
Brown, H. H.
Brown, F. J.
Boyd, H.
Burns, T. E.
Bryant, A.
Braden, G.
Barber, R.
Brown, R.
Baker, G.
Bush, C. H.
Bowen, W. N.
Bean, R.
Brown, W. G.
Baker, L.
Brown, J. H.
Burns, C.
Bright, C.
Bush, H.
Boler, J. C.
Boyd, H.
Berry, C. F.
Berry, E. V.
Botts, J.
Brown, J.
Courtney, J. F.
Carter, E.
Cooper, R. W. J.
Clark, E. W.
Culbert, J.
Cameron, J. T.
Cummins, G. T.
Carter, V. A.
Collins, J. A.
Cole, J. B.
Coleman, R. A.
Chavies, G.
Crawford, C.
Carson, J. L.

Coleman, S.
Dennis, L.
Davidson, W. T.
Davenport, D. G.
Dixon, R. L.
Davis, H. A.
Davis, M.
Dowtin, E. S.
Davis, C.
Davis, E. D.
Davis, J. H.
Denton, J.
Eglir, B.
Elston, B. J.
Edwards, H.
Foster, F.
Fowler, R. A.
Finch, F. D.
Finch, Pembrock
Farrar, Sam
Francis, J.
Foster, A. R.
Findley, C.
Fanning, W. M.
Green, C.
Griffith, J.
Gillard, R. J.
Gaines, A.
Grimes, R.
Griffiths, B. F.
Garrett, J. W.
Greer, N.
Greer, F.
Gray, J. W.
Garrett, W.
Grevious, N. H.
Greene, H. A.
Humphrey, J.
Harleston, R. W.
Hall, W.
Hamilton, J. P.
Harton, J.
Harding, J. F.
Howard, J. H.
Hughes, F. A.
Harris, A. B.
Hill, W. A.
Harrison, W. H.
Hall, F. C.
Herndon, A. D.
Hawk, A.

Harding, C. E.
Hubbard, A. T.
Harris, G. E.
Harris, J. C.
Hathman, E. R.
Hull, C. H.
Harden, E. A.
Halloway, C. B.
Haggard, S.
Hiddins, D.
Humphrey, J.
Irving, C. L.
Jones, B.
Johnson, J.
Johnson, W. H.
Jones, W.
Johnson, H.
Johnson, J. T.
Jordon, H. K.
Jelks, J. D.
Jefferson, J.
King, C.
Koyton, B.
Kilgour, H.
Lee, C. S.
Lewis, E. W.
Long, J. W.
Logan, J. C.
Lilly, F. D.
Lemon, K. G.
Morris, M. S.
Moore, W.
McKinney, L.
McFatridge, J. A.
Moody, C. C.
Morris, R.
Marshall, C.
McCaleb, W.
Malden, B.
Mann, B. L.
Miles, B.
McClure, W. B.
Marable, Thomas
McFarland, O.
Moore, H.
McNairy, E. D.
Martin, C. F.
Moore, J.
Morris, M. J.
McPheeters, D. D.
Moore, S.

McPherson, E.
Neale, E. H.
Owsley, W.
Paige, A. T.
Pitts, G. E.
Parker, J. H. Sr.
Palmer, J. E.
Poston, S. C.
Poston, C. L.
Phillips, W. R.
Power, R.
Phillips, W.
Parker, Q.
Ramey, F.
Rivers, R.
Richardson, L. L.
Smith, C. H.
Richardson, A. P.
Spires, R. B.
Smith, J. D.
Smith, R. L.
Smith, Amos
Simms, B. K. T.

Sweeney, N.
Smith, E. T.
Saunders, J.
Shannon, W.
Smith, A. A.
Stewart, J. W.
Shepherd, W.
Stowers, M. R.
Simmons, A. W.
Smallwood, C.
Stanley, C.
Taylor, C. B.
Travis, W. A.
Taylor, W. T.
Taylor, G. W.
Talley, V.
Thrasher, C.
Tolliver, J. H.
Thomas, C. S.
Taylor, K. A.
Travis, L.
Talbot, N.
Utz, E. B.

Washington, W. H.
Wilkerson, S. A.
Walker, P.
Wallace, W.
White, Chas.
White, L. H.
Wilson, J.
West, S. J.
Wyatt, G. M.
Williams, G. M.
Works, F.
Whipps, L.
Welch, F.
White, W. A.
Williams, B.
Williams, L. W.
White, C. G.
Webb, P. F.
Wilmot, E. B.
Winchester, N.
Whaley, J. C.
Wise, L.
Wynn, G. W.

SECRET FRATERNITIES

The colored Masons were for years as strong proportionately as the whites. "Sam" Clark was a pioneer; Lou Easton and others great warriors for the cause. They own property on West Sixth Street and on Gilbert Avenue, Walnut Hills.

The Oddfellows, also a strong body, owns splendid property on West Ninth Street.

The U. N. I. A. branch, in a few years, has become one of the strongest fraternal forces in this county.

U. B. F.'s and Galilean Fishermen are old societies.

There are scores of other orders and lodges doing well in the field of charity; were they to concentrate upon a public policy for the betterment of themselves and their race, they would have a glorious opportunity for improving general conditions in every way.

K. of P.

Dr. E. A. Williams and Dr. Stringer came up from New Orleans and founded the first lodge of K. of P. here in 1882. The ceremonies took place in the M. E. Church, then located where French-Bauer plant now stands on West Seventh Street. Later it was reorganized in a blacksmith shop on George Street. Lee H. Wilson and Arthur J. Riggs, a great orator of that time, were the leading promoters.

In the early nineties the Elks were formed by B. J. Howard and others.

Colored Masons were in Ohio from 1849 and most of the Southern states received their degrees from this community as the organization had many strong representatives in Cincinnati.

Masons

Corinthian No. 1
St. John No. 3
True American No. 2
Prince White Chapter R. A. No. 1
Simon Commandery No. 1
King Solomon Consistory No. 1

Mt. Sinai Temple, A. O. M. S. No. 59
St. John Chapter, O. E. S., No. 25
Corinthian Chapter No. 34, O. E. S.
True American No. 3, O. E. S.
Daughters of Isis, Sinai Court, No. 35

Elks

Alpha Lodge No. 1, I. B. P. O. Elks

Ettawah Temple No. 7

K. of P.

Garnet Lodge No. 32
Polar Star No. 27
Stith No. 54
Sifford No. 63
Court Calanthe, W. O. C.

Zenith Court No. 14, Elks' Hall
Wilson Court No. 45, Elks' Hall
White Lily No. 39, Elks' Hall
Shining Light No. 15, Elks' Hall
Odessa Court No. 15, W. H.

Knights and Ladies of Honor of the World

Lily of the Valley Lodge No. 84, 414G
Vigilant Lodge No. 302
Queen City Lodge No. 790

Laura's Daylight Lodge No. 556
Black's Delight No. 1081
Rose of Shannon No. 1124

FRATERNAL LEAGUE ORGANIZATIONS

Bell Flower Court No. 7
Crystal Fount Tabernacle
Crystal Fount Tent
DeHart Camp U. B. F.
Eclipse Co. F., K. of P.
Progressive Drill Corps
May Flower Juvenile No. 89
Marrietta Tent No. 19
Cincinnati Camp No. 1 A. W.
Ira F. Dixon Tent No. 213
Queen City Band

Polar Star No. 27, K. of P.
Light of Night No. 5 U. B. F.
Evening Star Juveniles No. 4
Star of Bethlehem No. 9 Tabors
Florence Crittenden Tent No. 260
Shining Light No. 79 Tabors
Covington Temple No. 6, S. M. T.
Cincinnati Camp No. 2, A. W.
Progressive Tent No. 10
Jeanette Star of the West
Bell Temple No. 13, S. M. T.

Queen Esther Court No. 1
Messiah Lodge No. 1641, G. U. of O. F.
Lelawanda Lodge No. 3195, Oxford, Ohio
Black Delight No. 1081
Quinn Lessa Juveniles No. 10
Ira Lodge Elks, Covington, Ky.
Josephine Mitchell Tent Tabors
Living Flower Lodge No. 6, G. S.
Brush Burners Tent No. 1, A. W.
St. Ann's Tabernacle No. 3
Virginia No. 28, U. B. F.
A. J. Lucas Paldtium Tabors
Progressive Tent No. 4
Golden Leaf Jewel Tent
Crispus Attucks No. 1650, Covington, Ky.
Kyra Temple No. 3, Covington, Ky.
Battalion Drill Corps
Juanita Drill Corps
St. Jacob's Temple
Ettawah Drill Corps Elks
Willing Workers Tent
Rebecca No. 14, G. S.
Samaria Drill Corps
Household of Ruth No. 92
J. Forsey Tabernacle
Mt. Tabor Tabernacle
L. F. Bedford Tabernacle
Eva Household No. 4176
Elizabeth No. 49, G. S.
Galilean Fisherman
Queen of Sheba
Garnet No. 32, K. of P.
Covington No. 6, K. of P.
Anthony No. 30, U. B. F.
Lockland No. 1710, G. U. O. of O. F.
Wilson Court No. 45
Household of Ruth No. 980
Queen City No. 3734, G. U. O. of O. F.
J. Fielding Juveniles

Zenith Court No. 14
Covington No. 35, U. B. F.
White Rose Household No. 1719
Patriarchy No. 29
St. Mary Marguerite
Excelsior Co. E., K. of P.
P. G. M. Council No. 64
Bell Davis No. 7, G. S.
Glittering Star No. 501
Carnation Drill Corps No. 1
Household of Ruth No. 2385
St. Mary's Tabernacle Tabor
Past Arcanum
Fraternal League
Co. I, Patriarchy No. 106
Langston Co. F., K. of P.
St. James No. 5, G. S.
Co. L., Patriarchy No. 165
Golden Rule Temple
Knights of Noah Circle No. 2
Ettawah Temple Elks
Saunders and Hubbard Tent
Golden Leaf Tabernacle No. 476
Palestine Co. B., K. of P.
Carmel Temple No. 66
Elizabeth Drill Corps No. 1
E. J. McCray Co. 2 Tabors
Daughters of the Venus Temple
Davis Camp No. 7, U. B. F.
Bright Light Court No. 59
Earhardt No. 19, S. M. T.
Golden Link Temple, S. M. T.
Jeanette Queen Tabernacle No. 44
White Lily Court No. 3906
Berkely Temple No. 1
Golden Hill Juveniles
Stith Lodge No. 54, K. of P.
Georgietta Juveniles No. 1568
Fidessa Court No. 54
Paris Council No. 132
Mosaics Temple of America No. 5065
Tube Rose Tent No. 26
Wanda Juvenile Class No. 68, Elks

CINCINNATI UNIVERSITY

STUDENTS

Mr. Scott
Francis Leslie
John Leland
George Crumwell
Harry S. Williams, Jr.
Lawrence D. Finley
Harry Smith
Mr. Ward
M. McMorris
Mr. Crump
Edward Hurst
A. B. McClure
Robert Brown
Raymond Bennett
Frank Rhodes
Ivan McLeod (Law)
DeWitt McCaleb (Law)
N. S. Roberts (Law)
Mr. Fox
Rev. Davis
Rev. E. W. Oxley
Theo. M. Berry
W. N. Lovelace
B. W. Overton
Wilson Berry
Herbert T. Miller
Mr. Rambo
Anna Musin
Elsie Austin
Corinne Eaddy

Louise Briscoe
Beulah Harris
Alma Hatfield
Anna Johnson
Laura Knight
Mary Busch
Mrs. Clara Huff
Elizabeth Hunter
Corinna Fuller
Rena Carter
Evelena Fourncy
Mrs. Rhea Cox
Isabel Menifee
Odessa Palmer
Miss Butler
Miss Brown
Miss Gilham
Ethel Gibson
Ruth Wilson
Nellie Hurley
Anette Sharpe
Dorothea Gross
Rebecca Chenault
Nancy Hawkins
Ray Parker
Miss Jennie Porter
Mrs. Zenobia Russell
Isabel Lawson
J. P. Monroe

FRESHMEN

Harry Smith
Alfonso McClure
Marjorie Hatfield
Dorothea Gross
Corinne Eaddy

Corinne Fuller
Roberta Clay
Elizabeth Hopkins
Edward Hurst

SOPHOMORES

Elsie Austin
Anne Estella Mason
Theodore Berry

George Cromwell
Lawrence Finley

JUNIORS

Alma Hatfield
Beulah Harris
Louise Briscoe
Odessa Palmer

Raymond Bennet
John Leland
Ann Johnson

Seniors

Mary Busch
Valeria Griffith
DeWitt McCaleb

Ivan McLeod
Mrs. Clara Hough

Cincinnati, Ohio, October 14, 1925

Mr. W. P. Dabney,
412 McAllister Street,
Cincinnati, Ohio.

Dear Sir: Miss Alice May Easton was the first colored graduate of the University of Cincinnati. She graduated in 1897 and is now a teacher. Mr. Francis M. Russell was the second colored graduate, having graduated in 1904. He is now Principal of Douglass School.

The following is a list of the colored graduates of 1923:

B. A.—Clinton Moorman, Thelma Moorman, Silas Rhodes, Angy Smith.

B. S.—Jennie Porter.

Grad. Dep.—Annie May Lee Houston (A. B. at Fiske University), Lena Norton.

The following is a list of the colored graduates of 1924:

B. A.—Breta Walker.

B. E.—Althea Chapman (A. B. at Howard University); Margaret Isby (B. S. at Howard University); Angy Smith; Zelma Tyler (A. B. at Howard University); Gladys Warrington (A. B. at Howard University); Leah Wright (A. B. at Howard University).

B. S.—Margaret Bowen, Beulah Farmer, Mary Rasor, Reseda Berry (Home Economics).

The following is a list of the colored graduates of 1925:

A. B.—Laura Clarice Knight, Costella Taylor.

B. E.—Wilhelmenia Butler, Lydia Crawford, Dorothy Sillam, Martha Holliday, Louberta Moore, Breta Walker, Janet Whitaker.

B. S.—Laura Troy Knight, Georgia Beasley (Home Economics).

M. A.—Lena B. Norton, Jennie Porter, Norton Roberts.

Very truly yours,
L. G. HARTMAN,
Registrar.

Charles Turner graduated from the University in 1891. He became an eminent Biologist.

Section IX
Prominent Property Owners

Many property owners in Cincinnati and vicinity own from one to half a dozen pieces of property. According to our office survey, there are about 3,000 houses and lots owned by colored people in this city and vicinity.

WEST END

Annie Harris
Hessie Carr
Stanley Knox
Harry Martin
Eva Brooks
Herbert and Edna Allen
Jas. and Goldie Montgomery
Sadie Samuels
Katie Boone
Perry Parker
Chas. Boyd
Mary Williams
Bessie Beaty
Elizabeth Nunn
Albert and Bertha Purcell
Chas. and Winnie Redwood
Mrs. Anderson Langley
Jas. and Inez McHenry
Cyrus Lindell
Maria Frye
Annie Bryant
Daniel Whitehead
Bessie White
Likel Madison
Wm. and Lalier Carr
Jno. and Fannie Franklin
Harry H. Jones
Elizabeth Long
Walter Jackson
J. Franklin Walker
J. H. and Mary Thompson
Cin and Ida Hardin
E. G. and Emma Braxton
Chas. and Esther Butler
Artie and Anna Matthews
Lauretta Embry
J. B. and Daisy Cole
Hattie Mae Hilliard
Phil and Daisy Burt
Wm. Hutchinson

Lucy Kirk
Elizabeth Roe Kelley
Arthur and Ella Houser
G. W. B. Conrad
Jesse and Bessie Thompson
LeRoy and Ruth Walker
Judge Knott
Mrs. Jas. Harris
Odd Fellows
Jas. L. Jones (Regalia)
Misses Taylor
John Savage
Spud Gates
Sylvanus and Belle Jefferson
Lillian Drayton
W. B. and Xzlema Young
Theo. and Esther Oxley
Nora Taylor
Bert H. Richardson
Rosa Thomas
Mamie Bacon
Priscilla Lee
Jack Tracy
Stephen T. and Mary Sneed
Jas. L. Harvey
Agnes Liggins
Mary and Rufus Williams
Mrs. Jas. Young
Houston Turner
Chas. McCoy
Marshall Hunt
Mrs. Gardiner
Josh Commer
Geo. and Maggie Tweety
America Mosely
Winnie Dempsey
Jennie D. Porter
Mary Johnson
Alexander Clark
Geo. W. Hays

CINCINNATI'S COLORED CITIZENS

Francis Wilson
Mitchel Bothman
J. M. Johnson
W. H. Wharton
Noah Kelley
Chas. L. Sanders
R. E. Hogeans
Joe Rogers
LeRoy Johnson
Chas. L. King
Albert Richardson
Mary Virginia Doll
Jno. W. and Cordelia E. Huffman
Sallie Jones
Daisey Slade
John Stargel
S. O. Shinnault
Will Minor
Annie Bryant
Ed Gaither
Thos. and Bertha Cooper
Virginia Keith
Louise and Ernestine Ray
Sam and Lillie Smart
Newman Sweeney
Mr. and Mrs. Chas. Trotter
Bishop Mary Mack
Mr. Davis
Compton Sisters
Robert Shropshire
I. W. Jackson
Mr. Smith
Mr. and Mrs. Geo. Johnson
Mrs. Jas. Phillips
Mrs. W. Thompson
Rev. L. H. Ingram
Mrs. Maggie Brown
Mr. Green Johnson
Samuel Montgomery
Mrs. Daisy Hughes
Mrs. Virginia Taylor
Mrs. Georgia Mae Branner
Mrs. Mary Taylor
Rose Lambert
John and Sadie Brown
Addie Kennedy
Monroe and Belle Scott
Mr. Henderson
Luke Matthews
Mamie Johnson
James W. and Maude Allen
John Lutie
James and Arnold

Jim Dales, Alex Hall
Ben Williams
St. Julian and Inez Renfro
Essie Williams
Will Dales
Cleveland Turnell
Lucy Maddox
Katie Brooks
Johnson Wallace
Nannie L. Saunders
Fred W. Payne
Leslie Towles
Julia Cassady
Wm. Casey
Guy Braden
Cecelia Savage
Edith Woffert
Rich Connelly
L. J. Woody
Mary Streets Moss
L. H. Ingraham
Mamie Johnson
Eliza Connelly
Annie Campbell
Mamie Barnett
Virginia E. Doll
Ruth Baltimore
Chas. Poindexter
E. N. Metts
John Parker
J. H. Thompson
Mrs. Humble
Luther Moore
Wm. Asbury
Chas. L. King
J. H. Thompson
Thos. and Jennie Fane
Jas. and Annie Murray
Andrews and Jordan
Virginia Bettis
E. G. and Emma Brackins
Annie Smith
Stanley Knox
J. F. Courtney
Walter Roberts
Wm. and Louise Mason
Ida May and Silas Rhodes
Laura Troy Knight
Bert H. Richardson
Annie Bryant
Chas. and Bettie Ball
L. B. Logan
Chas. E. A. Hunt

Margaret Nelson
Green Johnson
Mrs. Maggie Brown
Samuel Montgomery
Mrs. Daisy Hughes
Mrs. Virginia Taylor
Mrs. Georgia Mae Branner
Mrs. Mary Taylor
John Allen
Porterfield Clark
Mrs. Louise Allison
Mrs. Ada May
Blair Taylor
Mrs. Davis
Mrs. Jenkins
Mrs. Harry King

Mrs. Robert Jenkins
Mrs. Dennis Thomas
Mrs. Emma Baker
Mrs. J. C. Langley
L. R. Mitchell
Mrs. Samuel G. Henry
Mrs. C. King
Mrs. L. Brown
Mrs. Scroggins
Misses Cumpton
Mrs. Ethel Tate
Mrs. Sarah Haddex
Wm. Copeland
Mrs. Louise Saunders
Mrs. Sales
Edw. Davis

East End

Mrs. Wamack
Lida Holland
Major L. Zeigler
Emma Howard
Jennie Crummel and
  Susie Patterson
Lula G. Styles
Mollie Jarrell
Lizzie Campbell
Mr. Spicer
Chas. Humphrey
Mr. Pressley
Walter Jones
Henry Carter
Jas. Abernathy
Anna Bryson
John Brown
Mary Spells
Carpenter
Sandy McNair
Mrs. Savannah Janes
Mrs. Nick
Lee Wade
Thos. Williams
Mabel Ryder
Mr. Gentry
Mr. Nuckols
Nick Neblette
John McNair
Jim Bullocks
Geo. Beaty
Will Mills
John Bullocks
Lydia Fowler

Joe Sherwood
Geo. Smith
Chas. West
Pansy Davis
Mattie Swink
H. M. Carswell
Chas. Williams
Irwin Wilson
Clarence and Carrie King
Robt. and Maggie Campbell
Jessie McNair
Cleve Jones
Pearl Stanley
Rev. Geo. Williams
Matilda Diggs
Malinda Israel
Perry Cowan
Nick Saunders
James Hughes
Payne Wheeler
James Vinigar
Rev. J. T. Moore
Wood Fields
Bettie Tolbert
Homer Bullock
James Bullock
P. J. McBride
Nathaniel Armstead
Bettie Tolbert
Olivia Overstreet
B. Hutchins
Robert Rhodes
John Ezell
W. P. Dabney

Madisonville

Mrs. Lucy Acron
Mrs. Phoebe Allen
Mrs. Nancy Bush
Mrs. Cora Blue
Ben Blue
Annie Bowen
Ben Brown
Henry H. Busby
J. N. Bennett
Carol Beckwith
Lawrence Blackburn
John Blackburn
Wm. Cox
Wm. Combs
Sam Carroll
George Cockrell
George Compton
Angeline Copeling
Henry Dix
Cliff Davis
Tom Dutt
Rev. R. M. Davis
Rev. Dillard
Fred Donehoo
Charles Emery
Grandison Embry
L. W. Estill
Smith Estill
W. N. Frazier
Jacob Frazier
Rev. T. R. Fletcher
John Fultz
Wm. Franklin
Frank George
Percy Gifford
Eli L. Gifford
B. Glenn
George Hayton
Thos. Givens
Geo. Hayton
Richie Harris
Mr. Harrison
Mrs. Ollie Haney
Mr. Howard
Mr. Beal Howard
Charlie Howard
David Howard
Abe Henery
Ben Huey
Samuel Heiskin
Will Jackson
Mrs. Sarah Jackson
Mrs. Walter Jackson
Frank Johnson
Mrs. C. J. Jenkins
Mrs. Julia Jones
R. G. Kelly
Mrs. Sarah Kraft
Henry Looman
Mrs. Jane Logan
J. P. Logan
George Long
Dr. M. F. Leland
Collins LaMay
Mrs. Susie Miller
James Murphey
James Maupins
Horam Manns
Roy Miller
Mrs. Matthews
Zion McKinney
Edward Penman
Thos. Penman
Edward Prosset
Rev. Lee Phelps
R. E. Pattengall
Tom Reed
Wm. Rife
Ferguson Rife
Mrs. C. Rawling
Mrs. B. T. Richards
W. W. Smith
Rev. Wm. Simpson
Morris Simpson
Mrs. Cynthia Segar
Mrs. Frances Saunders
Mrs. Bell Sullivan
John Scott
J. Simms
Alfred Titus
Bennie Titus
George Turner
Mrs. Isom Turner
Jorden Tucker
Charlie Taylor
Rev. R. W. Thompson
Julius Thompson
Mrs. Nora White
Thos. White
Andy White
Mrs. Pearl Watts
Joe Waters

Joseph Winn
Jeff Walker
Mrs. Sarah Wallace
Allen Wallace
W. Williams
R. B. Woodford
Mr. Washington
Mr. Yates
Ben Rice

Geo. Nichols
Simms Olden
Geo. Roberts
Geo. Stone
Wm. Blackburn
L. Phillips
T. Duett
Mrs. Gertrude Ingram
Palmer Bomar

Walnut Hills

Lawrence Friason
Colored Women's Club
W. H. Enterprise Co.
Mrs. Jos. L. Jones
Mrs. Clara E. Hunster
Luther J. and Jennie C. Mills
Mrs. Hester Bennett
Jno. W. Lewis
I. Hill
Rankin Bros.
Chas. P. Miles
Ben Hughes
Henry Higgins
Mrs. Theopia Thompson
Miss Mamie Hawkins
Byron L. Mann
Caswell Ingram
Jno. and Susie Simpson
Chas. S. Taylor
Miss Lena Tabor
Geo. L. Kemper
Mrs. Jesse Alexander
Bishop I. N. Ross
Mrs. Minnie Moore-Waters
Mrs. J. Sample
Mrs. Harding
Wm. Hill
Henry W. Tate
Sylvia Wilks
Horace Sudduth
Lucy White
Wm. Tyler
John and Sabina Coleman
Fred Copening
John Owens
Wm. Douglass
Jas. Starks
Shirley Harris
Jacob and Anna Elders
Mr. Jackson

Leonard and Mattie Thompson
Dicey Smith
Wm. and Francis McFarland
Mary Estelle Kirksy
Elizabeth Hill
Benj. T. Lewis
Miss Lewis
Gertrude Franklin Tribue
M. F. Frazier
Sallie Frazier
Samuel W. Ball
Wm. N. and Nettie B. Phillips
John Runyan
Ida M. Glenn
Julia Shannon
Sanford and Nettie Moss
Ed. Knox
Frank P. Green
Eugene N. Clarke
Mattie Beasley
Jas. H. Jamerson
Robt. J. and Lena Evans
George Green
Rea and Ellery Cox
W. P. Chapman
Abram L. Willis
Allen and Minnie Davis
Dora Butler
Reed and Mamie Rowe
S. H. and Minnie Waters
W. O. Smith
Mr. Phelps
Mrs. Fountain Lewis
Mary Lee Tate
Helena Flats (George)
Gabriel B. Taylor
John C. and Elvira McLeod
Luke and Florence Edinbough
Eugene Cox
Allen L. Hinson
Robt. and Jennie Austin

Mrs. Fountain Lewis
Archie B. Adams
W. A. Johnson
Lee Davis
Geo. and Ella La May
Mrs. Hugh Carr
Honshell and Lizzie Ward
Andrew Hardin
Albert Ham
Henry G. Skillman
Jas. H. and Lizzie Branch
John M. Owens
Woodson S. Anderson
John W. Thomas
John Carson
Harry Jones
Henry Miller
J. T. and Mattie Cameron
Jno. and Julia Johnson
Lula Perry
Alzona and Anna Marmon
Norman and Evangeline Childs
L. W. and Katie Grey
Camille Friason Cole
Julia Douglas
Wm. and Dora Smith
Jerry and Carrie Guthrie
Francis McQuerry
Boyd W. Overton
Nelson Tribue
Wm. and Rosetta Reed
Wm. Van Hook
Katie Triplett
Rich T. Jones
Jos. and Sarah Paghe
Harry and Izella Washington
Shirley and Carrie Reynolds
Chas. Fields
A. M. Bean
Mr. Bradford
M. F. Frazier
John J. and Myrtle C. Johnson
Jas. H. Branch
Harry H. Friason
Samuel Johnson
Joseph Tucker
Katie Brown
Dr. E. B. Gray
Mr. Colvin
Wm. Hicks
Mr. Brown
Mr. McWhorters
Dr. E. D. Colley

Estelle and C. R. Davis
Jos. L. Jones
Henry and Carrie Curtis
Thos. O'Banion
Emma Baker
Walter G. Miller
Hannibal H. Hull
Robt. Blackburn
G. B. Conrad
Lummie Nichols
Wm. H. Howard
Fred J. Hamilton
Ernest Mitchel
Samuel B. Worthington
Pierce Reider
Elizabeth Williams
Walter Miles
Fred Bell
Linn Williams
Walter Brown
W. N. Ryder
Amanda Clarke
Dora Higgins
Annie Murphy
Clarence N. Johnson
Eugene Zimmerman
W. H. Hall
Howard H. Griffith
Mr. Bush
Jerry Guthrie
Thos. Hargrave
Alex Briscoe
Anderson Carter
Jas. H. Robinson
Mrs. Crewett
Wm. Hill
Lee and Lizzie Maxwell
Jas. Blanton
A. Kenney
Wm. Shelby
Andrew Blakeley
Pete and Mattie Anderson
Albert Herbert
Jean and Claudia King
Pauline Tribue
Jessie Heath
Howard Miller
Harry and Grace Baylor
John and Ella Merritt
Edw. and Florence Smothers
John R. Wilson
Fannie Smith
Carrie and Mary Scott

[14a]

Wm. Hooker
Mrs. Johnson
Jas. Milligan
Mrs. Byrd
Henry Underwood
Mrs. Salters
Marion Carr
John and Carrie Reider
John and Willana Channels
Ed and Fannie Champs
Sam and Mary Bowen
Frank and Lizzie Hall
Mr. Dells
Pearl Christian
Hattie Taylor
Martha West
Mattie Brooks
Abraham Prossett
Gilder J. Hill
Edith F. Miller
Wm. Winkfield
Margaret Isby
Tim Ray
Clarence N. Johnson
Cora Johnson
Roland Smith
Augustus C. Busch
Wm. Nance
Jas. Edwards
A. L. Ingram
Ernest Stewart
Emma Davis
Hezekiah Conway
O. B. Mitchell
Jas. and Lucy McLain
J. A. and Queen Crews
Mr. Gills
Ira Green Rollins
Mr. Willis
Ed. Birch
C. S. Jordan
Arthur and Sallie Hull
Wm. and Mozella Terry
John Buckner
Wm. N. Wilson
Hattie Moran
Herdon-Hammon
Bishop Mary Mack
Rev. Lee
Harry Adams
Wm. Mills
Robt. Greer
N. Greer

Oscar and Leanna Ingram
Wade Sanders
W. A. Page
R. A. Fowler
Andrew McFadridge
Alfred Carters
Henry Williams
Gus and Lucinda Goode
Fowler and Mamie Lowe
Anderson Jones
Rich and Lellie Moore
Lawson Johnson
Wm. and Amy Taylor
G. J. Jones
Albert Davis
Jas. Johnson
F. A. Hughes
Harden Spotts
Wm. A. Bush
Clifford Steele
Mary and Jno. Maupin
Eva Ricks
J. Jackson
Mr. Kalfus
Jas. Tolivar
Jessie Martin
Mr. Graham
Mr. Pellman
Golden Snyder
Mr. Johnson
Horace G. Pinkston
Mrs. Bogie
Edward Utz
Wm. Caliman
Minnie M. Jamerson
Ida B. Liverpool-Higgins
Mattie Gregston
Jas. Dunn
I. G. Penn
Dora and Wm. McCaleb
Hugh Carr
Mary Rasor
Mary L. Bean
J. W. Quisenberry
Jas. W. Thorpe
Dr. N. C. Vaughn
Wm. and Daisy Slade
Hezekiah Beasley
Lizzie Telton
Wm. Bradley
Wm. H. Mason
Ben Scott
John H. Johnson

Wm. and Ethel Smith
Mrs. Clay
E. B. Blackwell
Lottie Davis
Dora Scott
A. L. Dalton
Ferguson Sisters
Wm. Friason
Harry H. Friason
Wm. Bush
Rich Reed
Josephine McCracken
Jack King
Jacob and Anna Elders
J. H. Payne
Lucinda Whitlow Smith
Lucy Carr
Lucinda McKnight
Chas. Meyers
Frederick and Kitchen
D. D. McPheeters
Mr. Smith
Maurice Anderson
Ed. Davis
Robt. David
Fairchild Ingram
Jas. and Mary Robinson
Rena Payne
Ernest Chamlin
Sam Plater
Jessie Simpson
J. M. Green
Janie Bonner
Jas. R. Taylor

Frank Taylor
F. A. B. Hall
Allie Clarke
Sanctified Church
W. A. Johnson
Bill Pinkston
Essie Haynes
Jos. Horton
Hattie Simpson
A. L. George
Walter Cordell
Thos. Reed
Henry Ross
Josephine Smothers Offry
Sam and Lillie Smart
Ralph and Amy Hawkins
Mary Payne
Wm. and Amanda Robinson
Lottie Minor
Nancy Ruffin
Walter and Cora Jackson
Abel B. Hamlet
Mose Madison
Geo. and Jennie Carter
Lee Rollins
Edw. Townsend
G. D. Simpson
Dan Shelton
J. M. Green
Maude Gaines
Mrs. Parks
Hannah Smith
W. P. Dabney

East Sixth Street Hill

Eugene Stimpson
N. E. Taylor
Louis Pickens
Amos H. Watts
Sarah Smith

Dan and Jennie Harris
Richard T. Hester
Walter Counts
Allen Smith

Fairmount

Jos. Henderson
Wm. Price
Chas. Turpin
Mrs. Flowers
Jordan Carr
Mrs. Mays
Mr. Ira Favors
Wm. Drake

Frederick White
Andrew Jackson
Mrs. Rose
Mr. David Shaw
Stephen Blackwell
Mrs. J. Powell
Thomas Pinn
Jno. Lambert

Avondale

Walter Chenault
Israel Chenault
Kip Chenault
Mrs. Louis Thomas
Mrs. Perkins
Mills Forney
Chas. Bowman
Rev. J. Howard Jackson
Pillmer Gray
Mrs. Marshall
Carl Jackson
Mr. Lackey
Mrs. Patsie Jackson
Mrs. Kate Corvin
Mrs. Bowens
Mr. Huffman
Mr. Coleman
Isaac Williams
Jno. W. Ware
Mr. Cox
Mr. Scott
Mrs. Hattie Williams
Eugene Chenault
Mr. Phelps

Westwood

David Jacobs
Nettie Mearl

Hyde Park

Annie McCleod
H. S. Williams
A. G. Gaston

Cumminsville

Rev. H. M. Carroll
Mrs. K. Starr
Mrs. Eva Irving Bowles
Mrs. Stella Moorman
Dr. W. T. Nelson
Mrs. Maggie Bolden
Irene Holliday
Ella and Nora Pierce
Arthur and Marigold Lewis
John Wrenn
Mr. Johnson
Mrs. Givens
Geo. Williams
Reese Coleman
Jas. Reynolds
Calvin Howard
Chas. Henderson
Clay Porter
Mrs. Talbert
Granville and Alice Pease
Mrs. Price
Jas. and Clara Chalk
Mr. and Mrs. Moon
Mr. and Mrs. Logan
Clara Willis
Jackson Moorman
John Fitzgerald
Mr. Jenkins
Mr. Alexandria
Mr. Penn
Mrs. Mattie Kelley
George O'Bannon
Jas. Bryant
Maymie Johnson
Andrew Lee
Zella Owens
Mr. McFarland
Bert Crooks
James Greer
Scott Calimese
Fred Harris
Dr. E. A. Williams
Lee Coleman
Porter Bros.
Chas. Goode
Mrs. Williams
Geo. Drake
Ed. and Angeline Davis
Jennie Gray
Dan Williams
Samuel and Francis Jones
Wm. Brooks
Janie Boyd
Mrs. Josephine Akers
Dan Akers
Carrie Williams
Ed. and Serena Mason
Andrew Lewis
Wm. H. Harrison
Mr. and Mrs. Brennan
Eli and Luella Irving

College Hill

James Bailey
Mary Bennet
Lena Berry
Rev. Mack and Florence Berry
Samuel and Mary Biddle
Demus Brocket
John Brent
Mrs. James Oscar Brown
Martha Brown
Pattie and William Brown
Sallada A. Buckner
Ellen Bunch
George Burns
Eugene Burton
Eugene Butler
Elizabeth Buxton
Banks and Florence Byers
Lewis Byrd
Williams and Lalier Carr
Wade Chenault
George and Aline Choice
Harrison Coffer
Sarah J. Cole
Emmit Coleman
Mary Katie Coleman
William Coleman
Mary Conners
Pearl Conners
Anna M. Conway
Harriett M. Cook
Sarah F. Cook
Wm. H. Davenport
America Davis
Emma Day
Thos. H. Day
Amos Deadyler
George Depner
Mrs. Addie Dewey
Ida and James Ecton
Roland Edenburg
Jas. and Sallie Edwards
William Edwards
George Epps
Luzenia Even
Anna Ewing
Thos. K. Farnsworth
H. J. Feyn
Wm. H. Fishback
Mary L. Fitzgerald
Lovell Fletcher
James and Georgianna Foley

William H. Freidman
Harvey and Martha Gardner
Anna Gibson
Olivia Gill
Leonard Gill
Lizzie Goode
Mary Grant
Watler Gray
Mina William Green
Aaron and Lucinda Hall
Agnes Pauline Harris
Virgil and Tempie Harris
M. H. and Emma Hackins
Albert and Carrie Houston
Naomi Huff
John Irby
Alfred J. Jackson
Arthur W. and Georgette Jackson
Charles Jackson
George Andrew Jr. and Malinda Jackson
Mary R. Jackson
J. Walter Jackson
Sallie Jackson
Abraham Jenkins
H. M. Jentz
Eliza Johnson
John Johnson
Robert Johnson
Rosa Johnson
John Jordan
Lucy Jordan
Wm. and Mary Kattelmon
Ellen Keen
Lillian Keen
Connie Kenbo
William and Minnie Kimbrough
Thos. Kimbrough
Margaret Kincaid
Annie Lee
Lias and Lloyd Liggins
Margaret Liggins
William Little
Mrs. William Logan
Anna Lee
B. Leland
Edward and Sally Lynch
William Edmonds
Nathan McAllister
H. L. McClure
James McHugh

J. F. McWilliam
Lizzie Matthews
Francis C. Mercer
Maggie Merritt
Charles Middleton
John and Sarah Miller
Richard Miller
John C. Moor
Mark Neeley
Mrs. Sophia Wilson
Jessie Nesbit
Louvenia Newsome
Robert and Lizzie Owens
Jas. and Emma Pate
Florence and Harriet Pettit
Andrew and Almeda Price
J. Van Price
James William Quincy
John Raip, Jr.
Benjamin and Lula Ramsey
Charles Rath
J. H. Robinson
Edith Robinson
John and Nellie Robinson
Mitchell Robinson
Shady Robinson
Walter E. Robinson
Chap Ross
Joseph J. Schumaker
Addie Scott
Addie M. Scott
Chas. and Sarah Shields
Robert H. Shields
John R. Smith
Samuel C. Smith
W. O. Smith
Martha and Lilly Tye Safie
Edward Stepheny
Isaac W. and Eva Stewart
Ray and Eva Steed
Chas. W. Strawder
Mary M. Street
Wesley Swan
John W. and Alice Swan
Gertrude Thomas
Hester and Jas. Thomas
John and Georgia A. Thomas
Alexander Thompson
Lawrence Thompson
Jane Thurston
Peter Tollivar
Warren and Mary Towens
William Turner

Joseph Turner
Maggie Walton
Mary and Lincoln Ware
Margaret Warren
Louise Walkins
Lyda Waters
Joseph Weatherspoon
Thos. and Sarah Wiley
Alice and Jas. R. Williams
Arthur Williams
Henry Williams
Susie Williams
Oscar Willingham
George and Florence Willingham
Edward Wilson
John R. and Lillian R. Wilson
Archer Thos. Winfree
Wm. Lyons
Gary Conner
Oscar Wooten
Jas. Russell
Wm. Magee
Oscar L. Walker
Geo. Lee
Mr. Bevers
Nat Hill
Eugene Brown
Frank Stewart
Leonard Gill
Thos. Williams
Sarah Young
Sarah and Thos. Winters
John Rout
Mary and Eva Baker
John Jackson
Daisy White
Mr. Jiles
George Willis
E. W. Battles
Blanch Bradford
Mrs. E. Moss
Otho Holden
Wm. Royles
Chas. Green
S. H. Colquett
Will White
Dora Procter
Mr. Boros
Percy Bess
J. S. Nesbitt
John Hill
E. B. Burton
J. H. Smith

C. Coats
J. R. Wilson
A. R. Stewart
E. Bruce
Sam Jackson
A. Lee
Mr. Conners
C. Card
W. E. Edmond
E. Lewis
Mr. Threman
W. C. Johnson
Wm. Brown
C. Calhoun
R. H. Shields
Warren Towns
Gertrude Estes
Wm. Liggins
E. W. Battle
Susie Williams
Wade Chenault
C. W. Middleton
M. Cowan
Mr. Gill
M. H. Hawkins
O. Willingham
Wm. Bennet
Wm. Turner
Mr. Coffer
P. Young
A. Davis and Golden
Fannie L. Brown
Battle and Clayton
John Thomas
Geo. Willis
Annie Weathers
Wm. Lyons
Mr. Thurston
G. Fish
Alice Hill
Mr. Kimbo
Gary Conners
J. H. Miller
Daisy White
A. W. Jackson
Robt. Mason
Ray Steed
O. C. Mills
Mrs. Little

Robt. Johnson
B. L. Ramsey
C. W. Jones
M. E. Murphy
Bertha Tabb
Wm. Dancy
Sarah Miller
Mrs. Watkin
Mrs. Nancy Allen
J. J. Weatherspoon
A. T. Winfree
Sarah J. Robinson
L. V. Cunningham
Thos. H. Day
Robt. Taylor
S. Biddle and R. Hill
J. S. Foley
John Robinson
C. Shileds
Geo. Stewart
Mr. Collins
John W. Wrenn
L. W. Wrenn
Albert L. Imes
Clarence I. Smith
Chas. Mills
John Houston
John Brown
Julia Morris
Julia Hunter
Weston Casey
Jane Boughman
Elizabeth Locker
Jesse Locker
Nellie Robinson
C. I. Smith
Paul Ducksworth
Wm. W. Kinney
Mary Kinney
Nellie Liggins
Chas. Morris
Wm. Banks
Lucinda Evans
Garrett L. Thomas
Maggie Bailey
Caroline Ducksworth
Katie Kinney
Walter Parrott

Norwood

Mrs. Nellie Johnson

C. F. Letcher

O'Bryonsville

Frederick Ousley
Cecil E. Harris
Alexander Burkes
Phillip Daily
Edward Steward
Albert Blackburn
Anna Hughes
Leo Alsop
Aaron Sandipher
George Jones
Frank Keller
Harriet Johnson
George Turner
Rosetta Young
Lee Rogers
Andrew Sloane
Ada Grubbs
Walter Alsop
Mattie Minter
Minnie Harris
Nannie Burrell
Mr. Handy

Carrie Allen
Edith Green
Herman Wilson
Robert Washington
Jerry Johnson
Faith Holman
Robert Neall
William Hughes
James W. Jones
Lucy Ross
Harvey Dodge
Harry Shephard
Wm. Allen
Joseph Prince
William Fishback
Lee Turner
America Hodges
Richard Mason
Geo. Livingston
Irene J. Kirke
Alice Meads

Price Hill

Mr. and Mrs. John Crook
Mr. and Mrs. Ross Rivers
Mr. and Mrs. Robt. Belsinger
Mr. and Mrs. Neal Rasor
Mr. and Mrs. Warren Thomas

Wm. Beck
Mrs. Ella Dandridge
Mr. and Mrs. John M. Hays
Mrs. Isabel Boden
Mrs. Anna Harris

Lockland

Rev. W. H. Dickerson
Henry Spell
Mr. Chenault
Mrs. Katie Wallace
Mrs. Molly Merritt
Leslie Schooler
Isaac Johnson
Mrs. Rebecca Whitehead
Chas. I. Turner
Rev. Chas. Merrit
Anthony Walker
Mr. Levine
Mrs. Betty Pond
Mrs. Mahala Cook
Mrs. Henderson
Gilbert East
Mrs. Lidia Simms
Mr. Belt
Mrs. Lillian Morris

Henry Johnson
Richard Hurt
Mrs. Wicker
Tom Johnson
Mrs. Dunn
B. F. Baxter
Mrs. Leona Williams
Louis Collins
Mrs. Lula Turner
Mrs. Mamie Denny
Stone Francis
Mrs. Lillie Rice
Mrs. Anna Orr Strauss
Samuel Leavell
Mr. Carter
James Palmer
Rev. John Orr
Thomas Collins
Fred McFarren

Mrs. Wills
Mrs. Addie Roberts
Mr. Levine
Mrs. Lee
Mrs. Taylor
Leonard Brooks
Mrs. Mary Carr
Dr. Jas. Ross
Lafe Lunsford

Mrs. Matherly
W. S. Houston
Commodore Clay
Mrs. Eddie Harris
Wilbur Morris
Miss Ida Smith
Mrs. Daniel Fye
James Miller, Sr.
Mrs. Laura Earhart

Wyoming, Ohio

French Graham
Mrs. Alice Thornton
Mr. Gooch
P. A. Gray
M. V. Roberts
Mrs. Bessie Gentry
Mrs. Emma Carter
Miss Chanie Cavanaugh
Samuel Paxton
Mrs. Amanda Johnson
Mr. Mosely
Major Morris
William Stewart
Ulysses Walker
Mrs. Artie Cave
Daniel Walker
Fountain Pullins
Bishop Raymond
Rev. Watkins
Rev. Bowles
Mr. Mullins
Miss Nancy Hawkins
Hugh Smith
Richard Cammack
Mrs. Helen Pursawl
Mr. Coleman
William Jones
Henry Coleman
Isaac Miller
Arthur Coleman

Mr. Waldon
Attorney Ricks
George Phillips
Roscoe Elliott
Mrs. Myrtle Hann
Charlie Armstrong
Elwood Morris
Pierson Ritchie
Mrs. Chaney
Mr. Steve Hunt
Clarence Turner
Arthur Moore
Edward Blanton
Wallace Elliott
Stanley Guthrie
Mr. Williams
Eddie Phillips
John Derrickson
Jacob Laine
Mrs. Amanda Beasley
Edgar Burns
Mrs. Lydia Phillips
Walter Elliott
Orville Corneliuson
George Rice
Rev. Clarence Warner
Mrs. Abbey Hunter
Marshall Jones
Mr. Alsop

Elmwood Place

Mrs. Pearl S. Allen
Frank Dickerson
Mrs. Hull
Mrs. Crawford Smith
Mrs. Lewis

Rev. Grevens
Mrs. Mangum
Mrs. Thos. West
Rev. Fralice

Hartwell

Richard Books
James Cavanaugh
Mrs. Marie White
George Lewis
Mr. Oulds
Mrs. Bell Green
John Grey
Jacob Shearer
Will Black
Mrs. Dillingham
John Gentry
Mrs. Denny
Mrs. Gentry

Mrs. Niblet
Mrs. Ross
Mrs. Stella Zellars
Richard Gentry
Mr. Tribbus
Hobby Miller
Mrs. Lightning
Ed Minnis
Francis Minnis
Henry Dillingham
Houston Clark
Humphrey Martin
Mrs. Anderson

Covington

Levy Wells
Mr. Jones
John Coleman
Chas. Jackson
Tabby Jones
Laura Johnson
Phil Harris
Octavia Daniels
C. E. Jones
Henry Washington
Laura M. Jones
Tony Crosby
Thomas Holloway
Dr. A. G. Beam
William Scruggs
Minnie Harris
Sam Boggs
Cora Strings
Mrs. Robinson
Mr. Brooken
John Brown
Robetta Davis
John Conway
C. E. and Julia Jones
C. H. Robinson
Henry and Katie Marshall
Carrie Love
John and Eliza Tony
Dr. S. J. Watkins
Jas. and Luvenia Meyers
John Hill
Chester and Annie Hood
John and Helen Jones
Jas. and Helen Collins
Ida Lee

Chalotta Grant
Will H. Zealous
Nannie Singer
Effie Young
Anna Wells
Mary Humphrey
Frank Humphrey
Robt. Rice
Dr. N. H. Dunham
Thos. Young
Linsey Jackson
Geo. Young
Alonzo Pepper
Jenny Lightfoot
Lizzie Elkins
Katie Bryant
Mary Terrell
Mary Davidson
Hattie Wilson
Mary Taylor
Mrs. Contraul
Mary Pleasor
Nordell Burton
Boaz and Alice Jones
D. M. Smith
Geo. and Ethel Winn
Clark and Alice Alexander
Mack and Mattie McKenny
Maggie Stanton
Chas. E. Stewart
Bessie Rice
Dr. S. J. Watkins
Chas. and Lillian Davenport
Detroit Williams
Edw. and Rosa Jackson

Horace Sudduth
John Kilby
Martha Harris
Jennie D. Porter
Clarence and Lula Paxton
Wm. and Stella Shannon
Geo. and Jennie Thornton
Clara Hillman
Vena Smith
Jas. Strawder
Geo. and Kate Garrett
Albert Kilby
Bud Collins
Jacob Pinkom
Wm. Scruggs
Martha Page
Bell Taylor
Julius Conway
Rich and Mary Johnson
Georgia Saunder
Fred Davis
Warner Smith
Lizzie Allen
Dr. A. D. Kelley
Oliver and Elsie Russell
Dock Gregory
Josephine Russell
Wm. Francis
Jack Pinkam
Alex Sanford
J. Wilson
Clarissa Gaines
Dr. C. C. Smith
Jennie Craig
George Whipps
Mary Ziegler
Dr. J. E. Randolph
Jim Miles
Rev. Kelley
Hattie Lewis

Jennie Marshall
Eugene Lacey
Jas. White
Amos Smith
F. C. Locust
Tom Slaughter
Jennie Dickerson
Minerva Southgate
A. Davis
Addie Davis
Edith Estell
O. T. Martin
Maggie Slaughter
Dan and Laura Taylor
Hattie Mitchell
Russell and Bessie Connelly
J. C. Smith
Geo. Walker
Warner and Jewell Smith
Hardin Anderson
E. Z. Jones
Mrs. Riley
Tillie Price
Jas. and Lizzie Turntine
John Hill
John Webb
James Johnson
Herman Paxton
Ella Brown
Robt. L. Yancey
Minerva Bryant
Sue Wagner
Cal Clark
Mrs. Delaney
Molly Richardson
George Brooken
Jamie Smith
Richard Garrett
Alice Long
Chester Holloway

NEWPORT

Mr. Jackson
Mrs. Wilson
Nicholas Neblette
W. H. Sanders
Taylor and Charlotte Colston
Thos. and Ida Gee
Johnnie Johnson
Rev. Johnson
Chas. and Emma Horner
Maggie Fox

Nan Mayes
John Frazier
A. J. Mayo
Chas. Williams
John Pierce
Archie Grimes
Ode and Mary Grimes
Etta Hunley Wright
Alberta St. Clair
Frank Poynter

Mr. Edwards
Joe Nathan
Harry Jones
C. B. Strawder
E. Chapman
Chas. Young
R. H. Salters
Sarah Merritt
T. E. Heiskins
Wm. and Emma Blanton
Laura Greenway
Mary Patton
Francis Savage

Will and Hazel Lawrence
Dad Jackson
Mamie Walker
Mrs. Ozier
Sallie Robinson
Bessie Caldwell
Carrie Caldwell
Regina Brown
Albert Waugh
Grant Berry
Rufus and Rhoda Howell Estate
John Woods

Defunct Corporations

The Ohio Co-operative Company was formed nearly twenty-five years ago. Its charter empowered it to do any kind of mercantile business, including real estate. The many prominent citizens engendered too much friction for success.

The Gold Mine Company was formed to purchase a gold mine owned by the brother of Dr. Kerr. The amount of capital was too small and the distance from the mine too great.

Thousands of dollars were lost by our citizens in the stock of an eastern realty company. Most of the lots happened to be in the Atlantic Ocean instead of on the Jersey coast.

There have been numberless groceries started. Minnes & Grandison, then Underwood, Irvin & Arundel. The B. C. Grocery was owned by Speed Gates, George Wilson, George Mickey, Marion Bradford, Couley Powers and Chas. S. Chrystal. While the last named was manager, the firm did a big business.

Over twenty-five years ago, Wm. M. Porter, Geo. W. Hays, Edgar Watson and Warren King had a grocery in the Porter Building on Court Street. For a long time success reigned. Then came disaster.

The Royal Union, a branch of The Republican Union, bought a magnificent farm site on the Miami River. W. P. Dabney, the president, finally bought in all of the stock to prevent the land falling into the hands of the white mortgage holders.

A Word From The Publisher

Multitudinous delays from various causes have brought us to press the middle of February, 1926. "A plain, unvarnished tale" we have told, since for harmonious adjustment of inter-racial relations, inter-racial truth is absolutely necessary. Though our people have made in many ways most remarkable progress, yet they would be infinitely further advanced in citizenship had "white Americans" not depended upon dependent "colored Americans" for psychological and sociological racial knowledge, and had colored Americans not depended upon the same class for leadership and guidance.

'Tis a truism in all races, that, with few exceptions, those who receive or desire to receive salary, emolument or reward, invariably give to those from whom such blessings flow the kind of information and service most pleasing to them.

The ever increasing number of "just and gentle" whites, and the great development of real race pride among colored people, betoken the not distant dawn of a day so bright, that to coming generations there will be no conception of the lives and struggles of their foreparents, no realization of the conditions we have so frankly described, in "Cincinnati's Colored Citizens."

Finis

The Old Beecher Homestead, where Harriet Beecher Stowe wrote Uncle Tom's Cabin

Old Trustee Board of St. John A. M. E. Zion Church

Rev. Powell with Republican Union Committee on Dabney's Farm

Babies at Evangeline Home, a Maternity Hospital

Rev. "Dave" Irvin
"Father of Pythian Home"

Jas. W. Rawlins
Once Prominent Citizen and Business Man

www.ingramcontent.com/pod-product-compliance
Lightning Source LLC
Chambersburg PA
CBHW030315100526
44592CB00010B/434